Corporations and Citizenship

DEMOCRACY, CITIZENSHIP, AND CONSTITUTIONALISM

Rogers M. Smith and Mary L. Dudziak, Series Editors

A complete list of books in the series is available from the publisher

CORPORATIONS AND CITIZENSHIP

EDITED BY
GREG URBAN

PENN

UNIVERSITY OF PENNSYLVANIA PRESS

PHILADELPHIA

Published by
University of Pennsylvania Press
Philadelphia, Pennsylvania 19104-4112
www.upenn.edu/pennpress

Printed in the United States of America
on acid-free paper

10 9 8 7 6 5 4 3 2 1

A catalogue record for this book is available from the Library of Congress
ISBN 978-0-8122-4602-5

Contents

Chapter 1

Why For-Profit Corporations and Citizenship?

Greg Urban

In July 2011, Christopher Cristwell, a Starbucks barista in Chowchilla, California, posted a YouTube video. The video showed Cristwell, shirtless but clad in a green Starbucks apron, singing a song about the barista experience. The song delivers a steady rant about customers, his job, even his friends: "Hello rich white lady, I already know what you want / you want a skinny vanilla latte, young debutante / well that drink won't make you skinny, you gotta work for that / and just in case you're running, I just called you fat." Two months later Cristwell was fired. Alan Hilowitz, a Starbucks spokesperson, said: "While Christopher was expressing his own views in the video, the disparaging remarks about our customers and company are unacceptable and out of line with our commitment to our customers and partners."[1]

The right of free speech is enshrined in the U.S. Constitution. It is a right characterizing the relationship between citizens and their government. It is even a right, according to the 2010 Supreme Court decision in *Citizens United v. Federal Election Commission*, that business corporations seem to possess. The court ruled that the First Amendment to the U.S. Constitution prohibits the government from restricting political expenditures by corporations, because such restrictions might limit the range of viewpoints to which listeners would be exposed. Corporations, in short, have a right to free speech.

The Cristwell incident and the *Citizens United* case highlight a critical issue, one of central concern in this book: the relationship between for-profit business corporations and citizenship. Modern business corporations receive legal recognition from national (or constituent state) governments. They organize and regulate much of the daily lives of a considerable portion of humanity. However, they are not themselves typically constituted internally around ideals of national belonging, such as democracy, citizenship, and egalitarianism. Starbucks has the right to free speech in the United States, but Cristwell does not have the right to free speech as a "partner"—the term the company uses for "employee"—of Starbucks.

This book assembles a multidisciplinary group of scholars to address the role of modern for-profit corporations, as a distinctive kind of social formation, within democratic national states. In what measure do corporations promote the public interest? In what measure can and should elective governments shape corporations so as to promote the well-being of citizens? These are among the key questions taken up in the following chapters.

In his first annual message to Congress in 1901, President Theodore Roosevelt proclaimed: "Great corporations exist only because they are created and safeguarded by our institutions; and it is therefore our right and our duty to see that they work in harmony with those institutions."[2] However, corporations are not only regulated by citizens through their governments. They also regulate many aspects of the lives of the citizens who work for them, and they have profound influence over the lives of countless others. The question of regulation has become especially acute in the case of large multinational corporations. A study done more than a decade ago found that, of the hundred largest economies in the world, only forty-nine were countries.[3] The remaining fifty-one were business corporations. How and in what measure should corporations be regulated by nations? How much of the regulation of social life around the planet has been taken on by corporations themselves?

While business enterprises are self-organizing, requiring the initiative of individuals who expect or hope to gain financially from the endeavor, not all business enterprises are corporations. The Mexican drug cartels, for example, operate internationally and are estimated to have revenues of $10 to $25 billion annually, or as much as 2.5 percent of the Mexican gross domestic product.[4] They are definitely self-organizing, profit-seeking commercial enterprises. If the Mexican cartels were a single entity, they would rank on the Fortune 500 list somewhere between 100 and 250—that is, between Alcoa or Staples, on the larger side, and H. J. Heinz or Nordstrom, on the smaller. However, they are not corporations because they lack one key ingredient: legal recognition by national (or their constituent state) governments. The relationship between business corporations and governments, as well as citizenries, is central to the very nature of these social entities, as well as the main focus of concern for the authors of this book.

Are For-Profit Corporations in the Public Interest?

Lynn Sharp Paine, the John G. McLean Professor of Business Administration at Harvard Business School, opens the first of two sections in this book by observing: "The news is filled with cases of corporate mismanagement, influence buying, and wrongdoing that threaten the public interest." Yet, she continues, "corporations have done a great deal of good—even beyond their routine business of providing society with needed products and services—and could, if suitably led and governed, do even more." Those of us lucky enough to live in the developed world need only look around to see the benefits corporations bring to life, from lighting, air conditioning, automobiles, jetliners, and clothing to computers, smartphones, plasma screen televisions, video games, and movies.

On April 24, 2012, a newly formed company named Planetary Resources, Inc., announced that it planned to mine asteroids for resources. According to its website, the company aims to "develop low-cost robotic spacecraft to explore the thousands of resource-rich asteroids within our reach. . . . [and] then develop the most efficient capabilities to deliver these resources directly to both space-based and terrestrial customers."[5] This is not among the examples provided by Paine in her chapter, but it is one reflective of her general theme: that for-profit corporations are well suited to tackle many of humanity's problems and challenges, in the case of Planetary Resources, our need for minerals and other resources that are in limited terrestrial supply.

A 2006 article in the Proceedings of the National Academy of Sciences concluded: "Virgin stocks of several metals appear inadequate to sustain the modern 'developed world' quality of life for all Earth's peoples under contemporary technology."[6] In other words, if everyone in the world is to enjoy the standard of living found in the United States and Europe today, we need to find new sources for metals. Enter Planetary Resources, whose website explains: "Asteroids are filled with precious resources, everything from water to platinum. Harnessing valuable minerals from a practically infinite source will provide stability on Earth, increase humanity's prosperity, and help establish and maintain human presence in space."[7]

Of course, this new company may fail miserably, despite its substantial financial backing. It may never turn a profit. It may stray down the pathways of mismanagement and unethical conduct. But it is also indicative of the kind of adventurous, forward-thinking projects with which for-profit corporations have been and can be associated. Paine's examples include corporations working to develop waterless fabric-dyeing technology to conserve on water usage; to bridge the digital divide in China; and to counteract short-termism in finance in order to promote sustainability and long-term equity valuations.

The desire for profit is a powerful motivator, inspiring creative thinking and action, ingenuity, determination, and hard work. For this reason, profit can serve as a lever to pry humans out of their inertial pathways, introducing innovations that help us to adapt and prosper, and that therefore serve the public interest. So, to give a partial answer to the main question driving this section—"Are for-profit corporations in the public interest?"—we might say, "Corporations can serve the public interest."

In the opening to her chapter, Paine also notes: "Corporations are instruments. And, like most instruments, they can be used for good or ill." While her chapter focuses on the good corporations do, Chapter 3, by University of British Columbia law professor Joel Bakan, argues in stark contrast that corporations, in their single-minded pursuit of profit, can be harmful to the public. His view is not that corporations are immoral, but that they are amoral, pursuing profit without regard for society's values, getting away with whatever they can get away with, and incapable of feeling remorse. If they were persons, he proposes, we would classify them as "psychopaths," opportunistic individuals lacking in superego function.

Where in the scheme of social values do we place some of the online games, such as Whack Your Soulmate and Boneless Girl, that children manage to access despite (or even because of) age restrictions? Are large publicly traded for-profit entertainment corporations like Viacom, the parent company in this case, acting in the public interest when they support such games? Their AddictingGames.com website claims to be the "largest online game site in the U.S." "We are trailblazers," their website contends, "in the casual game territory, developing and distributing innovative, irreverent, and addictive online games."[8]

At the same time, these troubling games make up only a small part of the business of the parent company, Viacom, which can be said to perform a service the general public values—entertainment. The problem here is similar to that in the other examples Bakan discusses—namely, pharmaceuticals and chemicals. There can be little doubt that Zoloft, for instance, and the company that developed it, Pfizer, Inc., have contributed to the public good. Zoloft is an antidepressant medication that has helped countless individuals. Pfizer can be looked upon, in many ways, as a "profitable philanthropy."[9] However, and this is Bakan's question rephrased, can the profit motive cause generally good companies, such as Pfizer, to behave unethically?

What about tobacco companies? Do they serve the public interest? Cigarette smoking is estimated to have caused the deaths of 4.2 million people worldwide in the year 2000,[10] half as many as died in combat per year during World War II.[11] However, the world war had a defined beginning and end, whereas there is no end in sight for tobacco-related deaths. The U.S. Centers for Disease Control and Prevention refers to tobacco as "the nation's leading killer."[12] Philip Morris International, Inc., a publicly traded corporation based in New York, states on its website that it is "the leading international tobacco company . . . [with] an estimated 16.0% share of the total international cigarette market outside of the U.S." Does this company demonstrate the power of the corporation to do evil in the world, in contrast to companies like Pfizer or Viacom, which also do good?

Interestingly, in the late 1990s, facing litigation and public pressure, Philip Morris began to hammer out a Corporate Social Responsibility platform, initiated in 1996 in a statement by CEO Geoffrey Bible: "Our tobacco business may be controversial, but we are a principled people who are honest and straight-dealing. . . . That is an absolutely critical part of our corporate culture."[13] Bible noted that "cigarettes are a legal product," and that "smoking is part of an adult life style." The CSR campaign that got under way in earnest in 2001 emphasized these and other points.

In fairness, definitive public recognition of the health effects of smoking itself took hold in the United States only after the 1964 Surgeon General's report. Philip Morris traces its history as a company to a single tobacco shop opened in London's Bond Street in 1847. The company was acquired by U.S. stockholders in 1919, and introduced its most famous brand, Marlboro, in 1924. So it can perhaps be seen to have been a profitable philanthropy for most of its history. Did it suddenly turn evil after 1964, or did it simply endeavor to survive and protect shareholder value? Or is it today not evil, merely satisfying a demand for its products, with ethical responsibility for its destructive consequences residing with consumers exercising their right to free choice, as an economistic view of morality might have it?

In the political discourse coming out of Washington these days, there seems to be no dearth of definitive position-takings. However, in regard to the question "Are for-profit corporations in the public interest?" simple yes or no answers are inadequate. The truth is more complex, and surely it ought to be a key purpose of academic research to bring these complexities to light for public debate.

Jeffery Smith, founding director of the Banta Center for Business, Ethics, and Society at the University of Redlands, does just that in Chapter 4, tackling the question of corporations and the public interest from the angle of ethical philosophy. He begins with Howard Bowen, who some consider the "intellectual father of the contemporary 'corporate social responsibility' movement." Bowen's basic point, Smith explains, is "that business managers are stewards of the public good and are morally responsible for not only enhancing the value of their companies, but also for the realization of wider social goals such as distributive justice and the economic development of local communities."

This "corporate social responsibility" idea, however, clashes with a dominant view today, dubbed by some the "shareholder value theory" of the corporation. As Smith notes, this latter shareholder view finds resonance in Adam Smith's notion of the invisible hand: that people pursuing their own self-interest "without knowing it, advance the interest of the society."[14] The idea here is that producing profit for the shareholder overrides any other purpose the corporation might have, since that will (without the profit-seekers intending it) produce the greatest good for society. The shareholder value theory in the United States, however, is often given a legal rather than economic lineage.

In 1919, the Michigan Supreme Court issued a ruling in a suit brought by Horace and John Dodge, known as the Dodge brothers, as shareholders of the Ford Motor Company, against the company. Henry Ford, company president, had been cutting the price of the company's main product, the Model T, while increasing the wages of his workers. Even so, or perhaps because of this strategy, the company was flush with cash, which Ford proposed to use for expansion. He also wanted to stop paying dividends to shareholders, and so the Dodge brothers sued. Ford testified that his goal was to "employ still more men, to spread the benefits of this industrial system to the greatest possible number."[15] Of course, Ford also believed that his strategy would make more money for the company in the long run. The court, however, sided with the Dodge brothers, in their decision making the frequently quoted statement: "A business corporation is organized and carried on primarily for the profit of the stockholders."[16]

Economist Milton Friedman, in a 1970 *New York Times Magazine* article,[17] echoed this view of corporate purpose, in arguing that the social responsibility of the corporation was to produce profit. Yet, according to legal scholars, shareholder value was not the basis of the Michigan Supreme Court's decision. Moreover, the "business judgment rule" protects corporate directors against liability "so long as any plausible connection can be made between the directors' decision and some possible future benefit, however intangible and unlikely, to shareholders."[18] Lynn Stout, Distinguished Professor of Corporate and Business Law at Cornell University, concludes: "Corporations seek profits for shareholders, but they seek other things as well, including specific investment, stakeholder benefits, and their own continued existence. Teaching *Dodge v. Ford* as anything but an example of judicial mistake obstructs understanding of this reality."[19]

Present-day ethical debates over the corporation polarize around positions not unlike those contested in *Dodge v. Ford*. At one pole, the shareholder value theory proposes that the greatest benefits to society come from economic efficiency in provisioning goods and services, and economic efficiency can be best achieved when corporations maximize profits for stockholders. At the other pole in this debate is the stakeholder or "corporate social responsibility" theory: that corporations exist for the purpose of maximizing benefits for all stakeholders—employees and the communities in which the corporations operate and whom they serve—as well as the shareholders.

Even if the purpose of corporations were social responsibility, Jeffery Smith argues, it does not follow that managers must run corporations with that purpose in mind. Here he makes room for the economic shareholder value theory, acknowledging that corporate social responsibility might be best achieved by maximizing shareholder profit. To demonstrate this, he criticizes what he calls the "alignment theory"—namely, that managers should run the corporation with the same purpose in mind as the corporation actually has in society.

To attract investments, a relationship of trust must develop between investors in and managers of a corporation. The investors must feel that managers will operate a corporation in the most efficient manner possible, otherwise why would they agree to invest? The position at this point in Smith's argument is reminiscent of the Michigan Supreme Court's remark in deciding in favor of Dodge over Ford, or that of economist Milton Friedman.

However, Smith takes us on a journey through tangled complexities in the corporate ethics literature concerning the importance of law in ensuring a contractual foundation for stakeholder rights, and the necessity of managers to ensure the fulfillment of these contracts, in addition to striving for efficiency on behalf of shareholders; and from there to the imperative that managers avoid producing or exploiting market failures in the name of efficiency; and from there to a view of corporations as public, acting to advance social values in a way similar to lawmakers. Starting with market assumptions about the corporation, he ends up with a modified version of the alignment theory, that corporate executives are, in fact, the very individuals who have been tasked to decide how the social purpose of the corporation should be carried out in practice. Here he has moved closer to the side of Ford in the dispute with the Dodge brothers, and perhaps closer to the "business judgment rule" as articulated by Stout rather than the remark made by the Michigan Supreme Court.

If managers are ethically obligated to make decisions about implementing the social purpose of corporations, how have actual corporations fared to date in executing those obligations? In Chapter 5, Johns Hopkins business historian Louis Galambos teams up with Jeffrey Sturchio, former vice president for corporate social responsibility of Merck & Co., Inc., to offer an answer. Galambos and Sturchio provide an overview of corporate governance in the United States during the twentieth century, beginning with the Great Merger Movement that took place from roughly 1895 to 1905. Small firms joined with one another or with larger firms; sole proprietorships and partnerships were transformed into large corporations that dominated markets.

President Roosevelt's 1901 statement, quoted earlier, regarding the need to ensure that corporations work in harmony with governmental institutions, was a response to these developments, and signaled the beginning of a new era of governmental regulation of corporations, as well as the birth of a welfare state. As Galambos and Sturchio recount, corporate governance in turn evolved. By the 1940s and 1950s in the United States, corporations became multidivisional, with what is often known as a C-suite organization headed by a CEO (chief executive officer), with a COO (chief operating officer) running daily affairs, a CFO (chief financial officer), and others. Among the divisions were those responsible for public relations and public affairs, the former representing the company to the public as socially responsible, the latter lobbying Congress and state legislators regarding regulatory issues.

While some, if not much, of corporate social responsibility has been image management through PR, some has been genuine, the type case of the latter in this chapter being Merck, especially for its role in developing a treatment for river blindness, and distributing the medicine free of charge in sub-Saharan Africa and the rest of the developing world. Thinking of corporate management as ranging between the two poles mentioned earlier—social responsibility versus profit above all else—with Merck toward the former side and Enron toward the latter, Galambos and Sturchio see large corporations as arrayed between the two more or less in a bell curve, with the mean probably not that different from other institutions such as colleges and universities.

That colleges and universities might not be so different from large for-profit business corporations as regards socially responsible behavior is especially intriguing in light of current debates about the educational system in the United States today. The rise of for-profit universities, such as the University of Phoenix, a subsidiary of Apollo Group, Inc., a publicly traded company, has focused attention on the role of profit in relation to education. As Amy Sepinwall describes in Chapter 6, proponents of for-profit education underscore the role of profit as a powerful motivator for innovation. Where innovation is most needed, these proponents argue, is with populations in the United States not reached by the current system—that is, historically disenfranchised segments—and, globally, the less developed countries—namely, those outside the relatively prosperous member nations of the Organization for Economic Co-operation and Development (OECD), 34 countries out of the 193 currently forming part of the United Nations.

A 2010 jobs report[20] from Georgetown University concluded: "The future of employment in the United States comes down to this: success will require postsecondary education, in one form or another." Who can best provide that higher education to students not currently receiving it? In 2009, more than twenty million students were enrolled in U.S. higher education classes. Of those, 73 percent were in public institutions, mainly state colleges and universities. Another 18 percent were enrolled in private not-for-profit institutions. Major targets of for-profit institutions, like the University of Phoenix, are people not currently reached by state-sponsored and not-for-profit colleges and universities. In 2009, 9 percent of students were enrolled in for-profits like the University of Phoenix, a tenfold increase from 1980.[21]

At the same time, as Sepinwall points out, for-profit corporations have allegiances to shareholders that may trump their allegiance to students. The worry is that profit-seeking corporations may find ways to extract cash from their operations without fulfilling their educational tasks. George Washington University sociologist Amitai Etzioni describes the situation this way:

The [for-profit] schools' stripped-down curricula and poor instruction often make for nearly worthless degrees. When students graduate from these colleges, many cannot find jobs—or at least not the kinds they were promised—and eventually, many of them default on their loans. The federal government has estimated that for-profit university students, who make up just 10% of all American college students, account for about 44% of all student loan defaults. When the students default, you and I pick up the tab. But note: the money does not go to the students, but to the shareholders of the for-profit colleges.[22]

Current debates foreground the question of whether some social purposes, such as education or the military defense of a citizenry, should be sealed off from the reach of for-profit corporations.[23] Where some for-profit companies are operating, as in the case of higher education in the United States, the worry is that corporate managers may seek to boost short-term shareholder benefits at the expense of longer-term value creation, as well as at the expense of stakeholders, especially the students.

Galambos and Sturchio may be correct that large for-profit corporations array along a bell-shaped curve between good citizens and bad, and that the mean is not so different from that of colleges and universities, the large majority of which, in the United States, are either state-government-run or not-for-profit corporations. While the means may be similar, however, it is still arguably the case that the standard deviation is wider in for-profit corporations.[24] It is hard to think of not-for-profit colleges and universities that are as bad for their stakeholders as Enron was for its. In the case of countries, like the United States or the United Kingdom, that rely on an educated citizenry for self-governance, it seems no coincidence that generations of citizens have seen fit to create and maintain public higher educational institutions and to foster not-for-profit private educational institutions rather than to leave education entirely to market forces.

At the same time, this does not mean that there is no role to be played by for-profit higher education corporations. What it does mean is that, if the social purposes of higher educational institutions are to be fulfilled in part through for-profit corporations, then their success rides on the validity of Jeffery Smith's modified alignment theory. Managers of these corporations must be tasked, or view themselves as tasked, to make decisions about how the higher educational purposes of the corporation are to be carried out. They must not view their role exclusively in terms of producing short-term gains for shareholders.

The final two chapters in the section on for-profit business corporations and the public interest take up the central question not from a bird's-eye view, as in earlier chapters, but rather from the point of view of citizens affected by the corporation. In Chapter 7, Rosalie Genova looks at the Enron Corporation. Prior to revelations about it in October 2001 and its eventual bankruptcy in December of that year, Enron seemed the paragon of the modern business corporation, employing some 20,000 individuals and having revenues of over $100 billion per year. Indeed, between 1995 and 2000, Fortune magazine dubbed it "the most innovative company in corporate America."[25] The bankruptcy caused shareholders some $11 billion in losses, with company debt totaling $39 billion.

Genova links American responses to Enron with a deeper history of attitudes to corporations, admiration but also suspicion, reverence but also rebuke. In its rise to power, Enron was revered; in scandal, it was reviled. What Genova finds most intriguing, however, is a third response—satire or mockery. Americans exhibit a tendency to want to cut the powerful down to size. One way to do that is make fun of the mighty, including mighty corporations. This was certainly true in the Enron case, as, for example, in this widely circulated narrative/joke: "The Arthur Andersen partner was on his cell phone when he said, 'Ship the Enron documents to the Feds.' But his secretary heard, 'Rip the Enron documents to shreds.' The rest is history."[26]

Just how do public attitudes toward corporations take shape and circulate in a national matrix of citizenship? Genova proposes that citizen experiences of and attitudes toward the business world are shaped and transmitted by stories, gripping stories, stories of heroes (Steve Jobs and Apple) and stories of villains (Kenneth Lay and Enron), but also stories that mock. She cites in her chapter a 2000 poll revealing that 82 percent of U.S. citizens viewed corporations as having "too much power over too many aspects of American life." What more American response to the high and mighty than to poke fun?

Reverence, as well as suspicion, anger, and rebuke, ascribe power to corporations and those who run them, making them appear to be above ordinary citizens. Mockery, in contrast, has a leveling effect. Powerful figures seem inane and their actions absurd, rendering them thereby susceptible to public criticism, not somehow above everyone else, whether in a beneficent or nefarious light. Mockery may be a key attitude for a democratic public in its contemplation of modern business corporations, inspiring the feeling of citizen power: "We made them; we can change them."

We would be incorrect to conclude from Genova's account that the American public believes large corporations to be opposed to the public interest. However, her account does suggest that Americans, on balance, tend to be suspicious of large corporations. Even when corporations choose to act in an enlightened public interest fashion, as Merck did in developing and distributing free of charge its medication for river blindness, many Americans continue to suspect some sinister or self-serving motive.

Such American attitudes toward corporations contrast sharply with those in Japan, according to Cornell anthropologist Hirokazu Miyazaki. Based on ethnographic research among Japanese bond traders, Miyazaki examines Japanese orientations to the Tokyo Electric Power Company (TEPCO), owner of the Fukushima Dai-ichi nuclear power plant, where disaster struck in 2011. TEPCO is a publicly traded company. TEPCO bonds represent 8 percent of the total Japanese corporate bond market, and are, as Miyazaki reports, widely owned in Japan, though not internationally.

After the nuclear disaster, the price of TEPCO stock plunged, but bond prices declined more slowly. Japanese bond holders continued to have faith in the company; in the government; in domestic bond rating agencies as opposed to Moody's, Standard and Poor's, and Fitch; and in their shared willingness to sustain loss for a common good. As Miyazaki reports, there was also a shared sense of obligation on the part of market professionals to maintain this trust, imbuing financial transactions involving TEPCO bonds with the spirit of the gift and the feeling of solidary social relations.

That Japanese citizens, and, more surprisingly yet, Japanese financial professionals, could feel solidarity with a corporation in which they are not themselves employees, might strike Americans as remarkable. Such a relation between corporations and citizens has not been a prominent part of the American experience. And it may not continue for long to be part of the Japanese experience. As Miyazaki explains, the winds of change are sweeping across the land, and bond traders sense that an old world is coming to an end. Things will not be the same after the Fukushima Dai'ichi disaster.

These same financial professionals had already experienced a loss of faith in finance, or, at least, in the way they had been doing finance prior to the Great Recession. They had been making money through arbitrage. In an ideal market in equilibrium, price accurately reflects the relationship between supply and demand. Under non-ideal conditions, imperfections arise that can be exploited for profit by arbitrage. For example, if the currency exchange rates between U.S. dollars, British pounds, and Japanese yen are out of whack, a trader can profit by using the first to buy the second, the second to buy the third, and third to buy the first back again. For the Japanese traders, arbitrage became a way of understanding finance in general, and even a worldview through which everyday non-economic life could be understood. As opportunities for arbitrage dried up, however, these same traders suffered a crisis of faith, coming to see finance itself as illusory, and, indeed, to imagine an end to finance.

Miyazaki's traders see a world about to change course, though they cannot quite discern what lies around the bend. Will feelings of solidarity succumb to the cold, hard calculus of Wall Street-style finance? Will the current dominance of finance itself come to end, giving rise to new forms of sociability, ones distinct from traditional hierarchies in Japan? Will Japanese come to hold attitudes of suspicion toward corporations similar to those found in America today?

Even if attitudes are changing, public trust in corporations in Japan suggests that citizenries are not inherently skeptical of corporations, pace the American case. They may regard the corporations, without undue suspicion, as furthering the public interest. Indeed, it is possible that the skeptical attitude may be related to the dominant discourse in America—namely, the economistic view, as proposed by Milton Friedman, that the only goal of a corporation should be profit, regardless of the means, providing the means are legal.

Lynn Paine, Jeffery Smith, and Jeffrey Sturchio and Louis Galambos argue in this section for an alternative to the Friedman ideal, one in which the goal of the corporation is or should be providing society with the goods and services people want and need. While profit continues to be a central characteristic of the corporation, in such an account, it appears as a reward for achieving the corporation's goal of provisioning, not as an overriding purpose. Viewed this way, corporations are, indeed, in the public interest. But is it possible, in democratic societies, for elected governments to regulate corporations to ensure that they do act in the public interest?

Does Government Regulation of Corporations Promote Well-Being in a Democratic Society?

The corporation, as a social form, has roots going back to the Roman period, as distinguished labor historian Walter Licht observes in Chapter 9. In medieval Europe, various social entities—colleges, guilds, towns—received royal charters as "corporations." Royal charters were official recognition that the activities of the groups, while self-organizing and not directed by the state, were explicitly in the interests of the state. Corporations thus preceded the rise of democratic citizenries in the West, in which the ultimate political authority was thought to reside in the popular will.

Among the first specifically profit-seeking enterprises to receive royal charters were the joint-stock companies of the early seventeenth century, such as the English (later British) East India Company and the Dutch East India Company. These companies were also granted "limited liability," another characteristic of the modern business corporation, where individuals were financially responsible for a venture only to the extent of their investment in it. Shareholders, in other words, could not lose more than the value of their shares—a government decision designed to encourage the ventures and one that simultaneously acknowledged the interests of the state in them.

Chartering of a corporation prior to the latter half of the nineteenth century involved a formal legislative act. As Licht describes, this was the case even in the newly created United States, where a citizenry as the source of authority was explicitly recognized. Starting in the mid-1830s, however, and thanks in part to an economic collapse lasting into the 1840s, a wary American citizenry came to see the act of granting corporate charters as a collusion between the government and "men of influence." We see here, perhaps, the origins of some of the modern-day American skeptical attitudes Genova describes.

A democratic uprising ensued against this quasi-aristocratic privilege, leading to calls for passage of general incorporation laws. Such laws would enable ordinary citizens to incorporate their businesses through straightforward processes of registration, without currying legislative favor. The movement was, as Licht states, anti-statist: let people establish and run corporations without government intervening.

Readers will no doubt draw a parallel here to the creation, in the immediate aftermath of the 2008 economic collapse, of the "Tea Party," whose stated mission is "to restore America's founding principles of Fiscal Responsibility,

Constitutionally Limited Government and Free Markets,"[27] themes that appear as well in other chapters of this book.

However, Licht, who emphasizes the role of contingency and variation in the historical relations between corporations and citizenship in the United States, notes that, by the late 1890s, the attitudes of Americans had shifted. The latter half of the nineteenth century witnessed the rise of huge corporations—the American Tobacco Company, Standard Oil Company, the Union Pacific Railroad, J. P. Morgan & Company. As in the 1830s and 1840s, a populist movement again sprang up. However, unlike its predecessor, this movement was not anti-statist. Rather, the public pressured government to rein in the corporations through new regulations, again with parallels to the present calls for regulation of the financial industry, as well as to the Occupy Wall Street movement, dedicated to "fighting back against the corrosive power of major banks and multinational corporations over the democratic process."[28]

But can democratically elected governments effectively regulate corporations? The Sherman Antitrust Law of 1890, for example, appeared on the eve of the Great Merger Movement. Was it successful in regulating corporations? Arguably, it had unintended consequences. If it was designed to prevent monopolies, and thereby preserve competition, it could be viewed as limiting competition because it effectively keeps the winner from winning.

Such problems of unintended consequence are the subject of Chapter 10, by Cynthia Estlund, the Catherine A. Rein Professor of Law at New York University. Estlund is concerned, specifically, with the rights of workers. In Europe and the United States during the nineteenth century, democratic citizenries proliferated. Bondage—whether serfdom or slavery—came to be seen as antithetical to human rights. Despite the outlawing of bondage, profit continued (and continues to this day) to act as an inducement to unethical (and, in some cases, illegal) corporate behavior—that is, the exploitation of formally free workers.[29]

What became known as "wage slavery" in the late nineteenth century was popularized by Upton Sinclair for the meat packing industry: "Here was a population . . . hanging always on the verge of starvation, and dependent for its opportunities of life upon the whim of men every bit as brutal and unscrupulous as the old-time slave drivers."[30] Today we hear reports of sweatshop conditions in other parts of the world—for example, at Hon Hai Precision Industry's Foxconn plants in China, where Apple iPads are assembled. A New York Times article described "harsh conditions" at Foxconn factories, including "excessive overtime, in some cases seven days a week," "crowded dorms," and "under-age workers."[31]

The temptations for corporate managers to boost profits by short-changing workers was, in no small measure, what gave rise to the communist movements of the nineteenth and twentieth centuries, with their authoritarian regimes promising to rein in those temptations. It was in this context of exploitive corporate behavior and the rising tide of communism,[32] as well as fascism, that the U.S. Congress passed the National Labor Relations Act (NLRA) of 1935. "The high purpose of this Act," President Franklin Delano Roosevelt said upon signing bill into law, is "a better relationship between labor and management." "By assuring the employees the right of collective bargaining," he continued, "it fosters the development of the employment contract on a sound and equitable basis."[33]

While unions initially flourished under the NLRA—with workers gaining voice and influence inside corporations, and real wages increasing—union strength began to decline in the 1950s. By the mid-1960s American companies discovered they could cut labor costs and boost profits by exporting jobs to other parts of the world. They thereby ushered in the most recent phase of globalization—the transnational outsourcing of labor. Mexico and then other Latin American countries, followed by countries in South and Southeast Asia, and finally China, supplied much of the workforce for U.S. companies. Correspondingly, the influence of unions in the United States declined further, union membership dropped off, workers lost voice, and real wages deteriorated.

The NLRA's "company union" provision, Estlund observes, prohibits corporations from creating their own internal committees wherein management and workers participate to discuss issues of mutual concern, including the terms and conditions of employment. The original purpose of this provision was to prevent managers from preempting unionization. With union membership in the United States hitting its peak in the mid-1950s and declining steadily since,[34] however, workers were left with no forums to engage with employers and, hence, with no voice—an unintended negative consequence of the law.

Though technically illegal, many companies without unionized workers have organized precisely the kinds of employer-employee committees outlawed by the NLRA. Estlund furnishes evidence that employees on balance like these committees, preferring them, at the very least, to the absence of any mechanism for achieving voice. But can companies be trusted to ensure that such organizations, were they to be made legal, would be run in a manner that promoted worker interests?

The NLRA presupposed an opposition between "management" and "workers." However, the legislation did not only presuppose that distinction; it also helped to consolidate it and make it part of accepted understanding, occurring as it did around the time of the so-called managerial revolution.[35] Professional managers were coming to replace owner-managers in large corporations. Three years after enactment of the NLRA, in fact, Congress passed the Fair Labor Standards Act (FLSA), which formally recognized classes of employees who were exempt from the act—namely, executives, administrators, and professionals, who were "salaried" as opposed to "hourly" workers.[36]

While the consequences of specific legislation may be unintended, the actual internal organization of corporations reflects the stamp of government regulation and public opinion, as political scientist Peter Gourevitch argues in Chapter 11. In Scandinavia, Germany, and some other European countries, for example, legislation requires that trade unions be represented on the boards of directors of some companies, very different from the situation in the United States, as described by Estlund. We also see widely divergent patterns in trade union membership. In 2003, for example, 12.4 percent of workers in the United States belonged to unions, while that figure was 78.0 percent for Sweden, 74.1 percent for Finland, and 70.4 percent in Denmark.[37]

The basic form of the for-profit corporation has been copied around the globe, with its organization into shareholders, managers, and workers. However, within that form, an enormous range of variation is possible. Share ownership can be concentrated in the hands of a relative few, as is common in Germany and Japan, or widely diffused, with numerous distinct shareholders, as is more typically the case in the United States and the United Kingdom. Workers may be shareholders, especially through pension funds, and have representatives on boards of directors, as mentioned earlier. Even governments may be shareholders in private corporations, as witnessed in the United States, where the government, in 2009, received 60.8% of the outstanding shares of General Motors in exchange for $49.5 billion; as of September 18, 2013, the government had sold all but 7.3% of outstanding shares, with plans to sell the remainder by early 2014.[38] According to a 2010 Economist article, "about a fifth of global stock market value now sits" in government-controlled companies.[39]

How are we to explain such wide variation? In Chapter 11, Gourevitch argues that neither capital-labor dichotomy models (in political economy theory) nor market efficiency models (in economic theory) are adequate. Instead, we must look for answers to external political processes—most important, political processes taking place within national states.

In this context, it is worth recalling the political experiments of the twentieth century under communism, where attempts were made to rein in exploitation of workers by outlawing private property and, with it, the for-profit corporation. Upon taking over tsarist Russia, for example, "the Bolsheviks nationalized virtually all enterprises including those employing only one or two persons."[40] After an initial retreat, plans for "an economy of full state ownership run by administrative resource allocation" were put into place in the 1930s under Stalin.[41] After the 1991 collapse of the Soviet Union, rapid privatization ensued, but since 2003 state ownership of certain key industries has been on the rise again.[42]

Looking just at the parameter of degree of state ownership and control of corporations—and forgetting others along which nations vary, such as concentration versus dispersal of shareholding, and worker voice in management decisions as well as degree of worker ownership of corporations—there is a continuum between, at the one extreme, the full state ownership imagined under the 1930 Stalinist plan, and the laissez-faire agenda of Milton Friedman, at the other. The "Index of Economic Freedom" compiled by the Heritage Foundation more or less approximates this continuum. Their 2012 rankings show the United States as the tenth freest economy out of 179 (with Hong Kong as number one) and Russia coming in at 144 (with North Korea in last place).[43] The continuum dramatically illustrates Gourevitch's main point—the specific shape corporations assume reflects political processes, especially those occurring inside national states.

Even maximal freedom for corporations, all authors in this volume recognize, requires some state regulation—minimally, laws governing contract and property rights. In Milton Friedman's oft-cited argument that "the social responsibility of business is to increase its profits," he adds: "while conforming to the basic rules of the society, both those embodied in law and those embodied in ethical custom."[44] But how should a society formulate laws and rules regulating corporations? That is the question addressed in Chapter 12, by distinguished Yale law professor Jonathan Macey.

A special class of corporate regulations is those fabricated by converting "best practices" into government mandates—what Macey dubs "regulation by assimilation." The problem with this approach, he contends, is that a practice in the pursuit of profit becomes something altogether different when transformed into an obligation imposed upon corporations by law.

Take the corporate practice of risk assessment. According to Macey, before the 1970s, credit rating companies depended for their income on how well they performed for their clients, who were then investors. Investors used them as part of their strategy for maximizing their returns. This was a matter of prudence. To the U.S. Securities and Exchange Commission, such prudence seemed a good idea. So regulations were instituted requiring corporations issuing bonds to have their creditworthiness rated by a government-approved rating company, the big three today being Standard and Poor's, Moody's Investor Service, and Fitch Ratings.

According to Macey, once corporations were required to have themselves assessed, they shopped around to obtain the best ratings. Correspondingly, to attract business, credit rating companies sought to please the companies they evaluated, resulting in inflated ratings. The original purpose of the practice was subverted, and as a consequence, the agencies—and, we might say, also the regulations—contributed to the economic collapse of 2008.

A vivid illustration of the problem is the plight of the California Public Employees' Retirement System (CalPERS), which relied upon the big three rating companies in making decisions about how to invest the retirement funds for state employees. CalPERS suffered $1 billion in losses as a result of its investments in several companies, which had been given top ratings by the big three. A year later the companies defaulted. CalPERS is now suing the raters over their "wildly inaccurate" risk assessments.[45]

While Macey is concerned with a specific class of regulations, his argument points to a general problem concerning laws in relation to profit seeking. Corporations—when operating according to Milton Friedman's version of social responsibility—do not seek to comply with the intent of rules or laws, as if they were Kantian subjects acting in accord with duty. Rather, they factor the laws into strategies for pursuing profit, avoiding them or exploiting them like other obstacles or resources. This is true in the case of the National Labor Relations Act of 1935, whose intent, as articulated by Roosevelt, was "a better relationship between labor and management," but which, when factored into strategy, became an obstacle to profit and, consequently, led to the transnational outsourcing of labor. This is true also of legislation creating public assistance programs in California. A 2004 study found that Wal-Mart Stores, Inc., effectively exploited the programs as a resource. Employees were forced to use them, thereby costing the state some $86 million annually, converted, in turn, into Wal-Mart profit.[46]

Wal-Mart, however, to continue with this example, is not only an economic agent subject to government regulations. It is also itself a regulator, in fact, a regulator of precisely the sort Katharina Pistor discusses in Chapter 13. It is a multinational corporation doing business, according to its website, in twenty-seven different countries, with over 10,000 retail outlets, employing 2.1 million people, and having annual revenue for fiscal year 2012 of $444 billion.[47]

Wal-Mart has influence over worldwide production of goods by virtue of setting standards for its suppliers located around the globe. While allegations about its employee practices continue, the company has also taken a leadership role in sustainability, developing a "scorecard" for assessing the sustainability practices of its suppliers. The scorecard contains fifteen questions, related to environmental pollution (for example, "What are your total greenhouse gas emissions in your most recently completed report?"); resource consumption ("Have you set publicly available water use reduction targets?"); and labor standards and community relations ("Do you invest in community development activities in markets you source from and/or operate in?").[48] Wal-Mart has set specific goals it seeks to meet in each of the areas. As a result of the scorecard, according to greenbiz.com, "tens of thousands of suppliers increased their investments in sustainability."[49] And, just as Pistor suggests is true of multinational corporations more generally, industry watchers believe that Wal-Mart's "sustainability program will become a de facto standard for the industry."[50]

A key difference between government regulations and standards established by multinational corporations like Wal-Mart is that, in the latter case, employees and suppliers are strongly motivated to comply not just with the "letter of the law," so to speak, but also with its spirit. How well employees perform, in relation to these standards, affects how well they do economically, so they have a practical interest in advancing the goals set up by the company. Moreover, in the case of standards that promote social goals, the personal values of employees may give them added incentive to comply.

If managers view their role exclusively in terms of corporate profit maximization, then external governmental regulations appear either as obstacles or resources, but never as moral obligations with whose spirit the managers seek to comply. Curiously, therefore, standards, like those in Wal-Mart's sustainability initiative, operate more like duties, in the Kantian sense, than do governmental rules and regulations.

Why has Wal-Mart adopted the sustainability initiative? Doing so, obviously, makes the company appear socially responsible, a steward of the environment, and a high-minded public servant concerned with promoting a better world for all. Meanwhile, in July 2012, protestors marched in Los Angeles's Chinatown against a proposed opening of a new Wal-Mart store there.[51] The company is in a public relations struggle, and the sustainability initiative helps it to counter criticism.

Even if Wal-Mart's sustainability initiative is pragmatically motivated, however, there is little doubt that it is also real. It can have a significant positive impact around the globe—Wal-Mart being the central planner and regulator Pistor imagines, and also, in this area, a model for other multinational corporations. The company illustrates the power of the corporation for good, as Paine describes in Chapter 2. That power depends on corporate managers, as Paine suggests, taking a leadership role, seeing problems in the world that are in need of solution and solving them, seeing opportunities for bettering humanity and pursuing them. In these kinds of leadership roles, corporate managers act in accord with the ideals of citizenship in a globalized world, even if the pragmatic purpose behind those actions is to have the public look favorably on the corporation. Citizenship shapes the values and ideals against which entrepreneurs and managers are measured. Those entrepreneurs and managers, in turn, create and shape the values and internal regulations that guide corporate operations, even if only to look good in the eyes of citizens.

While Wal-Mart, as transnational regulator and central planner, has advanced a sustainability agenda, it has done less well in fashioning suitable regulations in other areas, notably labor relations. In 1998, the company aggressively entered the German market. Eight and a half years later it was pulling out, reportedly at a considerable loss. One of the main causes of Wal-Mart's failure, according to one study, was its " 'hubris and clash of cultures'-approach to labor relations."[52] Rather than endeavoring to hammer out a transnationally acceptable approach, it "imported its U.S.-style company ethic," resulting in "repeated clashes with unions."[53] The company also suffered accusations of "repeated infringement of some important German laws and regulations."[54] In short, Wal-Mart found itself in opposition to both German custom and German law, exhibiting its failure, in these regards, as transnational central planner and regulator.

If transnational corporations must perforce be regulators, as Pistor suggests, then they are effectively internalizing standards set up by diverse national governments, making them their own. This is in some ways the flip side of Macey's regulation by assimilation, in which governments formulate rules for corporations based on best corporate practices. In Pistor's transnational corporation, business managers adopt as internal company standards rules or laws formulated by governments to regulate the corporation. This latter option produces better results, since in these cases the corporations are not endeavoring to find ways around laws, but to make their own practices, in pursuit of profit, reflect laws.

Most of the chapters in this section concern the regulation of already established corporations. But we might also wonder about the general incorporation laws themselves, which in the nineteenth and twentieth centuries replaced chartering, the older system in which an explicit legislative act was necessary to create a new corporation. With the advent of general incorporation laws, citizens could create legal corporations by a more or less straightforward process of registration. The intent was to counter the quasi-aristocratic privilege involved in chartering. Have there been unintended consequences to general incorporation?

In Chapter 14, Harvard anthropologists Jean Comaroff and John Comaroff look at how ethnic groups make use of the legal corporate form to assert their place in society and, hence, to claim citizenship. The South African San, formerly and disparagingly known as Bushmen, are not culturally extinct, but they no longer, as the Comaroffs note, exhibit much of a "collective identity." In the San story, as well as others the Comaroffs recount, can be glimpsed the appeal or attraction of the corporate form, why it plays into the fantasies and aspirations of people. When first the South African government and then a global pharmaceutical company decided to develop and commercialize production of the Hoodia plant long used by their ancestors, the San, with help from a human rights activist, mobilized a collective identity to assert intellectual property rights and, hence, a share in the profits. The ethnic group was, in effect, reborn as a corporation.

Something similar has happened in case after case, not only in Africa but also in the United States and elsewhere. Whether ethnic groups have adopted the for-profit corporate form to secure proceeds from intellectual or artistic property, tourism, natural resource exploitation, or gambling, the phenomenon of "ethno-corporations" reveals another dimension of the relationship between corporations and citizenship. Citizens have desired the corporate form to promote their own aspirations for belonging in society. From this perspective, the desire for individual wealth appears as more than merely economic; it is also an aspiration for status within the community of citizens, a claim to self-worth. In the case of ethno-corporations, it is explicitly about the empowerment and recognition of ethnic groups as part of a citizenry. Such empowerment seems fully in keeping with the original anti-aristocratic spirit of general incorporation.

At the same time, ethno-corporations, while empowering ethnic groups within national imaginaries, also pose challenges for national belonging understood as citizenship. And this is perhaps an unintended consequence of general incorporation. As ethnic groups achieve wealth and power through the corporate form, they also sometimes, as in the case of many Native American communities, endeavor to assert partial or even full autonomy from the national government. Moreover, even if they do not strive for political autonomy, ethnic groups as corporations draw boundaries among national citizens, deciding who is and who is not entitled to membership in the corporation, disenfranchising some in the name of enfranchising others.

While these two problems—secession and exclusion—are especially obvious in the context of the rich forms of belonging associated with ethnic groups as corporations, they are actually typical of corporations more generally, as many of the chapters in this volume demonstrate. Corporations struggle against the regulations of the national states in which they are incorporated and operate, striving for greater autonomy and control; but they also struggle over boundaries: Who are the rightful beneficiaries of a corporation?

The Comaroffs show that general incorporation laws, as made use of by ethnic groups, have reorganized the senses of ethnic belonging and, with it, belonging within the nation. In the final chapter in this section, anthropologist Karen Ho looks at a different aspect of how government regulations affect belonging. She argues that "for much of the twentieth century, corporate institutions and employers were a main focus of social reform and amelioration." "Socially ameliorative policies, programs, and regulations," she continues, "from environmental protection to equal employment initiatives, were scaffolded upon bureaucratic institutions (framed as located in the private sphere). The corporation was seen not only as one of the foundations of a stable society, but also as an appropriate venue in which to further struggles for inclusivity." However, during the past several decades, precisely when ethnic groups were adopting the corporate form, "Wall Street-led financialization of the economy has catalyzed the demise and liquidation of corporate America."

Ho claims that, in this recent period of dominance, Wall Street has, effectively, dismantled or "liquidated" the corporation—or, at least, the U.S. corporation as it was known during the mid-twentieth century. From the perspective of Wall Street, she argues, the social value of a corporation is exhaustively measured by its stock price. Regulations and practices bolstering this view resulted in what she calls the "financialization" of the corporation, "where accumulation is mainly through financial channels as opposed to industrial production or trade." In the worldview of Wall Street, the social purpose of corporations as producers of goods and services society values transmogrifies into the profits corporations produce for their investors, or, more accurately, for short-term investors and for Wall Street itself.

It is worth recalling that the large financial companies—Goldman Sachs Group, Inc., JPMorgan Chase & Co., Morgan Stanley, Citigroup, and the like—are also themselves publicly traded corporations, most of them having gone public in the 1980s, after existing as partnerships in some cases for more than a century. During the past few decades, these publicly traded financial corporations have been the principal proponents of the shareholder value theory championed by Milton Friedman, and reflected in the Michigan State Supreme Court's opinion in *Dodge v. Ford*—namely, that "a business corporation is organized and carried on primarily for the profit of the stockholders."[55]

It is not hard to grasp that the shareholder value theory, as ideology, fosters the self-interest of the financial sector, helping to redirect profits from other industries into that sector. The great irony brought to light by the 2008 economic collapse, however, is that, rather than protecting the interests of their own shareholders, corporate managers at these financial institutions "transferred the ultimate financial risk from themselves to their shareholders,"[56] effectively leaving the latter, along with the American public, to absorb the losses.

Ho's chapter is not just about the financialization process. She is also concerned with its human consequences, among them the disruption of life expectations for corporate employees. Where mid-level employees could once imagine a career inside a single corporation, climbing "the corporate ladder," today they more typically find themselves "downsized," a process that increases the market value of the company, at least in the short term, and boosts profits for investors, but ignores employees as stakeholders.

Particularly for minorities and the underprivileged, Ho argues, the corporate ladder had come, during the mid-twentieth century, to furnish a pathway to social and economic advancement, and hence enfranchisement. Its dismantling during the past three decades, in turn, has disproportionately impacted these same segments of society.

Wall Street investment bankers drove the financialization process. What was their intent? The cynical view—and one, no doubt, not entirely lacking in validity—is that the bankers were simply out after profit, regardless of the damages they caused. As Ho explains, however, many of the bankers espouse the belief that they are benefiting society by contributing to efficiency and promoting competitiveness. This belief is bolstered by a "market knows best" attitude, in which the outcries of citizens can be ignored in principle. Ho concludes that, by dismantling the corporation, the bankers have, in fact, done just the opposite, thereby ultimately harming citizen-workers in the United States. It is important to recall that these banks serve a vital purpose: they help other corporations, as well as governments, raise capital through the issuance of stock and bonds.

As Ho explains elsewhere, investment bankers see themselves as enabling "the world to create mature financial markets, which in turn will raise the quality of life and teach the values of democracy."[57] Whereas other corporations, as profitable philanthropies, provide society with goods and services people need and want, the social purpose of investment banks is to stitch the world together into one gigantic marketplace by coordinating financial transactions, thereby enhancing the efficiency with which goods and services are provisioned.

So what precisely is the problem? A possible conclusion is that these same bankers may have placed too much faith in the dictum that pursuing short-term profits above all else necessarily promotes social good. As in the case of regulations propounded by governments, belief systems such as those subscribed to by investment bankers may have unintended consequences. Perhaps the Wall Street belief system is defective; if Ho is right about the American case, then investment bankers' pursuit of short-term profit harms rather than helps the typical American citizen.

At the same time, citizenries in democratic societies must be the ultimate judges of whether the short-term profit orientation benefits society. Through elected officials, they must decide on what laws should regulate financial institutions as well as other corporations. But, perhaps most important, citizens must also bear responsibility for the worldviews to which they subscribe, worldviews that figure the corporation as an institution with distinctive social purposes.

In the wake (if not the midst) of the Great Recession in the United States, both the Tea Party and Occupy Wall Street movements remind us of earlier eras in American history, when citizens rose up to demand fundamental change. Will epochal changes take place today as well, either in the regulatory environment for corporate activity or in public understanding of the social purpose of corporations?

What Do CEOs Think?

The regulatory and worldview challenges posed by corporations in relationship to the requisites of citizen-based polities like modern nations lead us to ask how the CEOs of for-profit corporations more generally see their role. Nien-hê Hsieh, formerly of Wharton's Legal Studies and Business Ethics Department and now a professor at Harvard Business School, takes up this question in the final chapter. Do CEOs see themselves as charged with making decisions about how best to fulfill the social purposes of their corporations? How focused are they on shareholder value and short-term profits?

The views articulated by some CEOs, like John Abele, co-founder and former director of Boston Scientific, the publicly traded medical robotics company, emphasize the social purpose of the enterprise. Abele thinks of corporations as "profitable philanthropies," making profits by advancing the well-being of people and society more generally. Fedele Bauccio, founder and CEO of Bon Appétit Management Company, which provides catering for many corporations and universities, echoes this sentiment. His company has long had commitments to utilizing locally grown foods and promoting sustainable agricultural practices, while simultaneously making a profit. William Cobb, CEO of the privately held JM Smith Company, a pharmaceutical distributor based in Spartanburg, South Carolina, in what could be a paraphrase of Jeffery Smith's modified alignment theory of management, describes the need for "balancing" the interests of "shareholders, customers, employees, vendors, and the community we live in."

Such views are characteristic of many, although by no means all, CEOs, as Enron and other cases remind us. Abele himself distinguishes between what he calls the "enterprise model," where entrepreneurs are in it for the long haul, and "serial entrepreneurship," where the interest of entrepreneurs is in selling the new company as soon as possible, getting out quickly and with a profit. We are reminded here of Wall Street's emphasis on short-term profits. Serial entrepreneurs may not conform to the modified alignment theory and, correspondingly, may be less concerned, as CEOs, with balancing the interests of multiple stakeholders. CEOs with long-term commitments to their companies, correspondingly, are more likely to see the self-interest of the corporation as dependent upon helping their employees, vendors, and consumers, as well as the local communities and governments in which they operate.

The long-term temporal horizon of CEOs in Abele's "enterprise model" is reminiscent of the view articulated by Henry Ford in *Dodge v. Ford*, and is consonant with the "business judgment rule" rather than the Michigan Supreme Court's remark. Such a temporal orientation can be seen in the remarks of other CEOs as well, such as Bon Appétit's Bauccio, who advocates for sustainability: "If . . . I have to give up profits to do something down the road . . . that's going to create more demand for what we do then I'm going to do it, even if profits [in the short run] suffer, because to me that's the economic engine."

At the same time, CEOs cannot, for obvious reasons, ignore profits—especially not CEOs of publicly traded companies. Gordon Bajnai, former prime minister of Hungary and also deputy CEO of a financial company there, noted that in times of economic crisis, CEOs must "principally seek to please shareholders by . . . raising shareholder value." Yet like Abele and other CEOs, he appreciates that "the company—for its own good—must also be mindful of its wider circle of stakeholders: employees, the environment, and the state," a position in accord with that articulated by Jeffery Smith as well as Jeffrey Sturchio and Louis Galambos in this volume.

As the chapters in this volume suggest, the key issue at the interface between corporations and citizenship is profit. Even prior to the rise of democratically organized societies, states recognized the value of permitting self-organizing groups to engage in economic pursuits that resulted in gain. The prospect of profit stimulates ingenuity, hard work, and determination, all of which can benefit society. Once the notion of citizenship took deep root, however, the ills produced by the pursuit of profit also came to public light. For democracies, controlled at least in theory by citizenries, the key questions have been whether and in what measure corporate activities in pursuit of profit have promoted the public interest; and can citizenries, acting through elected governments, establish rules and regulations capable of ensuring that profit-seeking does not harm citizens and undermine the public good.

These questions have become especially pressing in recent years, when short-term profit seeking is widespread and the dominance of financial institutions over productive ones so evident. The time has come to take stock of the modern business corporation. We need to consider not just regulations, which run the risk of backfiring, but also, perhaps even more important, how we, as citizens, should think about what the corporation is and what its proper role in society ought rightly to be. Should the overriding goal of the corporation, as democratically sanctioned social form, be profit? Or should its goal be the provisioning of society with the goods and services people want and need, with profit as the reward for provisioning? Our hope, in this volume, is not to offer definitive answers, but rather to provide readers with a better understanding of the issues involved, thereby contributing to more informed public debates and fostering the public interest.

PART I

Are For-Profit Corporations in the Public Interest?

Chapter 2

Corporate Power and the Public Good

Lynn Sharp Paine

Corporations are instruments. And, like most instruments, they can be used for good or ill. In this chapter, I focus on the corporation's power for good.[1] This might seem an odd choice of topic, especially at a time when the news is filled with cases of corporate mismanagement, influence buying, and wrongdoing that threaten the public interest.[2] In this context, getting to the root of corporate malfeasance might seem a more urgent task. Yet, while corporate malfeasance certainly merits attention and is a topic I have addressed at length elsewhere, it is also important to recognize that corporations also have enormous power for good.[3] Indeed, corporations have done a great deal of good—even beyond their routine business of providing society with needed products and services—and could, if suitably led and governed, do even more.

Consider, for example, that corporations were a driving force behind the dramatic rise in prosperity across many parts of the world in the last half of the twentieth century. Between 1975 and 2002, more than 97 percent of the world's countries experienced increased wealth, and almost half saw annual increases of more than 3 percent in real gross domestic product (GDP).[4] According to the World Bank, global income has doubled since 1980, and more than 450 million people have been lifted out of extreme poverty since 1990.[5] This achievement cannot be attributed wholly to corporations, of course. Credit is also due to liberalizing governments around the world and to multilateral institutions that opened up the international trading system after World War II. Improvements in education and the free flow of capital also played a role. But technology and advances in corporate management were also central. Most major corporations adopted a product divisionalized structure that enabled them to span the globe and grow to a massive scale. Today's large corporations are among the most powerful and capable actors on the world stage. They are also among our most dynamic and innovative. Focusing attention only on the ill effects of corporate power makes it easy to forget that corporations are a resource for addressing some of the major problems facing the economy and society today.

In this chapter, I argue that corporations not only can, but must, play a role in addressing these problems. Some companies are already doing so, and their experience offers useful lessons for others that would go down this path. Before discussing a few examples of such companies and drawing out some lessons from their experience, I will say something about the kinds of problems I have in mind and the potential threats they pose for the economy and society more broadly. I will then consider some of the standard objections to the idea that corporations—particularly publicly traded, for-profit corporations—can do more to serve the public good. I will conclude with a few observations about what it will take for more companies to embrace this role.

Critical Problem Areas

When I talk about major problems facing society and the economy, I have in mind a particular set of problems that came out of a project I conducted with my colleagues Joseph L. Bower and Herman B. Leonard in 2007. As part of the preparation for Harvard Business School's centennial summit in 2008, we organized a series of meetings with business leaders from different regions of the world to talk about the future of market capitalism. Our aim was to understand what issues were on the minds of these leaders and what that might imply for the school's agenda in its second century. To this end, we convened forums for a select group of leaders from each of four regions: Europe, Asia, Latin America, and the United States. In customary Harvard Business School fashion, we provided participants with a "case" to prepare in advance. The "case" consisted of excerpts from the World Bank's then just-published scenario for the world economy out to 2030 along with other data on long-term trends affecting the global economy.[6] In our meetings we asked participants for their views on the prospects for market capitalism, and we asked them to identify what they saw as the major threats and opportunities facing the system in the years ahead.

These forums, which were held *before* the financial crisis of 2008, yielded some findings that we found surprising. We learned that these business leaders were quite concerned about a number of forces that, left unchecked, could potentially lead to slowing the global economy's growth or, worse, reversing much of the twentieth century's progress in raising living standards across the world. As we listened to the conversation, we grouped participants' concerns into eleven major areas. Ten involve active forces that could severely disrupt the economic system. Although these forces are connected, they are reasonably distinct. The eleventh reflects an overarching concern about the adequacy of existing institutions to address these ten issues. Rather than going through each area in detail, let me highlight three that relate to company examples that will be presented later in this chapter.[7]

The Financial System

As mentioned, these forums took place before the subprime crisis and financial meltdown of 2008, so it is noteworthy that even then the assembled business leaders were concerned about the stability of the financial system. They worried about the system's capacity to handle the trillions of dollars flowing through it at lightning speed each day and about the lack of visibility into its workings and the forces driving it. Some questioned whether anyone truly understood the overall system and the financial claims being traded. More pointedly, they were concerned about the relative scarcity of information about the operations and governance of hedge funds and private equity funds, and they were troubled by the impact of what they perceived as an increasingly short-term focus among some investors. Many commented on the challenges posed by the increasing complexity of the financial system and, in particular, on the difficulty of regulating or controlling it given the lack of transparency and the lack of accountability among key actors and institutions. Little did these leaders know that their concerns would soon be validated by a global financial crisis that brought lending to a standstill and precipitated the largest decline in world trade since World War II, putting many people in both the "real economy" and the financial sector out of work and accelerating a recession worldwide.[8]

Income Distribution

Perhaps the most frequently mentioned concern was the growing gap between rich and poor both *across* countries and *within* countries. Business leaders in all regions spoke about the dangers posed by this phenomenon. To be sure, the World Bank's projections show economic growth that will expand the world's middle class and narrow the gap between incomes in developed and developing countries in the coming decades. More precisely, the world's middle class is expected to expand to 1.2 billion in 2030 (from 400 million in 2005);[9] average incomes in low- and middle-income countries are expected to rise to 23 percent of average incomes in high-income countries (from 16 percent in 2005);[10] and the number of people living on less than $2 per day is expected to decrease by some 800 million.[11] Nonetheless, growth will be unevenly spread, and the income gap between developed countries and others will still be considerable. Within the United States and other developed countries, the gap between high-income and low-income households is projected to continue widening, and more than two-thirds of the low- and middle-income countries studied by the World Bank are expected to see increases in inequality.[12] Moreover, most of the growth in unskilled workers is expected to be in developing countries, home to a projected 3.3 billion unskilled and underemployed workers in 2030.[13] Many participants in our forums saw these trends as threatening the market system's perceived legitimacy. As one put it, "You cannot have moral credibility—if large numbers of people believe that the system doesn't work for them."[14] But participants also worried that the widening income gap would lead to social unrest and generate pressures for governments to adopt populist policies that would ultimately destabilize the economy and retard growth, making everyone worse off.

The Environment

Yet another set of concerns centered on the natural environment. This area included a range of issues with potentially serious social, political, and economic consequences. Participants talked about increasing concentrations of greenhouse gasses in the atmosphere and evidence of rising temperatures around the world. Many were concerned about the potentially far-reaching impacts of climate change—breakdowns in global agriculture, rising sea levels, the flooding of heavily populated coastal areas, the increasing frequency of heat waves, and the spread of desert-like conditions in sub-Saharan Africa. These issues were particularly concerning in view of the disarray among national governments and the seeming impossibility of reaching international agreement on an approach to reducing carbon emissions. Air quality and water quality also emerged as areas of concern, especially among Asian leaders who worried about the effects on human health and the quality of life. Concerns about the availability of water and increasing water scarcity were another aspect of this discussion. Indeed, research suggests that two to three billion people around the world may face water shortages by 2020 if patterns continue on their current trajectory.[15] When the effects of climate change—less snowmelt and more frequent heat waves—are combined with other stresses on the water supply, the picture looks even worse. Although participants saw these environmental issues as quite problematic, they also feared the growth-limiting effects of excessive, or poorly designed, regulation that might be enacted in response.

As noted, these are just three of the ten first-order issues that emerged from the forum discussions. But perhaps this sample is sufficient to illustrate the large-scale nature of these issues and their potentially far-reaching impacts if they are left unaddressed. Through any number of mechanisms—natural systems collapse, excessive regulation, political upheaval, domestic and international conflict—these issues could evolve in ways that erupt into major disruptions for the economy and for society more broadly. This is not to say that these disruptions will in fact occur. But the possibility cannot be dismissed out of hand. A question, then, is what can be done to mitigate these risks—and by whom. In particular, what role can for-profit corporations play?

The Role of Business

Some readers might find it far-fetched to suggest that companies can play a role in addressing large-scale issues like these. Skeptics would say these are "public goods" problems that should be dealt with by governments. Indeed, that is a perspective that we heard from some participants in our forums. As one business leader with this view put it, "I think there is actually very little that business can do. It's above my pay grade."[16] But most participants in our forums had a more positive outlook on what business could contribute as well as a more negative assessment of what could be expected of government. These two positions on the role of business—the skeptical and the optimistic—reflect very different outlooks and assumptions.

The skeptical position owes much to neoclassical economic theory. As defined by this body of thought, "public goods" have certain features that make it difficult for individual companies to make a business of providing them. In particular, the enjoyment of public goods cannot easily be restricted to those who are willing to pay for it, and providing these goods at scale requires coordinated action among many parties, some of whom would just as soon leave the effort to others. Both features pose challenges for companies that seek to tackle public goods problems. For one thing, these companies put themselves at a competitive disadvantage by incurring costs that, by definition, are difficult to recover and that their less public-spirited rivals do not incur. For another, an individual company's efforts are unlikely to provide a complete solution since these problems, again by definition, are massive in scale and can only be fully addressed by multiple parties working together in sufficient numbers to have an impact. In other words, corporate attempts to deal with public goods problems are likely to be both futile and foolish. According to this line of reasoning, the most promising solutions are likely to come from government—the only party with the authority and ability to organize coordinated action on a scale adequate to make a difference and ensure that the costs of the effort are equitably borne.

This logic also leads to questions about managers' duties to shareholders. If corporate efforts to address public goods problems are assumed to be a net drain on company resources, then these efforts begin to look a lot like waste or misuse of corporate assets. Pouring corporate funds into projects with no prospect of a return to the company might even be deemed a breach of managers' fiduciary obligations and possibly a cause for litigation.[17] This, too, is a perspective that we heard from some forum participants who worried that investors looking for the next quarter's returns would frown on spending money to address public problems beyond what the law requires. These executives were not necessarily happy about having to rely on government, but they saw no alternative. Those with a more skeptical bent also questioned whether companies and their executives had the knowledge and capabilities needed to take on these large-scale issues. To paraphrase one, "Executives may know about sourcing inputs or achieving operational inputs, but what do they know about designing a regulatory system or reducing poverty?"[18]

In contrast to those who thought companies could do little, if anything, about these problems, other participants in our forums were quite optimistic about the contributions companies could make. Those with a more positive view tended to frame the problems less in macro or policy terms and more as day-to-day issues for business. As expressed by an executive who had chaired several major corporations, "It's companies [that] over and over and over again at the front lines pragmatically have to deal with [these] very profound problems."[19] Many in this group brought an entrepreneurial perspective to the discussion: where skeptics saw issues that could be dealt with only by governments, optimists saw unmet needs and opportunities for business leadership.

Indeed, most of the participants in our forums took the position that companies could have a significant impact on these problems through the management practices and business models that they adopt.

These leaders emphasized the scope and reach of today's companies. With operations that span the globe, companies have the power to tap into a worldwide talent pool for new ideas. At the same time, today's companies can enact organization-wide practices that raise standards and improve conditions for people in dozens of national jurisdictions at once. In many cases, the standards followed by multinational companies are higher than those imposed by local law. Similarly, a change in the sourcing requirements of a major global company has ripple effects in workplaces and communities around the world. And "best practices" often spread from company to company through the power of positive example as organizations compete for profits as well as reputation. Unlike those in our forums who envisioned the solutions to public goods problems coming from government via top-down actions and policies, this group envisioned solutions arising from the efforts of pioneering individuals and companies. This more business-focused group also saw the change process differently—as a bottom-up phenomenon driven as much by market, social, and cultural forces as by government-created incentives and penalties.

The proponents of a positive role for companies also questioned the wisdom of relying on governments to take up this work, pointing out that governments, too, have limitations. One of the most critical is their limited jurisdiction. Many of the threats identified at our forums span national boundaries and do not fall neatly within the authority of any single government. There is also the matter of time horizon: solutions to these problems require long-term plans and commitments that extend well beyond the election cycles followed in most democratic societies. Although companies are often (justifiably) accused of "short-termism," governments are no better, and sometimes they are worse. Then there is the question of resources: at a time when governments around the world are politically and economically weak, many simply don't have the wherewithal to tackle these problems even if they were otherwise so inclined. Too many governments are mired in debt or paralyzed by partisanship. In the United States, votes in Congress are said to be more polarized than at any time in the past hundred years.[20] When it comes to remedies, standard governmental tools tend to yield crude, one-size-fits-all solutions that are not particularly well matched to the operations of the companies they are meant to influence or to the complexities of the problems they are meant to address. Although it may well be true that governments *should* take on these problems, there is little indication that they actually can or will in a timely and effective manner.

Above all, this group emphasized the business sector's capacity for innovation. These leaders argued that by mobilizing this capacity more fully, companies could build the capabilities needed to address these large-scale problems without compromising their own growth and profitability. Indeed, some in this group argued that innovations aimed at these problems could actually enhance company growth and profitability. In other words, those who saw a positive role for companies rejected one of the skeptics' core assumptions: the belief that efforts to address public goods problems would inevitably be a net drain on company resources. Rather than assuming away the business potential of engaging with these issues, the optimists were open to exploring what kinds of involvement could make business sense. In this spirit, they called for more experimentation and more investment in new technologies, new organizational structures and practices, and new business models and strategies.

As for the investors who might question the wisdom of these investments, proponents of a positive role for business pointed to the importance of attracting the right kinds of investors and ensuring their alignment with the company's objectives. To this end, these leaders recommended a policy of open and ongoing communication with investors about the company's goals, strategies, and performance.

Corporate Power in Action: Some Examples

The dialogue between those who are skeptical that companies can be a force for good and those who are more optimistic reveals the intellectual fault lines between the two views. The dialogue also provides a roadmap to some of the practical challenges that companies operating in this domain are likely to face. Clearly, one challenge is devising strategies that are both profitable for the company and beneficial for the system. Another is developing the new capabilities that may be needed to implement such dual-purpose strategies. Yet another is achieving sufficient scale or influence to have a meaningful impact on the problem. But the debate between the two positions is unlikely to be settled by conceptual arguments. The best evidence for what is possible comes not from executives putting forth their views but from examples of what companies are actually doing. To the extent that companies are finding business

opportunities or pursuing promising innovations with the potential to ameliorate one or more of the problem areas, that is some evidence for the optimistic view. The following case examples speak to this point.

Nike and Water Scarcity

As an example of promising technological innovation, consider what Nike has
been doing to develop a water-free technology for dyeing textiles. As the
world's largest producer of athletic footwear and apparel, Nike recognized
some years back that water usage was a major issue for the apparel industry
and for its own business. At multiple points in the value chain—from growing
cotton or processing polyester to laundering apparel—water is a critical input.
Conventional processes for dyeing textiles, for example, use something like
twelve to eighteen gallons of water per pound of fabric.[21] Nike estimates that
textile mills use about three billion gallons per year to process cotton and
polyester for Nike brand apparel, and that material vendors in Nike's supply
chain (which serve many companies other than Nike) use roughly sixty billion gallons a year in total.[22] The polyester industry is expected to use over a
trillion gallons in the dyeing process in 2015—equivalent to the annual water
consumption of Los Angeles, Chicago, and Miami combined.[23]

In February 2012, after nearly eight years of exploring emerging technologies for dyeing textiles, Nike announced a strategic partnership with Dye-
Coo Textile Systems BV, a Netherlands-based startup that has developed a
waterless technology for dyeing polyester.[24] DyeCoo's process is similar to that
used for decaffeinating coffee. Instead of using water as a dispersion medium
for textile dyes, the process relies on recycled carbon dioxide (CO_2—hence
the name DyeCoo) at high pressure. By comparison with the incremental
improvements in water efficiency made by the apparel and dyeing machine
industry over the past few decades, the new process eliminates water from the
dyeing process entirely. For this reason, some commentators view the technology as a potential driver of disruptive change in the industry. DyeCoo aims
to sell its CO_2-based dyeing machines to textile mills and dye houses that are
part of the supply chain for global apparel retailers. Although DyeCoo's capacity to manufacture these new dyeing machines is currently limited, Nike's
management was intrigued by the potential to grow the company and leverage
its technology in a way that could have a significant impact on reducing water
usage not only within Nike's own supply chain but more broadly across the
industry. The technology, moreover, has other benefits. Besides saving on water, it also saves on energy (since water does not have to be heated and fabric

does not have to be dried) and eliminates chemical effluent discharge into the water supply. In addition to these environmental benefits, the new process is said to cut dyeing times in half and produce a better quality product.

DyeCoo's success as a business is far from assured, and its technology is currently costly relative to existing, water-based dyeing techniques. Nonetheless, Nike made a strategic minority investment with the aim of helping the young company address these changes and develop and commercialize its technology for widespread use across the industry. Although the results of this investment are yet to be seen, it illustrates the kind of dual-purpose thinking— aimed at producing both public and private benefit—that some companies are beginning to bring to their innovation agenda.

China Mobile and the Digital Divide

As another example, consider the case of China Mobile, the publicly listed subsidiary of China's state-owned China Mobile Communications Company and the world's largest mobile phone operator by revenue.[25] Through its innovative rural communications strategy, China Mobile helped narrow the gap between China's urban rich and its rural poor while driving the company's own growth and profitability.

The strategy emerged from a difficult situation. In 2004, when China's government stepped up pressure on the industry to extend phone services to the then more than 700,000 unconnected villages deep in the country's interior, the company reacted with grudging acceptance. China Mobile was growing rapidly, and the management team was fully occupied building up the company's subscriber base in the nation's cities and eastern seaboard regions. Moreover, many inside the company doubted that the rural poor would actually use the phone service and questioned the company's ability to reduce costs enough to make the expansion profitable. However, as saturation rates in the urban areas rose to 80 percent—and even 100 percent in some cases— China Mobile's management team had an epiphany: they realized that the company's future growth would have to come from these very customers. The management team began mapping out what would become the rural communications strategy and launched a series of "innovation competitions" among the company's thirty-one provincial subsidiaries to generate ideas for reaching these customers and making phone services affordable for the average rural resident. Pilot projects to test these ideas followed.

The result was an innovative, low-cost distribution system that reached even further into the countryside than China's postal system. Between 2005

and 2010 China Mobile added more than 220 million rural subscribers, introducing them to basic cell phone services and providing for the first time connections with current information on markets for their products. To help fuel
this growth, China Mobile offered low-cost handsets, convenient payment
systems, complimentary accident insurance covering personal injuries and
disability, and solar-powered charging stations where subscribers gathered to
socialize and recharge their phones. With access to basic communication
tools and information on topics ranging from weather forecasts and product
prices to pest management and job opportunities, millions of China's rural
poor were able to increase their incomes and improve their standard of living.
From 2006 through 2010, the rural market was also a significant driver of
China Mobile's growth, accounting for more than half of its new subscribers
each year.

Generation Investment Management and Sustainable Investing

Yet another example of an innovative business model aimed at addressing
large-scale societal issues comes from Generation Investment Management,
a boutique asset management firm based in London.[26] Generation's flagship
product is a $6 billion global equities fund that invests in publicly held com-
panies whose businesses are aligned with the needs of a sustainable economy.
Generation's innovative process for making investment decisions combines
traditional investment analysis with techniques drawn from the field of sustainability research, such as environmental and social impact analysis. In assessing the quality of a business, for example, the process takes into account
factors such as use of energy, handling of waste, and quality-of-life impacts,
as well as competitive position, pricing power, and technological strength.
Through research on global trends in areas such as climate change, water scarcity, demographic flows, poverty, corruption, and corporate governance, Generation develops road maps for how industries and companies are likely to
evolve over time. The investment team then seeks to identify those companies
that are best positioned to thrive over the long term relative to the risks and
opportunities presented by these trends.

The idea for Generation evolved from a conversation between David
Blood, a former head of asset management at Goldman Sachs, and former U.S.
vice president Al Gore. Blood and Gore were both concerned that the capital
markets were not giving due regard to critical challenges facing the global
economy. Gore was more focused on the environment and Blood on poverty
and development, but they both thought these issues were deeply intertwined

and would eventually present major problems for business and society. Blood and Gore also found common cause in their belief that short-term investing only aggravated these problems and was, even by its own terms, a poor investment strategy in any case. In 2004, they decided to set up an investment firm to test their hypothesis that companies able to manage the challenges facing the global economy would outperform for investors over the long term. Indeed, Generation's financial goal is to outperform the MSCI World index by 9 to 12 percent over a rolling three-year period.[27] Although the impact of Generation's investment model on the industry and on society more broadly is difficult, if not impossible, to determine, the firm's financial performance as of this writing has tracked to the high end of its targets.[28]

Some Common Obstacles

These examples suggest that corporations *can* play a role in helping address large-scale societal problems. This is not to say that corporations can do it all or that they can do it alone. But they can make a meaningful contribution. Moreover, without corporate engagement, the problems are certainly going to get worse. However, it is important to acknowledge that developing and executing an effective dual-purpose strategy or business model is far from quick or easy. The examples discussed above and others I have studied point to some of the recurring challenges that companies are apt to face in going down this path. These obstacles help explain why more companies are not pursuing these opportunities, but they also reveal what is required for success.

One of the most common obstacles is lack of organizational knowledge and information. To be sure, many people working in corporations recognize that environmental degradation, the growing income gap, and financial system instability pose serious threats. But in many companies this awareness remains in the minds of individuals; it has not yet been internalized as common knowledge among members of the leadership team or converted into information that is actionable by the organization. Moreover, few companies have departments or personnel charged with understanding developments in the global macro-environment and working out the implications for the organization and its business model. Developing this knowledge is not a trivial undertaking; it requires skill and resources—both human and financial.

The Nike case provides a good example.[29] The company's efforts to reduce its water footprint and its decision to invest in a partnership with DyeCoo did not happen on a whim. For over a decade Nike's sustainable business and innovation group had been developing an understanding of the company's water usage across the globe both in its own operations and in those of its suppliers. As noted earlier, Nike had some 900 suppliers in 2012. In 2006, the then-new vice president for corporate responsibility decided to dedicate a full-time position to a "horizons director" who was charged with scenario planning and trend analysis. Over the next three years, hundreds of executives and employees participated in a series of scenario-planning exercises that explored the implications of global trends in areas such as water availability, oil and energy prices, demographics, and increasing connectivity through technology. The scenario-planning exercises later evolved into a mainstream employee engagement program to build organization-wide understanding of macro-trends, their potential business implications, and the importance that Nike placed on collective accountability for creating a sustainable business. Once water was identified as a critical issue, Nike's management team dedicated further resources to modeling the company's water usage and analyzing the costs and benefits of different approaches to reducing it. As Nike's experience shows, converting general awareness of an issue into knowledge and information that is useful for planning and formulating strategy requires a significant investment of time and resources. Most companies are fully occupied dealing with the problems of the here and now and haven't given a great deal of thought to how large-scale systemic problems might evolve and affect their business in the years ahead.

Many companies are held back by organizational systems, structures, and processes that are inhospitable to the thinking and risk-taking needed to explore possible solutions. Short-term goals and quarterly performance metrics favor incremental improvements in existing ways of operating—not game-changing innovations that overturn those ways of doing business. As a method for maintaining discipline, short-term mechanisms serve a useful purpose, but by their very nature they crowd out long-term thinking and projects with more uncertain payoffs. Yet, longer-term thinking and more radical innovations are just what's needed to make headway on the large-scale challenges we are talking about. Moreover, the kinds of inclusive, wide-angle strategies likely to make a difference run up against many taken-for-granted assumptions hardwired into today's companies. For example, apart from information on certain environmental emissions, few companies today have in place information systems that track the negative externalities produced by their activities—presumably on the assumption, widely accepted in economic theory but dubious in ethical theory, that externalities are not a company's responsibility.

In some situations, such obstacles can be overcome by "rewiring" the organization—restructuring, creating new information systems, changing performance metrics, and revamping processes for planning, budgeting, and reporting.[30] In other situations it may be necessary or desirable to create an entirely new organization. Generation Investment Management is a case in point. The founding partners recognized the mismatch between their novel investment strategy and the organizational models typically followed by traditional asset management firms. So the founders decided to create a new organization designed from the ground up to support their strategy. They spent more than six months building a team with the right mix of expertise from the traditional asset management world and the newer field of sustainable investing. Once the new team was in place, they devoted more than a year—before accepting any third-party money—to developing new analytic models and an investment process that operationalized their investment thesis. During this period, traditional asset managers and sustainability experts worked in assigned pairs to learn each other's concepts and methods for analyzing companies and industries and to build a shared understanding of the new investment process. Although the insight that "structure should follow strategy" is hardly new, Generation's experience is a valuable reminder of the insight's practical implications for companies seeking to pursue innovative dual-purpose strategies.

This new organization helped Generation deal with another common obstacle to recognizing and developing opportunities that reside in these large-scale problems: incompatible frameworks and mental models. For executives, like some who attended our forums, trained to think that governments should take care of these large-scale problems, it is difficult to see them as potential sources of opportunity. Business proposals involving these areas are apt to be met with skepticism and resistance just as, for example, many inside the company questioned whether China Mobile's investment in extending its mobile phone networks into China's remote rural regions could ever be made to pay given the rural population's low incomes. To be sure, resistance to change is normal and expected. But resistance takes on a special character when it is grounded in deeply held assumptions and beliefs—or when serious customer demand for the planned product or service is not yet evident. In those cases, leaders must be particularly skilled at articulating and communicating their vision and engaging others—both inside and outside the company—in their efforts. A sense of timing is crucial. Getting too far ahead of key constituencies—be they employees, customers, or investors—can be as problematic as lagging behind them. And unconventional approaches may be called for: recall that China Mobile offered farmers complimentary disability insurance to encourage them to sign up for cell phone service.

The China Mobile example illustrates yet another obstacle that can deter companies from pursuing opportunities in these problem areas: the lack of critical infrastructure such as transportation, communication, or basic financial services. In order to extend mobile phone services to the millions of rural poor living in remote regions of western China, China Mobile first had to find ways to fund the building of base stations across a vast expanse of territory from the treacherous mountains of Tibet to the expanding deserts of Inner Mongolia. As part of its push for universal access, China's government offered the country's telecom companies support in the form of expedited approvals, tax credits, and access to energy, but each operator was responsible for funding the infrastructure needed to extend the system. Because these remote areas lacked established banking and payment systems, it was also necessary to develop convenient methods for would-be customers to pay for the services they purchased. China Mobile developed a payment system that also allowed remittances to be moved efficiently and securely from family members living in the richer eastern regions. Filling such voids in the larger societal infrastructure goes well beyond the work performed by the classic entrepreneur tinkering away in a garage or basement. But it is often part and parcel of the task when the entrepreneur is seeking to build a business that addresses a major societal problem.

A Matter of Leadership

This chapter has argued that corporate power *can* and *must* be brought to bear on some of the pressing large-scale problems facing society today. By marshaling resources and drawing on their capacity for innovation, companies can devise strategies that help address these problems and, at the same time, promote the company's own growth and profitability. In other words, companies can benefit from being part of the solution. Success in this endeavor, however, requires a deep engagement with innovation at all levels—products and technologies, organizational structures and processes, business models and stakeholder relations—and a willingness to deal with the obstacles that companies often encounter when pursuing such dual-purpose strategies. Perhaps the principal obstacle to widespread adoption of such strategies, however, is a shortage of leaders who understand why these strategies are urgently needed and who are inspired to act on this understanding.

Understanding and inspiration will spread only if more leaders are able to see beyond the narrow confines of business-as-usual. Three types of blinders are particularly problematic. One is the customary indifference to externalities—particularly, to the negative effects of corporate activities on the commons and the wider community of stakeholders. This indifference is not only harmful to the parties who are injured, but it also leaves companies in the dark about these effects and unprepared for the ensuing repercussions. Another is the narrow time frames imposed by the capital markets and other institutional structures that govern how business operates. Financial reporting periods, accounting rules, tax policies, instant communications, investor expectations—all of these institutions and practices tend to focus corporate attention on the here and now. The third, as discussed above, is the conventional belief that public goods problems will be taken care of by government. Taken together, these elements foster a kind of corporate myopia that makes it difficult to see certain types of long-term patterns and problems in the wider environment. Although a narrow focus undoubtedly has its benefits, business leaders need a more expansive view to understand the full range of risks and opportunities facing companies, the economy, and society as a whole.

Nonetheless, business leaders as a group are nothing if not pragmatic. When more business leaders come to understand the real threats posed by the problems discussed above—financial system instability, the growing income gap, environmental degradation—as well as other public goods problems, when more understand that these problems will only be solved if business plays a role, and when more recognize that business can benefit from being part of the solution, more will undoubtedly take up these issues. My hope is that by sharing examples of companies that are already doing so and drawing out the lessons from their experience, this chapter will contribute to accelerating this process.

Chapter 3

How Big Business Targets Children

Joel Bakan

It may appear that, as a constitutional scholar, I have strayed beyond my disciplinary boundaries by publishing a book entitled *Childhood Under Siege: How Big Business Targets Children*. However, in this age of "increasing convergence of public and private agendas," as the International Business Leaders Forum has described it,[1] I find it increasingly difficult to separate matters of constitutional governance from those relating to the constitution of private power. What I examine is one aspect of the relationship between these public and private domains.

My central claim is that in five different areas—marketing and media, pharmaceuticals, environmental toxins, child labor, and education—large for-profit corporations are, in their pursuit of profit, increasingly undermining children's interests, and challenging parents' abilities to protect them. I will be looking at just the first three here.[2] Even a brief exploration of these three areas, however, corroborates the view of the modern for-profit business corporation I put forth nearly a decade ago in my book *The Corporation: The Pathological Pursuit of Profit and Power*. The claim is that corporations, unlike the individuals who staff them, are "*singularly* self-interested and unable to feel genuine concern for others in any context"; they "often *refuse to accept responsibility for their own actions*"; they "try to *manipulate* everything, including public opinion."[3] If corporations are indeed persons, as they are often argued to be for certain legal purposes, I suggest, we would have to conclude they are psychopaths.

The topic for the book was inspired by a typical parenting moment. It occurred some four years ago when I asked my then eleven-year-old son what he and his friends were up to online. "There's this really cool site," he said, "it's called AddictingGames.com." My first response was—"Addicting games—you've got to be kidding—they actually call it that?" But that was just the start. When I paid a visit to the site, I found, listed among its most popular games, one called Whack Your Soulmate, which allows players to determine, to quote the teaser, "how . . . your soul mate meet[s] his or her untimely end." With a click of the mouse, a player chooses from a variety of brutal murder scenarios between two animated "soulmates." In one scenario the woman punches the man in the face, elbows the back of his head, and then defecates on him after he crumples to the floor dead and bloodied. Other scenarios are equally gruesome.[4]

Another popular game at the site, Boneless Girl, has players smash an apparently unconscious woman, wearing black thong underwear and a bra, against various-sized spherical objects, and squeeze her through impossibly narrow gaps that cause her limp body to be crushed and contorted. "Poke and pull this scantily clad babe all over bubble-land," the teaser exclaims. "You'll be amazed by the small spaces she can fit through, and throwing her across the screen never gets old."[5]

These games, it is important to note, are not hidden in some dark corner of the web, where children could only accidentally or sneakily stumble upon them; they are located at a site aimed specifically at tweens and teens, ten million of whom visit it each month. The site is maintained not by some shady operator, but by a leading children's entertainment company: Nickelodeon.[6]

I feature Whack Your Soulmate and Boneless Girl because they are emblematic of a trend in children's media and marketing. Especially over the past two decades, marketers have become increasingly brazen in their efforts to squeeze profit out of natural childhood emotions, desires, and curiosities. Indeed, the marketers I have interviewed are candid about this—they state in no uncertain terms that their job is to uncover and then manipulate the emotional hot buttons and desires of young people.[7]

Whether it's targeting the natural attraction of children to sugary and high-fat foods; or their love of pets; or their natural fascinations with violence, horror, and sex; or their obsessions with what peers think, their insecurities, forming identities, desires to be and appear older than they are, their tendencies to get obsessively hooked on games and social media—for marketers all of these tendencies and predilections are resources to be mined for profit, with the aid of calculated strategies, sophisticated techniques, the best psychological science, the latest technologies, and without regard for the consequences to children or for childhood. These marketers are targeting the young in these ways all the time and everywhere.[8]

According to a recent Kaiser Family Foundation study, children spend eight to ten hours a day on average engaged with commercial media on numerous platforms and devices, increasingly interactive, social, and mobile;[9] they buy, or influence their parents' buying, to the tune of $1 trillion a year, up from $50 billion twenty years ago and $5 billion twenty years before that; and companies now pay $15 billion a year to marketers and ad agencies to tap into this spending.[10]

No doubt such marketing has been around for a while, but its new reach and power, along with the increasingly brazen and uncaring strategies of its practitioners, make it something different than it ever was. It has, in the words of one of its leading practitioners, Martin Lindstrom, become "craftier, savvier, and more sinister."[11] The evidence suggests ill effects on children and childhood. Childhood obesity is on the rise—children's weight problems have tripled over the past few decades;[12] young people are becoming "addicted" to games and social media, drawn away from human connections and other important parts of their lives;[13] they are thinking more aggressive thoughts and feeling more aggressive feelings as they play more violent video and online games;[14] and girls especially are suffering from low self-esteem, insecurity, and eating disorders, partly as a result, according to a recent report of the American Psychological Association, of an oversexualized media.[15]

It is not only such tangible harms that are a concern; there is also the question of what values our youth are learning from the media and the marketing directed at them. With that media and marketing now the "new central curriculum of childhood," it bears asking: What are kids learning from that curriculum?

Imagine for a moment that this was an actual school curriculum—that for five hours each day students were placed in front of screens to be taught that boys and men are, and should be, brutally violent, and girls and women are sexual objects; that identity, self-worth, happiness, and good fortune are defined by what people buy and own; that it is best to eat foods with lots of fat, carbohydrates, and sugar, to smoke cigarettes, to drink alcohol; that parents are stodgy and uncool, useful only for getting the things you want; that obsessive and compulsive behavior is normal and right. Parents would be up in arms if this were an actual school curriculum. We would consider this a disaster for children and childhood. What I am suggesting is that, with the new

Internet "curriculum" of childhood taking up twice the amount of time and attention each day as school itself, perhaps we should be up in arms.

I will return to this issue in a moment to ask what we can do about it, but I want to first address another key issue—the medication of children with psychotropic drugs. In 1980, it was rare for a child to be medicated for a psychiatric disorder. Today it is common and unremarkable, with tens of millions of children in Canada and the United States, some as young as two years old—and even infants—being prescribed powerful and potentially dangerous psychotropic drugs for disorders that were not even diagnostic categories thirty years ago.[16] The question, of course, is why: Why are so many young people suddenly apparently ill and in need of pharmaceutical treatment?

My contention is that at least part of the reason may be an overeagerness, on the part of both physicians and parents, to medicate children for behavioral and emotional problems—an overeagerness that in turn is, at least in part, rooted in pharmaceutical industry marketing tactics, and also in the industry's growing influence over medical science.

In *Childhood Under Siege* I tell the story of Caitlin McIntosh, a twelve-year-old girl who died when she hung herself with shoelaces in the bathroom at her school. At the time she was taking Zoloft, an antidepressant that her doctor and parents—along with most other people—believed was safe. But what they didn't know—and couldn't have known—was that the drug companies' own studies had demonstrated that Zoloft, along with another drug Caitlin had been taking, Paxil, could induce suicidal thoughts and behavior in children and teens.[17] They didn't know this—and this is the truly disturbing part—because the drugs' manufacturers had buried the studies.[18]

Drug companies are under no legal obligation to publish in the medical literature the studies they conduct and sponsor. Needless to say, their business interests lie with publishing only positive results and burying negative ones. The larger and inevitable consequence of this is a systemic bias in the medical literature. The *New England Journal of Medicine* recently revealed, for example, that while nearly every antidepressant study published in a medical journal over several years had reported positive results, only half of all the studies actually done—unpublished as well as published ones—were positive.[19] In other words, when doctors read and rely upon medical journals, they are not—as was the case for Caitlin's doctors—getting the full story about the safety and effectiveness of antidepressants, and presumably other drugs.

The problem of partial information goes beyond just medical journals. It extends as well to medical conferences and seminars where leading research-ers are often paid by pharmaceutical companies to deliver speeches touting this or that drug to their medical colleagues. This is hardly the most reliable setup for ensuring full, unbiased, and impartial information. As one Harvard medical professor has described it: "The only reason companies hire doctors is to increase sales. They call it education and doctors call it education, but it's about making money. The focus may get away from what is best for pa-tients."[20]

It is not only the dissemination of science that is problematic; it is also the science itself. Over the past thirty years—partly as a result of legal changes in the early 1980s that effectively privatized much medical research—pharmaceutical companies have become more and more involved in and in-fluential over the conduct of research on the safety and effectiveness of their products. This increased control has become a problem because of the fact that medical research is not merely a mechanical enterprise. In any clinical trial, there are numerous variables that demand discretionary choices. As Marcia Angell, a former editor of the *New England Journal of Medicine* and a Harvard medical professor, describes it: "You can control what data you look at, control the analysis, and then shade your interpretation of the results. You can design studies to come out the way you want them to."[21] This is why it is a problem when those who have control over the various aspects of a clinical trial also have interests—as pharmaceutical companies certainly do—in ob-taining particular results.

My concern is that, taking all of this together—pharmaceutical companies burying negative results, sponsoring speeches, and controlling research, and there are other issues as well that I cannot go into here—the risk is that drug company influence is tilting the area of children's mental health problems toward greater reliance on drugs. My point is not that children should never be prescribed psychotropic drugs. It is that industry influence over medical science and practice increases the risk of drugs being prescribed when they may not be needed, or when other forms of therapy might be more appropri-ate, or when harmful side effects outweigh potential benefits, or when chil-dren's difficulties are rooted in problems at home, in the neighborhood, or at school, or poor nutrition, or learning disorders, or other areas that are not addressed by drugs.

I will discuss possible solutions to these problems later, but first I want to look at a third and final area—the unique vulnerabilities of children to indus-trial chemicals. Here are some scary facts:

- Over the past few decades, the quantity of industrial chemicals pro- duced or imported by U.S. companies increased seventy-five-fold, from 200 billion pounds to 15 trillion pounds.[22]
- Twenty-six thousand new industrial chemicals entered the market during that time, to make for a total of about 90,000 such chemicals currently in circulation.[23]
- Relatively few of these chemicals—as few as 200 according to some estimates—have been tested for safety, while many of them are known or suspected to be carcinogenic, neurotoxic, or hormone disrupting; growing numbers of chemicals, in increasing amounts, are being found not only in the environment, but in children's and infants' bodies, for some chemicals several times the amounts as are found in their parents' bodies.[24]
- Childhood asthma, autism, leukemia, brain cancer, and certain birth defects and behavioral problems are on the rise; babies are being born on average a week earlier than they were thirty years ago; and signifi- cantly more of them are born premature.[25]

Yet, despite all of these facts, the official line of industry and government re- mains that unless and until exposure to and body accumulation of this or that chemical is proven beyond a doubt to cause tangible and immediate harm, we do not need to worry about it, and nothing needs to be done. As the U.S. Centers for Disease Control and Prevention puts it, "The presence of an envi- ronmental chemical in people's blood or urine does not mean that it will cause effects or disease. Small amounts may be of no health consequence, whereas larger amounts may cause adverse health effects."[26]

The problem with this approach is that while it is true that small amounts *may* be of no health consequence, the latest science is suggesting there is a good chance they *are* having negative health consequences—especially for children. "The more we look," says Dr. Leo Trasande, a leading children's en- vironmental health expert:

the more we realize that the paradigm from the world of toxicology [and the regulatory system based upon it] does not fit the universe of experience. It may be that very high exposures don't matter in adult- hood for a certain health outcome. But a very exquisitely small dose can have tremendous consequences if it's at the wrong time window. In general, the prenatal period [and during childhood and adolescence as well] where so much development of organ systems is occurring, appear to be extremely vulnerable windows for chemicals to have profound and permanent lifelong consequences.[27]

"We are the humans in a dangerous and unnatural experiment," Dr. Trasande sums up, characterizing our currently lax oversight of chemicals entering children's environments. He adds: "It is unconscionable."[28]

I want to suggest that the characterization "dangerous and unnatural—and unconscionable—experiment," though perhaps most obvious in relation to industrial chemicals, extends to all of the issues I have been discussing. It is a "dangerous and unnatural experiment" that, in the most general terms, we are allowing corporations—institutions specifically designed to exploit anything and everything for profit, and to ignore whatever ill effects might be suffered by others—to dominate the lives of our youth, to define youth cultures, to push powerful drugs to alter the emotions and behavior of children, and, of course, to fill their environments and bodies with dangerous chemical toxins.

The difficult question is, what do we do about all of this? Some say it is up to parents to protect children from the threats outlined here. I don't entirely disagree. Of course, parents are the first line of defense when it comes to protecting their children's interests in the face of corporate-created harms. But—and this is one of my central claims—parents cannot do all of it on their own. The problems are just too great.

One moment in an interview I did with Bruce Lanphear, another environmental health expert, drove this point home. He was in the middle of explaining the intricacies of how chemicals affect biological systems. I just stopped him and said, "Look, you're a dad, I'm a dad; I think I understand the science, but how do we deal with all of this as parents?" His answer to the question was not comforting. "I feel totally ignorant about most of it," he told me. "I can't keep up with it, even if the data were out there, but the data are not out there for most of these things." And more than that, he said, there's a further problem: even in relation to what he did know, will his own children listen to him? "Do you really need to wear toxicant-laced rouge or eye shadow?" he asked his daughter, to which, of course, she replied, "Yes, I do." "The best I've been able to do," he said, "is to get her to use a nontoxic fingernail polish." At the end of the day, Lanphear said—and this is coming from a leading expert in the area—"Parents can't be expected to know—they shouldn't be expected to be chemists." "Some things," he said, "are beyond our control." Some things are beyond our control as parents, not just in relation to environmental toxins, but in relation to everything I have recounted.

Gregory McIntosh, the father of Caitlin, the girl who committed suicide while on psychotropic drugs, was told, he says, "that Paxil and Zoloft were 'wonder drugs' and they were safe and effective for children." It was beyond his control, and that of Caitlin's doctors, to know the truth about increased suicide risk when that truth was being deliberately buried by the companies producing the drugs.

What about children's media and marketing? Here too, I suggest, many things are beyond parents' control. It is no longer just a television set in the living room that we have to worry about, but an array of digital and social platforms that often defy parents' attempts to monitor and know what their children are up to, especially when, as is increasingly the case, mobile devices make media and marketing accessible to young people at all times and everywhere.

Take fast-food marketing. Parents may have some control over what their children eat, but they have far less control over what their children *want* to eat. And when the fast-food industry spends $4.2 billion a year targeting youth with slick campaigns designed to create appetites for its largely unhealthy products, that is not something we can just dismiss.

So what do we do, not only about this issue, but about all the others I have raised? How do we move forward? On November 2, 2010, the city council of San Francisco voted by an 8-3 margin to ban fast-food restaurants from giving away toys with most children's meals. The ban, which, among other things, made the sale of McDonald's Happy Meals illegal, was lobbied for, initiated, and justified as a measure to promote healthy eating habits and to fight childhood obesity. On November 5, three days after the board's vote, San Francisco's mayor, Gavin Newsom, announced that he would veto the law, which he did a week later. The law, he said, went "way too far in inserting government to try to be the decision-maker in someone's life as opposed to parents." In a similar spirit, McDonald's spokesperson Danya Proud complained, "Parents tell us it's their right and responsibility, not the government's, to choose what's right for their children."[29]

But the veto was overturned, and the law prevailed, and that is because the San Francisco city council believed—contrary to the mayor and McDonald's— that the ban actually *promoted* parental choice and freedom by countering a powerful source of pressure on parents—over which they had no control— namely, toy giveaways—that made children want bad food. The new law, rather than encroaching on parents' freedoms, in other words, could be seen as freeing parents from the grip of their kids' marketing-stoked appetites, and thus better enabling them to more easily choose healthier options—an example and approach that might shed light on broader debates around child marketing.

Pharmaceuticals raise different regulatory issues than child marketing, and thus require different remedies. Here the problem is distorted information that results from undue industry influence over medical science and practice. There has been some movement by regulators in this area, but not enough. In 2007, for example, largely in response to the scandals around buried clinical trial data, a mandatory public registry of clinical trials for drugs was created in the United States.[30] There are questions about how effective it is in ensuring that physicians have the full story on drugs, but it is at least a start.[31] The practice whereby pharmaceutical companies pay doctors to tout drugs at conferences and seminars has also been addressed by lawmakers in the United States. Since 2012, companies have been legally required to disclose to the government to which doctors they are making payments (or providing gifts, free meals, and so on) and what the nature of those payments is.[32] The government is, in turn, making the information available to the public. Neither of these changes, however, touches the core issue of pharmaceutical industry influence over medical research—namely, the control of clinical trials.

Some—including David Michaels, an epidemiologist who currently heads the U.S. Occupational Safety and Health Administration—have proposed that the funding of clinical trials be completely separated from the conduct of those trials—that while companies should be able to fund clinical trials of their drugs, those trials should be conducted by independent scientists under the oversight of independent agencies.[33] It is a proposal worth thinking about.

Finally, with respect to children's unique vulnerability to chemical toxins, there has been progress on the issue around certain chemicals. Canada, for example, has taken a strong regulatory stance on bisphenol A. Overall, however, the presumptions underlying regulatory regimes remain the same: chemicals are presumed innocent until proven guilty. In Europe, regulators have reversed that presumption, requiring companies that manufacture or import chemicals into Europe to run health and safety tests on those chemicals in accordance with government protocols and under government oversight. If a chemical is found to be hazardous, the manufacturer or the importer must demonstrate that it can be used safely, or that no safer alternative is available. This is an approach worth considering. It has been championed for some time by U.S. Senator Frank Lautenberg, but so far has not resulted in new legislation reflecting this approach.[34]

At the end of the day—and this is my concluding point—while parents make choices, they choose in conditions that are not always of their own choosing—conditions that increasingly reflect the choices of for-profit corporations and that work against children's health and well-being. Governments have a role to play in countering corporate influence and creating conditions more amenable to the well-being and health of children. Whatever else may be said of them, governments are the only institutions in our society that have the authority, legitimacy, and mandate to set and enforce rules and standards effective for protecting children from corporate-created threats to their health and well-being.

By no means am I suggesting that regulation is the answer to every childhood problem, nor that other measures should not be pursued, nor that parents are not also responsible, nor that traditional "command-and-control" models of regulation are always best (co-regulation models warrant consideration in some areas, as I have already suggested), nor that our current political and regulatory systems work perfectly, or even well. What I am suggesting is that the ideologically driven view that regulation is never, or at least very rarely, appropriate—a view that now dominates public policy debates—is wrong, and that it has served, over the past thirty years in particular, to forestall measures that could have improved children's lives, health, and well-being.

In the end, I am saying that being a good parent today requires more than just making good choices and decisions as parents. We also have to work to change the conditions in which we make those choices, to become active in demanding public measures that protect children from harms at the hands of corporations. Part of being a good parent today, in other words, is becoming an engaged *citizen* in the collective practice of re-making society, doing our part to ensure that the will of the people, not that of the corporation, prevails.

Chapter 4

Corporate Social Purpose and the Task of Management

Jeffery Smith

In the midst of the postwar economic boom—well before the field of business ethics was formally recognized in the academy—Howard Bowen wrote in *The Social Responsibilities of the Businessman* that managers should be evaluated not merely with respect to standard entrepreneurial goals but also with respect to "the objectives and values of our society."[1] Bowen's basic point was that business managers are stewards of the public good and are morally responsible not only for enhancing the value of their companies, but also for the realization of wider social goals such as distributive justice and the economic development of local communities. In retrospect, Bowen's work has turned out to be an influential precursor to more recent discussions of business's role in society. Indeed, it has prompted some to assert that Bowen is the intellectual father of the contemporary "corporate social responsibility" movement.[2]

A reoccurring feature of Bowen's position is the notion that the responsibilities possessed by managers are derivative of the business corporation's larger social purpose. The social goals of corporations "are the goals which businessmen [*sic*] are expected to consider . . . when making decisions on production, prices, personnel, inventories [and] investment."[3] It should therefore come as no surprise that scholars who invoke arguments similar to Bowen's almost uniformly seek to ground the responsibilities of business managers in an understanding of the social purpose of corporations. A quick survey of popular and academic discussions illustrates, however, that getting clear on the actual social purpose of corporations is still by no means a settled matter. Should corporate social purpose be defined in economic terms, tied to improvements in welfare through the availability of goods and services? Or are there corporate purposes tied to broader goods, such as innovation, liberty, progress, solidarity, or sustainability? These are difficult questions, to be sure, and I do not intend to answer them here with any rigor. I do nonetheless intend to focus on the supposed link between corporate social purpose and the content and scope of managerial responsibilities that are commonly presumed among advocates of greater corporate social responsibility. So for the moment let us assume that we could not only formulate what the social purpose of the modern corporation is, exactly, but let us also assume that such a formulation was held in agreement by all who bothered to consider the question. What would this consensus view tell us about the responsibilities of corporate managers?

I focus on this question to highlight an implicit challenge raised by certain business ethicists regarding the relationship between a corporation's social purpose in a well-ordered society and the responsibilities undertaken by those individuals who are charged with directing its operations. The challenge is roughly that corporate social purpose says little about the responsibilities of managers. A corporation's social purpose, whatever it is, does not necessarily entail that managers deliberately manage the corporation with this purpose in mind. In the following pages I hope to provide a response to this challenge by examining theoretical perspectives that presume a strong relationship between corporate social purpose and managerial responsibilities as well as those that attempt to divorce the two concepts. In the end, while I do not forward any definitive answer to the question regarding what social purpose the modern corporation serves, I aim to question the soundness of those positions that maintain a normative separation between the scope and content of managerial responsibilities and the social purpose of the modern corporation.

The Alignment of Social Purpose and Management

Consider first the category of views that implicitly reject the aforementioned challenge and maintain, along with Bowen, that there should be a strong alignment between corporate social purpose and managerial responsibility.[4] I will refer to this as the *Alignment Thesis*. Freeman's influential stakeholder theory of corporate responsibility is illustrative. He maintains that the responsibility of executive management is to undertake efforts that "enhance value" for all "stakeholders" simultaneously, where a corporate stakeholder is defined as a constituency that is either impacted by, or instrumental to, the success of the corporation.[5] The most obvious examples of such constituencies are employees, equity investors, managers, suppliers, other financiers, and local communities. In one of Freeman's initial discussions of stakeholder theory, he asserts that the purpose of the firm is to serve as a mechanism for mutual stakeholder interest satisfaction.

> [The] stakeholder theory of the firm must redefine the purpose of the firm. The stockholder theory claims that the purpose of the firm is to maximize the welfare of the stockholders, perhaps subject to some moral or social constraints. . . . The purpose of the firm is quite different [for the stakeholder theory]. If a stakeholder theory is to be consistent with the principles of corporate effects and rights, then . . . the very purpose of the firm is . . . to serve as a vehicle for coordinating stakeholder interests. It is through the firm that each stakeholder group makes itself better off through voluntary exchanges.[6]

Note the degree of integration between corporate purpose and the function of management when corporations are understood in this light. Managers have a primary responsibility to institute and administer policies that, to the greatest possible extent, avoid "tradeoffs" and "conflicts" between stakeholders and create as much "value" as possible for each constituency in accordance with the purpose of optimally coordinating stakeholder interest satisfaction.[7] Advocates of stakeholder theory who have been influenced by Freeman have offered principled guidelines for management that identify practices that assist in the implementation of this overarching purpose. These include, for example, consultation and communication with stakeholder groups, processes to minimize health and safety risks to consumers, fair treatment of employees by balancing risks and rewards, and the imperative that managers avoid conflicts between their private interests and the interests of other stakeholders.[8]

The problem with this integration of corporate social purpose and managerial responsibility is that it presupposed rather than defended. There may indeed be a strong pragmatic case that one can develop for techniques that fall under the umbrella heading of "stakeholder management," which tend, over

time, to fulfill the defined social purpose of corporations to improve stakeholder welfare; but the prior, more basic question regarding what *moral responsibilities* managers possess in their special role is not necessarily answered
simply by what optimally promotes the welfare of stakeholders, either individually or in the aggregate. Even Freeman's early attempt at providing a normative foundation for stakeholder management failed to provide an argument
that established a conceptual relationship between corporate social purpose
and managerial responsibility. There he focused on the responsibilities that
managers have in how they treat others. His route emphasized how management involves moral responsibility based on the nature or effects of stakeholder relationships within a firm rather than examining if, and how, the
social purpose of corporations bears any relation to the scope and content of
what responsibilities managers possess.[9] Freeman seemingly equivocates on
the matter; he presumes either that corporations are purposefully designed to
improve the welfare of each stakeholder group, and therefore managers shoulder this responsibility, or that managers shoulder the responsibility to improve the welfare of each stakeholder group, and therefore this is precisely
what society should expect of corporations. The possibility that the institutional architecture supporting the existence of corporations is designed to rely
upon *different* managerial responsibilities is not seriously entertained.[10]

The alignment of managerial responsibility with corporate social purpose
continues to receive support throughout the literature in management and
business ethics. Porter and Kramer have spent the past few years making the
case for what they call "shared value" creation, which directs management to
see their role as developing business strategies that unify the interests of investors, employees, and the larger communities in which corporations operate.[11] Again, comparable to Freeman's more recent pragmatic justification of
stakeholder theory, they claim that managers should internalize the purpose
for which the corporate form has been designed—the optimal satisfaction of
"society's needs"—as a guiding norm for their operational planning and decision making. Still other academic discussions of corporate social responsibility emphasize how management should deliberately merge social with
strategic imperatives to articulate a company's aspirations to "do well by doing
good." The very mantra "doing well by doing good" is itself a succinct, if nonetheless vague, statement of the alignment view's conviction that the betterment of society should be a criterion by which corporations are properly
managed.[12]

The challenge to the Alignment Thesis identified in my introductory remarks rests on the plausible observation that an institution may rely upon subordinate social mechanisms that operate autonomously from the design principles of the institution itself. There is sometimes a difference—and even explicit separation—between the norms that define an institution and the norms governing conduct or decisions within that institution. Take a parallel case inspired by Rawls's seminal introduction of this distinction. Attorneys utilize criminal procedures, standards of evidence, and norms of conduct to vigorously defend clients even though they may have intimate knowledge regarding the true nature and extent of their client's crime.[13] The institutionally defined purpose of the criminal justice system to punish guilty individuals in proportion to their actual offense is not an aim that necessarily guides the day-to-day decisions of defense attorneys. Their role as an advocate for their client sometimes relies on responsibilities—such as client confidentiality to prevent the disclosure of guilt-confirming statements—that are separate from the institution in which their profession resides. Similarly, it seems possible to maintain that the institutionally defined purpose of a corporation may be specified quite independently from what is expected of its executive managers. Managerial tasks may be functionally distinct from the social goals that are ultimately served by fulfilling those tasks.[14]

This point is slightly reminiscent of Adam Smith's historically significant observation that the collective benefits of free trade are actually made more secure by individuals who act with motives that pay little attention to whether those collective benefits are realized. Indeed, critics of the Alignment Thesis, such as John Boatright, characteristically begin with a comparable starting point—that is, self-interested bargaining and exchange can actually support the interests of society's members. They offer a rich, detailed, and thorough analysis of the economic purpose of corporations, which are taken to serve the goal of making goods and services available in more and more efficient ways.[15] But, unlike Freeman and others' use of the stakeholder concept, this purpose does not settle the question as to what the motives of management should be; positioning himself in opposition to Freeman's approach, Boatright concludes that Freeman's position suffers from the stakeholder fallacy: "passing from the true premise that corporations ought to serve the interests of every stakeholder group to the false conclusion that this is the task of management."[16]

Boatright's view of the modern corporation is a contribution to the economic or financial theory of the firm that emphasizes that the corporation is an institutional form that preserves and extends the overarching aim of the market to improve social welfare.[17] A corporation is a nexus of exchange relationships between rationally self-interested individuals where the terms and conditions, as well as contributions and rewards, of each individual's participation in the productive activities of the corporation are contractually specified. What each individual contributes to the corporation is a function of his or her skills, abilities, interests, and bargaining position; the type of contribution and level of compensation offered by each individual is typically determined through specific contracts—as in, for example, the wages received by employees, the salary negotiated by managers, the prices paid by customers, or the rate of interest paid to bondholders—but, for those willing to assume the costs and benefits of control over the operation of the corporation, compensation comes in the form of ownership, or an entitlement to residual income. Nothing rules out that the nexus of contracts in any particular corporation could confer ownership rights to employees, customers, or suppliers, depending upon their willingness to exercise control and defer some, if not all, of their compensation to residual income; however, Boatright follows the work of others to argue that ownership is typically assumed by equity investors because of their (relatively) homogeneous interests, tolerance for risk, and ability to forego current or short-term compensation for longer-term welfare gains.[18] Other stakeholders, too, tend to recognize that their interests are better served when investors assume an ownership position. In all of this, so the thought goes, corporations coordinate lower transaction costs between economic actors and enable the efficient production of goods and services while providing rewards to individuals who contribute in various capacities to the productive activities of the firm.

How does this picture challenge the Alignment Thesis? In a typical corporation, ownership and the concomitant right to residual income is something that equity investors accept only on the condition that they have a reasonable expectation that those who manage the corporation will do so in a way that protects their interest in residual income, or profit. In the absence of contractually guaranteed compensation, investors will seek confirmation of this protection and, apart from attempting to gauge the actions of particular managers themselves, will rely on features of corporate law that provide assurances for the heightened levels of trust that are needed to secure investor confidence. Thus, the fiduciary responsibility that managers owe to shareholders is one important feature of the institutional makeup of corporations, along with such things as the fiduciary duties of board members, the limited liability of shareowners, and enduring corporate identity over time. But if investors reliably provide capital only on the condition of management fulfilling its fiduciary obligations to enhance profitability, and corporations generally achieve their cost-lowering, efficiency-enabling function, then the purported institutional purpose of corporations to enhance social welfare is largely an outcome of whether managers understand their role as primarily defined by their responsibility to ensure profitability. While this responsibility is shaped and constrained by other ethically derived responsibilities to stakeholders, it would, for Boatright, be a mistake to say that the responsibility of management is to serve the interests of all stakeholders simultaneously. Improvements to welfare result from management's primary, institutionally specified responsibility to manage the corporation on behalf of investors' interests.

None of this implies that managers have license to neglect the interest satisfaction of other non-owning stakeholders, or that it would not be good strategy to tend to the well-being of employees, suppliers, local communities, and the like. Kramer and Porter may be exactly correct. Neglecting to manage for stakeholder interest satisfaction may run counter to long-term viability of the corporation. The critic of the Alignment Thesis can retreat to a position that views stakeholder management as strategically enlightened but nonetheless one that provides an inadequate answer to a more basic normative question: *for whom should the corporation be managed*?[19] For Boatright the answer to this question is the stakeholder group that contractually negotiates for the rights of ownership, which typically, over time, will be equity investors.

I am not prepared in this discussion to provide a systematic critique of Boatright's or any other advocate's version of the economic theory of the firm, at least as it relates to questions of managerial responsibility or business ethics. But I do want to examine an important limitation to the position that will have implications for whether we accept some version of the Alignment Thesis.

Alignment and the Economic Theory of Corporations

The limitation I have in mind centers on the way in which various ethical concerns manifest themselves within the economic theory of the corporation. The normative leverage of the economic theory of the corporation—if it purports to have any—is located in its account of contracting between different stakeholders. The terms of how individuals are treated, the conditions under which productive activity takes place, the contributions offered, the roles that are assumed, and the compensation that is owed to various individuals are determined by the free agreement of individuals who seek to enter into a relationship with other members of the corporation. It is not difficult to see, however, that there are conditions that accompany contracting in actual cases that call into question the degree to which contracts are free or fair. Sometimes, individual lenders or customers make decisions without complete information. Others, like prospective employees, may be led to accept less than preferable terms due to geographic limitations, poverty, or highly specific job skills. Suppliers may find themselves in positions of unequal bargaining when dealing with a corporation that maintains a position of market dominance.

This type of problem prompts Boatright to offer an important set of qualifications. In order to turn the economic theory of the corporation into a normative theory, there must be an *idealized* account of the process of contracting. What would, in other words, each stakeholder negotiate as terms for their participation in the firm, assuming that conditions of freedom, fair bargaining, complete information, and competitive alternatives were present in the market? Idealizing the conditions under which contracts take place in this manner not only would tend toward greater efficiencies, but it would address the latent concern that the contractual terms under which a particular corporation operates sometimes fail to pass a basic test of ethical suitability.

The need to idealize the contractual circumstances in this way should come as no surprise. Normative theory is distinguished by the need to make many assumptions. Some of these assumptions are designed to abstract, or remove information from a consideration in order to eliminate the possibility that a theory is built upon specific cases or instances of a problem. Other assumptions made in normative theorizing do not abstract information, but add idealized information about the world we experience.[20] Rawls is again instructive in this regard.[21] He notes that citizens in the original position assume that they are drafting principles of justice for a "well-ordered" society—that is, a society where citizens are full participants in society's system of cooperation and who fully comply with whatever principles are selected. Although such an assumption causes consternation among many who read Rawls's work, it seems almost necessary to get the normative project off the ground in the first place. Once the principles tied to idealizing assumptions have been established, then the theorist can move to the more complicated task of exploring what the ideal theory may prescribe with respect to actual practices and actual social arrangements where full cooperation and compliance with principles of justice are not assured. Boatright's recognition that there are idealized contractual circumstances that may not obtain in all actual cases should not be viewed as a problem in and of itself. It, like Rawls's need to posit a well-ordered society, is arguably an essential component from moving the economic theory of the firm from its explanatory origins to a full-blown framework with prescriptive force.

All of this yields an important result. The terms and conditions under which any stakeholder participates in corporate life will be a function of how well their interests are protected relative to the types of contracts into which they would ideally enter. This still leaves open the question as to how these terms and conditions will be carried out and, if need be, enforced. Boatright provides a characteristically institutional response to this question.[22] The law should set the basic terms and conditions for participation in corporate life. This is not only because it tends toward more efficient results (given that corporations achieve their social welfare function when there is a single, dominant managerial objective) but also because stakeholders themselves recognize greater security and consistency through the law as form of protection of their interests.[23] In both respects—on grounds of efficiency and stakeholder recognition—managerial judgment and discretion is not the primary mechanism through which the ethical ideals of contracting should be secured.[24]

Elsewhere I have scrutinized this answer on the grounds that the call for law-driven, institutional protections for idealized contracts is insufficient.[25] The law, after all, is itself an imperfect institutional form, and the mere fact that the law is well developed in a particular area (for example, occupational health and safety) does not eliminate the need for managers to exercise judgment and discretion in how legal constraints are satisfied. There are other concerns that are commonly cited. The law is incomplete, slow to react to changes, and, importantly, is shaped by the very corporations that are the subject of its scrutiny. None of this is a surprise, and Boatright himself acknowledges how management still retains the ultimate authority when it comes to flouting regulations or taking advantage of the built-in bargaining power that management may have over a particular stakeholder.[26]

All of this may leave us feeling a bit ambivalent, if not confused. On the one hand, an economic theory of the firm that leverages the ideal of contracts to develop a normative account of managerial responsibility develops a plausible alternative to the Alignment Thesis. Managers are to manage on behalf of owners' interests because over time this will lead to improvements in social welfare. And although this social purpose is what justifies the social and legal arrangements that constitute a corporation, the functional task of management need not focus on this overarching purpose but, rather, primarily on the interest satisfaction of owners. On the other hand, even with this alternative picture in place, there are ethical qualms some will have as to how the preferred interests expressed through ideal contracts can be sufficiently protected. As long as management exercises discretion over how and when the terms of contracts are satisfied—as well as how and to what extent legal requirements are instituted within the firm—then there will be moments when the welfare of stakeholders remains (or should remain) under the mindful oversight of management.

Market Failures and Corporate Purpose

Does this result require that the normatively restructured economic theory of the firm align the social purpose of the corporation with managerial tasks, despite aspirations to the contrary? We seem to have arrived at the point where managers have the task of caretaking stakeholders' interests as a necessary condition for justifying the division of their specific role within a corporation from the social purpose of corporations in general.

I think Boatright may reply that such a worrisome alignment between corporate social purpose and managerial task does not occur, at least in the same way that it occurs for Freeman or other advocates of stakeholder theory. As long as the role of management is defined in fiduciary terms as advancing the interests of owners, or slightly more expansively in terms of administering contractual relations within the firm's internal hierarchy to preserve freedom and fairness, then any ethical constraints regarding what would, ideally, be needed to secure normative legitimacy of stakeholder contracts are exactly that—constraints. They do not replace the aim of management, which remains to advance owners' interests, not to advance the interests of all stakeholders at once.

This response still begs an important question, however: at what point do a corporation's economically defined aims become a conscious factor in managerial decision making? I am not simply asking whether managerial decision making at the level of the firm proceeds according to norms such as cost reduction and efficiency. The answer to this is an obvious affirmative. I am asking, rather, whether the larger social welfare goals that justify the existence of the for-profit corporation in the first place should become part of the sphere of concern of management.

Joseph Heath, who is sympathetic to many of the normatively spun dimensions of the economic theory of the firm, takes up a noteworthy position on this question.[27] He begins from the premise that modern society is "institutionally differentiated," which allows actors within economic institutions to adopt different motives and live by specialized norms that may not be the same as the motives and norms that guide action within political institutions or within other domains of social life. Business ethics, for Heath, is therefore a set of moral standards that pertain to the nature of corporate management as one social relation housed within the economic sphere of modern market-oriented societies; as such, a responsible manager is someone who carries out the actions necessary to serve this special role. This involves fulfilling the trust that is owed to owners to pursue profit and ensuring, like Boatright, that the terms and conditions necessary for membership in the corporation's internal hierarchy remain free and fair. But it also involves making sure that profit does not come through the exploitation of "market failures"—that is, the situations where markets fail to coordinate efficient outcomes due to lack of competition, information asymmetry, the presence of public goods, or the inability of market prices to reflect the true costs (or benefits) of certain transactions. To profit through the exploitation of market failure would be to undermine the market's aim of enhancing welfare, which ultimately justifies profit-seeking behavior in the first place.[28] Thus, Heath offers a code of sorts that spans a number of market failures for which managers should ideally act to prevent, or refrain from exploiting, in the pursuit of profit. These include imperatives to minimize negative externalities, reduce information asymmetries between firm and customers, ensure that prices are exogenously determined by demand, compete only on price and quality, refrain from political action that thwarts market-correcting regulation, and avoid anti-competitive practices such as erecting barriers to market entry.[29]

These constraints are ultimately derived from the institutional norm, or purpose, that corporations should improve overall social welfare. So we should not live under any illusions that the market failures code is a set of imperatives that express intrinsic value in distributive justice, employee autonomy, fidelity, or environmental sustainability; instead, Heath is quite clear that

what distinguishes the market failures approach from other such proposals is the specific account of how these constraints should be derived. Rather than trying to derive them from general morality . . . the market failures approach takes its guidance from the policy objectives that underlie the regulatory environment in which firms compete, and more generally, from the conditions that must be satisfied in order for the market economy as a whole to achieve efficiency in the production and allocation of goods and services.[30]

This account of the market-derived constraints placed on managers is one explanation as to why there are ethical responsibilities that fall to management that extend beyond simply ensuring that the terms and conditions of the corporation's internal hierarchy are free and fair.

Heath remains a proponent of separating normative responsibilities that come with the administration of an institution from the purpose of the institution itself. Managers' "administered transactions" define their responsibilities internally, with respect to owners and employees, but their "market transactions" demarcate their responsibilities externally, with respect to stakeholders that are affected by—and instrumental to—the firm's activities.[31] Notice, however, that the moment where market failures materialize is the same moment where management's role is expanded and coincident with the social purpose of the market. Responsibilities arising from the role of being a manager are responsibilities that arise because the corporation—as an arrangement within the market—fails to achieve the outcomes from which it receives justification. It is at this point where some version of the Alignment Thesis is operative, even for business ethicists who advocate an institutionally differentiated, economically grounded account of business ethics. Management is to be judged not only by how well they administer the corporation with regard to owners' interests with which they are entrusted, but also—from time to time—by how well they enhance the welfare of parties affected by corporate activity in the marketplace.

Heath may be comfortable with this result. The ability to differentiate economic institutions from institutions that serve other public purposes is more difficult to maintain, however, if the value of social welfare serves as a constraint on managerial decision making. Let us think about this inference by contrasting it with the parallel case previously discussed. Above I suggested that managerial responsibility, like the responsibility of criminal defense attorneys, could be separated from the social purpose of the institutions in which the tasks associated with those roles were normatively defined. The ends with regard to which roles are assessed can be separated from the ends that constitute the institutions in which those roles are housed. But notice that in the legal domain the criminal defense attorney is thoroughly insulated in her responsibilities from the purpose of the legal system to appropriately punish those guilty of criminal infractions. A vigorous defense of criminal defendants against prosecution by the state is so important that the actions of attorneys are never evaluated with regard to the *outcome* of the defendant's actual guilt or innocence. This is the result of a system that strives to protect individual liberty in the face of evidentiary uncertainty. So the process under which a defendant is defended, as well as the associated judgments made by a defense attorney within this process, are the sole criteria by which an attorney is professionally evaluated. She is not evaluated as to whether appropriate punishment has been administered to those who are actually guilty. While this is the aim of the institution of criminal justice, it is not functionally part of how the conduct of attorneys is evaluated. True, if the system of criminal justice was found to produce results inconsistent with the aim of appropriate punishment for the guilty, then that would serve as a strong reason to revise the mechanisms employed by the system to evaluate guilt or administer punishment. It would be a reason for redesign of the institution. But it would not be an obvious reason to criticize attorneys as failing in their role as advocates in a system of justice.

This stands in contrast to the responsibilities of managers on Heath's market failures approach to ethics in business. The welfare outcomes of the free market become part of the deontic constraints set out by the general principle that ethical corporations should not profit from market failures. The ends of the market, in other words, are normatively relevant in our evaluation of managers when they have the opportunity either to take advantage of failures in the market, or to institute practices that avoid taking advantage of situations where the discipline of the market cannot function on its own. In this respect the social purpose of the market becomes institutionally internalized; managers should take the market's ends as appropriate constraints on their planning.[32] Recent extensions of Heath's market failures account of business ethics further evidence this result. Norman argues that business ethicists have failed to provide a coherent story regarding the values that ground the regulation of the market and the values that ground that evaluation of ethical conduct of market actors.[33] Part of his solution—inspired by Heath—is that we conceptualize ethical conduct in business as a kind of self-regulation, grounded in the very same values that support the regulation of corporations in the marketplace. This has the effect of creating greater "symmetry" between the normative constraints expressed in regulation and the normative constraints expressed in platitudes about the need for the truly ethical corporation to move "beyond" mere compliance. It is this symmetry that I am arguing prompts the need to align corporate social purpose with managerial responsibility.

An Alternative for Alignment

Recall that part of the reason that Heath presumptively separates the norms governing the administration of an institution from the norms justifying the institution is that institutions are "differentiated" in modern, market-oriented societies. This means not only that behavioral norms between institutions are varied, but that institutions are often designed to accomplish specific purposes. In the case of corporations, however, the presumption of differentiation is cast somewhat into doubt. If I am correct in the preceding section, then the internal, administrative aspects of management cannot be so sharply distinguished from the external, market-oriented purpose of corporations. The *task* of management does indeed become constrained by a consideration of the ends that corporations have been purposefully designed to realize through law and public policy.

More generally, one might also begin to question whether it makes sense to suppose that corporations fit so neatly into institutional frameworks with exclusive—and precisely differentiated—economic purposes. Social welfare is certainly one value (perhaps the dominant value) that is used to evaluate whether corporate managers are fulfilling their responsibilities. Yet it is clear that corporations serve an array of values that are not necessarily tied to social welfare. As Christopher McMahon puts the point, the decisions of corporate managers impact a range of "morally important social values"; these are not themselves moral norms but simply the ends or values that corporations have a role in promoting through their productive activities.[34] "They include social justice, the defense of national territory, the maintenance of the rule of law (or more generally social peace), the promotion of social [welfare] (that is, the prosperity of the population as a whole), the protection of the environment, the fostering of community, the preservation of the health of the population, the advancement of knowledge, and the development of culture."[35] If we are inclined to understand these values in non-economic terms, and corporations have a role in promoting them, then it is not unreasonable to think that corporate social purpose may need to extend beyond merely the promotion of social welfare.[36]

McMahon uses this observation to explain why managerial decisions are in an important sense *public*. They are public because how a company is managed will often carry the effect of promoting or diminishing morally important social values, much like a lawmaker that weighs and balances competing considerations in deciding whether to support a particular piece of legislation. This seems especially true in industries for which these morally important social values are constitutive of the enterprise. Managers of pharmaceutical firms and other health care organizations have productive discretion over goods and services related to public health and must consider how to price certain products so as to make those products affordable. Aerospace contractors obviously play a dominant role in shaping plans for national defense and maintaining the public's trust. Prisons are now routinely owned and managed privately and scrutinized for practices that, while efficient, may impact the administration of justice. Automotive companies' willingness to integrate fuel economy goals into long-term planning will have some of the most lasting impacts on air quality and the reduction of greenhouse gas emissions. For-profit educational corporations are increasingly seen as a uniquely convenient opportunity for nontraditional students to acquire job-specific skills and satisfy career goals. Media corporations (still) ostensibly advance public knowledge despite the need to maintain profitability.

The point here is not simply that corporations engage in activities that impact (positively or negatively) this range of morally important social values. This is self-evident. The point is that market institutions are intentionally designed to afford corporations and their managers discretion over these social values through the market. At the most abstract level, markets are constructed to promote social welfare, and for-profit corporations are a mechanism through which this value is realized; but at a more concrete level, polities also decide what specific goods and services are to be traded in a market and ultimately produced and distributed by market actors. Utilities, transportation services, and health insurance are typical examples in this regard. They have been subjected to a public decision process as to whether the social welfare gains provided by the profit motive are compatible (enough) with the morally important social values to which these goods contribute.

The appeal of thinking of corporations as public in this limited sense is that it supports the intuition that the social purpose of corporations is not merely a by-product of some natural set of events. Purposes are fashioned intentionally. Whether or not national defense, education, public health, or other morally important social values ought to be administered through public institutions, private corporations, or some combination of both is a difficult public choice. The point worth underscoring is that it *is* a public choice. It is a choice about how institutions should be designed and how they may have features that require interaction with one another or features that express cross-institutional purposes. McMahon's insight suggests that corporations are not merely economic actors but actors that share institutional features in common with public entities. This presents a picture of corporate social purpose that militates against the assumption that institutions within market societies are, or necessarily should be, sharply differentiated in the sense outlined by Heath.[37]

A lack of sharp differentiation between corporations as economic actors and other actors who serve as administrators of non-economic public value offers yet another perspective on the Alignment Thesis. The alignment between corporate purpose and managerial responsibility makes sense under the foregoing picture because corporations are not merely economic actors, but economic actors that have been delegated limited public tasks. Corporate managers are essentially agents of the public good because their oversight over morally important social values "takes on a kind of legislative character."[38] What could otherwise be the sole work of a public agency has been effectively decentralized and turned over to corporations under the expectation that an array of morally important social values can be effectively realized. Put differently: the values that have been delegated to corporations require that managers manage a firm for the interests of investors only under the condition that these social values are preserved. But "it is not [always] plausible to . . . suppose that the courses of action that maximize profit . . . will always be optimal from the standpoint of [other] social values."[39] Managers thus face the added responsibility of balancing their concern for profit, and the associated value of social welfare, with the other values that corporate activities impact.

Notice that this account of the alignment of corporate purpose with managerial responsibility need not imply that corporate managers have the defining responsibility to "create value" for all corporate stakeholders or that managers owe anything like fiduciary duties to any group other than investors. It is more helpful to think about decisions related to morally important social values as context-sensitive ends that shape how the fiduciary responsibility to investors is fulfilled. In this respect it shares something in common with Heath's market failures account of managerial responsibility. The internal responsibility that managers have to act on behalf of owners remains a definitive responsibility; however, there are external responsibilities that arise from the ways in which corporate activity advances (or retards) the realization of morally important social values. This is most pointedly the case with corporations that assume positions of authority in the maintenance of specific social values.[40] Thus, for instance, defense firms bear special responsibilities regarding transparency and openness in contracting with public agencies, pharmaceutical firms are thought to bear special responsibilities in the area of medicine availability, and for-profit educational organizations have duties to uphold quality in pedagogy, instruction, and career placement.

I suspect this publicly oriented variant of the Alignment Thesis goes a long way to explaining why the separation of corporate purpose and managerial responsibility seems problematic for so many. There may be some institutions for which the responsibilities associated with internal administration and the ends of external purpose can be kept separate. Perhaps the criminal justice system can continue to exemplify this phenomenon. With respect to corporations, however, executive managers that have administrative roles are the very individuals that have been granted oversight to explore how purposes should be instituted in practice. The policies developed by management are themselves specific ways that a corporation's purposes are satisfied.

Chapter 5

Corporate Purpose and Social Responsibility

Jeffrey L. Sturchio and Louis Galambos

What is the purpose of the corporation? Who should control its decisions? Who should allocate its resources? And does the corporation have obligations beyond those of investing its shareholders' money and providing them with returns? These issues have been perennial topics of debate in boardrooms and business schools for decades, at least since the classic analysis of Adolf A. Berle and Gardiner C. Means on *The Modern Corporation and Private Property.*[1] We address these questions in this chapter through a historical analysis of the changing institutional, economic, and political contexts that shaped the evolving understanding of corporate purpose and social responsibility in the United States since 1900.

We begin with a look at corporate governance at the beginning of the twentieth century and how it changed in response to legal, regulatory, and competitive trends in the American economy, leading by the 1930s to a set of institutional adaptations that provided specialized expertise to deal with increasing concerns about the external environment. Those changes persisted after World War II and the division of labor within the firm continued as demands to address the pressures from a broad array of stakeholders in addition to stockholders mounted. In the following decades, these changes created a new gestalt among the leaders of American business, a setting in which those on the leading edge adopted a new view of social responsibility as an important part of how they did business. We explore the implications of this evolution in thinking and practice by examining the case of health care policy and the extension of expectations of corporate leaders to address related questions in the international arena beginning in the 1980s.

Inevitably in a brief chapter like this, we can only suggest key factors that shaped the trends that interest us, providing apposite examples and offering an explanation of the phenomenon that we hope will guide others as they pursue these questions at a more detailed level. We hope that our argument will encourage others to fill in the picture through more systematic studies of the range of behaviors of different firms in different industries over time. We need to know more about how the pattern of their behavior helps us to understand both what drove firms to become more socially responsible, what limited their movement in this direction, and how their decisions were shaped by market forces, government regulation, public opinion, bureaucratic imperatives, and changing leadership values. A more dynamic history of the creative tensions around different concepts of the corporation will result. This chapter, then, can serve as an introduction to that story.

U.S. Corporate Governance and Corporate Purpose, 1900 and Post-1940 Compared

Between 1900 and 2000, the patterns of corporate governance in the United States changed dramatically. By "governance," we are not just referring to the legal nature of governance (for instance, the American practice of giving one vote to each share of voting stock); we are also referring to the nature of the internal and external structures and operations of corporations.[2] At the beginning of the twentieth century, in the midst of the Second Industrial Revolution and the Great Merger Movement,[3] most corporate enterprises were led by a president who exercised straight-lined authority over both the internal operations of the organization and its external relations with various levels of government, with customers, with universities, and with other nonprofit institutions. These U-Form (for "Unitary") corporations were quickly replacing partnerships or single-proprietor businesses in the heart of what had recently become the largest industrial power in the world. The speed with which the transformation took place was surprising to some and shocking to many, especially those who found themselves displaced (for example, wholesalers in many industries) or marginalized (for example, many skilled workers in iron and steel) by this transition.

The leading scholar in studying this new type of business was the late Alfred D. Chandler, Jr., whose work was so influential that the successful mass-production, mass-distribution corporations are often called "Chandler firms." In a relatively short period of about eight years, the Great Merger Movement made these organizations the rule and not the exception in America's industrial economy. While most businesses were not organized in this manner, those that were played the leading role in such leading industries as chemicals, electrochemicals, oil, most metals, land transportation, and electrical communications. Even those companies that continued batch production (as opposed to mass production) were organized and governed along similar lines.[4] By exercising substantial economic power over their markets, the U-Form corporations of that era were able to amass sufficient wealth to finance their own further expansion and to fend off or buy off many of the entrepreneurial firms that attempted to enter their markets. They had what Chandler referred to as first-mover advantages.

The private sector in America at this time dwarfed government at both the state and federal levels. It was of more than symbolic significance that in 1907, J. P. Morgan (the nation's leading investment banker in the pre-World War I economy), rather than the United States government, intervened to prevent a major financial collapse.[5] Since the nation lacked a central bank or federal reserve system, the private sector played the role that the Federal Reserve ("the Fed") would be expected to play after 1913. Symptomatic of the balance between the private and public sectors was the fact that the combined debt of America's railroads exceeded the debt of the United States government.[6] Given a relatively unchallenged position of great power and wealth, the leaders of American business focused primarily upon the interests of the stockholders (including, of course, themselves).[7] Charity was generally an individual, not a corporate responsibility, as were the problems that might be created by pollution or injuries on the job.[8]

This corporate paradise didn't last very long—by the historian's standards of time.[9] Like all of the developed nations, the United States began in these same years at the turn of the new century to create a regulatory administrative state at the federal level and, more slowly, a federal welfare state that attempted to advance the values of equity and economic security in a society long primarily dedicated to economic efficiency, innovation, and the great opportunities America's abundant resources created.[10] The politics played out in a series of surges labeled by participants and historians as the Populist and Progressive Eras. Along with a larger, more active public sector came a tremendous expansion of interest and professional groups dedicated to influencing in various ways the public and private policies of a society that was increasingly urban and industrial. By 1930, there were almost 45 million Americans still in rural areas, but there were more than 69 million living in urban centers.[11]

The growing pressures from outside the large corporation to consider social and political issues brought about changes in the institution. The breadth of the market for corporate social responsibility began to determine the degree of business specialization, although not the particular form that it took.[12] Within large U.S. corporations, the growing demand for a new means of handling these responsibilities brought about the creation of several new staff functions, all of which came gradually to be organized as separate functional departments. One was public relations, which was already a well-defined activity in the era of the U-Form corporations. Progressive Era regulatory and antitrust legislation prompted companies to pay more attention to their public images. The public relations staffs helped ensure that a corporation's public statements were consistent with corporate policy and were unlikely to create new problems with the company's external or internal environments. No longer was a corporate president likely to say, "The public be damned."[13] The gap between corporate rhetoric and corporate reality probably grew larger as the public relations departments matured and secured stable positions in their respective corporate hierarchies.[14]

The other supporting organizations included public affairs (under various names), which handled the political activities of the corporation, including lobbying, and managed the growing number of policy issues related to the expanding engagement of the firm with national, regional, and local regulatory agencies and legislatures. In an earlier day, the president of a company did much of the lobbying in an American political system that emphasized face-to-face, personal relations. Now, however, large firms needed specialized lobbyists, and they began to create separate offices in Washington, D.C., to deal with Congress, the Executive Branch, and even the Judiciary.

Relations with the workforce began to be handled by departments of industrial relations, which later evolved into "human resources," with broader concerns involving the entire workforce. These new departments began to formalize and bureaucratize the firm's relationships with its workforce, including the new layers of professional managers needed to run these very large organizations.[15] In some cases bureaucratic authority reinforced union authority, but it also could function as an alternative to the shop steward and the labor organization. So too with company unions, which became popular in the 1920s.

In a few large firms, including AT&T, management developed a "social welfare system" in an effort to reduce turnover in the workforce. The program in the Bell System included sports teams, an insurance plan, a stock-purchase plan, and new forms of communication, all designed to buttress the orientation of the company's massive workforce to the firm. The Bell program was consistent with the company's efforts to protect its near-monopoly by accepting and working with public authorities on both the federal and state levels.[16]

All of these specialized organizations fed information back into the modern corporation and at times helped line officers work out compromises over the stance the corporation should take on social and political issues. Some of the compromises were rhetorical, but others were substantive, as was certainly the case with the Bell System. The System was eased toward accommodation by the fact that its expenses were included in the rate base used by state regulators to set the prices for Bell services. With other large companies in oligopolistic industries, corporate welfare was treated like any other expense and thus was ultimately paid for by the business's customers.

While many of the corporate welfare innovations quickly disappeared after the economy collapsed in the 1930s, the new internal structure of staff functions persisted. Whatever the motives for its creation, it provided an institutional base within corporate America for the significant transformations that took place in the 1940s and the postwar era.[17] Then, the institutional framework for corporate social responsibility expanded to include many of the rapidly growing university business programs—first in the United States and then, gradually, abroad in Europe. Later, the academic wing of the movement became even more international as a global economy developed.

By that time, organized labor was also an active participant in the political and economic processes that characterized America's brand of democratic capitalism. The so-called New Deal settlement between the unions, the federal government (represented now by a National Labor Relations Board), and corporate enterprise gave labor the strongest voice it had ever had in American national affairs. Union strength steadily increased, beginning in the late 1930s and increasing as labor markets became very tight during World War II. Labor's share of national income increased as well. The membership of the movement peaked (as a percentage of the nonagricultural workforce) in the latter years. Then, industry-wide negotiations were yielding significant advances in job security and fringe benefits and to a lesser extent in wages and weekly hours in major manufacturing industries.[18]

In this setting, it is not surprising to find that a new stakeholder concept of the corporation began to emerge in the United States. As the challenges of operating diversified, often global, organizations and the many regulatory and political issues that confronted them on a daily basis grew, corporate leaders also faced increasing demands from another direction. Public expectations mounted for corporations not only to prosper economically, but also to demonstrate social responsibility to employees, communities in which they did business, various nation-states, and their present and potential customers, among others. Corporate leaders now found it difficult to handle all of these concerns and run their businesses on a day-to-day basis.

To deal effectively with external pressures, as well as their highly diversified, national and international activities, most large U.S. companies in the 1940s and 1950s adopted the M-Form (for "Multidivisional") style of organization with a CEO (chief executive officer) responsible for strategy, links to the board of directors, and most matters external to the firm—including most aspects of social responsibility. Assisted by a COO (a chief operating officer who ran the firm on a daily basis) and a CFO (a chief financial officer), the CEO of the post-World War II era focused on corporate strategy, budgets for the divisions, and what might be called the firm's diplomatic relations.[19]

The new structure and new pattern of governance can be seen as a product of the sort of functional specialization that Adam Smith said was related to the breadth of the market. Multidivisional, multinational firms were now frequently as large (economically) as many of the world's nation-states. Even in industries in which vertical integration began to give way to other forms of organization, the companies still had CEOs, COOs, and CFOs to direct company business.[20] These organizations were accommodating to new environments and adjusting to the growing demands for socially acceptable performance, at home and abroad. New international governance institutions— the United Nations and its World Health Organization, the International Monetary Fund, and the World Bank Group—and thousands of nongovernmental organizations were now vitally concerned with every significant move that America's largest public and private organizations made. The stakeholder environment was far more complex, vocal, and demanding.

So too was the intellectual environment, as the subdiscipline of corporate social responsibility (CSR) became a teaching program and academic discipline. Whether it was called CSR or corporate citizenship or stakeholder theory, the new body of knowledge and the new array of practitioners developed another set of pressures on corporate executives. Increasingly, corporate managers and executives came through undergraduate and master of business administration (MBA) programs and were thus given opportunities to study subjects such as business ethics, human rights, and community affairs. It became increasingly obvious that CSR could be an important component of a multinational firm's public image—and maybe its sales and profits.[21]

Responses to a New Environment

As you can well imagine, changes of this magnitude in organizations central to America's style of capitalism did not take place without substantial resistance both inside and outside the modern corporation. One product of the resistance in the post-World War II years was an ardent defense of the stockholder strategy of corporate affairs. The most eloquent and learned of those advancing this strategy was Milton Friedman (of the University of Chicago's economics department), who argued vehemently that the stockholders' interests not only should be paramount, they should be the *only* significant interests of a law-abiding corporation. We'll call this the Chicago School position, the most extreme form of the strategy.[22]

The opposition to the Chicago School position can be framed as the Social Responsibility strategy, which in its most extreme forms called upon every American corporation to consider the social implications internally and externally of every corporate activity in this country and abroad. The definition of those social responsibilities would be primarily done outside of the firm by interest groups (hereafter nongovernmental organizations, or NGOs) and political organizations of various sorts functioning at various levels of government.

We actually do not know of any large American corporations in the postwar years that maintained pure Chicago School or pure Social Responsibility positions, but these categorizations can be used to define a simple scale on which we can array various companies at various stages in their evolution. If we place the pure Chicago School position on the far right-hand side of the scale and the pure Social Responsibility position on the far left side, we believe that most American corporations in the post-World War II era would be in the middle of the curve, which would come close to resembling a normal bell curve of the sort you usually get when, for example, you grade a large class in the university. We would like to be able to state with authority where the median firm was positioned and how the median shifted over time between 1945 and 2012, but we cannot do that in any systematic, quantitative way in this chapter. We believe on the basis of our personal experiences and institutional research that the median gradually and unevenly drifted to the left, but we can only illustrate that trend—we cannot measure it. We can, in this context, merely offer some illustrative examples of firm behavior that enable us to push ahead with this treatment of social responsibility.

Even without a good quantitative analysis, we can suggest on the basis of anecdotal information that size mattered. Most of the nation's largest companies were, we believe, grouped to the left side of our bell curve, toward the Social Responsibility position.[23] More small companies, faced in general with greater resource constraints and less flexibility in where to invest those resources, were grouped toward the Chicago School position. As pressures mounted for greater gender and racial equality in employment and advancement in the private sector, for instance, small corporations in industries like construction appear to have resisted change more actively than large, multinational firms.[24]

Environmental policy was another area that evolved in a way more attuned to the stakeholder view where large corporations were involved. The rise of the environmental movement in the 1960s and the advent of new regulatory approaches—symbolized by the creation of the Environmental Protection Agency under President Richard Nixon—led to a new sustainability movement in the corporate world. More and more large companies began to see the benefits of managing to a "triple bottom line" of financial, environmental, and other social concerns.[25]

This characterization of a drift toward a stakeholder strategy is weakest where organized workers were involved. As global competition intensified in the 1970s, and as abundant opportunities arose for production outside of the United States, the New Deal settlement between unions and corporations broke down. Large companies could lower costs by producing with non-union labor in Mexico or the Far East.[26] As a result, union strength was in decline on both a relative and absolute basis, except for labor organizations in the public sector. In industries using computer controls, like oil and many chemicals, the managerial staff could now run the plants, and unions were forced to give concessions to management or risk complete defeat. The results included a loss of job security and a long-term tendency for the distribution of income to shift toward upper-income groups—a shift that seems to have left the economy less stable.[27]

During the 1980s and 1990s, these problems became particularly acute as American corporations went through an extended struggle to adjust to global competition and rapid technological change. De-conglomeration, re-structuring, and re-engineering left many blue-collar and white-collar workers without jobs. This was the first downturn since World War II in which significant numbers of white-collar workers and managers lost their jobs. Later, the loss of job security and the erosion of a sense of equity became particularly acute issues after the economy sagged into the Great Recession in 2008. Today, the slow recovery of employment remains a serious social crisis for which neither U.S. corporations nor the U.S. government seems to have convincing solutions.[28]

Corporate Social Responsibility and Health Care in the United States

We would like to illustrate some of the major patterns of change by looking at one of the nation's most important social responsibility issues, health care. As the American economy experienced a successful recovery from World War II regulations and demand, two issues moved up near the top of the social responsibility agenda: one was environmental protection (as noted above), and the other was health care. In the depths of the Great Depression, neither of these issues had seemed paramount. That was also the case during World War II. But in the prosperity of the so-called American Century, both of these issues acquired new saliency.[29] In the Cold War context, the United States was now heavily engaged with foreign countries, many of which had extensive public programs for providing health care. Britain's relatively new National Health Service (NHS) offered a particularly appealing model for those organizations and individuals who wanted more extensive federal/state involvement with health care in this country.

Instead of the NHS model, the United States followed its characteristic pattern by opting for Medicaid, Medicare, and a private/public insurance system that covered many of the employees of American businesses. About 85 percent of America's population came to be covered by one or more of these systems. Typical of the new setting was Blue Cross/Blue Shield, a quasi-public medical insurance system organized on a state-by-state basis. Large corporations were deeply involved with this style of medical insurance, as they were with the provision of health care for their growing ranks of retired employees.[30] By the 1980s, innovations in how Americans paid for their health care were matched by a transformation in the delivery of care. Independent physicians and hospitals marked by fee-for-service practices were replaced in short order by national networks of managed care organizations consolidated into a few major corporate competitors.

There were other important developments in these years. Large companies were heavily involved with pharmacy benefit managers (PBMs), a relatively new American institutional innovation that developed in an effort to carve out and systematize the provision of prescribed medicines to employees and retirees.[31] As these and other public and private programs and institutions evolved, large corporations found it almost impossible to ignore completely what was happening in their health care environment. None that we know of did.[32]

The large U.S. pharmaceutical companies became very attentive to their stakeholders as the HIV/AIDS crisis developed in the United States. AIDS activists were intense, and they organized creative lobbying groups that the firms involved in researching HIV/AIDS treatments or vaccines could not ignore. Nor could the government turn its back on the calls of the HIV/AIDS lobby for the research needed to save the lives of their members, friends, and partners. One measure of their success was the amount of public and corporate money devoted to HIV/AIDS research and the extent to which those funds exceeded the relative importance of the mortality/morbidity figures for HIV/AIDS in the United States.[33]

The successful efforts of the HIV/AIDS lobbyists were an extreme but very important example of the changes taking place in the environment of the large corporation in the recent past. While CEOs of the involved companies might have wanted to focus their attention on their next New York session with the financial community, it was impossible to ignore the fact that people were chained to the gates in front of your business or were dumping blood on your booth at an international medical conference. Media attention to these events made public relations officers at the companies cringe and quickly counsel compromise.

Corporate Social Responsibility and Health Care in the Developing World

Nor when effective treatments became available could the pharmaceutical companies ignore the demands for lower-cost medicines for the developing world. This was an intricate problem for the corporations, which were already engaged in serious struggles over pharmaceutical pricing at home. At first, they tried to take a legal position, claiming correctly that they were under no obligation to lower prices on drugs still under patent protection. The companies explained that deep discounts to expand access to the millions affected by the AIDS pandemic in the developing world would impede their ability to gain the financial returns necessary to continue investing in risky research and development (R&D) for new and improved drugs for HIV/AIDS and other unmet medical needs.

But that approach soon wilted under NGO and media pressure. The cool rhetoric of corporate policy statements was no match for the apocalyptic metaphors and confrontational politics favored by passionate advocates for the cause. The results included corporate philanthropic contributions at first and, more important, tiered pricing systems that made drugs more affordable for many developing countries. These responses involved a complex series of events that unfolded over more than a decade of intense engagement that yielded (among many other things) a significant learning experience for many of the corporate executives involved. The successful research efforts that transformed the therapeutic possibilities for treating HIV infections; the seemingly relentless spread of infection through poor and marginalized populations across the globe; the disparity between outcomes in countries like the United States, where patients did have access to life-saving therapies, and Africa, where millions did not; the unprecedented growth in foreign assistance and health programs dedicated to meeting the challenge of HIV infection (such as the Global Fund, established in 2002, and the U.S. President's Emergency Program for AIDS Relief, created the following year); changes in global trade rules to enable countries faced with public health emergencies to gain access to needed medicines more efficiently—these were key elements of the environment that moved pharmaceutical companies to find new policies and practices to ensure that their antiretroviral medicines would indeed reach those in need. Between 2000 and 2011, the number of people treated with combination antiretroviral therapy in low- and middle-income countries rose dramatically, from a few tens of thousands to more than eight million.[34]

During the same period, American companies supplying the drugs also began increasingly to become involved with the health care systems in the nations of the developing world. Market trends were favoring this development, as opportunities for continued growth were shifting from areas of traditional strength (North America, Western Europe, and Japan) to growing economies in Brazil, Russia, India, China, and South Africa (the BRICs) and other emerging nations. This interaction was successful, but there was and still is a learning curve for partner countries, the international health care institutions, and the companies as well as their national governments.

Other situations arose with other diseases, including onchocerciasis and lymphatic filariasis, among the so-called neglected tropical diseases. Both diseases occur in relatively poor societies, especially in sub-Saharan Africa and parts of Latin America. Onchocerciasis causes river blindness, and the disease was rampant along African rivers, where marshy land provided ideal breeding grounds for the black flies that carry the microfilariae that cause the disease. In researching an animal health treatment in the late 1970s, Merck and Co., Inc., one of America's largest pharmaceutical firms, discovered that ivermectin could also be used to treat onchocerciasis. After developing a formulation of ivermectin for human use (Mectizan) and testing it in extensive clinical trials in West Africa to establish its safety and efficacy for treating river blindness, Merck obtained regulatory approval for Mectizan in France in 1987. But neither the individuals in affected communities nor the governments of Africa could afford the treatment. Dr. P. Roy Vagelos, CEO of Merck at that time, knowing that Mectizan would address an unmet medical need for tens of millions of people, made a decision to provide the treatment free to as many people who needed it, for as long as necessary, to eliminate river blindness as a public health problem. Later, it turned out that the same drug could be co-administered with albendazole to prevent lymphatic filariasis (commonly referred to as elephantiasis), and Merck expanded the coverage to that population in countries where the diseases are co-endemic. This ongoing campaign—which observed its twenty-fifth anniversary in 2012 and now reaches more than 100 million people in more than 100,000 communities each year—clearly positioned Merck down the left-hand tail of our theoretical bell curve on social responsibility.[35]

So, what large firms would we put on the right tail of our bell curve? The easy choice is Enron, a company that in the final stages of its collapse took down both its stockholders and its stakeholders. Enron started out as an innovative energy company that became involved with various CSR initiatives. Enron took advantage of a transition in the natural gas industry to build a great fortune trading in gas supplies. After becoming the dominant player in that market, however, the firm's leaders tried to apply the same approach more broadly in the energy field and ran the company toward bankruptcy. Struggling to prevent a collapse, they engaged in fraudulent accounting practices but were unable to avoid a massive bankruptcy.[36]

Today, on the other side of our bell curve, companies (as well as an astonishing array of national and international public agencies, universities, and NGOs) are attempting to build on the experiences with HIV/AIDs and other diseases and mount a new campaign, an effort to reduce mortality and morbidity from noncommunicable diseases (including cardiovascular diseases, cancers, asthma, and diabetes, for example), which are a growing burden for health systems around the world. These diseases cause about three-fifths of all deaths globally, and 80 percent of those deaths are in developing countries.[37] Once again, U.S. corporations are being called upon to have a very broad, international sense of corporate responsibility. The authors of this paper, Sturchio and Galambos, are involved in that effort, working with a group of international public health experts and the support of the International Federation of Pharmaceutical Manufacturers and Associations and AstraZeneca (a British corporation with operations in the United States and elsewhere) to develop specific, well-defined policy recommendations to help carry this general plan forward.[38] It is hard to imagine any such effort being mounted in the years before World War II, when the developing world was primarily a site for empire building.

A New World

Our contention is that modern U.S. corporations have responded in highly varied ways to the calls for social responsibility but that no large, public company is likely to ignore those calls completely unless it is sinking toward bankruptcy. The academic interest in CSR has meanwhile spread around the world and created a form of intellectual, cultural, and ideological change in the institutions training the next generation of business executives and managers. The pressures on the chief executive officers of public corporations are intense and relentless and cannot all be delegated to vice presidents for social responsibility.[39] Even the vice presidents are overloaded in the contemporary setting, and this has resulted in another round of functional specialization. There are now a range of investment advisors, indexes, special investment funds, and conferences to bring like-minded investors together to assess just how socially responsible businesses are (examples include FTSE4Good, the Dow Jones Sustainability Index, the Calvert indexes, the Goldman Sachs ESG [for environment, social, and governance] Fund—and SRI in the Rockies, an annual gathering of hundreds of socially responsible investment funds). There are now also specialized consulting firms and other organizations, including Rabin Martin, FSG, Business for Social Responsibility, Sustainability, and CERES (to name just a few), that assist corporations in developing and implementing social and environmental programs; these organizations provide an informal learning network that helps corporate managers understand the range of approaches they can take to address challenges in this area successfully and sustainably.

The fact that this is a growing field of corporate endeavor suggests to us that while the Chicago School alternative has not been abandoned, it is certainly not the dominant strategy among large, public companies in the United States today. Indeed, the most progressive corporate leaders—those on the left-hand tail of our bell curve—have come to understand that incorporating social responsibility into their thinking about the challenges facing their organizations can lead to new solutions and opportunities that strengthen business results while adding value to the communities and societies in which they operate.[40]

Neither most American companies nor their CEOs or other officers are, of course, able to meet all of the demands for a socially responsible approach to their business. Indeed, we locate the midpoint of this bell curve about the same place that we would find it for our professorial colleagues and our institutions of higher learning. Look carefully at the trend toward part-time faculty—a national trend in the United States that cuts fringe benefits for the schools. Look carefully at the big-time athletic programs and their serial scandals. If you separate rhetoric from reality, most of the schools are in the middle, meeting some but not all of their social responsibilities.

Let us end on a personal note. We have applied that test to ourselves and have noted that both of the authors of this paper benefited from the academic variety of insider trading, the Old Boys' Network, early in our careers. Today, almost all positions are publicly announced, but that innovation was not a product of the Old Boys themselves. It was a product of the same type of social and political demands and pressures that have resulted in corporate efforts to serve society as well as the firm, to serve their stakeholders as well as their stockholders.

Chapter 6

Education by Corporation

The Merits and Perils of For-Profit Higher Education for a
Democratic Citizenry

Amy J. Sepinwall

For-profit colleges have elicited wildly divergent reactions, with critics vilifying them and their executives, and supporters seeing in the institutions a necessary and laudable complement to public and nonprofit institutions. As I propose in this chapter, the truth likely likes somewhere between these extremes.

The for-profit educational sector has become an increasingly prominent and powerful presence within higher education. For-profit (FP) colleges have seen an average rate of growth of 9 percent per year, over each of the past thirty years.[1] Today FPs educate roughly 1.4 million postsecondary students in the United States, accounting for 7 percent of all postsecondary students. The largest FP college system—the University of Phoenix—enrolls more students than do all of the Big Ten schools together, and is second in student population only to the State University of New York.[2]

The growth of FPs can be gleaned not just from increasing student enrollments over time, but also from increasing revenues. Thus, for example, the for-profit sector generated $9 billion in revenue in 2000, but $29.2 billion in 2010;[3] most of this was earned by thirteen large, publicly traded companies that dominate the for-profit higher education market.[4] The sector has attracted the attention of both venture capitalists and large institutional investors, who see an unprecedented opportunity in the confluence of new technologies and interest in nontraditional educational platforms.[5]

While the public imagination casts the FP educational institution as brutishly profit-oriented, and its not-for-profit (NFP) counterpart as highmindedly unconcerned with revenues, the distinction between the two on this front is not so stark. NFPs need to be concerned about generating enough revenue to fund their activities. To this end, they often pursue profit-making activities—most obviously by fundraising and applying for grants, but also by securing patents for university-created products or technologies from which they can yield royalty fees, or by offering expensive degree or certificate programs for which the university does not extend financial aid.[6] The key distinction between the FP and NFP entity, then, pertains not to whether the entity is permitted to earn revenue that exceeds operating costs but instead to what the entity may do with this surplus. In particular, the NFP must reinvest any surplus in the institution, whereas the FP institution is permitted to distribute the surplus to its owners or shareholders.[7]

The key source of revenue for FPs is student tuition. These institutions tend to cost less than private NFPs, but more than public colleges or universities. In 2010-2011, for example—the most recent year for which national figures are available—the average cost at a public university for in-state students living on campus was $20,100, while the average cost for a four-year nonprofit college was $39,800 and $30,100 for a for-profit college. (Community colleges, the cheapest options, averaged $7,900.)[8] The FP's reliance on student tuition, in addition to the profit-making imperative that the FP institution owes its investors, accounts for many of the FP's worst abuses.

This chapter incorporates considerations raised in the context of a panel discussion held at the University of Pennsylvania featuring three leaders in the for-profit education world.[9] I propose here to amplify the conversation with reference to the existing literature on for-profit higher education. Commentary on for-profit education proceeds along three narratives: the first views the for-profit college as a kind of villainous, unstoppable monster; the second, contrastingly, sees the for-profit college as a kind of savior; and the third takes a more nuanced position, identifying virtues of for-profit education while expressing concern about its compatibility with education's traditional democratic aims. I present and critique each of these narratives in turn.

For-Profits as Villains

Education, including higher education, is often seen as sacred—above base concerns about making money, and crucial to the advancement of the individual and the society to which she belongs. To the extent that for-profit institutions problematize, if not pervert, this vision, these institutions are cast as enemies of the public good. Thus one critic likens the FP higher education sector to "the blob,"[10] threatening to swallow and replace traditional institutions, and another refers to the University of Phoenix in particular as "the anti-Christ."[11]

Some of this criticism is fueled by those cases in which a for-profit college has willfully engaged in acts of deception or fraud. But for other critics, for-profit higher education is inherently repellent, even if not out-and-out criminal, since the quest for profits is, they contend, necessarily in tension with educational quality. In its worst manifestation, the profit motive entails exploitation of the students whom these institutions target. But even when the institution's conduct does not rise to the level of exploitation, the for-profit college is nonetheless alleged to shortchange those it is intended to serve, by privileging owners or shareholders over its student-consumers. I elaborate on each of these concerns in turn.

For-Profit Colleges and Illegal Activity

FP colleges have been charged with two kinds of statutory violation. First, some have offered incentive-based compensation to recruiters, keyed to the number of students the recruiters succeed in enrolling, in contravention of the Higher Education Act, which forbids this kind of compensation to entities receiving federal funds. For example, in 2004, the government sued the Apollo Group, parent company of the University of Phoenix, for its alleged pay-for-performance recruitment incentives. The company denied wrongdoing but nonetheless settled with the government for $78.5 million, believed to be one of the largest pay-for-performance compensation settlements ever reached.[12]

Second, many FP colleges have been found to have engaged in fraudulent or deceptive marketing practices. In 2010, for example, the Government Accounting Office released a report based on an undercover investigation of fifteen FP colleges. The colleges in question were selected only because they received at least 89 percent of their funding from the federal government; prior to the investigation, there was nothing about the colleges that had alerted the GAO to any wrongdoing. Nonetheless, the GAO discovered that all fifteen misled prospective applicants about the cost or value of the education they would receive. For example, recruiters commonly stated that students attend classes twelve months a year yet reported the tuition costs for just nine months of classes, thereby misleading the potential recruit about the full cost of tuition.[13] In one instance, a recruiter told a prospective student that the massage therapy certificate program about which she was inquiring was a good value at $14,000 in tuition, yet a nearby community college offered the same certificate program for just $520.[14] Worse still, four of the fifteen colleges encouraged prospective students to lie on their financial aid application forms—in one case urging the applicant to omit information about $250,000 that he had in savings,[15] and in another advising the applicant to fabricate three dependents in order to appear more needy.[16]

These examples involve clear ethical and legal breaches. Nonetheless, a few bad apples do not make for a bad tree: it is easy to see how the profit motive might make such breaches more likely, but there is nothing in the for-profit structure that renders fraud or deception necessary or inevitable. The merits of FP higher education cannot be decided on the basis of these lapses alone. However, if it turned out that the FP college's quest for profits entailed widespread abuses—whether the ones just detailed or instead efforts to exploit prospective students' vulnerabilities, or sacrifice the quality of their education for the sake of lining shareholders' pockets—we would then have more reason for concern. And indeed, FP colleges have been charged with just such abuses.

For-Profit Colleges and Exploitation

Tales of FPs' predatory recruitment practices abound. The University of Phoenix and Chancellor's School of Professional Studies, both for-profit institutions, have targeted homeless shelters and halfway houses for potential students, seeking to enroll individuals who are recovering drug addicts or alcoholics, or convicted felons.[17] Recruiters have also sought to prey upon minorities and other members of historically oppressed groups,[18] and they have been especially keen to pursue military veterans, since veterans enjoy federal education benefits that do not count toward the 90 percent cap on federal funds imposed upon FP institutions.[19]

Recruiters are alleged to overstate the economic benefits of the degrees their institutions offer, and to minimize or fail altogether to disclose the difficulties in repaying loans that their students face:[20] many more students at for-profit institutions than at not-for-profit institutions carry federal loans—86 versus 63 percent.[21] And, while students at for-profit universities compose just 10 percent of all college students in the United States, they represent 44 percent of those who default on their federal college loans. Critics attribute the higher default rate to a greater rate of attrition at FPs—the graduation rates there are 28 percent, compared with 65 percent at NFPs.[22] The low graduation rates result, in turn, from the poor instructional quality and lack of support that FPs provide, critics contend. Yet even those who do graduate from FP colleges default more often than their NFP graduating counterparts, a disparity that critics attribute to the (purported) worthlessness of a degree from a FP institution.[23]

Because of these alleged abuses, Senator Tom Harkin, D-Illinois and chair of the Senate Health, Education, Labor, and Pensions Committee, sought to investigate the for-profit higher education sector. The investigation culminated in a report, issued in August 2012, that contained, in Harkin's words, "overwhelming documentation of exorbitant tuition, aggressive recruiting practices, abysmal student outcomes, taxpayer dollars spent on marketing and pocketed as profit, and regulatory evasion and manipulation."[24]

To the extent these abuses exist, they have been likened to the free riding and moral hazard that precipitated the housing market crisis. As Amitai Etzioni quips, FPs "are making money not by producing a product and marketing it, but by loading consumers with loans they cannot pay and then sticking the taxpayers with the bill. Only this time, it's not houses and mortgages but 'higher' education and student loans."[25] One former admissions officer grew so disenchanted with the aggressive recruitment strategies he was expected to pursue that he decided to dramatize his experiences in a one-act play called *For Profit*, which toured the United States in 2012.[26] In an interview, the playwright, Aaron Calafato, recounts that he was being pushed to enroll single mothers, recovering addicts, and others who had barely earned their high school equivalency diplomas, or could barely read—and all would come to carry heavy student loans.[27]

Far from enhancing the financial prospects of the members of these vulnerable groups, it is clear that saddling them with loans that they will be unable to pay off imposes yet another obstacle on their paths to prosperity. But these unseemly and exploitative recruitment practices are not a necessary part of the for-profit landscape. Like the illegal activity detailed above, the predatory practices of some for-profit educational institutions ought not to impugn the industry as a whole. We can readily imagine a for-profit college that engages in a stringent vetting and admissions process, selecting only those students who show the requisite promise, and who are made aware of the burdens that college studies impose. Along these lines, Kaplan Higher Education allows students to try out its college programs for three weeks, free of cost and with no record of matriculation should the student choose to leave after the trial period. In this way, prospective students are given the opportunity to see firsthand whether they can handle the work.[28] Similarly, there are FP colleges that have developed a solid track record of placing their graduates in well-paying, secure jobs.[29] Further, in addition to self-restraint, we can turn to government regulation to minimize opportunities for predation, through mandated disclosures to prospective students. Such initiatives are already under way. For example, the U.S. Department of Education has proposed tougher rules forbidding colleges from paying recruiters on commission.[30] And, a recently issued Executive Order on recruitment of veterans also seeks to reduce their exploitation.[31]

Given the fact that FPs rely far more on tuition as a source of revenue than do public and NFP institutions, exploitative recruitment practices may be more common in the for-profit sector. But again, there is nothing about for-profit education that requires these practices. In any event, even if self-restraint or governmental regulation were to curtail these practices, there might still remain concerns with for-profit higher education, as we shall now see.

For-Profit Colleges and Shareholder Primacy

FP colleges need not resort to illegal or exploitative conduct in order to invite the suspicion that there is something untoward about their business model. For one thing, many people tend to view money-making as antithetical to the intellectual pursuits that we take to typify a university education. I defer consideration of such concerns to a subsequent section, where I address the question of whether FP higher education illicitly commodifies a good that should be beyond market value. Here, I consider whether the premium FPs place on generating financial returns for shareholders negatively affects the quality of the education they provide.

The traditional view of the for-profit corporation grants pride of place to the corporate shareholder: the purpose of the corporation, in this view—often called the shareholder primacy view—is to earn money for shareholders. Measures that benefit constituencies other than shareholders—employees, consumers (e.g., students of the FP college), society at large, and so on—are to be pursued only if, and to the extent that, they redound ultimately to the benefit of shareholders. Correspondingly, initiatives that would diminish shareholder returns are to be avoided.

Because of the near-hegemony the shareholder primacy norm enjoys, critics of FP higher education are led to believe that the FP institution will sacrifice student welfare whenever doing otherwise would lead to a loss of potential shareholder or managerial profits.[32] Thus, for example, David W. Breneman, dean of the Curry School of Education at the University of Virginia, contends that "Wall Street has put [FP colleges] under inordinate pressure to keep up the profits, and my take on it is that they succumbed to that."[33] Prominent educators, students, and some of the University of Phoenix's own former administrators say the relentless pressure for higher profits has diminished academic quality[34]—for example, by propelling FP institutions to hire less experienced teachers, who do not command as high a salary, or deny admission to special needs students given the additional costs of accommodating them.[35]

Further, in addition to engaging in morally dubious cost-cutting measures, there is a concern that the FP college might incur expenditures that divert resources away from the students it does enroll. For example, given the extent to which FP colleges rely on student tuition for revenue, these colleges spend vast sums on marketing and advertising. Thus, the Apollo Group, which owns the University of Phoenix, spends roughly 20 percent of its revenue on "selling and promotional" expenses.[36] And according to the Harkin report invoked above, the investigated colleges had ten times as many recruiters as career-services staff members—32,496 and 3,512, respectively—suggesting that these institutions are more intent on taking in tuition funds than training and placing their students.[37] In contrast, FP advocates point out that the traditional sector is not without its own marketing imperatives. As Peter Smith quips, athletic directors at public and nonprofit institutions have to sell their schools to potential recruits too.[38] And outreach efforts can benefit members of underserved communities that might not otherwise have the wherewithal or resources to access information about higher educational opportunities.[39]

More generally, FP advocates reject a zero-sum view of the FP entity, according to which shareholder gains necessitate reductions in educational quality. Instead, at least some see student satisfaction and success as a key to shareholder wealth. Thus some FP advocates insist that at their institutions students absolutely come first—and they contrast this priority with the reigning hierarchy at traditional institutions, which, these advocates maintain, tend to indulge and pander to the often prima donna-like attitudes of their faculty.[40]

To the extent that shareholder primacy entails that the firm *maximize* shareholder returns, the concern about the for-profit form has traction; a norm of shareholder maximization would entail that the firm pursue whatever initiatives benefit shareholders most, and it stands to reason that shareholder value can sometimes be maximized only by sacrificing some amount of educational quality. For example, seniority pay and tenure help to retain better and more experienced faculty, but increase costs and thereby diminish shareholder profits; similarly, a well-stocked library, landscaped grounds, and state-of-the-art computer labs and athletic facilities can all enhance the quality of the student's experience, but these too increase costs at shareholders' expense.

By contrast, a norm of shareholder *primacy* need not be so demanding; so long as the firm attends to and seeks to augment shareholder value, it has satisfied the norm. And it can do so consistent with sometimes foregoing more profitable opportunities, in order to ensure that its students receive a good-quality education. Nor does the law mandate maximization of shareholder value. Instead, prominent statements of law permit corporate officers to pursue ethical objectives even if doing so fails to enhance shareholder value *at all*.[41] To be sure, the corporation will fail to attract and retain investors if it does little or nothing to seek to turn a profit. But the quest for profit need not operate to the exclusion of the quest for quality.

The question, then, is not whether the FP college can afford to provide adequate quality, but instead whether it can provide an education or degree equal or superior in value to that provided by traditional colleges. Does the FP college have unique capacities or competencies that should cause us to welcome its presence on the higher education scene?

For-Profit Colleges as Saviors

In 2009, President Barack Obama called for a doubling of the number of college graduates in the United States by the year 2020.[42] For-profit advocates contend that public and NFP universities cannot meet that goal alone. In particular, only by enrolling nontraditional students could the country increase the number of degree holders so significantly.[43] Enter the FP college.

Yet the FP's aspired role is even loftier than that. The supporter of FP education aims not only to award college degrees to more people but in particular to recruit individuals who have historically, and in some cases systematically, been excluded from traditional colleges, and to rescue them from their positions of relative disadvantage with the leg-up that a college degree provides. As one FP entrepreneur put it, the industry wants "to put 'the flying car of higher education in the driveway of every student.'"[44] In this way, champions and purveyors of FP higher education operate with a near-messianic vision.

More specifically, supporters of FP institutions believe that these institutions are uniquely placed to serve the needs of traditionally underrepresented students. Thus, these supporters highlight the FP college's ability to accommodate the needs and schedules of nontraditional college students. For example, whereas traditional colleges undertake lengthy admissions processes and have students matriculate at just a handful of fixed times over the course of the school year, FPs boast that they return prospective students' requests for information within fifteen minutes, and can have the student begin courses within a month of the call.[45] The FP colleges schedule courses in four-hour blocks, running from 8:00 a.m. to 10:00 p.m., which makes it easier for students to combine a full-time job with their studies.[46] Many also offer courses online, which students can pursue on their own time, thereby further accommodating students' work lives.[47]

FPs provide flexibility not just in terms of scheduling but in terms of course offerings as well. Unlike their traditional counterparts, FPs can readily add classes or programs in response to changing demand. This greater responsiveness results in no small part from the FPs' governance structure—typically centralized at corporate headquarters and uniform across campuses, unlike at traditional universities, where, for example, curriculum changes must be approved by faculty and can therefore take months if not years.[48]

More generally, supporters of FP colleges note that market-based competition can motivate for-profit entities to deliver better quality at a smaller cost.[49] FP institutions also have incentives to innovate, and their innovations can permeate the public domain or else motivate public institutions to produce innovations of their own, so as to compete. And FPs seem better able to make constructive use of new technologies than their traditional peers, as can be seen, for example, in the case of massive open online courses (MOOCs). These courses, typically taught by all-star professors at elite institutions, have the power to vastly improve the educational quality at FPs by allowing their students access to excellent instruction in courses rigorous enough to meet recognized accreditation standards. By contrast, MOOCs threaten to worsen the educational experience at a traditional institution, by eliminating intellectual diversity and rendering live instruction obsolete. Thus, for example, San Jose State University invited pushback when it proposed that its philosophy department replace some of their traditional ethics offerings with an online course entitled "Justice" taught by Harvard professor Michael Sandel. "The thought of the exact same social justice course being taught in various philosophy depts. across the country is downright scary," the philosophy department wrote in an open letter objecting to the initiative. In a similar vein, Amherst College's faculty voted against their school's producing MOOCs out of concern that MOOCs threatened to impose too much uniformity and centralization on higher education. Diversity is the welcome corollary of the intellectual freedom that pervades the traditional higher educational institution. As one commentator has put it, "When three great scholars teach a poem in three ways, it isn't inefficiency. It is the premise on which all humanistic inquiry is based."[50] But FP higher education, for good or ill, is founded on a franchise model. If calculus 101, or poetry or ethics 101 for that matter, is to be taught in the same way to all of the FP institution's students no matter what, it is best that the instructor and course content be drawn from the top ranks of the traditional institutions.

In sum, FP colleges promise benefits that traditional institutions currently fail to provide, and may even be structurally incapable of providing. The consumer orientation of the FP institution may in principle increase traditionally disadvantaged groups' access to higher education, and thereby enhance their socioeconomic status. And the centralized governance structure and market incentives of the FP sector may create more dynamic and innovative institutions. At the same time, through the use of MOOCs, FPs may be able to offer their students the star power and quality instruction that elite institutions provide, without shortchanging their students by denying them the spontaneous and sometimes unique experiences emerging in the live classroom, since the FP was never going to offer its students those experiences in the first place.

What this means is that, in theory, there may be much to celebrate about the ideal FP college. Unfortunately, however, the reality may look far different from the ideal. The promise of FP colleges, and the self-congratulatory market rhetoric of which it is a part, depends upon ideal market conditions that may not and, in some instances, do not obtain. For one thing, champions of the free market assume no information asymmetries between suppliers and consumers. But it is notoriously difficult for prospective students to weigh the value and costs of particular higher education programs.[51] It is for this reason that Congress is currently contemplating legislation that would require all colleges to provide financial aid applicants with a "shopping sheet."[52] And to the extent that competition itself motivates greater transparency, so that consumers can compare options, there arises a concern that the competing institutions will privilege quantitative indicators of success, thereby neglecting or deemphasizing softer but no less significant attributes.[53] The dramatically increased importance of standardized test scores provides evidence of this concern.[54]

A second reason to be skeptical about the adduced benefits of market competition arises in light of the possibility that the requisite competition is absent: where the market is dominated by one entity, or supply is otherwise limited, the entity (or few entities) in question has fewer incentives to cater to its consumers. Students cannot readily transition between colleges: each institution may have different requirements for admission, or each may decline to award credit for courses completed elsewhere, or particular financial aid packages may not be transferable between institutions, or there may be only one game in town and the costs of moving elsewhere may be prohibitive. In short, exit is not a viable option for many.[55]

In any event, concerns about the fairness of the market are just one piece of the puzzle; there is a more foundational issue—namely, whether there should be a market in this arena at all. Thus, even were perfect market conditions to obtain, and even if FP colleges were genuinely and robustly consumer oriented, there would remain a question about the propriety of the market dynamic. For it may be that consumer satisfaction ought not to be an ultimate aim, let alone *the* ultimate aim, of higher education. No one doubts that individual welfare gains constitute one worthy goal of a college education. But higher education has traditionally conferred benefits on society as a whole, both economic and political, and these may be threatened by the increasing presence of FP colleges.

For-Profit Colleges and the Public Good

For-profit institutions boast that they can provide students with better job training than their traditional counterparts. "You don't go to one of our schools to be a classics major," the president of the Career College Association quips; their schools excel instead, he maintains, in conferring upon students skills "related to a real job in the real world."[56] This difference in educational focus invites questions about what the goal of higher education should be and, indeed, whether the higher education landscape can accommodate diverse visions and aims, with some institutions more practically oriented and others furnishing a more traditional liberal arts education.

It is undoubtedly true that the workforce needs individuals who have received highly specialized training—in culinary arts, medical and lab technology, computer programming, and so on.[57] But the concern is that students, as members of a democratic populace, should also be exposed to a particular canon of subjects, and trained in particular modes of critical thinking. Some maintain that a college degree—unlike a proficiency certificate—implies just this kind of training, and that institutions that fail to provide it should not be permitted to confer the degree. Further, we might also worry that education is too lofty or sacred an arena to be governed by market forces; the notion that disinterested investors may earn a buck off the backs of students threatens to taint higher learning not because (or just because) FP colleges will have an incentive to pander but because money-making seems to be fundamentally at odds with higher education's foundational premises. I address each concern in turn.[58]

Higher Education as a Public Good

From the time of the nation's founding, higher education has been seen as a critical public good, developing students who could go on to serve the public as a result of the training they had received.[59] Thus, for example, the Continental Congress insisted that some portion of land in the Northwest Territories be reserved for public institutions of higher learning.[60] Further, at least two delegates to the Federal Convention of 1787 advocated for the federal government's power to establish a college at the national level.[61] Their cries were echoed by the first six presidents of the United States, each of whom beseeched Congress to establish a national public university. Contemporaneously, several state constitutions provided for the establishment of public universities within the state in question.[62]

The Founders, and their political successors, were committed to higher education because they saw in it "an extra-constitutional mechanism to preserve the republic by broadening the diffusion of learning across social classes and enlarging the population of persons possessing the skills required for democratic governance and useful in diversifying the economy."[63] In this regard, it is worth noting that the American Association of University Professors, from the time of its formation in 1915 through to the present day, has in its successive articulations of its Declaration of Principles envisioned the university as a "public trust," given the role of "education [as] the cornerstone of the structure of society."[64] And the Campus Compact, an association of the presidents of more than 1,100 public and private universities, has issued and reaffirmed a Declaration challenging "higher education to re-examine its public purposes and its commitments to the democratic ideal."[65]

To be sure, a college degree confers upon the graduate a set of personal benefits—for example, it formally certifies that the degree holder has completed a particular course of study, it inducts the degree holder into a network of alumni who may function as useful personal and professional contacts, and it tends to allow the degree holder to earn more money than she would have earned without it. But higher education also enhances individuals' preparation for the duties and activities of citizenship. Those with college degrees are more likely to vote, and exhibit a greater interest in civic and political issues, even controlling for social background and personality traits.[66] College-educated citizens also display more social awareness, more political activism, and more humanitarianism.[67] And society benefits from these outcomes as well, as greater numbers of college graduates generate increased charitable giving, lower public health costs, and a more diverse set of leaders.[68]

Education, like health care, is, for all these reasons, taken to be a prerequisite for both fulfilling one's life plan, and creating and preserving a well-functioning democracy.[69] Further, the more educated the populace, the greater the nation-state's global standing. Even Milton Friedman, who advocated a market-based approach to education through vouchers, argued that a "stable and democratic society is impossible without widespread acceptance of some common set of values and without a minimum degree of literacy and knowledge on the part of most citizens."[70] Or, to put the point even more succinctly, as Martha Nussbaum does in her bid to preserve a place for the humanities in higher education, "Without support from suitably educated citizens, no democracy can remain stable."[71]

FP institutions undercut a connection between higher education and democracy by neglecting to prepare students for citizenship. As a dean at one FP college unabashedly stated, "For-profit universities do not have as their primary mission the shaping of a more informed citizenry, or creating a more cultured population, or helping young people understand their heritage, their society, and its values."[72] And it is not just that at least some FP institutions fail to enhance their students' civic engagement; they may even worsen it in some regards. In particular, an exclusive focus on educating for specific professional or vocational ends—what Martha Nussbaum calls "educating for profit"—denies college students the opportunity to acquire or refine the rhetorical and critical thinking skills that democratic engagement requires.[73] And the consumer satisfaction model might encourage or further entrench existing class, ethnic, and racial divides, as students vote with their feet in selecting institutions close to their already segregated neighborhoods, or whose student bodies consist largely of other students like them, thereby insulating themselves from a more diverse student body that could improve cross-class and cross-cultural understanding. As Martha Minow writes, "Without regulation, more choice—including private religious options, for-profit options, and alternatives serving specialized interests—could produce self-segregation along the fault lines of race, class, gender, religion, disability, and national origin. As a result, schools could exacerbate misunderstandings among groups and impede the goal of building sufficient shared points of reference and aspirations for a diverse society to forge common bonds."[74] Elizabeth Anderson echoes the worry when she insists not only that public leaders "must be drawn from all sectors of society, including the less advantaged" but also that "these diverse members must be educated together, so that they can develop competence in respectful intergroup interaction."[75]

For these reasons, it is perhaps no wonder that "research suggests that students in the for-profit sector are less likely than students at nonprofit community colleges to vote, participate in political activities, or become involved in their communities."[76] To the extent that this is true, the loss is not society's alone. The relative lack of civic engagement threatens to undermine the promise of providing upward mobility for the underprivileged student that the FP college holds out in justifying its existence. For that mobility results not just from the enhanced material benefits that a college degree can confer but also from participation in public life with an eye to eradicating other kinds of structural barriers currently impeding the underprivilegeds' success.

And beyond the substantive ways in which FP colleges might deny their students the democratic training that students at traditional colleges receive, there is a further worry that FP education threatens the very ethos of democratic citizenship. As one commentator has evocatively stated in the context of K-12 school choice, "The struggle is not between market-based reforms and the educational status quo. It is about whether the democratic ideal of the common good can survive the onslaught of a market mentality that threatens to turn every human relationship into a commercial transaction."[77] The concern loses no force when what is contemplated is higher education rather than primary and secondary schooling.

Commodification

Worries about the incursion of a market discourse and rationale into the realm of education take many guises. For one thing, there is a general unease in subjecting something as (purportedly) lofty as education—especially higher education—to the base cost-benefit calculations that govern the market.[78] Further, delegation of a traditionally public function to a private entity, or the use of public dollars to fund a private entity, raises fears about a loss of public control and trust. The private school need not be responsive to the public will in the way that the public institution must be. To be sure, this concern arises for both FP and NFP colleges, but the former occasions it to a greater degree, since the FP college may be subject to fewer government constraints and since it affirmatively has obligations to a constituency other than its students or the public at large—that is, its shareholders. "Public control and review—whether through administrative or political processes—diminish as previously public activities fall under private management and control."[79] And the consequences of the delegation might extend beyond a sense that the FP institution may proceed with indifference to the public will; delegation may undermine public trust more generally. As Martha Minow notes, "The appearance of private motives in a public domain can undermine respect for government and even generate doubt whether the government is sincerely pursuing public purposes."[80]

More disturbing still, allowing for-profit entities to bridge the gap that traditional institutions have created obscures the fact that the public might bear responsibility for the gap in the first place. As Mark Rosenman writes, "Our elected leaders steadfastly refuse to generate the revenues government needs to do what needs to be done and instead favor an increasingly inequitable distribution of wealth . . . ; politicians cut the funding of cost-saving programs [like those that would keep students in school or improve their performance there] to come up with new avenues for capital to make private profit in meeting public needs."[81] The incursion of profit-making entities into spheres traditionally occupied by the government undermines individual altruism, may lead to fewer charitable donations overall, and diminishes public spiritedness more generally, Rosenman argues.[82]

These are all compelling concerns. We have good reasons to worry about an erosion of public trust or altruistic sentiment, especially in light of the economic downturn, which has diminished individual largesse and heightened voters' resentment of those groups (for example, unions) that are seen as reaping undeserved concessions or social assistance.

But it is not clear that the concerns mandate a ban on FP higher education, for it is not clear that the other-regarding sentiment that is (on this line of argument anyway) preserved or enhanced where the profit motive is absent will tend toward funding of higher education, less still that it will do so with the innovation and flexibility that the FP sector can provide. In other words, it may be unduly optimistic to think that the public will improve the educational opportunities of historically underserved populations when it has heretofore failed to do so; the FP market for higher education would not have arisen were traditional colleges already serving all of those who were candidates for higher education as well as they could. As Martha Minow states, "The persistent failures in existing forms of social provision—in schooling [among others] . . . —supply powerful reasons for government to work with the private forces of for-profit, secular nonprofit, and religious organizations." The FP sector may provide a much-needed complement to traditional colleges and universities. It remains to be seen just what role the FP sector should play.

Conclusion: Ideal Versus Non-Ideal Worlds

In an ideally just world, every student has the opportunity and the resources to obtain a higher education—one that prepares the student both for the realities of the job market into which she will enter and for the project of self-governance of the polity of which she is part. We do not currently inhabit that world (if we ever did). We should not abandon hope of realizing it and, indeed, we should work toward its realization. But we cannot in the interim repudiate any and every alternative that fails to meet the standards that we would impose in this ideal world. To do so would be to fetishize purity over practicality, with the burdens of the repudiation falling disproportionately on those whom the current system already marginalizes or excludes. We should instead welcome institutions, like FP colleges, that can fill in the current gaps.[83] As Kevin Carey, policy director for Education Sector, an independent think-tank in Washington, D.C., writes: "The difference between what higher learning should be in theory and what it really is in practice (and what's feasible given the current economic and funding environment) is vast. And it's in that space that new organizations are going to thrive."[84]

At the same time, we should seek to ensure that the presence of FP institutions does not entrench existing inequalities or otherwise impede progress toward a more ideal world. The general strategy flows from those theorists who view justice along two planes. The foundational plane articulates a conception of justice that we would impose in a world where we could be assured of a material surplus and where individuals recognized the equality of all. This is the ideal world. A second plane begins at the point where we acknowledge that we do not live in this ideal world, and that we need to enact temporary measures that both respond to the current non-ideal circumstances and allow us to make progress toward the ideal world.[85] In particular, these measures should "hinder the empowerment [of the disadvantaged] the least and further it the most."[86]

FP colleges can play a part in this non-ideal world, and so we should embrace them—but only with some careful qualifications and constraints. One element of this approach requires that we secure a robust opportunity for the public will, arrived at through democratic deliberation, to guide and constrain the operation of the FP higher educational sector. This is the suggestion Jeffery Smith advances in this volume,[87] and others have expressed it as well.[88] But there is a prior question—namely, what the public *should* will on this score. The concerns about FP higher education described above provide the components of a response.

Most obviously, there must be greater governmental regulation and oversight to protect against the worst abuses—fraud, deception, and exploitation. It is permissible, and even desirable, for FP colleges to target traditionally marginalized populations. But they should do so in a manner that allows the targeted populations to arrive at a robustly informed decision about the benefits and costs of the education on offer, and without imposing undue pressure to consent.[89]

We might also seek to ensure that FP colleges do good by their students even as they try to do well by their shareholders. To this end, we might mandate that some percentage of the school's profits be reinvested in the institution itself, or we might insist that FP colleges qualify for an accreditation, retention of which would require that the college meet certain barometers of student success.

It is less clear that we could or should seek to insist that FP colleges provide (more) training for civic life. As niche institutions, FP colleges might focus on subjects having nothing to do with self-governance in a democratic polity, or they might recruit students from predominantly one social class, or ethnic, racial, or religious group, thereby denying their students the opportunity to mingle in a diverse environment. They could be encouraged to do otherwise, but the business model may make it unreasonable to demand that they do otherwise.[90] Thus we might have to resign ourselves to having some other forum or institution encourage and prepare citizens for civic engagement. (We could, for example, seek to improve the democratic training currently offered in K-12 institutions, or insist that at least some not-for-profit entities, like churches, tax-exempt social clubs, and so on, devote some time and resources to fulfilling this role in exchange for their tax-exempt status, and consistent with the constitutional guarantee of freedom of association.)

Concomitant with pursuing the specific measures aimed at the FP colleges themselves, we must seek to reform the background conditions that make FP colleges as attractive as they are. This is not the place to articulate a full-fledged plan, but we can identify some rough and ready ideas. First, we must find ways to make traditional colleges more accessible to underprivileged students—for example, we might enhance the amount and quality of academic guidance students at public high schools receive, so they are better informed about their options and more effectively led through the various admission processes, or we might encourage colleges and universities to maintain more flexible schedules or to promote work-study opportunities in other ways, or, again, we might offer a year of postsecondary, college preparatory education to students who have attended failing public high schools. (This last measure would be more affordable than more widespread reform of the failing public schools, and would at least allow the students who suffered through these schools an opportunity to catch up.)

More significantly, we ought to remedy the background inequalities that put at least some traditional institutions beyond the reach of those students whom the public schools have largely failed. In an ideal system, the quality of primary and secondary education would not vary anywhere near as widely as it does currently, nor would the worst providers be anywhere near as dismal as they are now. More generally, there would be far less inequality of wealth, and the quality of the schooling available to children would not depend on the resources of their parents.

In short, the background circumstances that set the stage for FP higher education are themselves deeply entrenched, and they will likely, and unfortunately, persist for too many years to come. Given these circumstances, and the possibility that FP colleges can function at least as a stopgap measure to ameliorate their effects, we ought not to insist upon a wholesale rejection of for-profit higher education. But we can require that FP colleges and universities operate in ways that do not worsen the unjust conditions that currently obtain; better still, we can seek to ensure that FP institutions actually help those who are disadvantaged to improve their lot. Profit making may be inimical to the ethos of higher education, and FP colleges may shortchange their students when it comes to training them for citizenship. But we do not now have the luxury to repudiate FP higher education altogether. To deny the disadvantaged student access to an FP college may well be to deny her access to any college at all, and so to consign her to the impoverished conditions she already inhabits. We should instead support a more highly regulated and constrained FP college sector, even as we seek to reform the injustices that provide the demand for FP colleges in the first place.

Chapter 7

Enron and the Legacy of Corporate Discourse

Rosalie Genova

Enron's bankruptcy filing in 2002 and its widespread repercussions did not seem likely to be soon forgotten. Yet the financial crisis beginning in the fall of 2007 eclipsed the Enron scandal and others of that time. Furthermore, as of 2010, the Supreme Court's ruling in *Citizens United v. Federal Election Commission* and the Dodd-Frank financial reform law supersede 2002's "post-Enron" regulations. Still, Enron's name echoes in commentary and analysis, from popular media sources to academic studies in corporate governance, securities law, accounting, and business ethics.

In this chapter, I situate Enron's collapse as a historically meaningful event. The "meaning" of the collapse derives not only from what came before it, but also from what followed. I argue that narratives of Enron's bankruptcy described a particular moment in the political economy and business culture of the United States, tracing historical American attitudes toward large corporations and their officers culminating in the Enron case. Reactions to big business have ranged from celebration to condemnation, but I hope to show that neither provides an appropriate foundation for relations between citizens and corporations. This leads me, at the end of the chapter, to a third alternative: a conception of big business articulating not only its power—for good or bad— but also its vulnerabilities.

Initially spurring this inquiry was a fascination with how people perceive, understand, and talk about large corporations in the contemporary United States.[1] Yet as a research question, this interest was both overly broad and methodologically impractical. Under normal circumstances, average citizens do not leave documents recording their attitudes toward particular companies or corporations in general. Additionally, big business today is ubiquitous and taken for granted—though this was not always the case.

Since such a general study was impossible, I chose instead one catalyzing event, one that brought ordinary people into the discussion about business in American politics and society; one that inspired commentary from unexpected quarters; and one about which people were sufficiently informed and impassioned to have opinions. Initially, Enron seemed too iconic, almost clichéd, but I came to see that as precisely the reason that it makes for an apt case study. It was a scandal, yes, with all the inflated rhetoric and tawdry personal intrigue that scandal usually manifests. But scandal also brings into relief a society's standards for behavior and accountability.[2] Because a large corporation stood at the center of this scandal, it prompted exactly the kind of reflection and debate I sought.

The more I read about Enron as a firm—from human resources policies to office nicknames—the less unique it seemed. There was nothing special about its corporate culture that condoned or even encouraged fraud. I do not argue that Enron was a prudently managed company, or even a comfortable place to work. But I do suggest that people's reactions to Enron, as facts and details became public, revealed how they viewed big business more generally. Many of Enron's practices at which people balked were, in fact, standard—suggesting systemic rather than episodic failings. Enron was out of the ordinary in only some respects, but due to these aberrations and the ensuing bankruptcy, people had occasion to learn about and comment upon the norm. Thus the extraordinary gives way to the ordinary—both in what goes on inside large corporations, and also in how people generally feel about it.

Despite all that was unexceptionable in the norms of large corporations, I quickly understood why Enron was so iconic for a public audience, and thus how it became (as its officers so loudly complained) the "poster child" for a spate of dramatic business failures during the first few years of this century. Enron's failure was outstanding, to be sure, in its speed, complexity, and ramifications. Widely admired and wildly successful, the company also had farther to fall than most of its peers. Further, given Enron's well-known political connections, there was genuine suspense as it falteringly attempted to get back on its feet.

But most importantly, the Enron collapse made for a singularly good story. Its human interest elements included not only greed and deceit but also arrogance, grudges, cronyism, power struggles, sex, and suicide, lending journalistic legs and political punch. Narratives emerged that used popularly accessible language and concepts, rendering this bankruptcy—dazzlingly complicated even to expert analysts—coherent and thereby contestable for just about anyone. It was the closest that the American public had come for decades to an inclusive national discussion on the practices and effects of large corporations and their top executives.

Ultimately, popular understandings of Enron affected American culture and politics more enduringly than the company's actual errors, blunders, and lies. Accordingly, narratives about Enron overwhelmed the associated "facts." And where numbers and data, even when expertly compiled, fell short of a holistic explanation, narratives have a life of their own. Business scholars are often so absorbed with what actually happens in the commercial sphere that they tend to overlook what people *believe*. Yet the stories people tell—however incomplete, misinformed, or biased—are crucial in the shaping of public perception, the crafting of legislative reforms, and ultimately the composition of history.

Public Perceptions of Big Business: Past as Prologue

Among average Americans without business expertise or affiliation, the word "corporation" almost always connotes blame or suspicion.[3] Tack on "mega-" or "multinational" and it is even more certain, unless the context is technical, that we are hearing about something bad. It is as if the corporate form itself were tainted—and the larger the entity, the stronger the presumption of guilt. Common journalistic substitutes like "giant," "behemoth," "juggernaut," and "Goliath" convey not only that the corporation is vast, but also that it is fearsome. We stand in its long shadow and challenge it at our peril. One poll in 2000 showed that 82 percent of Americans believed "business has gained too much power over too many aspects of American life," with 74 percent agreeing specifically that "large corporations" enjoyed too much influence in politics and public policy.[4] Yet despite this negative image, historical scholarship on American attitudes toward big business reveals a general progression toward acceptance of, or at least resignation to, large corporations. People have come to acknowledge that not only will large companies continue to exist, they will also dominate their industries, often holding great economic and political sway.

Studies of small enterprise trade journals, the popular press, politics, and entertainment suggest that, by the turn of the twentieth century, a majority of Americans were complacent on the issue. By 1929, writes business historian Louis Galambos, most Americans "accepted the giant corporation as a permanent feature of their society."[5] In 1932, Adolf A. Berle and Gardiner C. Means published *The Modern Corporation and Private Property*, affirming for a wide audience the ascendancy of big business and its penetration of every mundane event in the reader's daily life.[6] Guido Palazzo and Andreas Georg Scherer call this "cognitive organizational legitimacy," by which corporations and their activities come to be recognized as inevitable and necessary.[7]

How, then, to explain persistent complaints about mega- and multinational corporations and their unscrupulous ways? The resentment today is impossible to ignore. It is also (and often self-consciously) connected to shrill protestations of Americans past. Indeed the historical trajectory toward acceptance of and reliance on large corporations would be difficult to measure were it not for a strong and persistent tradition of criticism and resistance—and where positive statements about large corporations do occur, they are typically defenses against attack rather than spontaneous celebrations. Such defenses endeavor to ascribe to the corporation what Palazzo and Scherer term "pragmatic legitimacy"—that is, legitimacy grounded in the claim that large firms serve people's interests.[8] That is, before Americans came to take large corporations for granted, they focused on their benefits, while warning of their potential ills and trying to curb or preempt them.[9]

To revisit old debates about big business in the United States is to discover constituencies and concerns that seem sometimes grimly familiar, in the context of present-day controversies, and at other times bewilderingly foreign. During the nineteenth century, small Midwestern and Southern farmers feared that the trend toward business "combination," as cartel practices were then called, threatened their way of life.[10] Voters questioned the ethics of government leaders who seemed readily to accept favors, contributions, and even bribes from railroad executives.[11] And almost everyone resented the dearth of competition in "natural monopoly" industries (such as oil, steel, and rail transport), which enabled large companies to manipulate markets.[12] All of these complaints make as much sense now as they did then. Indeed some seem, in retrospect, remarkably prescient. "Under the American form of society, there is now no authority capable of effective resistance," wrote Henry Adams in 1886. "The national government, in order to deal with the corporations, must assume powers refused to it by its fundamental law."[13]

Other strains of past discussions of big business, by contrast, are almost unrecognizable today. Yet these too are instructive, revealing contingent elements of American political economy. Two patterns in commentary, while perhaps counterintuitive, appear consistent over many generations. First, there was a pervasive and firm linkage made between big business and Christianity. The discipline of political economy first appeared, in the eighteenth century, within academic departments of moral philosophy, with many of the field's early scholars recruited from the ministry.[14] In churches, what clergy had to say about large corporations went far beyond the question of morals—and their comments were usually approving. "Captains of industry" such as George Baer and John D. Rockefeller, in turn, went out of their way to discuss their careers and business strategies in a spiritual context.[15] Disgraced executives often do this today for political blessing or legal absolution, but most of these earlier instances occurred under entirely normal circumstances. In the infancy of big business, it seems, all parties considered commerce and church to be substantively similar, rather than just awkwardly reconciled or pragmatically allied.

A second connection also persisted, in historical commentaries, between big business and, of all things, socialism.[16] Most surprising about this theme is that it was advanced seriously both as a fear and as a hope. To today's detached analyst the large corporation is a consummately capitalist entity—the product of private, competitive calculations in strategies of entry and exit, market penetration, economies of scale, and so on—one not possible under a more interventionist state. But many commentators, in context of communist agitation, apparently saw the corporation's symbiosis with federal government as a potential precursor to nationalized industry and the state-directed allocation of resources.[17]

Socialist conceptions of the corporation also applied to labor. Today we typically assume that large corporations, with their flexible, decentralized operations and strategically oriented top brass, are able to maintain leverage over employees. If worker unrest occurs, we assume that the corporation will emerge and adapt more or less unscathed. In the 1920s, however, socialist activists argued that, as companies grew larger, they became more susceptible to worker takeovers.[18] The more concentrated the means of production, they contended, the easier to seize control from those who had done the concentrating.[19]

Extinct lines of thinking, like extinct species, are useful in studying the evolution of all. To discover ideas about big business that have *not* survived is to illuminate those that have—even tracing the mutations over time by which older notions gave rise to current ones. Like the remarks, complaints, and connections just outlined, no doubt some recent arguments about large corporations will, in the future, sound wiser and more reasonable than others. But all are relevant in synthesizing their particular historical moment.

In the sum of historians' reports on Americans' resistance or acceptance toward big business over time, two factors emerge that have most often quelled public concerns and even fostered support. The first factor is good economic times.[20] Periods of stability and growth, from the later nineteenth century to the present, may or may not be directly attributable to large corporations. But regardless, prosperity has usually won them approval. In the twentieth century, big business has been credited with employing people, often with better security and wages; with increasing output to meet increased demand, thereby keeping a downward pressure on prices; and with innovating new technologies and modes of organization that made life, from household chores to organizational administration, more efficient.

The second factor driving public favor for big business—not unrelated to the first—is war. During and after World War I Americans tended to be complacent and even welcoming toward big business, with agitations of the Progressive Era suddenly seeming passé.[21] Indeed this period's integration of industry and government for purposes of organization and logistics may have eased the way for Americans' view of their country as one integrated "economic unit." This development was hailed and even furthered during the administrations of Herbert Hoover and Franklin Delano Roosevelt.[22] In context of the Depression, the industrial upswing brought about by World War II was more than welcome, leading the way to a consumer-driven postwar boom. Finally, when American corporations dominated the scene of multinational commerce, they protected a crucial front in the Cold War. Despite Eisenhower's warning about the military-industrial complex, the latter survived and flourished, facing no serious political or economic threat through the Vietnam War and into current conflicts.

These historical patterns point to another factor making Enron particularly instructive as to public sentiment on big business: this scandal happened at a time when circumstances should have discouraged any major hue and cry. For most of the 1990s in the United States, inflation was in check, unemployment low, and productivity rising at an impressive rate. The bursting of the dotcom bubble in 2000 portended problems, but that incident was understood more as comeuppance for a young and pompous industry (and its giddy speculators) than as a sign of systemic problems.

Despite a brief recession during that year and a major decline on the NASDAQ index from its 2000 peak, the economic climate—always measured at least as much by crude psychology as by anything else—was in 2001 still relatively healthy.

Yet Enron, unlike so many doomed dotcoms, was neither a new nor an untested company. Moreover, after going down in disgrace it was followed by a number of other large and respected firms in completely different areas of business, such as Adelphia, Qwest, Tyco, and WorldCom. Owing to the relatively upbeat economic context, people were not spoiling for a fight against large corporations. At the same time, we can see how willing American citizens and public officials remained, even during a period of economic optimism, to take seriously a corporate bankruptcy involving foul play.

The variable of war, too, favored big business more than it had for over fifty years; Enron bankrupted less than three months after the September 11, 2001 attacks. The global "war on terror" was, at this time, still new and widely supported. The "rally effect" brought exceptionally high approval ratings to both president and Congress even on domestic issues. Large corporations in the United States have often been informally equated with a patriotic front, as well as formally involved in war efforts. Correspondingly, Americans regard them with increased faith and loyalty during times of national strife. Insofar as people were angry about Enron, then, they were bucking a historic trend. Indeed the post-9/11 discourse of national pride sat awkwardly alongside rage and embarrassment surrounding the scandal.

The Enron bankruptcy might have occurred during an economic slump when the United States had no foreign enemies to speak of. In that scenario, voices of protest and urges toward reform would likely have been stronger than they were. In fact, for every complaint aired and every reform enacted, after Enron, there were numerous arguments and proposals placed firmly outside the realm of consideration. For example, no one seriously suggested nationalizing the energy industry or forcing corporations to remain small and managerially simple. Such ideas probably strike present day readers as preposterous, but here again historical comparisons are useful. While reactions to Enron's collapse were more impassioned than we might have predicted, they were muted compared to their forebears' populist and socialist rhetoric. Thus while the proven calming effects of economic prosperity and war morale may have been overridden for Enron, the long-term trend of acceptance toward big business was not reversed.

What Was "New" in Enron's Political Economy?

Many concerns coming to the fore after the Enron bankruptcy were familiar from previous business scandals, such as Teapot Dome in 1922-23, the electrical equipment price-fixing conspiracy of the 1950s, and the savings and loan crisis of the late 1980s and early 1990s. Laypeople and politicians alike voiced concern over the treatment of lower-ranked employees and other stakeholders, who had no fault in the fiasco. The competence and character of top executives were questioned, with allegations rife. Anxieties about the size and sway of corporations found their way into many complaints. Citizens questioned the integrity of political leaders, including legislators and even the president, who appeared to have condoned practices leading to the disaster—perhaps out of self-interest. Constituents prodded these same officials to implement reforms in order to avoid similar incidents in the future. Despite numerous similarities with earlier scandals, however, a number of novel conditions at the turn of the twenty-first century were also at play, making Enron a test case for changes in civic climate.

Securities Market Participation

At the time of the Enron bankruptcy, more Americans owned stock than ever before: some 50 percent of the population, although most of these holdings were through institutional investments, as in mutual or pension funds. The figure represents a far greater proportion of the country than in the past with direct interest in the securities market.[23] Stock ownership was also more widely dispersed in the United States than in nations such as France, Germany, and Japan, making ownership more thinly diffused, and real control more decoupled from ownership, than in the corporations Berle and Means observed eighty years ago.[24] A corporation's obligations to its shareholders, on the one hand, and to the broader "society," on the other, came to overlap as growing numbers of employees, retirees, and customers owned its equity.[25] An idealized "investors' democracy," long enshrined in American economic life as a metaphor for popular economic sovereignty, was firmly established in rhetoric opposing government regulation.[26] Meanwhile, however, people could and did participate in financial exchanges without understanding their technicalities or even their fundaments.

Complexity, Expertise, and Democratic Authority

While more Americans held a stake in large firms and the markets on which they were traded, these companies' internal structure had become more complicated than ever. And if big business was by numerous measures more arcane, Enron epitomized all its complexity and opacity. Not only were Enron's management and financial structures indecipherable to most outsiders; by the time the company bankrupted, there was urgent controversy even over the question of what business Enron had actually been in. With so much potential for confusion, claims about who did or did not know what was going on at Enron became crucial in establishing or undermining credibility. Lack of comprehension became not only a practical problem—as laypeople struggled to understand what had happened—but also itself a normative issue of charged debate.

Enron vividly illustrates the linkages between expertise, authority, and accountability in political economy. In a forthcoming study of the work of clerks, historian Michael Zakim documents the shift to a knowledge economy in the mid-twentieth century, as accounting helped to create modern markets through information and its representation. "Productivity" now referred to making profits rather than things. But profits, when substantiated only by ledger, were subject to revision as well as to dispute. Accountants claimed total neutrality and objectivity, but laypeople, from the beginning, questioned their assignments of value.[27]

Progressives in the late 1800s embraced the concept of managerial expertise, part of a trend toward greater faith in scientism overall. With that embrace, however, came anxieties about rule by elites.[28] Jennifer Alexander shows that as a "mantra of efficiency" achieved ascendancy in the industrial era—from manufacturing, to management, to macroeconomic functioning—authoritative experts asserted the primacy of numbers, announcing that their unique quantitative expertise licensed them to make sense of complex issues on behalf of untutored audiences.[29] Such self-designation as translator comes with immense political power: discretion over what will be communicated to the lay audience, and on what terms. This role is still assumed in discourses on the economy and financial system whenever academics, industry authorities, public relations professionals, corporate spokespersons, or business leaders themselves address the general public.

To be credible, high-profile executives often need to manifest competence in knowledge, trustworthiness in character, or both. The current postindustrial structure of commercial value encourages greater overlap between these two criteria than was necessary in previous historical periods. Paul Adler suggests that in traditional commerce, managers' authority could rest upon an innate "positional prerogative," by which they commanded hierarchical organizations engaged not in innovation or knowledge production but in rote industrial functions. In an information economy, business leadership hinges on "expertise and functional necessity," giving the slippery concept of trust new importance.[30] Managers today are expected to be personally brilliant and organizationally indispensable, with both qualities evident rather than simply assumed.

Applying similar analysis to the realm of government, Yaron Ezrahi shows that in a liberal democracy, scientific/technological empirics—including high finance—form the foundations of accountability for public authorities as well. Impersonal standards of evaluation override claims of power by birthright; reasoned deliberation replaces personal passions in politics. Accordingly, transparency assumes greater value because, at least in theory, it enables objective judgment, by informed monitors, on the merits of particular policies or officeholders.[31] In sum, therefore, leadership in both business and politics has become more technocratic, and authoritative legitimacy can be both predicated on and verified by specialized expertise.

Ezrahi highlights the democratizing potential of such a regime, but expertise also bolsters elitism and opacity in a manner all the more dangerous for its purported monopoly on pure, incontestable "fact." Under intense fire, Enron executives showed a national audience what it looks like when the veneer of exclusive expertise is breached. No degree of savvy would exonerate them. The claim to superior knowledge appeared either as a failed attempt to deflect criticism or as a liability in itself: observers simply could not believe that such sophisticated businessmen did not know of, or could not have recognized, misconduct in their own ranks.

Behavioral Incentives in and Among Public Corporations

Norms and standards of performance within large companies had changed as well, presenting not the first opportunities for fraud, but some new and different ones. Large modern corporations in the post-World War II era had initially thrived with the help of legions of "organization men"—also called "sound men" and "yes men"—middle managers who faithfully submitted to the ideas of their superiors and the long-term interests of the company in exchange for career security. Here loyalty and a collectivist mentality were prized and rewarded.[32] Yet toward the end of the twentieth century, a new ethic of skepticism, contrarianism, and even irreverence came into vogue. The ideal business professional was increasingly an innovator, someone who would readily challenge those above him or her, and who recognized untapped profit opportunities or inefficient working models.[33] This is not to say that more conventional business structures and management cultures did not persist in the late twentieth century. However, they no longer represented the "cutting edge."

Enron is an apt case in point. The company, which adopted the slogan "Ask Why," took pride in experimenting with business strategies and creating markets where none existed before. Even as it grew larger and more established, Enron identified itself with the entrepreneurial wave of small, New Economy startups. Its internal practices in many ways followed suit. Employees moved between units frequently; projects were abruptly launched and shut down; rules might be bent or ignored; and the company's performance review system abandoned loyalty or consistency, pitting colleagues against one another in a mandatory zero-sum game. Top executive Jeff Skilling, who gained first fame and then infamy, personified the daring of New Economy entrepreneurs. His story began with an admissions interview for Harvard Business School in which he salvaged an initially lackluster first impression by famously declaring: "I'm fucking smart." Skilling and his colleagues ultimately illustrated the dark side of their era's exalted "innovation," and lay onlookers were quick to condemn their brash manners after misdeeds were uncovered. The uncomfortable reality, however, was that such audacity, translated into business strategy, made millions. It had also been almost universally rewarded, foremost by those same investors who would later wrinkle their noses.

If Enron executives caused people to question what the market valued in individuals, Enron itself cast doubt on how the market judged corporate performance. While giants like Coca-Cola or IBM may attract and keep investors by maintaining a stable value and paying reliable dividends, companies espousing a growth model must ply their promise instead with a stock price consistently trending upward. Increasingly, the latter scenario was normative, especially for young companies. Partly by choice and partly by market pressure, therefore, these publicly traded firms faced higher performance expectations over shorter increments of time. Meanwhile, the growing emphasis on quarterly financial reports forced management to make decisions on a shorter time horizon than ever. These new standards, plus the premium on "innovation," do not force fraud onto executives, but they may facilitate or even at times seem to justify it. They can also blur the boundaries that supposedly delineate which behavior is ethical, legal, or even competitively advantageous.[34]

Politics: Old Connections, New Constituencies

The direct relationship between Enron and the White House made another distinguishing feature of this business scandal. The Bush family had long-standing ties to CEO Ken Lay and to his company, and those relationships flourished, to the benefit of all involved, when George W. Bush prevailed in the election of 2000. Past American presidents have treated big business as both friend and foe—and often simultaneously cooperated with large corporations while pretending to condemn and chasten them.[35] However, by this time several terms had passed since the nation's highest officeholder had cultivated any image as corporate antagonist. (Jimmy Carter had so striven, to some extent, with more obvious predecessors being Theodore Roosevelt and Franklin Delano Roosevelt.) Indeed the White House, regardless of which party occupied it, seemed increasingly friendly to big business. If Ronald Reagan and George H. W. Bush had pushed privatization and rolled back regulation, Bill Clinton adopted many of their approaches—and he too played golf with Ken Lay. When George W. Bush took office as the first president to hold an MBA, it was in general a culmination of business-government cooperation, and in particular a culmination of Enron-Bush synergy. For Americans who felt uncomfortable with either of these dynamics, the bankruptcy scandal may have helped to articulate why.

Thus the context of business fraud had changed—both in what might give rise to errant behavior and in how people were likely to react to it. Constituencies in the nation's political economy had also transformed by 2001. Clergy, unions, socialists, and farmers, vocal in previous eras, had shrunken or fallen quiet, and none had much to say about Enron. To the extent that a few individuals did, they were so narrowly heard as to be politically ineffectual. Meanwhile other groups, formerly too small, homogenous, or rhetorically predictable, had grown in numbers and also in the variety of perspectives they offered. The terms "investor" and "stockholder" now applied to half the American population, including millions of working people with major stakes in, but little understanding of, big business and securities markets. Likewise, while farmers and union activists had dwindled in number, office workers were now more numerous than ever. The nearer someone's own profession is to the realm of "business," the more moderate his or her attitudes toward it, according to one historical study.[36] Thus the increase in office workers, like the increase in stockholders, may have tempered public reactions to Enron and other recent business scandals.

A New Challenge in Corporate Self-Defense

But the most fundamental shift that made reactions to Enron unique to their own time involved no names, no numbers, nor even any single development in business or the economy. In most U.S. industries today, the presence and indeed the dominance of big business is a given. Huge, integrated companies control the markets for telecommunications, information technology, transportation, entertainment, and most other products and services used in daily life—and people simply do not remember, nor can they imagine, what life would be like without them. For large corporations, this signifies unprecedented acceptance but also a new vulnerability: Americans are no longer thankful to big business because they no longer consciously recognize what it provides.

In earlier historical debates, the most consistent and strongest argument in favor of large corporations was that they furnished goods and services to the American people that would otherwise be more expensive, or unavailable altogether.[37] Farmers in the 1880s appreciated products the corporations offered, and praised railroads for their competitive lowering of freight rates.[38] Skilled workers of the same period welcomed large companies' products and services; they even found that, in some cases, corporate wage scales and labor policies brought change for the better.[39] Such sentiments led the way toward consensus: the costs and threats of big business were outweighed by its advantages. Corporations benefited not just the government, or even the nation in its competition on a global scale, but also "ordinary" men and women as they went about their daily lives.

In the aftermath of the Enron bankruptcy, a few of the company's leaders and champions attempted to defend it along similar lines. They argued that the company had brought new amenities (usually energy sources) to people and regions otherwise going without. No groundswell of popular support emerged for Enron, or companies like it, based on their gifts to humanity. Indeed, only large firms whose core business is conducted directly with retail consumers—Wal-Mart, for example—elicit arguments from unaffiliated individuals that big business has made them better off. In this latter twist on populism, large corporations actually favor and empower common people. With a company like Enron, which had almost nothing to do with lay consumers and at its peak dealt mainly in finance and information, such arguments held little sway. The American public no longer questioned the right of large corporations to exist, but neither did it have much regard for their "value add" to the general population. The case had to be made anew, and the corporation's defenders were not prepared to do so.

Analytic Themes

Narratives of the Enron bankruptcy and scandal were remarkably varied. Yet from sobbing news testimonials, to indignant speeches in the halls of Congress, to irreverent amateur cartoons, to legalistic sentence splicing, three consistent themes emerge as the points of most intense disagreement. These are also the three elements of this scandal—common to many others like it—that speak most directly to Enron's historical significance.

First, the legitimacy and accountability of leadership, within both business and government, fell into question. People debated (and most condemned) the role of the company's leaders in the bankruptcy and its fallout. How had the company failed, and why? What were the obligations of its top executives to employees, shareholders, and the public? Who had had sufficient authority either to solve Enron's problems or to deserve blame for failing to do so? Americans were led to wonder, beyond the Enron case, what kinds of people become celebrity tycoon power brokers in the United States? What can the public expect of them? What happens when they fall short?

When the topic is businessmen of great influence, especially discomforting is the fact that corporate leaders are not elected. Indeed, they are not formally public servants of any kind.[40] Even their oft-touted "shareholder value" may be tossed aside, sometimes brazenly—to say nothing of concerns among employees or other community stakeholders. Yet the Enron case also provoked arguments about the role of public officials in relation to private business. Controversy abounded as to the types and degrees of responsibility of legislators and even the Bush administration, both having allegedly coddled the company in exchange for campaign contributions. Blame was also heaped on regulatory agencies, such as the Federal Energy Regulatory Commission and the Securities and Exchange Commission. Had Enron been allowed to break rules? Were the country's leaders and regulators doing their jobs? Moreover, had the real authority of their positions been compromised, in part, because money and favors from companies like Enron subvert the democratic process?

A second theme in the Enron scandal, rarely articulated directly, was questioning of who did or did not "understand" business, finance, and the law.

Even before its problems were exposed, Enron's business models, financing, daily functioning, and organizational structure were highly complex. To grasp what went awry could be more difficult still. The bankruptcy and its fallout witnessed a fascinating scramble over who was knowledgeable enough to make pronouncements on what had happened. When non-experts—including employees, investors, and legislators—made judgments on Enron executives, they claimed to understand enough to assign blame. For their part, the company's executives—once so revered in all their expertise and ingenuity—sometimes insisted that the people most angry with them did not grasp relevant issues; at other times, they claimed that they themselves were completely unaware of key elements of their own company's business and accounting.

Nor was there consensus about whether specialized knowledge or comprehension was even useful, much less necessary, for interpreting and responding to Enron's collapse. Recognizing that exclusive standards of expertise are often deployed to silence unwelcome questions and opinions, some people most outraged by the bankruptcy framed their narratives in moral rather than technical terms.[41] All that one needed to comprehend Enron, they insisted, was a basic sense of right and wrong. Yet other narrative makers—satirists—also rejected the premium on business arcana by contending that neither technicalities nor moral reasoning was particularly relevant. Pragmatic common sense enabled anybody to get their jokes, and, in some cases, to envision change.

A final theme in the Enron scandal is that commentators revisited and even reconsidered conceptions of the "American way" and U.S. civic culture. The issues under debate in this case were most abstract, and invocations of them least direct. People had to think in terms of systems and processes rather than, as comes more easily, in terms of individuals and incidents. How much influence did large corporations enjoy over American government, society, and individual livelihood? Was this level of influence earned and deserved? Did it comport with the values of the nation's imagined community? What happens when traditional admiration for businessmen's ambition, innovation, and self-made success collides with traditional disdain for businessmen's greed, manipulation, and entitlement?

Large Corporations in America: Reverence, Rebuke, and Something In-Between

Studies of business and attitudes toward it, from the era before independence through to the present, have consistently demonstrated a tension: on the one hand, Americans respect—often idolize—individuals who achieve dramatic success and fabulous wealth through business enterprise. Demonstrated time and again, the vast socioeconomic gulf between "average" citizens, such as themselves, and celebrity executives, is tolerable so long as the upward mobility doctrine of the American dream persists. On the other hand, Americans have been suspicious of business from the very beginning—indeed, wary of the corporate form itself, from the earliest days of charter granting in the American colonies.[42] With every development in U.S. business came a wave of resentment and resistance, often related to the same mechanisms of concentrated money and influence that at the very same time earned admiration and applause.

The American colonies were conceived as a profit-making project. Many of the first Europeans who committed to settling here did so, at substantial risk, in hopes of making money—far more money than the Old World would offer to non-nobles. It should not be surprising that these people and their descendants would admire the spirit of enterprise. With the market revolution, Americans of all regions and stations routinely praised growing corporations for the amenities they brought. They also appreciated corporations as providers of employment. By the late nineteenth century it was also suggested that corporate leaders served the interests of cultural betterment. By the logic that "material well-being must [precede] social and cultural progress," Morgan, Carnegie, et al. could be viewed as more valuable than the nation's most esteemed thinkers and artists.[43]

The more people identified as consumers and as wage earners, the more immediate their recognition of how big business affected their livelihood. Renowned for his innovations in manufacturing and labor policy, Henry Ford ranked slightly below Jesus and Napoleon in 1920s public polls concerning "the greatest men in history."[44] Philanthropic giving by famous executives has also been a constant, allowing business leaders to salve their conscience and/or public image. Whatever the philanthropic motive, the recipients have been grateful for the funding they received.

In recent years, with the "question" of big business long settled in the affirmative, some scholars argue not just for acceptance of large corporations, but for appreciation of their role in establishing and maintaining the United States as a national society. For example, in "The Prospering Fathers," Paul Johnson argued that the same titans of industry and finance so often called "robber barons" were actually patriots—economic pillars and civic exemplars—to which Americans past and present owe a considerable debt.[45] Most "household names" of the New Economy, likewise, are recognized not only in association with their companies' successes, but also in connection with their (often massive) philanthropic efforts, the readiest example being Microsoft founder Bill Gates. Enron's best-known executives, Ken Lay and Jeff Skilling, were outright celebrities during the company's heyday, considered geniuses of trading and management, and consulted constantly on matters of business and policy. Lay's philanthropy would come to public attention primarily after his criminal indictment (and then again after his death), but it reflected the same tradition of noblesse oblige—and the public appreciation it evoked.

Yet early in America's history, along with its zeal for commerce and the fruits it would bear, was an intense skepticism toward the capitalist ethos and the sometimes reckless ways of businessmen and their corporations. The Puritans' Calvinist doctrine admonished both idleness and over-commercialism, leaving in between a narrow strait of industrious piety that, as historian Perry Miller noted, ultimately proved too difficult for a burgeoning capitalist society to navigate.[46] Anxieties ran rampant in the early national period about the Bank of the United States' consolidation of capital and power.[47] Mark Twain's 1873 novel *The Gilded Age* depicted businessmen buying off legislators with nonchalance. Where captains of industry had appeared as "folk heroes" in many films of the 1920s, Hollywood during the 1930s often portrayed them as villains.[48] By the 1970s, business executives were allegedly the only demographic whose mass vilification on television was still acceptable, portrayed as "unadulterated bad guys."[49] More recent films such as *The Insider, Erin Brockovich,* and *Michael Clayton*[50] carry on this tradition, presenting large corporations and their heads as unscrupulous, even violent, in protecting and enriching themselves.

This long-standing duality in American thinking about business and large corporations—admiration alongside suspicion—would be rich enough to sustain a study on its own, but I find there is also a third tradition in treatments of big business. I was not looking for it, but during my research on Enron narratives it became impossible to ignore. This third kind of narrative about corporations has been not only highly influential; it also has a long history. Yet while business historians sometimes acknowledge it anecdotally, they seem to find it unworthy of synthesis or even comment.

When more academically inclined, I call this third narrative style "satire." At times it seems more accurate to dub it "mockery." The overall pattern is the deployment of humor, with business the butt of the joke. Americans who make fun of business and business people engage directly neither in admiration nor in derision. In fact, satire seems simultaneously to reject both attitudes and to sample selectively from each.

First comes mockery of the capitalist endeavor and its promises of wild success. In the 1605 play *Eastward Hoe!* a tavern patron bragged that, thanks to profit-making ventures in "VIRGINIA, Earth's only Paradise," its denizens had "chamber-potts" of "pure gould."[51] A folk song from the early twentieth century had Jay Gould's daughter begging, before she died, to try the only two beverages in the world that she had never tasted: water and tea. There is also grim acknowledgment of the dehumanization (figurative and sometimes literal) that business logics beget. Charlie Chaplin's 1936 film *Modern Times,*[52] for example, satirized factory mechanization, featuring a boss who decided not to feed his employees by machine only because the machine's tendency to clobber them made it "impractical."

Moving toward more accusatory fun, Will Rogers said, around the same time, "a holding company is . . . where you hand an accomplice the goods while the policeman searches you."[53] Likewise, on February 2, 1960, somebody bought advertising space in the *New York Times,* under fake sponsorship, to sneer at a recent price-fixing scandal that had germinated at the Barclay Hotel. "Antitrust corporation secrets are best discussed in the privacy of an executive suite at the Barclay," the "ad" said. "It is convenient, attractive and financially practical."[54]

Finally, the effects of office work at a large corporation on social relations and personal values presented ample opportunity to make fun of people who seemed to take themselves excruciatingly seriously. Impersonating a high-powered manager in a large company, author Joseph Heller in 1974 described the ridiculous company politics that would become fodder for many later send-ups, including films like *Office Space,* television series like *Arrested Development* and *The Office,* and of course Scott Adams's long-lauded comic strip *Dilbert.*[55] Heller also lampooned businessmen's notorious self-importance in a caricature that lives on vigorously today. "I enjoy my work," he wrote, "when the assignments are large and urgent and somewhat frightening and will come to the attention of many people."[56]

To mock someone who occupies a privileged place in society is to impugn, in one way or another, his or her right to be there. The grounds for doing so can be as superficial as poor looks or as serious as criminal allegations. But while satire, obviously, departs from praise when it describes high-profile executives and their world, it also avoids the ominous tone that characterizes straight polemic. To decry some public harm from commercial practices, or warn of its threat, one has to believe that business leaders wield great power. Only through the perception that "ordinary" people, by default, are at the mercy of corporate maneuverings, does any complaint or resistive activism appear even logical, much less necessary.

Thus expressions of suspicion and anger toward big business actually share one important element with expressions of reverence: a sense of wonder. Both earnestly positive and urgently negative characterizations of big business attribute to its prominent figures a special prowess and mystique. Each, likewise, lends credence to the notion that finance and commerce are esoteric domains, only for the elite few expert enough to understand them. Any account in exaltation or in polemic suggests that business activity is deft, arcane, and impossible to pick apart. Successful businessmen may be exceptionally driven and brilliant, or exceptionally greedy and conniving, but both traditions in commentary agree that they are exceptional.

Not so the concomitant procession of satire and mockery. With humor, the world of massive-scale, arcane business activity is revealed to be the same as our own. It has no distinct or impenetrable language, logics, or potencies. It contains neither heroes nor villains. There may be some actions worth taking at a given juncture, but either way the first priority is perspective. The subjects of these jokes are not so lofty as to deserve our idolatry. But neither are they imposing enough to disturb us—or even to be taken seriously, at least for now.

Each of these three views of big business emerged in descriptions of Enron: admiration for business success, outrage at business recklessness, and amusement encompassing both. By virtue of their unique, elegant resolution of the struggle between technicality and morality, humorous accounts may be more insightful than their alternatives. It is perhaps ironic that the most lighthearted interpretations of Enron were often the most capacious. They took into account myriad factors, insisting that technical decisions and moral judgments were equally relevant, but neither all-encompassing. They offered a platform for a more inclusive discussion. And they approached the most powerful figures in the United States—in both the private and public sectors—as people rather than as titans.

Accordingly, making fun of Enron, and of other sorry episodes at the intersection of business and government, can actually be a serious, conscientious, and productive public response. While simply equating humor with citizen empowerment would be too romantic, the political possibilities that open with laughter should not be discounted. Most Americans have stopped expecting, much less proposing, any radical revision to the scope and position of large corporations in economic and civic life. In such a political climate, mockery and satire may be uniquely adaptive: forms of critique that express learned realism alongside persisting dissent.

Chapter 8

Saving TEPCO

*Debt, Credit, and the "End" of Finance in
Post-Fukushima Japan*

Hirokazu Miyazaki

The recent global financial crises suggest the era in which finance served as a site of vigorous intellectual and socioeconomic experiment may be coming to an end. Finance has always been about uncertainty, and financial market professionals have devised a variety of models, tools, and techniques for managing uncertainty by translating it into the language of calculable risk. But the global financial crisis of 2007-2008 and the subsequent European sovereign debt crisis have demonstrated the ultimate limitations of risk-based models, tools, and techniques, and of the human actors that use them.[1]

The sense of the end of finance created by the global financial crisis has particularly intensified in Tokyo. The theories, techniques, and tools of finance designed to manage and profit from uncertainty have served as a means of socioeconomic reform in Japan since the deregulation of Japan's financial markets in the mid-1980s and especially after the burst of the economic bubble in the early 1990s.[2] In particular, Tokyo-based global investment bankers had been a major force behind the promotion of a new culture of risk-taking and the associated brand of individualism. By the middle of the first decade of this century, however, Tokyo had begun to lose its prominence as a global financial center. Many of the Tokyo offices of global investment banks have reduced their operations significantly, and some of them now report to their Hong Kong offices rather than to their London or New York offices directly.

Tokyo's financial market professionals now face new challenges ranging from frequent layoffs and downsizing to a sheer lack of intellectual excitement.

In this context, Japan's March 2011 earthquake, tsunami, and nuclear disasters, and the profoundly uncertain and unknowable character of the world that the triple disasters have revealed, have presented a new layer of challenges to Tokyo's financial market professionals. As with many other natural disasters, Japan's earthquake and tsunami are not simply "natural" disasters.[3] At 2:46 P.M. on Friday, March 11, 2011, an earthquake of magnitude 9.0 struck eastern Japan, and within an hour a massive tsunami devastated Japan's northeastern coast. It was later confirmed that a series of explosions and meltdowns took place at the Fukushima Dai'ichi nuclear power plant during the first few days following the earthquake and tsunami primarily due to damage caused by the tsunami to the plant's cooling system. Tokyo Electric Power Company (TEPCO), the operator of Fukushima Dai'ichi, was widely criticized for its slow and inadequate initial response to the trouble with reactors at Fukushima Dai'ichi. The company's apparently incompetent handling of the accidents and failure to provide timely and accurate information triggered public outrage and panic. The impact of the nuclear disaster far exceeds the immediate vicinity of the power plant from which residents have been evacuated with no prospect of returning to the area in the near future. A massive amount of radioactive substance spread over a large area of eastern Japan and the Pacific Ocean. Cesium contamination has been detected in a vast area of ocean water and agricultural and farming land, and health concerns have been raised regarding a wide range of food and food products.

In addition to the social, cultural, and political implications, the disasters have had profound economic and financial consequences. The estimated cost of the reconstruction of the tsunami-devastated areas of northern Japan is twenty trillion yen (approximately $200 billion at the exchange rate of the time of writing). The cost of the cleanup of the areas contaminated by radioactive substance has also exceeded 1.5 trillion yen (approximately $15 billion).[4] The disasters thus have imposed a major burden on the country's already massive sovereign debt.[5] Japan's disasters immediately spurred debates about many economic and fiscal issues, such as whether to increase the country's consumption tax.

The nuclear crisis has also created a significant debt and credit crisis of a sort. Immediately after the accidents at the Fukushima Dai'ichi nuclear power plant, TEPCO's financial liability surfaced as a contentious issue. TEPCO, one of Japan's ten electric power companies, is virtually the sole supplier of electric power for the greater Tokyo area and the biggest utility company in the country.[6] Before the disasters, TEPCO was widely regarded as one of Japan's most financially stable companies. This meant that many Japanese mega banks, insurance companies, pension funds, and individual investors held TEPCO shares or bonds, and in most cases both, in their portfolios.[7] In particular, TEPCO had financed itself primarily through debt, and it had been the largest issuer of corporate bonds in Japan. At the time of the disasters, TEPCO had bank loans worth about 1.6 trillion yen (approximately $19 billion at the exchange rate at the time of the disasters) and had issued corporate bonds worth over 4.4 trillion yen (approximately $53 billion).[8] After the accidents at Fukushima Dai'ichi, TEPCO's creditors—that is, major Japanese financial institutions—therefore were suddenly exposed to a wide range of risks associated with TEPCO's large debt as well as lawsuits and massive compensation claims against the utility company. Following the crisis in Fukushima, in other words, TEPCO quickly came to be seen as a threat to the entire Japanese economy.

The disaster has highlighted the problematic nature of the previously widely shared assumption that nuclear energy is cost effective. For example, economist Ken-ichi Oshima has gained widespread acclaim for his recent calculation of the "costs" of nuclear energy in Japan. Following K. William Kapp's work *The Social Costs of Private Enterprise,*[9] Oshima goes beyond the conventional calculation to include the "social costs" of nuclear energy, such as various kinds of damage caused by the nuclear disasters, compensation for such damage, taxpayers' money invested in the promotion of nuclear energy in the past, and the future costs of managing and disposing nuclear waste.[10] Oshima's inquiry is ultimately driven by the question of whether "the benefits of abolishing nuclear energy exceed the costs of doing so."[11] Oshima effectively reframes Japan's reenergized antinuclear activism in the language of cost-benefit analysis. According to Oshima, the conventional calculation of the relative cost effectiveness of nuclear energy vastly underestimates the total social cost of nuclear energy, and as a result, the relative cost-effectiveness of alternative energy sources is not adequately considered.[12]

In this chapter, drawing on my ethnographic field research in Tokyo in 2011 and 2012, I examine two contrasting forms of financial market activism orchestrated by Tokyo's debt and credit market specialists in the months following the disasters, as manifestations of these professionals' conscious efforts to redeploy theories and techniques of finance in a newly found sphere of profound uncertainty. I offer these examples as illustrations of a more general question of how theoretical, technical, and professional commitments are made anew at the limits of expert knowledge.

Debt in Japan: The Gift in Finance?

The current anthropological debate about debt and credit triggered by the global financial crisis of 2007-2008 largely takes for granted the distinction between debt in the gift and debt in finance.[13] The distinction implicitly capitalizes on a popular indictment of financial technologies and techniques used to transform debt and credit of all kinds, such as subprime mortgages, into tradable securities for causing the global financial crisis of 2007-2008.[14] The mainstream anthropological impulse has been to broaden the debate about debt with a view to exposing the narrow vision of debt associated with finance to a broader and more humane vision of debt entailed in the idea of human economy.

What makes the Japanese case intriguing is the way it challenges this anthropological impulse. In the crisis of TEPCO, the problems of financial debt, and the moral and political debate about the "Too Big to Fail" problem,[15] are superimposed on the widely acknowledged cultural specificity of the gift-based sociological fabric of Japan's debt and credit markets. Here the distinction between debt in the gift and debt in finance, or even the gift and finance, seems to break down quickly. The anthropological broadening of the problem of debt becomes redundant to the popular culturalist argument about the distinction between U.S.-style capitalism and "Japanese" capitalism reenergized in Japan after the Wall Street-originated global financial crisis of 2007-2008. As Holly High notes, "Debt ... can perhaps best be defined as an on-going moral reasoning about the obligation to repay,"[16] in the Japanese case as well. My turn to financial market professionals' own responses to Japan's nuclear crisis and associated debt crisis reveals their own moral and philosophical reflections on the competing cultural logics of the gift and finance. For example, seeing company shares as gift-like forms of debt with a less rigidly defined temporal structure, as opposed to bonds and loans, potentially opens up a new space of debate in which general ethical, moral, and political problems associated with corporate ownership and governance may be rethought.[17] A closer examination of Japanese financial market professionals' responses to the crisis of TEPCO described below points to the need for a different kind of analytical framework altogether.

The very evening before Japan's triple disasters of March 11, 2011, I had dinner with Nakada, a credit analyst working for a global investment bank's Tokyo office. My purpose was to gain insight into Japan's debt and credit markets. My inquiry focused on what happens in large yet highly specialized markets, such as the market for Japanese convertible bonds, in which market participants, mostly professional investors, know one another personally, monitor one another closely, and occasionally help one another in the name of a morally empowered sense of "indebtedness" (*kashi kari,* or "lending and borrowing").

The conversation focused on the difference in the nature of debt and equity.[18] Unlike Japan's equity markets, Japan's bond markets are largely domestic: Japan's government, municipal, and corporate bonds are held mostly by domestic investors. Domestic institutional and individual investors hold over 90 percent of the Japanese government bonds (JGB). Likewise, domestic investors hold nearly 99 percent of corporate bonds issued by Japanese corporations.[19] In particular, Japanese corporate bonds are not traded actively because most institutional investors "buy and hold" bonds until their maturity dates.[20]

Nakada complained bitterly about the closed and nontransparent nature of the Japanese world of bank loans and corporate bonds compared with the far more globalized, open, and transparent Japanese equity markets. Nakada noted that the nominal size of bank loans and corporate bonds far exceeded the size of the value of corporate shares, but in Nakada's view, Japan's debt markets were closely anchored in long-term social relations, and from a purely economic perspective, the terms of loans and bond issuing were set arbitrarily. Moreover, in Japan, corporate bonds are traded over-the-counter (not at exchanges), and pricing information is not readily available in the market. This lack of transparency has further fed the image of Japan's corporate bond markets as highly relational. For example, Nakada mentioned that if an analyst from a global investment bank like himself visited TEPCO, the person would be told by TEPCO's financial officer in charge of bond issuing to keep visiting the company for at least ten years before he could hope to be taken seriously. Nakada offered this as an example of the closed nature of Japan's debt and credit market.

Nakada also noted that for a variety of historical reasons, the issuing of corporate bonds had been generally limited to a certain class of corporations with high credit ratings.[21] In the 1990s, over 50 percent of corporate bonds were rated AAA at the time of their issuing, and over 85 percent were rated above AA.[22] The issuing of bonds rated below BBB has increased only since the late 1990s.[23] The virtual absence of "high-yield" bonds and "junk bonds" has made the Japanese corporate bonds market exceedingly unattractive from overseas investors' point of view. Nakada pointed out that there was a widely held assumption that only financially healthy corporations could issue corporate bonds. Moreover, banks, as both underwriters and investors, played a major role in the corporate bond market. They also implicitly agreed to purchase back the bonds issued from their investors at the time of default.[24] Default had been rare, and creditors and bondholders had almost always been compensated. Among these generally safe investments, bonds issued by electric power corporations were regarded as particularly safe investments and accounted for over 20 percent of the total outstanding corporate bonds. TEPCO bonds were unattractive to foreign professional investors specializing in high-yield bonds, but for the same reason, they were popular with risk-averse domestic institutional investors.

The conversation I had with Nakada on the eve of Japan's triple disasters reflects his own long-standing frustration with Japan's debt and credit markets. Nakada further complained about a strong pervasive assumption that corporate bonds entail no risk. Nakada asked, "Is this situation really appropriate for financial giants like Japan?" Here Nakada positioned himself as a reformer and an activist of a kind, committed to the further deregulation and optimization of Japan's debt and credit markets. There was a long-standing tradition for this position. Finance had served as a form of political activism in Japan since the 1980s. Tokyo-based global investment bankers like Nakada had embodied new values associated with global capitalism and neoliberal ideals of risk-taking individualism.[25] For Nakada, the relational, and gift-like, quality of Japan's debt markets represented the core of Japan's problem that the globalizing logics of finance were supposed to overcome and resolve.

Saving TEPCO: Too Big to Fail?

It quickly became clear to policy makers and financial market professionals that TEPCO was "too big to fail."[26] Yet, it became so in a particular fashion in the particular context of the nuclear power plant disaster and in articulation with a pervasive nationalistic urge to unite, persevere, and even sacrifice for the sake of victims of the disasters. TEPCO shareholders responded to the disaster by selling their shares immediately. TEPCO shares were traded at

2,121 yen on March 11, 2011. They had plunged to 148 yen by June 9, 2011. Some TEPCO shareholders showed up at the first shareholders meeting after the disasters on June 28 demanding that the company withdraw from nuclear energy, although TEPCO's powerful institutional shareholders rejected the motion.

In contrast, TEPCO bondholders responded profoundly ambiguously. The yield of TEPCO's bond with a maturity date of July 2021 had jumped from the pre-earthquake level of 1.4 percent to 4.366 percent by May 20. Relatedly, the "spread"—the difference between the yields of TEPCO bonds and comparable Japanese government bonds—had also widened from the pre-earthquake level of 5.9 basis points to 321.2 basis points by May 20. But despite the fact that the credit rating of TEPCO bonds (to be more precise, TEPCO's long-term issuer rating) had been lowered to Baa1 and BBB+, respectively, by both of the major global rating agencies operating in Japan—that is, Moody's and Standard & Poor's—by April 1 (which gave Aa2 and AA-, respectively, before the disasters), a majority of TEPCO bondholders held on to their bonds.[27] Subsequently, Standard & Poor's downgraded TEPCO bonds further to junk status (B+) on May 30, and Moody's followed on June 20 by downgrading them to B1, but the market did not respond dramatically.[28]

In fact, the prices of TEPCO bonds did not fall as drastically as the price of TEPCO shares. According to bond market insiders, the trading price of TEPCO bonds fell 40 percent at one point. But they did not see the loss as significant. That is because not many bonds were available for trading anyhow. No more than approximately 1 or 2 percent of TEPCO bonds previously held by banks and insurance companies were actively traded in the months immediately following the disasters. The price of the bonds bounced back fairly quickly as some trading in TEPCO bonds began to take place (see below).

Shareholders' and bondholders' divergent responses to the crisis of TEPCO themselves are perhaps not surprising, at least superficially. In fact, some market participants saw bondholders' response as another manifestation of the highly domestic, inward-looking and relational quality of Japan's debt and credit markets. However, my ethnography shows that the status quo was the artifact of conscious effort among Tokyo's financial market professionals to sustain this quality in the midst of the crisis.

In mid-May, I met with Nakada again. Our conversation naturally focused on the TEPCO crisis. Nakada had written his first report to institutional investors on TEPCO on March 23, and by the time we met in mid-May, he had circulated over ten reports on the TEPCO crisis. Nakada told me that in his observation his colleagues and other market professionals were trying their best to maintain their own "faith in the system" (*taisei wo shinjiru*) by helping TEPCO to avoid default. Nakada clearly had a certain sense of solidarity with other analysts and credit market specialists. TEPCO needed to be protected from default. This was surprising to me given the fact Nakada had been part of the broader effort among global investment bankers to deregulate and globalize Japan's debt and credit markets and promote the further financialization of the Japanese economy.

Initially, there was ambiguity concerning the significance of the magnitude of the disaster for TEPCO's responsibility. The Japanese law governing compensation for damage associated with a nuclear accident has a clause that exempts the nuclear power plant operator from liability in case of a natural disaster of an unprecedented scale. However, an agreement was gradually reached that this clause would not apply to the nuclear disaster in Fukushima, and this in turn triggered speculation as to the size of compensation and its potential impact on TEPCO's balance sheet. Moreover, it quickly became apparent that the cost of de-commissioning the four reactors at the Fukushima power plant would be enormous.

Nakada pointed to a constellation of reasons for TEPCO bondholders' refusal to sell their holdings after the nuclear disaster in Fukushima. First, there was a vague shared sense of "trust" (*shinrai*) in the ability of Japanese mega-banks and life insurance firms, TEPCO's long-standing major sources of financing, to continue to support TEPCO. Indeed, Japanese mega-banks injected 1.9 trillion yen ($23 billion at the exchange rate of the time) on March 31, 2011. The loan was reportedly non-secured, low-interest, and long-term. Second, there was yet another vague sense of trust in Japan's two major domestic rating agencies, Japan Credit Rating Agency (JCR) and Rating and Investment Information (R&I), whose ratings a majority of Japanese institutional investors monitor more closely than ratings released by the two major global rating agencies, Moody's and Standard & Poor's. Indeed, both JCR and R&I refused to downgrade TEPCO bonds too quickly. Third, there was a similar collective sense of trust in the government's commitment to upholding the laws related to the rights of TEPCO's bondholders to receive compensation ahead of other creditors and possible compensation claimants, such as victims of the nuclear disaster, should TEPCO go bankrupt. This meant that the government would never allow TEPCO to default at the expense of victims of the disaster. Fourth, among TEPCO bondholders, there was a vague trust in one another's willingness to sustain losses together. Fifth, and perhaps most important for present purposes, there was a concerted effort on the part of financial market professionals, like Nakada, to sustain this vague sense of trust itself.

The collective effort to sustain trust in the system reached its climax when chief cabinet secretary Yukio Edano suggested on May 13, 2011, that bank loans made to TEPCO prior to the March 11, 2011, disasters be written off.[29] In Nakada's and other market insiders' view, this would lead to the further downgrading of the TEPCO bonds and would create a chaotic situation in the markets. For Nakada, Edano's statement served as evidence of the emergence of politics as a major risk factor in the market. Nakada's subsequent work focused on circulating more credit analysis reports in which he sought to reaffirm the vague sense of trust he shared with many market participants. When that trust or faith fell apart, the system would fall apart, he observed.[30]

At the least on the surface, it is easy to see in this episode a manifestation of the gift-like quality of Japan's debt and credit markets. Nakada's and other market professionals' concerted effort to save TEPCO from default may be also interpreted as a demonstration of the pervasiveness of Japan's post-earthquake and tsunami nationalism in the Japanese financial markets and even among market reform-minded Tokyo-based global investment bankers like Nakada. Before examining Nakada's seemingly contradictory financial market activism further, I now turn to another equally powerful and yet less vocal campaign among Tokyo's global investment bankers. This campaign focused on selling TEPCO bonds overseas.

Selling TEPCO's Debt Overseas: Arbitraging Japan?

By late March 2011, some global investment banks' Tokyo offices had begun to capitalize on the TEPCO crisis. Okada, a Tokyo-based veteran credit trader long committed to stirring up and opening up Japan's debt and credit markets, told me in July 2011 that he had been able to buy TEPCO bonds from a midsized insurance firm and had sold them to an overseas, high-yield fund within a month after the disasters. Okada observed that the sale was possible because of the particular location of global investment banks like his. The midsized insurance firm would never have sold the bonds to a Japanese securities firm at that time because the firm would not want other market players to know of the sale. The firm therefore went outside the closely monitored network of bond brokers and investors to find a broker for the sale. Okada also noted that

Japanese securities firms would not have entertained playing the role of middleman for this transaction, either. They had TEPCO bonds themselves in their own portfolios of bonds they maintained for market-making purposes, and pricing the TEPCO bonds would adversely affect their market position. As Okada recalled in April 2012, the role of global investment banks like his was to get the paralyzed thinking of market participants after the disasters moving again. Here it seems that Okada executed his own long-standing activist spirit.

By May 2011, however, Japanese securities firms had also begun to follow suit. In early July, the credit analyst Nakada introduced me to Yamane, a pioneering Japanese credit derivatives specialist. Yamane, who specialized in structuring credit derivatives and associated synthetic products for repackaging various kinds of debt—both domestic and foreign—in the 1990s, now worked for a Japanese securities firm. Yamane believed that the global financial crisis of 2007–2008 marked an end of the high finance of complex derivatives products he once designed and marketed to Japanese investors. Yamane's sense of the end of finance resulted from his own personal bitter experience with credit derivatives during the first decade of this century.

In the 1990s, the idea of credit risk had surfaced as a concern even for risk-averse Japanese institutional investors in the Japanese corporate bond markets. The increase in cases of default in the late 1990s further sharpened Japanese investors' attention to the need for risk management in this sector. As a result, Japan's markets for credit derivatives and credit-related structured products grew rapidly during the late 1990s.[31] Tokyo-based global investment bankers, like Yamane, initially marketed structured products, such as collateralized debt obligations (CDOs), using domestic loans and corporate bonds, to Japanese clients (mostly domestic regional banks). However, partially in response to his clients' demand for a better return as well as to his team's expansion, Yamane started marketing products from the United States whose contents were not transparent to either him or his clients. Eventually, some of his clients lost money in subprime mortgage-related products and lost interest in these products altogether. Their negative experience with these structured products had resulted in the enhanced form of risk-averse conservatism in Japan's debt and credit markets discussed above.

The TEPCO crisis, however, was a blessing to Yamane. He was having "fun" with TEPCO bonds, he said. Unlike Nakada's active campaign to save TEPCO, Yamane's excitement about the TEPCO crisis sounded shocking to me to the extent that it was out of sync with the national collective sentiment of mourning, suffering, and resignation. At the same time, it was rather refreshing in the context of the suffocating emptiness of the pervasive collective determination to *ganbaro* ("let's persevere and not give up") and emphasis on *kizuna* ("social bond," "togetherness," or "relatedness"). In selling TEPCO bonds previously held by Japanese investors to hedge funds overseas, Yamane told me that he found joy in stirring up a sense of "risk" (and associated need for techniques and tools of finance) as opposed to the constellation of vague and irrational senses of "trust" (and associated logics of sociality/relationality) discussed above. He wanted to shake up the "preexisting framework" (*kizon no wakugumi*) of Japanese society by shaking Japanese investors' irrational confidence in TEPCO (and the system that supported it) and selling their assets off to overseas risk-takers. This was exciting to him.

Yamane's excitement perhaps represented his renewed commitment to the logics and techniques of finance and associated utopian dream of financial globalization he had cultivated during his previous careers in global investment banks. Yamane's project to sell TEPCO bonds overseas in the midst of the national collective effort to persevere and work together to overcome the crisis, and to rekindle his passion to break open Japan's closed financial system, was reminiscent of the kind of utopian urge that drove his and many other financial market professionals' earlier financial market activism before the financial crisis of 2007–2008 I have described elsewhere.[32] During this period, Yamane often noted the anger Japanese people shared toward TEPCO. Although he did not express it directly, his excitement in selling TEPCO bonds had much to do with his sense of this popular sentiment toward TEPCO. He clearly felt that TEPCO did not deserve the kind of collective financial protection it was receiving and that this sentiment might eventually translate into government action against TEPCO, as shown in cabinet secretary Edano's controversial statement. In attempting to buy TEPCO bonds from Japanese institutional investors, he hinted to risk-averse Japanese institutional investors who might have bonds to sell about the possible future downgrading of TEPCO bonds. In selling TEPCO bonds to overseas high-yield funds, Yamane emphasized the high possibility of the government's rescuing TEPCO eventually. Here Yamane was essentially seeking to arbitrage TEPCO, if not Japan's financial system as a whole, where the discrepancy between the ways TEPCO's risks were evaluated in Japan and elsewhere surfaced as an arbitrage opportunity. In the logic of arbitrage, arbitrageurs profit from such discrepancy, and in the process of profiting from the discrepancy, they eliminate it. To the extent arbitrage is supposed to propel the market to a condition of "no arbitrage" in which there are no such arbitrage opportunities and hence the market is perfect at last, there is a latent form of utopianism in arbitrage.[33]

But there was something different in Yamane's endeavor. He himself did not expect any radical change as a result of his and his like-minded global investment bankers' efforts. After all, according to market insiders, only a fraction of TEPCO bonds became available for such trading. Even Okada, who had been known for his aggressive trading, seemed to be satisfied by the fact that he was one of the first traders to price and trade TEPCO bonds after the disasters. This was very different from the kind of intellectual excitement and grand utopianism about the possibility of transforming the Japanese economy through new financial technologies and techniques I had observed in Tokyo in the late 1990s and the first half of the first decade of this century.[34] In the aftermath of the global financial crisis of 2007-2008 and Japan's triple disasters, no utopian vision was in view. After all, as Yamane admitted to me with a sigh in April 2012, TEPCO was "too big to fail." For Yamane, however, his own excitement in selling TEPCO bonds overseas was personally significant. It was important for Yamane to re-experience that sense of excitement he once felt routinely in structuring and marketing complex derivatives products in the 1990s, in the midst of a national crisis in which he, his wife, and their small child lived with the constant daily reminder of the radical uncertainty of their life now contaminated by cesium.

It is important to note at this point that the credit analyst mentioned above, Nakada, himself was equally cynical about the trust-based market activism he himself led. No one believed that TEPCO would collapse or default. Moreover, TEPCO bonds were secured bonds. This meant that TEPCO bondholders would be one of the first groups of creditors to be able to claim TEPCO's assets in case of default. There was something redundant about his and his colleagues' effort to uphold Japan's "system."

Nakada admitted to me in May 2011 that his frustration with the situation had led him to start drinking heavily since the disasters. He was concerned about the unknowable potential effect of cesium contamination on his primary-school-age children's health. He and his wife had asked his children's school not to let them play outside during recess. He was also deeply concerned about other nuclear power plants, such as Monju, a controversial fast breeder reactor in Fukui Prefecture. At Monju, a not so widely reported and arguably highly risky operation to retrieve a device that had fallen into the reactor was scheduled to take place in June 2011. Nakada told me that his initial impulse had been to run away from the crisis situation in which he found himself. He cited the "loss-cutting" instinct he had cultivated in his long career in the financial industry.[35] But that would not be an option for him and his family because it would not be easy for him to find a comparable job elsewhere. Like Yamane's urge to sell TEPCO bonds to overseas investors, Nakada's campaign to save TEPCO then was an effort to try to keep going in an impossibly uncertain situation.

The two seemingly contrasting responses to the crisis of TEPCO then might not be contrasting cases after all. Perhaps they are comparable examples of what Annelise Riles, Yuji Genda, and I have called "retooling," the conscious redeployment of professional tools and techniques one has long worked to master at the very limits of the efficacy of those tools and techniques—that is, in a condition of profound uncertainty.[36] In these specific cases, tools and techniques of finance are no longer regarded as transformative. In the case of Nakada, it was no longer the market, but politics, that would determine the future of TEPCO and its creditors. In the case of Yamane, TEPCO was "too big to fail" in any case, and there were no real arbitrage opportunities.

Retooling rather served as a tool for personal survival. This is a version of the problem of hope I have explored elsewhere: the problem of how to reorient oneself in a condition of profound uncertainty.[37] However, Nakada and Yamane did not seek to find hope on the horizon of utopian visions their tools and techniques, whether credit analysis or arbitrage, had before been able to bring into view. Rather, it was their commitment to those tools and techniques itself that enabled and sustained their hope, if only for the moment.

Seeing Nakada's and Yamane's efforts—the former's apparent alliance with the gift-like relational, collectivizing, and even nationalistic logic of *kizuna,* and the latter's apparent alliance with the sensibility of arbitrage and the globalizing logic of finance—as comparable examples of retooling has a particular consequence to my own engagement with the situation in which I found myself in the months following Japan's disasters. My family and I left Tokyo a few days after the disasters but returned to Tokyo in May 2011. Leaving Japan in the midst of the crisis created in myself a personal crisis. I developed an inexplicably strong, and irresistible, urge to go back to Japan immediately. Volunteers were rushing to the scenes of destruction and devastation. Was there something I could do? Upon returning to Japan in May, however, I found myself in a situation in which the pervasive, collective urge to unite and persevere intensely suppressed voices of dissent. I was naturally attracted to the market movement that Okada, Yamane, and others led to sell TEPCO bonds overseas. I was increasingly uncomfortable with the overwhelmingly strong movement to save TEPCO that Nakada and others led—a movement that echoed a more general sense of solidarity represented by the spirit of *kizuna* and "All Japan," a rather awkward English phrase (previously used in the context of World Cup soccer games) used widely at that time. I found the former liberating and the latter oppressive.

In redeploying their respective professional tools and techniques in the context of Japan's debt and credit crisis following the country's triple disasters in which no end of the crisis was in view, both Nakada and Yamane sought to keep going through their reengagement with tools and techniques of finance that they knew had exhausted themselves. Seeing them as comparable cases of retooling perhaps effectively "arbitrages" the difference between the two individuals (and the two equally unsustainable broader positions—nationalism and financial globalism—they initially seemed to represent). For me, personally, as a result, I find a glimpse of hope, albeit only in retrospect, in my own retooling of a sort. In my own retooling, I decided to resume my longitudinal ethnographic fieldwork on financial market professionals and document their responses to Japan's crisis. In this light, the three projects—Nakada's campaign to save TEPCO from default, Yamane's effort to sell TEPCO bonds overseas, and my own ethnographic engagement with them—may surface as parallel responses to the unbearably uncertain situation in which we all found ourselves in the months following Japan's triple disasters. This possibility seems hopeful to me, not because any of our responses achieved anything good, but because it has confounded both what looked oppressive and what looked liberating to me at the outset. If there is a way forward illuminated by this ethnographic episode, it should be this sense of unpredictability and unknowability that calls for a calm and gentle embrace of it.

PART II

Does Government Regulation of Corporations Promote Well-Being in a Democratic Society?

Chapter 9

The Rise and Embedding of the Corporation

Considerations for American Democracy and Citizenship

Walter Licht

A remarkable accident of history: in the United States in the second half of the nineteenth century, an extraordinary set of men miraculously appeared, who through their uncommon determination, foresight, innovativeness, and daring built the mammoth business enterprises that propelled the United States to economic majesty. The names are familiar—Carnegie, Rockefeller, Ford, Morgan, among others—and they serve in high school textbooks and popular histories and biographies as the explanation for the rise and embedding of the American corporation: the subject matter of this chapter.

Hardly a scholar today subscribes to the Great Man Theory of History ingrained in the narrative sketched above; in fact, as will be noted soon, our famous (or infamous) titans of enterprise all but disappear in recent scholarly analyses. Yet, these men did have impacts that speak to the subtitle of this essay—to the question of democracy and citizenship—and to the essay's larger argument. Consider the following at the outset.

The behemoths created by the likes of Carnegie and Rockefeller, the imperious ways of these men, and the unfathomable wealth they accumulated generated vast resistance. In the late nineteenth and early twentieth centuries, middle-class citizens joined striking workers in their communities in tumultuous protests against corporations and the threats they posed with their concentrated economic and political power to cherished notions of the United States as a small producers' republic. Simultaneously, American farmers vociferously organized to fight monopoly, placing public regulation of corporations on the political agenda, and reform-minded politicians followed suit in establishing regulatory agencies on the state and federal levels. The putative Robber Barons in this way spurred democratic mobilizations.[1]

But, the great business figures of the American past played another role. As presumed Industrial Statesmen, their lives and accomplishments provide a powerful and enduring message: that American economic prosperity and well-being rests on entrepreneurialism and that businessmen who can effectively organize and manage productive capacities require and deserve leverage and leeway. Heroic individuals, they know best how to create wealth for all. In anointing business leaders, of course, the public sector gives way to the private. And with their very looming selves and enterprises—to be understood as just part of the realities of modern life—average Americans are placated somewhat, but also stilled as to their own senses of power and in their ability to imagine alternatives to a hierarchically managed world. In this regard, corporations inhibit democratic citizenship.

The impacts of the corporation are thus indefinite, and as formations, corporations are not simply characterized as well; they are not cast in cement, in other words. For example, corporations shift organizationally, oscillating periodically between highly centralized management and divisionalization and decentralization, between the reining in and letting out of control; administration fattens and flattens, and in effect, the oscillations reflect a tension between managerialism and democracy. Corporations can achieve economies of scale and scope, providing cornucopias of affordable goods and services, but in their complexity, they can also be marked and marred by gross inefficiencies. With their great resources, corporations serve as fonts of invention and innovation, but they can be inflexible, inert, and sluggish—with the imperative of organizational stability stymieing change. Corporations operate impersonally according to plan, rules, and systems of accountability—well-oiled and regimented machines—but responsibility can be obscured in their bureaucratic mazes, and they can be riven by discord and conflict of both the personal and formal kind.

The complexity of the corporation will be highlighted in this chapter by examining the genesis of the American business corporation—largely through the lens of recent scholarly debates—and by peeking inside, tracing the history of labor relations in American corporate enterprises. In consideration of the issue of democracy and citizenship, the corporation presents one additional complication for analysis that needs note. What exactly is it about the corporation that raises concerns? Is it simply a matter of size? In this regard, privately owned firms can be large, bureaucratically structured, and able to exert market and political power—and act in societally damaging ways. Supposed-impersonally operated big corporations, in contrast, can succeed through charismatic leadership and operate with social responsibility. Or is it the very essence of the corporation, its chartering and privileging by the state and form of ownership—by shareholders—that is the critical problem? This speaks to the great privilege extended by the state to the owners, limited liability: that shareholders remain not personally liable financially for the societal wrongdoings of the corporation, at a distance from operations, practically powerless, and not a force to check corporate chicanery and misuses of power.[2] The issue here is as hard to pin down as is the corporation.

The concept of the corporation dates to ancient Roman times. The word itself derives from *corpus*, the Latin term for "body" or "body of people." Roman authorities recognized certain associations of individuals as distinct legal entities with privileges, assets, and liabilities apart from those of their members. The Romans had a set of names to apply to these specially sanctioned organizations, including *universitas, collegia,* and *societas.* The corporate form of endeavor appears to have developed independently in other parts of the world, notably in ancient India.[3] In its original conception, the corporation represented an aggregation of individuals and resources—a collective entity— with authorization from the state (having a public dimension). Centuries later, it would take a good deal of legal fancy footwork and juggling to convey personhood to this construction: courts extending to the corporation many of the same constitutional rights guaranteed to an individual.

In medieval Europe, such diverse bodies as colleges, guilds, churches, and cities received corporate entitlement. The great joint-stock companies chartered in the first decade of the seventeenth century by English and Dutch authorities—the English India Company and the Dutch East India Company— are normally cited as the world's first business corporations (the world's first transnational corporations as well).[4] Both companies received sole authority respectively to seize and manage overseas trading zones and colonies. They represented a historic collusion between national sovereignties and groups of merchants to build the wealth and power of nations through achieving global commercial dominance (the coffers of crowns expanded through the taxing of external trade in the process, the incomes of the investors and managers of the corporations similarly enhanced through the monopoly rights and securities afforded them by the state—with the protection of navies proving especially critical). "Mercantilism," of course, is the short script for this momentous development. The exploration and settlement of the Western Hemisphere by western Europeans and the coercive control of trade routes and centers in Africa, the Indian Ocean, and East Asia by western European powers starting at the turn of the sixteenth century was accomplished through the agency of mercantile corporations deputized by the state. As a tidbit of this history, remember, the so-called Puritans arrived in New England under the aegis of the Massachusetts Bay Corporation.

American colonists seceded from the British commercial empire in 1776, but in rebelling against mercantilist controls, citizens of the new nation—or more precisely, the elite among them—did not dispense with the notion or practice of the government chartering of merchant-inspired and -formed corporations with the aim of promoting national economic development. During the first decades of the new republic, corporations were thus established for the building of turnpikes, bridges, canals, and railroads and the establishing of banks. Since the U.S. Constitution did not provide for the chartering of companies by the federal government, the process devolved to the states, and the ability to petition for incorporation at the more local level led to the greater proliferation of the corporation in the new country than in Europe, where granting powers remained in the hands of central authorities and successful petitions required great influence and resources. In the Commonwealth of Pennsylvania alone, between 1790 and 1860, special acts of the state assembly created 2,333 corporations. State government charters at the time included clauses that mandated that significant percentages of the stock offerings of the new companies be subscribed to by the states. The Commonwealth of Pennsylvania invested in $100 million of state revenues in canal and railroad construction in the antebellum period. In New York, 315 municipalities pledged more than $37 million for the purchase of shares in transportation companies chartered in the state (as required in chartering of these firms).[5]

The corporations created in the early republic for the greater good—for public purposes—were superseded in the late nineteenth century by the big businesses associated with the likes of Carnegie and Rockefeller. Popular and scholarly attention focuses by and large on this phase of long history of the corporation—and understandably so. In recent decades, considerations of the emergence of the large-scale, corporately owned, bureaucratically managed business enterprises that have dominated the economic landscape since the turn of the twentieth century have been shaped by the scholarship of the preeminent business historian of our times, Alfred D. Chandler (Chandler died in 2007)—and it is Chandler and his critics that provide grist for complicating the corporation as a subject of inquiry and concern.

Chandler bequeathed a model of the rise and embedding of the American corporation that casts the Great Robber Barons/Industrial Statesmen to the very far sidelines. Chandler emphasized the role of impersonal forces, demographic, technological, and market. Human interventions are critical to the story, but his heroes are not the headline-capturing founders but rather the middle-level managers who conceived the administrative schemes that allowed the behemoths to run efficiently and on sustained bases (small "g," small "m," great men, if you will).[6]

Chandler's account starts with the vast growth in population in the United States in the mid-nineteenth century—due almost entirely to immigration—and the growing concentrations of people in urban areas, city dwellers beholden to markets for their very livelihoods and even the bare necessities of life, much less creature comforts. A great stimulus simultaneously occurred with the building of a national transportation and communications infrastructure—including canals, railroads, and telegraph systems. According to Chandler, this major development created a national marketplace where firms no longer could operate parochially with known, loyal suppliers and customers. Heightened competition then demanded that companies transform themselves and that necessarily entailed growth. Here, Chandler points to standard avenues of expansion, vertical and horizontal integration, but it is vertical integration that is the key for him: a realm of remarkable innovativeness.

To maintain competitive advantage, achieving efficiencies through control of the accessing of raw materials often proved critical. If suppliers cannot deliver parts on time, of required quality and tolerance, and at low price, then companies move to establish departments for the direct ownership and administration of the supply function—and greatly expand in the process (U.S. Steel, formed in 1901, provides a classic example with its acquisitions of iron ore fields, coal mines, fleets of vessels, extensive rail facilities, coke works, and steel mills). Of course, there is no imperative to assume the high costs of so-called backward integration if there is a competitive world of suppliers in reach. Chandler, in this regard, devotes much greater attention to the "forward" side: the pressure placed on all firms by a developed national marketplace on the merchandising of products. With no guaranteed customers, companies had to allocate significant resources to distribution, warehousing, advertising, and wholesale and retail selling. Entirely new branches of operations with sizable work forces had to be created. In some instances, as Chandler shows with one of his favorite case studies, the meat-packing enterprise of Gustavus Swift, the merchandising end of the company far outgrew the production side. Chandler rarely dealt with the financing of expansion—finance capital is a missing, even a dismissed element in his works—but a safe assumption is that growth required substantial investments, that expanding firms eventually had to resort to raising funds in equity markets, and that big business and incorporation went hand in hand.

Chandler thus attributes the *rise* of the corporation to impersonal demographic, technological, and market forces. But, that is not the entire story. To succeed, to become *embedded* required the intervention of professionally trained and capable managers, men who developed the organizational flowcharts, accounting systems, and information feedback mechanisms that allowed firms to achieve efficient through-processing—economies of scale and scope—from the accessing of raw materials through the automated production of goods to the purchasing of brand-name products by eager customers and consumers. Permanence, however, involves a further step in Chandler's narrative: the seizing of strategic decision-making, not just day-to-day administration, by the new managerial class. Less wedded to the intentions and accomplishments of the original founders and owners, the managers analyzed circumstances and saw especially the potential problem of overproduction and saturated markets—of sticking with success, in other words. They developed new strategies of diversification, of using accumulated knowledge and capital capacities to create new product lines and, effectively, new markets, spreading risk in the process. Diversification also required fresh organizational arrangements, and innovative managers developed accordingly decentralized schemes of operation, including fairly autonomous product divisions and central offices charged with overall coordination and long-range planning. Chandler illustrates these developments with two other of his favorite cases, Du Pont, the great chemical works, and General Motors, the giant car maker. With Du Pont, company managers faced the great loss of business after World War I as the firm lost customers for its prime product, gunpowder; decisions were then made to use the massive chemical facilities of the enterprise to produce a vast range of consumer products—paints, nylon, and so on—and with a centralized structure of management in place, the task remained to create an effective divisionalized one. While Du Pont thus built downward, GM built upward. The firm originated through the merger of five automobile manufacturing companies. Here, managers developed a strategy world resources—the American workplace came under close scrutiny. Government investigations, newspaper reports, and scholarly works pointed to great losses in productivity and growing job dissatisfaction and alienation among American workers. Critiques of American corporate enterprise then ensued that underscored the inflexible and sclerotic state of the country's vaunted mass producers. The critics of what was dubbed "Fordism" found alternatives: enclaves of thriving small- to medium-size, nimble firms that honored skill and quality (the industrial north of Italy and the Silicon Valley of California served as prime examples); they similarly honored large companies that produced on the basis of empowered teams of workers (Toyota was thus extolled).[10]

Historians joined the dialogue, but largely in response to Chandler and less to the economic crises of the times. New historical research increasingly challenged notions of the inevitability of corporate dominance and pointed to alternative paths to economic development and growth; frequently cited, this work provided ammunition to critics of late twentieth-century corporate America. Historians took Chandler to task on two fronts. Statistically minded scholars analyzed data that indicated that large-scale, corporately owned, bureaucratically managed firms operated no more efficiently than their smaller counterparts, nor were they necessarily sites of greater invention and innovation.[11] More important, local historical studies revealed that Chandler, in focusing on big business, entirely discounted the vast amount and variety of goods produced outside the corporate realm in family- and partnership-owned and -managed specialty enterprises operating in small-town and metropolitan America alike. Philadelphia, for example, emerged by the turn of the Civil War and remained into the twentieth century as a premier industrial center with the following features: a prevalence of small- to medium-sized proprietorships, product diversity and diversity of work settings, custom production, and reliance on skilled labor. Philadelphia manufacturers prospered not by competing with mass producers of goods in other parts of the country, but rather by operating in niche markets fashioning high-quality wares or by concentrating in single aspects of production (in textiles, for example, separate establishments emerged to spin special fibers, weave fine clothes, and dye elaborate fabrics). Even in the case of Philadelphia's famous (but relatively few) large firms, specialty production remained the hallmark (as did noncorporate forms of ownership).[12] In diverse manufacturing centers throughout the United States—and Philadelphia is just one example—networking also benefited small- to medium-sized firms as they symbiotically bought and sold to each other, shared information on technology and markets, and, as their workers moved among them, augmented and spread expertise.[13] Evidence of the salience of networks—even in places where corporations dominated the economic landscape, Chicago, a notable case in point here—has contributed to theoretical revisions of the Chandlerian perspective.[14] Throughout the United States, theorists have proposed, firms operated in different milieus, pure market forces shaping operations and prospects in some instances, networks and hierarchical administration in others.[15]

The "small is beautiful" critique of Chandler has its own fault lines and detractors. Small specialty businesses persist, for example, but, as has been argued, they increasingly become beholden to corporations that exploit them for supplies and outsourcing; a "dual economy" has emerged in this way of thinking, with a corporate core and a periphery of fragile, supplicant small firms. Chandler's critics have also tended to over-romanticize the world of proprietary capitalism, especially in imputing harmonies between owners and employees and among networked firms. Petty producers can operate insularly and in sweatshop fashion, a cutthroat rather than a mutualistic order prevailing. Consumers, too, broadly benefit more from the cornucopia of goods that issue from well-heeled and -oiled corporations than from their small-batch-producing lesser competitors. Finally, exposés of America's bureaucratic workplaces spurred reforms—with the flattening of hierarchies and greater authority and input afforded so-called quality work teams—but research has shown that recent "re-engineerings" of the American shop and office floor have been cosmetic at best, and ephemeral structures of power hardly budged.[16]

Skeptics and naysayers aside, the "small is beautiful" challenge to Chandler has succeeded in giving due respect to the significant place of small-scale specialty production in the grand history of American enterprise and shaken notions that corporations are inevitable, necessary, and unalterable fixtures of modern life. Nonhierarchical workplaces have existed, excelled, and added greatly to the economic well-being of Americans. There are good grounds to argue for the virtues of democracy and citizenship at the settings where most adults spend the greater parts of their waking hours.

Contingent Moments: The 1830s

If corporations are not inexorable by-products of modernization, then they must be creations of particular circumstances. With that point of view in mind, scholars have isolated moments in U.S. history where a confluence of ing the McCormick Harvesting Machine Company and the Deering Harvester Company to form the mega International Harvester.[21]

The history of the American corporation was thus written anew in the 1890s—with mammoth corporations now embedded—and this occurred, again according to scholars who point to the contingent nature of developments, through specific events and circumstances, including: the ironic impacts of antitrust legislation; a shift in the activities of finance capitalists; and an economic downturn that pushed financiers to be agents of corporate creation and mergers in the industrial sector (with declines in stock values and widespread bankruptcies during the great depression of the period, firms could be acquired cheaply, another inducement to consolidations). One last ingredient can be added to the mix of circumstances. In the 1890s, competition prevailed among states to house the headquarters of major corporations. As a result, there was pressure for the writing of permissive codes of incorporation, and New Jersey assemblymen, followed by their counterparts in Delaware, proved most willing to oblige. Legislators in both states revised general incorporation laws that allowed for the chartering of holding companies that operated across state lines and permitting companies to purchase potentially controlling stock in other firms.[22] This, too, proved an impetus for business consolidations.

Government Structures, Politics, Judicial Rulings, and Power

Chandler's well-managed corporations arose in a political vacuum, as many of his critics have noted. Impersonal demographic, technological, and market forces may have generated corporations and managerial innovations embedded them, but the entire process was shaped by the American political order. A federal system of government, for example, contributed to the widespread adoption of the corporate form of enterprise, liberal incorporation laws, and procedures enacted by some states furthering the process; legislation inspired by antimonopoly politics erased notions of the public purposes of corporations, eased access to the privileges of incorporation, and drove mergers. Key judicial decisions also played critical roles, most famously the Supreme Court's ruling in the 1886 case of *Santa Clara v. Southern Pacific*, where the court held that corporations were "persons" covered by the equal protection clause of the Fourteenth Amendment (which had been written to guarantee the rights of freed slaves). This decision and subsequent rulings did not deny government regulation of corporations, but in not defining corporations as servants of the commonweal, they legitimized the private nature of their existence. Court decisions in antitrust suits also functioned to ensconce the corporation. The courts could have read the Sherman Antitrust Act strictly: to wit, that mergers leading to significant market-share control inherently restrain trade and inhibit competition. Through a series of cases in the first decades of the twentieth century, capped by a decision in a suit brought against U.S. Steel, the Supreme Court wended its way to a fixed but middle position: business combinations were not illegal per se; the issue would be the means—"reasonable" or illicit—by which market dominance was achieved. Business consolidations were here to stay; only clear conspiratorial activity would be punished.[23]

Considerations of the role of government, politics, and law in the history of the corporation raises the larger issue of *power*, a matter not broached at all by Chandler and one raised by his critics. The control and influence of corporations through the liquid and capital resources at their disposal are manifold: the abilities to create and structure consumer preferences and markets, quell labor unrest, appear as inevitable (even beneficent), and leverage the state are obvious examples. The latter capacity speaks to a tricky subject, "corruption." There is literal and measurable corruption: the purchasing of the favor of state officials. Here, some scholars have argued that the rise and embedding of the corporation in the United States in the nineteenth century was due in no small part to not just persuasive lobbying, but the buying of the assistance of governors and state legislators (add this to the list of contingencies).[24] The role of corruption can be simply dismissed as one of the costs of doing business, the necessary greasing of the wheels of commerce. In this regard, influence and incorporation have always gone hand-in-hand since the first group of men of means had the wherewithal to petition the state for corporate privileges. The greater symbolic effects of corruption on democracy and citizenship, of course, are harder to determine. Corruption can rankle and mobilize opposition to corporations as well as deflate senses of power and affect and immobilize citizens. The impact of the corporation, again, is indefinite.

Finance Capital

Alfred Chandler dismissed the role of financiers in the rise of big business, and criticism of his work on this score is well warranted. To be sure, until the 1890s, the extraordinary growth of American manufacture did not rest on the raising of capital in equity markets (the story is entirely different for the development of the nation's extensive transportation infrastructure). The great consolidation movement of the late nineteenth and early twentieth centuries (and merger upsurges of later times) did transpire through the interventions of finance capitalists, and their inclusion in the history of the rise and embedding of the American corporation is essential. However, qualification is in order (of a sort not provided by Chandler). The great merged enterprises fabricated by the likes of J. P. Morgan did not necessarily succeed. Scholars have estimated that at least 40 percent of corporations formed in the period of the Great Merger Movement failed within twenty years.[25] Some had been created not for straightforward economic reasons, controlling competition, or achieving economies of scale, but for the quick paper profits to be captured by Wall Street promoters. Others failed to achieve either steady profits or market dominance, because an expanding American economy at the time prevented monopolization. Poor management did in the rest (perhaps, they did not follow Chandler's recipe for success). The key here is to understand the unsteadiness of the corporation.

Labor Conflict

Chandler wrote his influential studies of American business at a time of the flowering of American social history, of writing history from the "bottom up," and, in some sense, he can be considered a social historian, because he delved below the famous, went into the black box of the firm, and discovered important actors who had escaped the eye of scholars, middle-level managers (although they remain fairly nameless and faceless in his work and it has remained for researchers following in his footsteps to bring them fully to life).[26] Chandler, of course, never went below the managerial ranks to determine the place of labor relations and conflict in the rise and embedding of the corporation. Corporations in the late nineteenth century certainly stirred labor and populist unrest, but a question arises as to whether conflict itself contributed to business consolidations in the period. The issue remains unexamined by and large by historians, but the few studies suggest that replacing labor, particularly skilled labor that exerted critical controls on the shop floor, with automated technologies manned by low-paid workers, was seen as a solution to the tumultuous strikes of the period.[27] This required substantial investments, another incentive for consolidation of resources. Labor conflict is another contingent element in the history of the emerging place of the corporation in American life, perhaps of lesser weight. The subject does provide segue into looking inside the corporation—to its internal dynamics and their impacts on democracy and citizenship.

In the 1950s, the American corporation drew the attention of social scientists, popular writers, and even filmmakers. The economic performance of the country's great firms was not at issue—as during the 1970s. Rather, what triggered concern was a much profounder matter: totalitarianism. Immediately after World War II, American intellectuals and pundits fixated on the rise of Fascism in Europe and the succumbing of people to demagogues and authoritarianism. Could it happen in the United States was the question. Some commentators found solace in the exceptional, nonideological, consensual underpinnings of American life—it could not happen here. Others saw potential and pointed a finger at the corporation as a breeding ground for conformism and submissiveness. Success in these organizations required allegiance to company goals and ways, agreeableness, and sacrifice of one's personal instincts and values to group norms: to be "other-directed" rather than "inner-directed," an "organization man" in a "gray flannel suit," in the great phrases of the day (the sociological exposés of the times always cast male, white-collar figures). In the late twentieth and early twenty-first centuries, there has been an interesting return to viewing the corporation as problematic in terms of personality development/disorder (not in terms of economic functionality, again as during the 1970s). With glaring examples of wrongdoing in the inner sanctums of these organizations, concerns have been raised as to how the internal dynamics of the corporation contribute to dishonest, illegal and immoral behaviors.[28] In either instance, the corporation as breeder of conformists or lawbreakers, there is little delving into the question of what it is about the corporate form of enterprise that makes for such personal orientations. Is it a matter simply of bureaucracy: bureaucracy as the source of submissiveness or behaviors that compromise better moral judgment ("I was only following orders," that infamous refrain)? Or is it not a matter of bureaucracy per se, but of corporate bureaucracy? Perhaps it is separation of ownership from management, the imperative to keep share prices high and shareholders receiving their dividends at all cost, the very confusion of stakeholders (investors, boards of directors, managers, employees, suppliers, and customers)—all that induces hazardous behaviors. Commentaries that link the corporation to personal dereliction rarely push the issue.

Concerns about the internal workings of the corporation at various moments in the post-World War II period are a far cry from the anxieties of earlier times. From the late 1870s and the rise of big business to World War II, the issue was pure and simple: labor conflict (nothing to do with personality here). Relentless, violent labor strife accompanied the rise and embedding of the American corporation. There are the famous confrontations: the great railroad strikes of summer 1877 that paralyzed the commerce of the nation; the strike at the McCormick Reaper Works in Chicago that led to the Haymarket Riot in May 1886; the Homestead Strike in 1892 that saw pitched battles between workers at Andrew Carnegie's major steel mill and hired Pinkerton guards; the momentous Pullman Strike of summer 1894 that brought the economy to a standstill and fame to Eugene Victor Debs; the extraordinary Anthracite Coal Strike of 1902 that also paralyzed commerce and required the mediating interventions of President Theodore Roosevelt and financier J. P. Morgan; the dramatic strikes led by the Industrial Workers of the World in Lawrence, Massachusetts, in 1912 and Paterson, New Jersey, in 1913; the mammoth strike against U.S. Steel in 1919 (during a year of radically tinged strikes throughout every sector of the economy and region of the country); the Railway Shopmen's Strike of 1922 that required presidential intervention to restore business activity; and, of course, the remarkable drives to organize workers in the mass production industries under the aegis of the Congress of Industrial Organizations (CIO) in the 1930s. These are the just some of the legendary strikes, but countless other small battles erupted in every year and in every nook and cranny of the United States as the American business corporation came to dominate the economic landscape. In the earliest moment of this history, for example, the decade of the 1880s, government investigators counted 1,000 strikes per year on average, with 125,000 workers involved and 12,000 businesses affected on average per year. These numbers more than tripled in the decade of the 1890s.[29]

The threat that corporations posed to cherished notions of independent producership, economic hard times (depressions practically every twenty years), low wages, long hours, and poor working conditions: all contributed to the great labor unrest of the period (and radical ideas and radical organizers fueled the flames). But the source of conflict can also be found in the internal workings of the corporation—with all sorts of implications for the issue of democracy and citizenship—and nowhere was this more evident than in the stations, yards, and shops and along the tracks of American railroads.

Alfred Chandler placed a spotlight on American railroads not just because they created the transportation and communications infrastructure for a national marketplace, but because they also were pioneers in the corporately owned, bureaucratic-managed form of business enterprise in the United States. Railroad managers developed the divisionalized organizational structures and accounting systems and feedback mechanisms that served as models for later industrial conglomerates. Chandler, however, documented all the charts and official procedures, but never looked to see whether the railroads operated according to plan at the ground. He was not, in effect, a labor historian.

Nothing, in fact, operated according to the plans of Chandler's innovative managers on America's railroads in the early years. In spite of articulated rules and regulations, authority in the new behemoths devolved to local foremen, who took full charge on their own terms of hiring, training, disciplining, rewarding, firing, and retiring of railway employees. Even with posted manifests of pay rates and hours of employment, local foremen paid the men and allocated workloads as they saw fit. Nepotism and extortion were rampant. Critically, in the case of injuries and fatalities on the job—which were everyday occurrences—local supervisors at their discretion saw to the needs of the families affected—keeping favored workers on payroll, employing their older sons, and offering company monies for medical and funeral expenses. As government investigators discovered in trying to fathom the intensity of labor conflict on American railroads in the late nineteenth and early twentieth centuries, the issue was not wages and hours, but the capricious rule of foremen inside the supposed impersonally administered railroad corporations. The testimony of Franklin Mills, a railway employee discharged by the Baltimore & Ohio Railroad Company for his participation in the Pullman Strike of 1894, to a special federal commission investigating the upheaval is revealing and representative on this score:

> *Commissioner Kernan:* What was the feeling among the men on the Baltimore & Ohio with regard to striking prior to the time they struck?
> *Mills:* It was not very favorable.
> *Commissioner Kernan:* Had there been any cuts in wages about which they were dissatisfied?
> *Mills:* Not lately. The most of difficulty on the Baltimore & Ohio was favoritism, pets and maladministration of some of the petty officers.[30]

To counter the whim of supervisors, railroad workers starting in the late 1870s began to organize by craft (in so-called Brotherhoods) to gain union contracts aimed at a modicum of justice and security. Top managers of the railroads found the rule of foremen to be disruptive to operations, and they began to recognize the Brotherhoods and accept the rules for hiring, training, disciplining, rewarding, benefits in cases of injury and fatality on the job, firing, retiring, and pensioning advocated by union negotiators. In effect (and famously for the railroads), union work rules became management rules. Bureaucratization came as much from below as from the top. There were gains and losses for workers in this détente: the end of the rewards of nepotism for some and routinization of work for all, on one hand; fairness and security, on the other.[31]

The history of labor conflict and relations on American railroads, the country's largest corporations by far before the 1930s, complicates the subject of the corporation. For one, corporations were sites of contest, with opposition from the outside, notably from farmers, and inside from workers. Second, railroad corporations were not set entities, in spite of all the organizational flowcharts and rules and regulations; they were pliable and workers had agency. Citizens engaged the corporations, but their actions—whether in successfully petitioning for government regulation of their market activity or for rules written by and for employees—did not challenge their very existence and worked to further embed them. The history is thus best understood dialectically.

The history of labor conflict in American's major industrial corporations took a different course than on the railroads, but the endpoint is fairly similar. The thorns in the side of the major manufacturers were skilled workers who maintained, through their knowledge, expertise, and solidarity, significant controls over production processes. Top managers initially fought back with the stick: they used every means at their disposal, including armed guards, to rid their operations of the fairly powerful craft unions of the skilled men (the Homestead Strike of 1892 was such an epic battle); they formed trade associations to exchange information about labor agitators and collectively blacklist them; they hired the likes of Frederick Winslow Taylor to come into their plants, study tasks, break them down into elements which less skilled men could perform, and then develop incentive systems to boost productivity (with all the publicity surrounding the implementation of scientific management techniques, Taylor and his disciples could count few successes as foremen and workers sabotaged the experiments of the consultants and executives discovered Taylorism to be an administrative nightmare when there were shifts in product lines and needs for retooling); top managers at great expense could also invest in technology to produce on mass assembly-line bases, supposedly reducing the need for skilled workers (this too proved chimerical, as Henry Ford discovered—he needed the skilled men to produce the finely fab-

ricated parts that could be easily installed by semiskilled assembly-line workers, and high turnover of these workers due to the demands and ardors of
conveyor-belt production forced Ford to offer his famed $5 a day). After all
these experiments, most manufacturers recognized or continued to recognize
the craft unions, engendering the loyalty of their needed aristocrats of labor
through negotiation.[32]

As to other workers (lower-level managers, white-collar employees, and
semi- and unskilled workers), corporate leaders also faced the problem of
engendering discipline and loyalty in their mega operations. The old incentive
to work hard with the end in mind of eventually achieving mastership just did
not work anymore. People would have to be convinced that they could have
successful lives within the corporation. Corporate executives applied the stick
in certain instances, but they also began experimenting with carrot approaches: offering a panoply of fringe benefits to which one was vested after a
period of duteous service (everything from turkey giveaways at Thanksgiving
and company picnics to profit-sharing, health insurance, and pension plans).
The 1920s thus saw the heyday of so-called welfare capitalism. Corporate
leaders also brought "democracy" to the shop floor at the time with suggestion
boxes and employee representation committees (the latter an obvious ploy to
avoid unions). And to encourage ongoing loyalty, corporations also began to
develop career lines within firms, with promotion systems, often creating new
titles for the same old jobs in the process.[33] Unfortunately, for the workers in
these benevolent firms, practically all of the "carrot" programs and initiatives
of the 1920s were jettisoned in the 1930s with the exigencies of the Great
Depression. In fact, part of the dynamic of the mobilizations of mass production workers in the nation's major industrial firms involved the restoring of
benefit programs that had been established in the 1920s, but this time as part
of union contracts and with union management of them.[34]

From approximately one million workers having the benefits of unionization at the time of Franklin Delano Roosevelt's ascension to the presidency in
1933 to ten million men and women working under union contract at the
time of his death in 1945—from less than 10 percent of workers unionized to
35 percent writ large and upwards of 80 percent in the mass production
industries—the organization campaigns of CIO unions in the period represented a great sea change. There are any number of ways to explain these
advances—citing political, demographic, and economic developments (and
efforts to restore lost benefits)—but the issue here is what labor organizing in
the 1930s tells about the place of the corporation in American life. As with the

railroads, industrial corporations were not set institutions. In the face of labor conflict or the need for new incentive systems, corporations constantly experimented with programs to engender discipline and loyalty, and laboring people had agency in the process. Even mass-assembly technologies installed to embed the pace of production in machinery did not work according to plan. As the great sit-down strikes in General Motors plants in the winter of 1936-37 showed, all workers had to do was flip the electric switches to "off"; throwing monkey wrenches into the cogs of the conveyor belt system was not necessary. CIO unions also brought democratic practices to the shop floor, with grievance procedures administered by shop stewards and union work rules that put an end to the capricious actions of foremen. As with the successes of the railroad Brotherhoods, there were gains and losses in achievements of the CIO. As executives in industrial firms discovered that working with CIO leaders could bring needed peace to the factory and that it was easier to work with single industrial unions rather than a multiplicity of craft unions, labor conflict became rationalized, legitimized, and bureaucratized; management and union officialdom could meet in hotel rooms with government mediators if need be to work out complicated contracts; grassroots involvement and insurgency thus stilled. Contractualism brought fairness and security, but did not challenge the existence of the corporation, as had earlier antimonopoly protests; in fact, it contributed to the corporation's further entrenchment in the American landscape.[35]

The accommodations reached by so-called Big Business and Big Labor entailed in the compacts signed between CIO unions and the likes of U.S. Steel and General Motors as of the late 1930s can be pinpointed as the final step in the embedding of the American corporation. However, there are other moments and developments that could earn the distinction. Some scholars argue for World War I and the extent to which the participation of corporate leaders in wartime planning and mobilization of the economic resources of the country placed a damper on muckraking attacks on them as they emerged as true patriots. Alternatively, the 1920s (or the 1950s) and the efflorescence of mass consumerism can be touted: when a consumerist ethos supplanted producer values (let the treats flow; why care about where and how they are fabricated?). It might also be the coming of Keynesian macroeconomic policies and practice and the focusing on purchasing power. The point here is that the history of the embedding of the corporation is ongoing.

This chapter has been a foray into the history of the American corporation and its internal workings—with an eye to the issue of democracy and citizenship. The writings of Alfred Chandler and his critics have served here as a means for examination. What now is to be concluded?

The corporation is an unsettled institution. The organizational configurations of corporations shift; they are not carved in stone—in other words, they have histories. Impersonal demographic, technological, and market forces may have impelled the rise of the corporation, but its embedding has been enabled and shaped by government structures, politics, legislation, judicial decisions, and sets of circumstances and interventions (including those of administrative innovators and finance capitalists). Tensions within corporations persist between impulses of managerialism and democracy. American corporations have been sites of intense conflict, with opposition from without and pressures from within from employees (less so from shareholders). The resistors to corporate hegemony have historically had great agency in forcing government regulation and just labor practices—though in the process, they have contributed to the entrenchment of the corporation. Corporations have rankled citizens and spurred democratic mobilizations; they need not be pacifiers. These stirring words may ring hollow in an age of labor defeats and concessions, where antimonopolism as a deep strain in American political life is seemingly long gone, and where CEOs are unaccountable for their destructiveness—in their environmental practices, financial shenanigans, and leavetaking of communities through capital flight—and obscenely rewarded whether they succeed or fail. History holds some messages for us, though: there is nothing fixed or ineluctable about the corporation.[36]

Chapter 10

Citizens of the Corporation?

Workplace Democracy in a Post-Union Era

Cynthia Estlund

Once upon a time, in the cauldron of economic depression and widespread labor unrest that produced the New Deal, the idea of "industrial democracy" burst into mainstream discourse and helped produce the National Labor Relations Act (NLRA). The NLRA, still the foundation of U.S. labor law, created a framework for industrial democracy through union representation and collective bargaining. Of course, unionization was not mandatory; it was an option that could be exercised by a majority of workers in a particular bargaining unit, and that employers (at least since the 1947 Taft-Hartley amendments to the NLRA) could freely and quite aggressively oppose. And that they did. For unionized operations, with their higher wages and benefits, had to compete with nonunion operations.[1] Globalization and deregulation gradually ramped up product market pressures, which stoked employer resistance to unionization, which in turn outstripped the reach and deterrent capacity of the aging NLRA.

That, in short, is the story behind the drastic decline of union density to less than 8 percent in the private sector. It will take a monumental effort by organized labor, and a political economic sea change, to bring that figure back up to double digits. That battle is worth fighting, but it would still leave 90 percent of private sector workers without any semblance of what we once called industrial democracy.

It is telling that we can barely entertain the notion of a democratic form of workplace governance today without backpedaling: we do not really mean "democracy," of course, but only some form of collective worker "voice" or participation. We cannot quite conceive of workers as citizens of the workplace with a right of collective self-determination, but only perhaps as "stakeholders" of firms that are governed by managers who are chosen by and accountable to the firm's shareholders. Nor is there much currency these days to the notion that citizens in a democratic society must enjoy a measure of democracy in their economic lives. We have become accustomed to thinking of work as a domain of economic relations—of market forces, supply and demand, entry and exit—rather than a domain of politics. And yet perhaps there is still a case to be made for a form of workplace democracy that can meet employee needs and aspirations without provoking vehement employer resistance—a domesticated version of workplace democracy to supplement (and not to replace) the essential right of workers to go into opposition against their employer by forming a union.

This essay explores the question of what workplace democracy could mean in the twenty-first century for the overwhelming majority of private sector workers that are destined to remain without union representation. It first takes up the questions of "what workers want,"[2] and what they have by way of representation in today's workplace. It then turns to whether and why workers still need a collective voice in the modern workplace, given the rise of employment mandates and improved workplace management practices. Finally, it suggests a role for responsible *corporate* citizens in supplying a measure of what workers want and need as workplace citizens (if only the law would allow them to do so).

What Kind of Workplace Representation Do Workers Want, and What Do They Have?

The decline of unions has opened up a large democratic deficit, or a "representation gap," in the workplace. But the nature of that representation gap is contested and open to interpretation. In their massive, in-depth survey of worker attitudes in the 1990s, Freeman and Rogers found support for the labor movement's view that many workers (30 to 40 percent of nonunion, nonmanagerial employees in the private sector) wanted independent, unionlike representation, and that labor law reform was needed to make that choice available even in the face of management opposition.[3] But the survey found that 85 percent of workers wanted a less adversarial type of organization, one that is "run jointly" by employees and management.[4] Indeed, when asked to choose between an organization with which management cooperated but that had no power, and an organization that had more power but that management opposed, employees said they preferred the former by a margin of 63 percent to 22 percent.[5]

Employees' preference for cooperative nonunion forms of representation is partly an "adaptive preference": employees know that employers vehemently oppose unions, and that makes unionizing difficult, risky, and less likely to yield gains.[6] For some employees, employer opposition is simply a fact of life; others may trace it, as many employers themselves do, to increasingly intense product market competition from near and far-flung sources. Either way, that is the world these employees live in. In that world, workers' preference for a form of participation that is cooperative by design, and that elicits management's cooperation, seems entirely sensible. Workers want a collective voice at work, even if it is a less powerful voice than unionization and collective bargaining would bring.

Unfortunately, the NLRA prohibits the very form of representation that most workers say they want; that is, an organization "run jointly" by employees and management. The NLRA's "company union" provision, Section 8(a)(2), prohibits employer domination of or assistance to "labor organizations"; that term is defined to include any organization "in which employees participate," and that "deals with" the employer on terms and conditions of employment. To be sure, there are no serious sanctions for violating 8(a)(2); at worst an employer may be ordered to disestablish an unlawful organization. The fact remains, though, that federal law prohibits employers from maintaining representative structures through which employees can meaningfully discuss workplace concerns unless they are entirely independent of the employer.

Section 8(a)(2) was the most controversial provision of the NLRA, partly because it prohibited not only representative structures that were designed to fend off majority-backed demands for union recognition, but also those that pre-dated any union organizing and that enjoyed strong support from employees. For a New Deal Congress that sought to promote collective bargaining throughout the economy, all company-backed representation schemes appeared to discourage the growth of independent unions. The "independent union or nothing" approach of the NLRA remained in place even after Congress in 1947 recast the goal of the labor laws as the protection of employee "free choice," and even today when union density has fallen to single digits.

Under U.S. labor law, it is legitimate for employees to choose not to be represented by a union, and for employers to pay good wages and treat employees fairly in hopes of avoiding unionization. But it is not lawful for employees to choose, or for employers to supply, a less adversarial, less independent, and less powerful form of employee representation than a union.

In the meantime, the rest of the world has moved in a very different direction. Most developed countries now *mandate* some form of employee representation, apart from union representation and collective bargaining.[7] No country broadly prohibits voluntary forms of nonunion representation or worker-management cooperation as does the United States.[8] Even Canada, whose labor laws are largely modeled on American ones, maintains a narrower "company union" ban; it permits, even requires, forms of worker representation that are illegal in the United States.[9]

So what most workers say they want in the United States is not legally available. And yet consider what U.S. workers say they have. In one recent study, 34 percent of nonunion respondents reported having some form of management-established representation structure at work.[10] These are not identity-based affinity groups (which were tracked separately), nor are they mere "quality circles." Many (42 percent) involved discussions of wages and benefits.[11] Workers mostly seem to like these representation schemes (as one would expect given their expressed preferences). Most participants rated them highly in terms of consulting with workers (54 percent) and standing up for them (51 percent).[12] These schemes were also correlated with employee perceptions of modestly greater security, dignity, fairness, and justice (though that appeared to reflect their coexistence with other employee-friendly human resources practices).[13] These structures are almost certainly illegal under the NLRA.

We do not know much more about how these management-established schemes function. Many employers appear willing to violate Section 8(a)(2) by creating these structures, but few are willing to discuss them publicly. Moreover, it seems certain that the law discourages some employers—especially large, high-profile firms with strong "compliance" structures and norms—from setting up such organizations. It is fair to assume that more employees would have access to these forms of representation, and we would know more about them, if they were not illegal.

So we find that the overwhelming majority of workers say they want a form of collective representation that the law says they cannot have, and that a significant minority of employers are in violation of the law by giving employees what they say they want. These are facts worth reckoning with. But perhaps workers' own stated preferences are not a sufficient basis for reform. In some accounts of the modern workplace, workers no longer need collective representation because their interests are adequately protected by a combination of legally enforceable mandates and self-enforcing norms. I will argue in the next section that these accounts are wrong and workers are right: most workers not only want but need some form of collective representation in order to enforce the mix of legal mandates and informal norms by which they are currently governed at work.

The Rise of Workplace Mandates (and Why They Are No Substitute for Collective Voice)

The New Deal launched three forms of legislative intervention in private sector employment: support for collective bargaining through unions, construction of a floor on wages and working conditions, and elaboration of rights and liberties at work.[14] The three branches of the New Deal settlement have obviously met divergent fates. Employers have mostly won their battle against collective bargaining. But they have had less success in resisting the encroachment of mandates, as both minimum labor standards and nonwaivable employee rights have proliferated modestly but steadily since the New Deal.

On some accounts, legislative mandates function as a kind of union substitute, giving workers much of what they might have sought through unionization. But most minimum standards are quite minimal, and are often under-enforced, leaving most terms of employment for most workers subject to individual "bargaining" and labor market forces. Moreover, the enforcement of mandates is largely in the hands of employees themselves, and is beset by both collective action problems and the fear of reprisals. That is partly because U.S. law does not mandate protection against unjustified dismissal. Employees' lack of legally enforceable job security, whatever its economic benefits,[15] undermines employees' ability to enforce other workplace rights.[16] So the regime of mandates on which we have come to rely for the protection of employees is itself plagued by a "representation gap." I have elaborated on this problem at length elsewhere,[17] and will be brief here.

Minimum Labor Standards and Their Limitations

The New Dealers believed that market mechanisms for the allocation of goods, services and labor, though worth preserving, were intrinsically flawed.[18] Competition needed to be "fair" rather than "free," lest it generate a destructive "race to the bottom" in which responsible firms were undercut and the public injured by exploitative cost-cutting.[19] In particular, in the midst of the Great Depression, labor market competition had pressed wages too low and hours too high to satisfy the legitimate needs of workers and their families. The NLRA of 1935 and the institution of collective bargaining was part of the New Dealers' answer. But in addition, the Fair Labor Standards Act of 1938 (FLSA) set a nationwide minimum wage and mandatory overtime premium and banned most child labor across much of the private sector labor market. Above that fairly low nationwide floor, states were free to demand higher standards, and private parties were free to bargain, either collectively or individually.

For a few decades, Congress left the field of employment to collective and individual bargaining, subject to a periodically adjusted minimum wage level. But some gaps between public demands and private bargaining gained political salience in the 1960s. Congress responded with the Occupational Safety and Health Act of 1970 (OSHA), which sought to take workplace safety out of competition by establishing publicly enforced minimum standards; the Employee Retirement Income Security Act of 1974 (ERISA), which regulated the administration and funding of employee pension and benefit plans; the Worker Adjustment and Retraining Notification Act of 1988 (WARN), which required advance notice of plant closings and mass layoffs; and the Family and Medical Leave Act of 1993 (FMLA), which required modest periods of unpaid parental and medical leave. Notwithstanding persistent complaints from employers about the burdens they impose, none of these mandates has ever been significantly cut back.

These employment laws have conferred on employees a modest measure of protection from the vicissitudes of the market. Yet those laws have proven inadequate to the task of regulating labor standards in millions of workplaces across the country. In part that is because no uniform standards can meet the needs of workers and the capabilities of employers across the breadth of the labor market;[20] minimum labor standards fall well below the level that many employees demand and many employers could supply. But even those minimum standards are under-enforced, especially in the lower reaches of the labor market.

The problem under the wage and hour laws is illustrative: whenever there are workers willing to work for less than the law requires—as poor and undocumented immigrants often are—employers are sorely tempted to pay them less. Traditional enforcement mechanisms fail to raise the cost of non-compliance high enough to outweigh the immediate savings from noncompliance, and employers risk little by underpaying employees in violation of the law.[21] Some simply ignore minimum wage and overtime requirements; others misclassify workers as exempt from the law's requirements or exact "off-the-clock" work. These practices are found even in major firms—Wal-Mart, for example, became notorious for its "off-the-clock" work policies—but they are especially common among marginal producers with little fixed capital or stake in their reputation.[22]

Occupational health and safety laws confront a more complex economic calculus; clearly the law is not all that drives firms to invest in safety. But to the extent that the law is needed to deter dangerous practices, it is not up to the job. OSHA enforcement is plagued by rare inspections, low penalties, and long delays.[23] Some firms invest seriously in compliance and worker safety, but some firms compete by squeezing labor costs, and in part by skipping safety precautions, or by driving workers at a pace that forces them to cut corners.

The problem of under-enforcement under the FLSA and OSHA reflects in part a chronic shortfall in public enforcement capacity. There is simply no way for public agencies and inspectors to monitor and enforce compliance with labor standards in millions of covered workplaces. Rather, employees themselves must take the lead role in monitoring and enforcing their own labor standards. But that points to another problem: decent labor standards are "public goods" within the workforce. The public good dimension of workplace safety is especially clear.[24] But collective action problems plague many terms of employment, for employers manage their workers largely through policies and practices, not individualized agreements. So if an employer demands "off-the-clock" work from a group of employees, a single employee who challenges that practice faces a "free rider" problem: both the cost to the employer and the benefit to employees of correcting the practice far exceed the benefit to the individual complainant. A complaining employee bears all the costs and only a fraction of the benefits of confronting the employer.

The public goods nature of workplace terms and conditions suggests, and empirical studies confirm, the value of a collective voice for workers in achieving compliance with minimum labor standards.[25] And that brings us back to the problem of union decline and the "representation gap": most employees have no legally sanctioned vehicle for collective participation in labor standards enforcement; they have only the individual right to file a complaint or contact regulators.[26] The NLRA poses a legal obstacle to efforts by states or regulatory agencies, as well as by employers, to institute health and safety committees in the nonunion workplace.[27] The decline of unions and the lack of any lawful alternative vehicle of collective voice contribute in turn to the under-enforcement of labor standards.

Employee Rights and Their Under-Enforcement

The idea of the workplace as a domain of civil rights and liberties animated the NLRA and its version of industrial democracy. But that idea was dramatically extended and transformed with the Civil Rights Act of 1964, Title VII of which banned discrimination in terms and conditions of employment based on race, sex, religion, color, and national origin.[28] The banner of equal opportunity has proven to be politically formidable and adaptable. Congress has extended it to new categories (age, pregnancy, disability, and genetic endowment), added new remedies, and overruled court decisions that restricted liability.[29] State and local laws protect additional groups and provide additional avenues of recourse. Most of these statutory equality rights are enforceable both by public agencies and by individuals; a jury trial is generally available, and remedies include compensatory and exemplary damages, as well as attorney fees.[30]

Employment discrimination laws gave birth to a plaintiffs' employment bar, which in turn helped employees claim rights of privacy and dignity on and off the job, and of freedoms of belief, association, and expression at work. Those claims were up against the employers' presumptive power under employment at will to terminate employment at any time for good reason, bad reason, or no reason at all.[31] But the civil rights laws had already dealt a mortal blow to the legitimacy of firing employees for "bad reasons," and opened the door to legislative and judicial recognition of other unacceptably bad reasons for discharge. Beginning in the 1960s, common-law courts began to invoke public policy to afford redress to employees fired for refusing to violate the law, for claiming a legal right, or for "blowing the whistle" on illegal conduct.[32] Legislatures also entered the fray, particularly with the protection of "whistleblowers" from retaliation. Wrongful discharge law thus became a major source of litigation.

The expansion of employee rights should not be overstated. The scope and strength of those rights vary from state to state and are often quite restricted. Moreover, enforcement is left largely to employees themselves. Given the cost of litigation and the difficulty of proving an unlawful motive, many employees are unable to find an attorney to challenge employer actions they believe to be illegal. Some workers, especially low-wage immigrants, may be so unlikely to sue that employers can safely ignore their rights. In short, some employee rights, like labor standards laws, are under-enforced, at least at the bottom of the labor market.

Part of the problem is that even individual employee rights have a "public goods" dimension, so that enforcement faces collective action problems. That is particularly true of many discrimination claims. First, the very nature of discrimination lies in treating individuals differently based on their group identity; absent "smoking gun" evidence, discrimination may not be recognized, much less provable, unless employees can share and collect information about how other group members are treated. That information is a public good. Second, as Title VII law itself recognizes, discrimination often occurs not through one-off personnel decisions, but through policies and practices that affect many employees at once. Those policies and practices may be challenged through both "pattern-and-practice" lawsuits and "disparate impact" claims, and the law allows for aggregate litigation to mitigate the collective action problems that face such claims and to spread the considerable cost of proving them. Yet workforce-wide theories of liability and aggregate lawsuits face many hurdles, legal and practical, especially in the wake of recent Supreme Court decisions overturning class certification in the Wal-Mart case, and upholding employers' power to use mandatory arbitration clauses to bar group claims.[33]

So aggregate forms of discrimination, and the collective action problems that follow, are not matched by effective aggregate forms of redress. Nor are they matched by effective collective mechanisms for addressing discrimination internally, and for pooling employees' information and interests regarding discriminatory policies and practices. Once again, the "representation gap"—and the lack of a meaningful collective employee voice in most workplaces—undermines effective enforcement, here, of employee rights.

For a variety of reasons across a wide range of employment mandates, both above and below official minimum standards, the individual employment contract and the market forces that operate on parties to the contract effectively govern most terms and conditions of employment most of the time for most employees. That is especially true at the top and the bottom of the labor market. So let us turn briefly to the nature of that employment contract.

Norms in the Nonunion Workplace (and Why Workers Still Need a Collective Voice)

The employment contract is highly incomplete. Most of its terms are relegated to employer discretion, informal norms, and reputational sanctions, and are not legally enforceable. On one account, that is as it should be. In any event, that is how it is. The question is whether employees in the nonunion workplace are adequately protected against the risk of employer opportunism in this norm-based regime, or whether they need some form of collective voice to help police against opportunism.

The Incomplete Employment Contract in Theory

According to the economic theory of the firm, firms "make" rather than "buy"—they employ labor internally rather than contracting with other market actors for the relevant products or services—when the nature of the work requires close monitoring, firm-specific knowledge, or both.[34] In such cases, both the transaction costs associated with the negotiation and enforcement of detailed contracts with outsiders and the productivity gains from workers' accumulation of firm-specific skills are likely to be very high. In such cases, it is more efficient to hire employees to perform the work within the firm, subject to managerial control, than to contract with outside actors.

So the boundaries of the firm are defined by the choice of managerial control within the firm over formal contracting with outside parties. As a result, employment relations within the firm, though contractual in nature, are fundamentally different from ordinary contracts for goods or services. Their raison d'être is the avoidance of explicit contracting costs, and their terms are largely open-ended or "incomplete"; they leave much to employer direction and discretion. The resulting "internal labor markets" generate joint gains that can be divided between the firms' owners and employees. Yet internal labor markets are also characterized by "match-specific investments" and information asymmetries, and by risks of opportunism that are generally thought to be absent in competitive external labor markets. In particular, employers may be tempted to exploit employees' firm-specific investments and lack of external labor market options, and keep too much of the joint surplus for themselves.[35]

One solution lies in discerning and enforcing the terms of the individual contract. But the economic theory of the firm suggests that legal enforcement of the terms of individual employment contracts is presumptively inefficient because it imports into the employment relationship many of the costs that the relationship was formed to avoid.[36] Crucially, legal enforcement is also said to be unnecessary to protect employees, for workplaces are governed by norms of fairness backed by the threat of informal sanctions.[37]

We should pause for a moment to observe that the quality of "human resources management" (HRM) in the nonunion workplace has undoubtedly improved since the conflict-ridden 1930s. Under the pressures of legislation, litigation, and the "union threat effect," modern corporate employers have developed fairer and more humane modes of managing workers.[38] Clearly, harsh (and illegal) labor practices still prevail at the bottom of the labor market, including within major corporations and their supply chains (and observers will disagree over how to define that "bottom" and how high up it goes). But at least relative to the levels of exploitation and arbitrariness that prevailed up to the New Deal, most employers in both the union and nonunion sectors have cleaned up their act. It is against that backdrop that some economists contend for the superiority of nonlegally enforceable norms of fairness over formal contract.

Rock and Wachter thus argue that legal enforcement of employer promises of job security is unnecessary, costly, and ultimately counterproductive for workers.[39] It is unnecessary because employers already face reputational sanctions for breaching norms of fair treatment: current employees may punish the opportunistic employer by quitting or reducing their effort, and prospective employees will avoid those employers or demand higher wages. Legal enforcement is also costly: both the sheer expense of litigation and the risk of error by outside decision makers are high given the open-endedness of many terms of employment and the difficulty of monitoring employee performance. All that being the case, legal enforcement is ultimately counterproductive for workers because its costs are greater than the incremental gain in job security, and those costs will be borne by employees in the form of lower wages. In short, workers are *and rationally should be* unwilling to pay for the benefit of legal enforceability; it is simply not worth the price.

So there is a theoretical case to be made for reliance on nonlegally enforceable norms within internal labor markets—a case that we will revisit more critically below. (For one thing, to the extent the union threat effect is responsible for "self-enforcement" of norms, the waning of that threat is a source of concern.) But does the law comport with the theory? In fact it has come to do so, by a somewhat roundabout path.

The Incomplete Employment Contract in Fact

Although courts are hardly guided by the "theory of the firm" when faced with employee claims of unfair treatment and broken promises, they reach much the same result through doctrines that ensure a high degree of managerial discretion over how employment relations are to be governed. Managerial discretion and the predominance of norm-based governance was supported by one set of legal doctrines for much of the twentieth century, and then, after a decade or two of transitional uncertainty, by another set of doctrines.

Until the 1960s or 1970s, individual employee claims of unfair treatment were mostly kept out of the courts by a very robust presumption of employment at will. As long as employees were free to quit at will, courts were loath to find employers bound even to express promises of job security, and as long as employers were free to fire employees at will, they were also free to impose virtually any terms they wanted as a condition of continued employment. The result was that, except in rare cases, employers were constrained only by non-legally enforceable norms and informal sanctions, not by enforceable contracts.

Starting in the 1970s, the legal fortifications around employment at will began to crumble, and courts began to see broken employer promises as breaches of contract. Few employees had secured individual written promises regarding job security, but many could attest to oral or implied promises of job security, or could point to employee handbook provisions promising fairness in discipline and discharges. There was much wrangling over whether these promises were sufficiently definite and of the proper form to be legally enforceable. But by 1990 or so, courts in most states had opened one or more avenues of legal recourse to employees claiming that employers had broken promises of job security in discharging them without justification.

Employers were alarmed to learn that past assurances and existing policy documents might open them up to employee lawsuits over discharges.[40] But even as courts opened the door to employees' contract claims, they instructed employers on how to close the door: all they needed to do was to include in any employee handbook a clear "disclaimer" explicitly denying any intent to make binding promises and reaffirming the employer's right to modify its terms and to terminate employment at will, with or without cause.[41] A reasonably prominent boilerplate disclaimer in employee handbooks or job applications would foreclose nearly all contract claims, whether based on an oral contract, implied contract, or handbook.[42]

Once employers rewrote their manuals and job applications to incorporate the requisite disclaimers, they largely defused the threat of contract litigation for newly hired employees. For incumbent employees who already had (newly) enforceable expectations of job security, employers sometimes had to jump through some legal hoops to modify those prior promises. But one way or another, employers were generally able to condition continued employment on employees' acceptance of new (at-will and nonlegally enforceable) terms for the future. It took a decade or two in most states for the new legal rules to be worked out and for employers to modify their employment practices accordingly. But in the end, employer prerogatives were largely intact. The new law of the employment contract, much like the old, allows employers to adopt a regime of norms without legal enforceability.[43] For at the end of the day, contract law is about enforcing promises, and employers largely decide for themselves what to promise employees.

So under the modern law of the employment contract, employers can and generally do choose to govern the workplace largely on a discretionary basis, subject to market forces, external mandates, and informal norms, but without the constraints of legally enforceable contractual obligations. Unlike the old days, employers now have to make explicit their commitment to employment at will and their avoidance of contractual constraints.[44] If employees read and understand the disclaimer language by which they are bound, they now realize that their expectations of fair treatment are backed up only by their employers' reputation, and not by the courts. (Unfortunately, many employees appear to believe otherwise.)[45]

In theory, again, this should work out just fine for employees—better, in fact, than a costly regime of legal enforceability. In theory, if employees observe employer opportunism, they can go elsewhere or simply put forth less effort, or they can form a union and opt for a regime of collective contract and arbitral enforcement. Those informal, nonlegal sanctions may induce most employers to live up to their promises most of the time. But problems remain.

Prospective employees may have difficulty gaining reliable information about employment practices. They may not see employee manuals, noncompete covenants, or arbitration agreements until starting a new job, when their options have narrowed.[46] Even as to current employees, employers may be able to conceal opportunistic behavior (for example, by portraying an unfair discharge as fair or turning it into a "voluntary" resignation), and they may be able to detect and deter employees' countermeasures (reduced effort, for example) by closer monitoring and the threat of termination. Employees' primary recourse in response to unfairness is the right to quit, but quitting may be quite costly, especially for employees who have accumulated firm-specific skills and knowledge, and especially in slack labor market conditions.

The vagaries of nonlegal enforcement are exacerbated by the fact that employers' compliance with informal norms and promises of fair treatment, as well as information about compliance, is a public good within the workforce. Compliance is usually a wholesale and not a retail matter—a matter of policy, not individual case-by-case decision making. The cost of compliance to the employer is often much greater than the benefits to any one employee, so that, even apart from the fear of employer reprisals, each employee is tempted to free-ride on others' efforts to enforce norms or promises made to a group of workers.

The point is not that informal sanctions do not work at all, but that they work imperfectly and to varying degrees. Informal norms and reputational sanctions will better protect the expectations of workers with scarce and higher-level skills; workers who lack those skills are easier to replace and easier to monitor, thus reducing the cost to the employer of its own opportunism. So, too, informal norms and sanctions will be more effective in disciplining the behavior of larger and more established firms with robust reputations, and less effective in disciplining smaller and more marginal firms with less history, less of a public profile, and less of a stake in cultivating a good reputation. In other words, even if informal norms and sanctions were perfectly adequate to protect the expectations of most skilled and valued workers in Fortune 500-type firms, they would come up short for less skilled workers, especially in smaller and more marginal firms. All employees, but especially those in the latter group, would benefit from the existence of collective structures for pooling information, monitoring conditions, and asserting complaints.

Is There a Future for Workplace Democracy or Worker Voice?

So there is good functional sense in employees' desire for more and better forms of collective voice in their working lives. The decline of unions in the past sixty years, and the lack of any lawful alternative structures of collective voice, have opened a representation gap that has not been filled, or rendered irrelevant, by the simultaneous rise of employer mandates, better HRM practices, and stronger norms of fair treatment.

Unfortunately, that is not enough to get employees what they want. It is not even enough to remove legal obstacles to cooperative forms of employee representation. The well-grounded demand for labor law reform that facilitates union organizing has a powerful institutional advocate in organized labor, yet it has (again) failed in the face of unanimous and vehement business opposition. An effort to meet employees' well-grounded desire for more cooperative forms of collective voice at work would provoke far less opposition, and even some support, from employers. But that effort does not have a strong institutional champion. (Indeed, unions have long opposed any narrowing of the "company union" ban on the grounds that it would expand employers' anti-union repertoire and impede organizing.[47] Nor are employee desires for greater collective voice (in union or nonunion forms) spilling into the streets and disrupting the social and economic order. The case for the NLRA was clinched in 1935 not by idealistic appeals to the value of industrial democracy, but by widespread labor unrest—some of it infused with anticapitalist ideologies—and the claim that union recognition and collective bargaining were necessary to secure labor peace and social order.

I do not want to digress too far into the realm of politics here. But I do want to explore the question of whether "responsible corporations" could themselves become the champions of meaningful yet cooperative forms of employee representation in workplace governance. The template that I have in mind is the corporate embrace of workforce diversity.

The quest for workforce diversity originated in legal demands for equal opportunity. But it grew into an independent movement, one emanating largely from inside corporate HR departments, for institutional reforms that go far beyond what employment discrimination law demands (and perhaps even beyond what its "colorblind" version permits).[48] Lawsuits, threats of federal contract debarment, and damaging publicity surrounding complaints of bias all played crucial parts in motivating corporations to embrace a commitment to equal opportunity, especially in the beginning of the civil rights era. But in the decades since, "compliance" motivations have receded, and corporate diversity efforts have moved up the organizational chart and into the management suite. Having a diverse and inclusive workforce, and following "best practices" to promote diversity and inclusion, has become an important part of how corporations and their managers define their corporate identify and promote their reputations as good corporate citizens.

The story of how corporate America came to champion diversity and equal opportunity is fascinating and complex. A major part of the story lies in how personnel and HR managers both embraced the antidiscrimination norm and adapted it to fit organizational imperatives and minimize internal conflict (and incidentally to elevate their own role within the firm).[49] The antidiscrimination norm has proven "digestible" by organizations; it has been accepted and internalized into the corporate body, both transforming corporations and being transformed in the process.

We should not paint too rosy a picture, even within the Fortune 500; after all, number one on that list is Wal-Mart, Inc., sued in 2004 in the largest sex discrimination lawsuit of all time.[50] Still, progress is undeniable. Overt barriers to entry and advancement at work have been largely dismantled, and the more subtle barriers that remain are less exclusionary. For black and Hispanic workers who make it to adulthood with an education and a decent basket of skills, their prospects for employment and advancement in a wide variety of jobs and organizations are far better than they were fifty years ago.[51] Title VII and the norm of equal opportunity must be judged at least a qualified success.

Is something like that possible with a norm of workplace democracy or "voice at work"? That is another complicated question, and one that I only begin to explore here. The analogy between a right of "equal opportunity" and a right of democracy or collective voice at work is hardly seamless; there are many reasons why the former was more "digestible" than the latter can possibly be (unless it is reduced to meaningless pabulum). But one thing is quite clear: collective voice will never be embraced as an element of responsible corporate citizenship as long as it is identified exclusively with unionization. The right to form a union and bargain collectively, even as it has been rebranded as "freedom of association" and elevated to the status of customary international law, has proven "indigestible" by U.S. employers. They uniformly and aggressively resist the exercise of that right even if they concede it in principle. They do so largely, though not entirely, in response to market incentives and pressures that are endemic to a decentralized system of collective bargaining like ours,[52] and that have become intensified in most of the private sector economy.

Let me be clear: the right to form a union should not be abandoned; it should be fortified. Employees' right to go into opposition, and to do economic battle with their employer, is an essential protection against abuse. At a minimum, the possibility of unionization must be part of the punishment that awaits employers on the "low road." Collective bargaining need not take such an adversarial form, but that is how most employers see it, and that adversarial possibility is an essential inducement to better workplace behavior.[53]

But unionization and collective bargaining as we know them in the United States will never be embraced as essential features of responsible corporate citizenship.

The idea here would be not to replace the right to form an independent union and bargain collectively, but to reframe that right as one embodiment of a more encompassing right of participation that employers would be not only allowed but encouraged (or eventually even required) to internalize and institutionalize. Such a right might be championed by the sort of coalition of civil rights and employee advocates and forward-thinking corporations that supported the enactment and expansion of the antidiscrimination laws. A campaign for workers' right to participate—collectively and cooperatively—in workplace decision making has the potential to divide the business community, and to attract "responsible" employers, in a way that no union-backed labor law reform effort has ever done (not even in 1935, when the future of capitalism seemed to be on the line).

Conclusion

These musings are likely to be rejected as naïve at best and insidious at worst, by many in the labor movement. Some see all professions of corporate social responsibility (CSR) as a snare and a delusion—a cynical and self-serving public relations juggernaut that deflects workers and activists from the need to build a movement that is based on solidarity and that can exercise countervailing collective power on behalf of workers. Others may believe that, while there are sincere corporate proponents of social responsibility, they are fooling themselves (and the rest of us) because corporations in today's world, and their top managers, cannot help but pursue profits at the price of human values. Like many reluctant converts to the belief that CSR can be a progressive force, I vacillate between the fear that the anticorporate crusaders are tragically squandering an opportunity to accomplish something good for workers, and the fear that they are right.

The skeptics are surely right in part, at least where it comes to enabling workers to exercise collective voice and influence at work. There are enormous risks in a strategy that would expand corporations' freedom of action and engage them in the process of promoting and shaping a norm in favor of affording employees a voice at work. Corporations are quite certain to use that greater freedom of action in part with an eye toward avoiding union organizing. If the risks are worth taking, it is only because the path we are now on appears to be leading to a grim place, with unions on life support (or beyond) and alternative outlets of employee voice under a shadow of outlawry. At some point, the existing labor movement will be too weak to stand in the way of reforms that allow a broader range of vehicles of employee representation. Unfortunately, at that point the labor movement will also be too weak to play a constructive role in shaping reforms in the interest of employees.

Chapter 11

Politics and Corporate Governance

What Explains Policy Outcomes?

Peter Gourevitch

The enormous influence of modern business corporations on contemporary society has been widely recognized. Less recognized, but perhaps equally important, has been the role of society in shaping corporations and affecting their internal operations. In this chapter, I examine the influence of political processes outside the corporation on corporate governance. By "corporate governance," I mean the political system inside the firm—that is, the allocation of power to make authoritative decisions regarding the elements of production—capital, labor, profit, and income. My contention is that the political system inside the firm is shaped by the political system outside the firm. Firm organization and activity reflect incentives derived from political processes that give rise to laws and regulations, as well as their patterns of enforcement. Values, such as stewardship, get reinforced or undermined by policy behavior.[1] Arguments that derive corporate forms and behavior from purely corporation-internal processes fail to account for the incentives shaped by laws and regulations, as well as by norms and social structure.

The impact of society on corporations can be seen in the variation in firm organization around the world. Corporate governance systems differ among countries in well-known ways. The United States and United Kingdom have diffused shareholder patterns and lively markets for control; Germany and Japan, along with most of the world, have concentrated shareholding, or extensive cross-shareholding, and weak markets for control.

Controversy about the strengths and weaknesses of these systems remains high. The U.S. and U.K. pattern encourages rapid shifts to new economic activities, but it also generates high executive pay, income inequality, unemployment, and decaying firms. The German-Japanese system protects people from rapid change, but locks up labor and capital in older technologies, thereby inhibiting product innovation, but at times encouraging process innovation.

A 2012 vote at Citibank rejecting management's proposals on executive pay foregrounds what is today a hot issue and evokes images of effective shareholder monitoring.[2] However, executive pay remains high, shareholder resolutions are nonbinding, and few people have been punished for transgressions in the financial crisis of 2008. Substantial formal change has occurred in many countries—for example, passage of the Sarbanes-Oxley Act of 2002 and the Dodd-Frank Act of 2010 in the United States. In recent decades, Germany and Japan have also enacted legislation that formally allows governance change.[3] Just how much change has occurred in practice, however, remains unclear.

The variety of practices around the world suggests a diversity of ways of solving incentive problems. There seems to be no single optimal solution, but rather multiple ways of constructing an effective corporation. To understand what forms prevail, we need to investigate why countries differ in their policies concerning corporate governance.

Many policy ideas, of course, originate from research communities, especially from fields such as law, economics, and management science. Based on theory and on empirical research, the various communities develop strong opinions about optimal policies. Despite the brilliance of many of these researchers, optimality arguments seem never to finally resolve policy disputes in the larger political arena where legislation is enacted and implemented. Some policy ideas are followed; others are not. Why the difference? What gives some of the ideas the leverage—"the legs," in journalism parlance—to become policy and practice?

The answer lies in the role of politics: political processes shape regulatory policy. Indeed, for political scientists, the very notion that the best ideas win because they are "best" seems dubious. Policies carry payoffs—rewards and punishments. Because of these payoffs, they attract support and provoke opposition. What gets through the political process will thus be influenced by political struggles. Studying politics—that is, studying "the authoritative allocation of value," in David Easton's well-known formulation—is necessary if we are to understand how corporations are governed internally.[4]

Optimality specialists are often hostile to the study of politics. Having demonstrated what policy is optimal, researchers must surely find it frustrating to see political forces intervening. Having shown the merits of an idea by efficiency arguments, the researcher wants politicians to simply implement it. Politics and political processes seem to them only to get in the way, to interfere with optimality. No wonder they are hostile to and dismissive of politics, as well as, indeed, political science.

In my view, however, politics should get in the way. There are always unresolved issues in the search for optimality. Optimality research assumes more certainty than we have. More significantly, optimality researchers are reluctant to confront the value judgments involved in their formulation. Many economic issues turn on value judgments: What are the acceptable levels of unemployment, of inflation, of income inequality, of environmental degradation, of risk in banking regulation? Value-neutral law or economics or management theory cannot answer these questions. Serious value choices are at stake, choices that affect different individuals in society differently. Politics is a way of negotiating these different points of view and of making collective value judgments.

Accepting the validity of politics necessitates a sea change in assumptions about optimality. We might note similar sea changes under way in related areas: emotion, for example, does not appear to block reason, as has been typically argued; rather, as Kahneman observes, emotion is necessary for reason to work.[5] It is not nurture versus nature, but how nurture elicits responses from and shapes nature. Similarly, it is not politics versus law and economics, but how politics molds our understanding of what is optimal.

My contention, in this chapter, is that we need to examine the politics surrounding the conflict of ideas about corporate governance. Knowing who supports or opposes what arguments about corporate governance regulation in the political arena provides insight into the value choices at stake. How much leeway should we give managers to innovate versus how much should we limit them to prevent excessive risk taking? How are managerial claims for flexibility to be weighed against the claims of employees whose pension shares are controlled by management? "The market decides" is not a sufficient answer in an era when the public is so acutely aware of market imperfections.

Within the existing corporate governance literature, there is some recognition of the role of corporation-external politics, with disputes centering on how best to understand the impact of political processes. A central question in this literature concerns what political actors want and how political institutions aggregate these wants or preferences to produce collective outcomes.

Most of the literature focuses on investors, with some attention being given also to managers, employees or workers, and other stakeholders. These actors are typically assumed to be uniform in their preferences, an assumption I will challenge in what follows.

Analysts have presumed that the self-interests of investors would lead to good corporate governance practices. Markets would favor good ideas about corporate governance because firms adopting those good ideas and turning them into practice would attract investor money. Consequently, the firms would prosper. Correspondingly, bad ideas would be punished. Firms adopting them would flounder, and engaging in practices based on them would not attract them. However, when countries differ in regard to their uptake of good ideas, some type of corporation-external explanation is called for.

I begin with an explanation of variability in corporate form coming out of legal scholarship. I then consider a political account that provides an alternative to the legal explanation. I argue, however, that political analysis needs to be taken further. We cannot assume that the categories of actor normally discussed in the literature—investors, representational intermediaries, and labor—are unitary. In fact, as I show subsequently, these categories are internally diverse, driven by political forces.

The "Legal Family" Theory of Variability

Perhaps the most widely held view explaining differences in corporate governance outcomes has been "legal family" theory. A "legal family" is a collection of national legal systems of the same type. One principal family consists of systems operating according to civil law or code law, such as is found in France and related countries. Another principal family consists of countries operating in accord with common law—that is, law built up by precedents, such as is found in the United Kingdom and the United States, as well as related countries. The legal family school of interpretation takes the position that country-by-country variation in corporate governance practices can be explained by the type of legal system the country has. Such an interpretation leaves no role for political process in explaining policy formation except in the initial choice to adopt one kind of legal system or another, and also fails to account for significant variability within a legal family.

Using a large cross-national data set, La Porta and colleagues observed that countries differed in the degree of shareholder concentration as well as in the protection investors have from managerial agency costs.[6] Concentration versus diffusion refers to the amount of stock owned by large or block shareholders (usually considered to be those owning 5 percent or more of the total company stock) versus small or individual investors. Shareholder protection refers to laws, regulations, and practices that prevent company managers or other insiders from exploiting their status to the detriment of investors.

The important argument La Porta and colleagues made was that shareholder diffusion—resulting from the willingness of investors to take a minority position in a firm—happened only if investors felt protected from insiders using their status to their own advantage.[7] La Porta and colleagues viewed shareholder diffusion as a positive indicator of pro investor conditions: the more diffuse the shareholding in a country, the more protection investors feel they have. Protection attracts capital.[8] Stock markets are deeper under these conditions. Stock market depth in turn contributes to economic growth. There is thus an efficiency driver at work: markets reward arrangements conducive to investment; minority shareholder protection encourages investment from a broad spectrum of the population in a society.

Armed with these variables—shareholder concentration and investor protection—La Porta and colleagues were then able to compare countries in a systematic way.[9] In so doing, the legal family researchers revolutionized the study of corporate governance: they took it from comparison of legal doctrines across countries to correlating observed behaviors (degrees of shareholder concentration versus diffusion) with regulatory provisions (shareholder protection laws).

Quite problematically from my view, however, the researchers went one step further: they offered an explanation of the provision of investor protection based on the type of legal system. They argued that the degree of minority shareholder protection (MSP), reflected in the collection of regulations that protect minority shareholders from exploitation by insiders, derives from the type of legal system. Common law systems provide stronger shareholder protections than do civil law systems. The evidence provided by La Porta and colleagues confirms the intriguing "eyeball" observation that the United Kingdom and its former colonies, including the United States, are grouped in the high shareholder diffusion and high minority shareholder protection quadrant, while France, Spain, and their former colonies tend toward the blockholder and low-protection quadrants.

While the data do reveal a general correlation between legal family and stock market development, closer inspection of the findings provides grounds for challenging the causal account. On the empirical side, we observe substantial variance in corporate governance patterns within countries over time, even though the legal family to which they belong remains constant. We also observe considerable variance among countries within the same legal family.

In their important paper "The Great Reversals," Rajan and Zingales show that France and Japan developed robust stock markets prior to World War I, apparently moving toward the diffuse shareholder quadrant, but then swung sharply toward bank dominance and shareholder concentration afterward.[10] The United States looked much like Germany prior to the war, but policy changes, beginning with the Sherman Antitrust Act before World War I, and a number of changes afterward, created banking regulations and minority shareholder protection provisions, thereby producing the system we know today. Within the same legal family, moreover, considerable variance exists among countries, notably within the civil law group.

On the conceptual side, the legal family argument's causal mechanism remains unclear: why does the legal family produce the claimed effect? The legal family type—whether a legal system is based on case law or code law—does not explain the content of the actual laws passed. Even more important, it does not explain the pattern of enforcement. Nothing about common law guarantees that countries will enact vigorous minority shareholder protection provision, nor that they will enforce them. Nothing about civil law systems prevents countries from enacting strong minority shareholder protection laws, nor from enforcing them. Other variables are needed if we are to explain the content of actual regulations or the patterns of their enforcement.[11]

The deepest flaw in the legal family argument is the absence of a politics. Membership in a legal family is a "one-shot event." At some past moment, countries evolved in the direction of one or another legal family. In the case of the United Kingdom, the common law evolved over the course of centuries, making it impossible to pinpoint a single year or discrete moment. In France, the formation of formalized code law happened at the time of the French Revolution, thus with great specificity of date. For the former colonies of France, Spain, and the United Kingdom, the choice was made by the colonizer, thus again with high specificity.

In each of these cases, the legal family approach suggests that once the legal system choice is made, no further political process is at work: the logic of the legal family imposes itself. Countries have little leeway in how or whether to improve protections for shareholders or to shape the role of corporate boards. This seems to me implausible. Countries vary considerably in regard to what they do with their legal heritage. Nothing in the legal tradition prevents civil law countries from expanding investor protections, and nothing prevents common law countries from undermining these protections. Numerous examples within each legal family back this up.

We need an explanation for the variability in shareholder protection within legal families as well as across them. A useful place to look for such an explanation is to the political variables of preference and action. What do interest groups or political parties want, and how do they go about getting it?

Interest Groups and Partisan Politics

A political explanation of corporate governance outcomes invites us to look more directly at what groups actually do in politics concerning rules and regulations, as a way of testing and also checking what theorists imagine them to do. Using economic theory, we can posit a preference; using political data, we see if the behavioral data fit the theory.

The modern literature on managerial agency costs, for example, assumes that investors are the key drivers favoring cost containment, as famously articulated by Berle and Means in their study of the separation of corporate ownership from corporate control.[12] The owners—assumed to be the investors and not other stakeholders—seek shareholder protection. The market, in this view, should reward firms and countries that provide it.

If investors seek shareholder protection, it is not hard to imagine that labor is on the other side. Correspondingly, political parties that support labor should be against minority shareholder provisions, while parties that are pro investor will support it. Labor seeks a world that protects jobs, wages, and welfare benefits (such as health and retirement). Labor therefore supports political movements that reduce managerial autonomy in relation to jobs, wages, and benefits.

Starting from these suppositions about investors versus labor, Mark Roe tested the expected correlation, and, of course, in so doing tested an alternative political explanation to the causal account in legal family theory.[13] He sorted governments, according to their ideological orientation and support constituencies, into left and right. He then correlated the politics with the policy outcome: he found a strong correlation, with left governments less inclined to support shareholder protection than right ones. In his tests, Roe broadened the items he included. He looked as well at restrictions on labor market freedoms and income inequality. (Investors were not likely to be friendly to any of these, as they limited the ability to optimize capital.)

This allowed Roe to locate corporate governance patterns—including the rules concerning boards, managers, and managerial agency costs—in a political context. He found that the "world's wealthy democracies have two broad packages: (1) competitive product markets, dispersed ownership and conservative results for labor; and (2) concentrated product markets, concentrated ownership, and pro labor results. These three elements in each package mutually reinforce each other."[14] Roe's goal was to provide a political account of corporate governance outcomes that could be contrasted with the "apolitical account" in legal family theory. His empirical results do, indeed, support his interpretation over legal family theory, and I have found this persuasive.

The controversy continues, however, with support for the legal family interpretation continuing. The legal family explanation has "legs," no doubt, in part for reasons of research strategy: it is based on a data set enabling comparison across a very large number of countries. Political variables involving parties and institutions are harder to study cross-nationally in this way. But the legal family interpretation lives on also, I suspect, because it provides a way of avoiding politics. It posits a fixed element—legal family membership—and derives behavior from that element without recourse to the messy world of political processes as causes of deviation from optimization ideas. There is no politics in the legal family interpretation.

Alternative Political Models

While Roe has made a substantial contribution in his critique of legal family theory, I want to examine here some alternatives to his formulation of political alignments. He sees the cleavage in class terms, left versus right. There is considerable merit to this view, as shown by the voting patterns in his data. But his account underplays the "cross-class" patterns we also observe. Business and labor groups can be found on both sides of a given issue: in some cases, business groups ally with labor to support extensive regulations of the firm, and in other cases labor groups support the liberal market side.

Pagano and Volpin observed, some years ago, that labor and business sometimes converge in seeking to preserve the firm from outside takeover and breakup.[15] Hall and Soskice detected a broader pattern, with capitalist systems exhibiting two principal varieties: liberal market economy (LME) and coordinated market economy (CME).[16] Firms in the LME model maximize the advantages of flexibility but pay a price in high transactions costs. The CME firms reduce transaction costs through strong inter-institutional linkages (cross-shareholding, for example) but pay a price in losing flexibility for shedding labor costs in times of recession. Firms invest in production strategies that take advantage of whichever system the regulatory environment favors. They acquire specific assets in that environment, which then gives them incentives to preserve those assets.[17]

Support or opposition for regulations that deter or encourage hostile takeovers, fluid labor markets, mobile capital, and other aspects of corporate governance are thus linked to the policies that various groups both inside the firm and outside the firm prefer and lobby for. Preferences can be deduced from intra-firm logic, but to actually affect regulations in the larger political system, these groups must find allies. Social and political processes, therefore, are key ingredients of any explanation that seeks to account for the origin and existence of regulations that shape the firm.

Politics shapes even the application of seemingly otherwise unitary doctrines, producing different results. Theorists of governance have sought to derive policy from a well-worked-out theory, yet specific theories often support alternative policy prescriptions. Two papers make this point forcefully, each dealing with major figures in the literature. Glaeser and colleagues argue in "Coase vs. the Coasians" that the ideas of the well-known theorist Ronald Coase could be seen as justifying conflicting policy recommendations.[18] One reading of Coase argued for a weak regulatory regime for the creation of stock markets in Eastern Europe after the collapse of the Soviet Union; this interpretation proposed the use of ordinary tort law developed by legislatures and generalized courts. Another reading of Coase, however, called for a more proactive supervisor through a regulator with specialized powers, such as the U.S. Securities and Exchange Commission. Comparing Czech Republic, which followed the former, to Poland, which followed the latter, Glaeser and colleagues concluded that Poland has had more success in growing its financial institutions.

The second paper, an essay by Dobbin and Jung[19]—entitled "The Misapplication of Michael Jensen: How Agency Theory Brought Down the Economy and Might Do It Again"—argues that theorist Michael Jensen's ideas were unevenly applied. Jensen and Meckling pioneered the idea that the mission of corporate managers should be to maximize shareholder value.[20] They undermined the notion that managers have a "social duty." Instead managers should focus their energy on high share prices and dividends. Fund managers could contribute to the application of these ideas by rewarding managerial behaviors they liked through the purchase of shares, and punishing behaviors they did not by selling—the classic market mechanism. In practice, investors chose to reward those managerial behaviors that helped them in the short run:

> Shareholder value stood for industrial focus, debt financing, board independence, financial transparency, executive pay for performance, and executive equity holding. Fund managers publicly backed all of these reforms, but we argue that behind the scenes they did not push reforms designed to protect owners that were inconsistent with their own newfound interest in short-term share price gains. They pushed for financial transparency, which helped them to pick stocks and prevented unexpected earnings reports that could cause stock price to tank, and they favored stock options and bonus pay, to align executive interests with their own material interest in boosting share value.[21]

From about 1970 on, the assets controlled by institutional investors grew substantially.[22] Investors did influence practices: they helped to propel the breakup of conglomerate-model firm organizations, and to smooth earnings reports, and thus to provide some stock price stability. Firms did become more focused in their core competencies. Investors responded by driving market valuations substantially upward; the percentage of shares held by institutional investors rose as well.

At the same time, investors were not pushing quite as vigorously for other items in the Jensen arsenal, such as greater board independence from managers and executive equity-holding over long periods of time. Boards have remained under the de facto control of the managers. Outside of venture capital firms, there were few claw-back provisions to contain adventurism. The investors did not pressure boards to demand longer-term equity holdings, or to be more cautious about options repricing, where part of executive compensation is an option to buy stock in the company at a specified price, in theory below the market price at the time the option can be exercised. These measures might have reduced the incentive to take excessive risks. Instead of aligning executives' incentives with shareholders—the sensible goal of the payment strategy—the options pay system led to a divergence among types of shareholders. Lacking incentives to worry about the long run, highly paid executives moved to make big gambles that destabilized the financial system and hurt small shareholders.

Board independence is another goal underdeveloped by the investor channel. Boards remain dominated by CEOs and groups of self-perpetuating insiders. It is hard to penetrate boards and inject outside voices. Financial institutions have not united in pushing for stronger independent board members.[23]

In several areas, investors have disagreed on what elements of firm organization to reward and which to punish. We can infer from this that there is no intrinsically unitary category of "investor." By extension, we might wonder whether labor and the other traditionally conceived actors in the corporate governance drama might also be internally diverse, subject to differing political orientations in different circumstances.

Reputational Intermediaries

Reputational intermediaries, such as bond rating agencies, were expected to play a substantial role in governance by providing and evaluating information. They have been disappointing in this regard, though their conflicts of interest should have made us wonder long ago about the likelihood that they might actually help investors. Bond rating agencies have provided little value added, giving if anything a false sense of security, profiting handsomely from the rules requiring their use without obligating them to pay a price for being wrong (a sure violation of Coasian ideas) and contributing to the financial bubble. Accounting firms have provided weak supervision, helping to inflate profits and providing options strategies for executives.[24]

Courts, too, have interpreted laws in ways that cut in different directions. Delaware law allows takeovers but slows them down in ways that tend to increase bids. Takeover defenses have to contend with fiduciary duty doctrines. Courts (and indeed regulators and legislators) have stayed away from compensation issues, save to require information about the amounts and about shareholder approval. In countries like Germany, compensation and related conflicts of interest having to do with golden parachutes, options, and side payments are more heavily regulated; this dampens the incentives for takeovers and mergers and acquisitions. Courts move with the political times, as party politics influences appointments. The primacy of Delaware has been undermined by federal legislation.[25]

Institutional investors are another heterogeneous category. The dream that they would overcome the collective action problems of diffuse shareholding has dimmed.[26] Many institutional investors vote automatically with management. Recent legislation required that institutional investors reveal openly how they vote. This has led to further challenges to management, though it remains to be seen how far this will go.[27] The 2012 proxy season suggests some pressure on executive pay, but these are advisory votes, and, over time, they can be evaded. The regulatory battle over the implementation of Rule 14a-11 continues, with controversy over *Business Roundtable v. SEC* in the U.S. Court of Appeals, D.C. Circuit.[28] Rule 14a-11 was part of the Dodd-Frank amendment to the 1934 Securities Exchange Act. The rule would have given shareholders the right to nominate board members and have their nominees on the official company ballot, but the court sided with the Business Roundtable in opposing the rule.

Institutional investors differ among themselves in interesting ways.[29] The profit-making private sector ones have conflicts of interest with their investors: making the best returns for the investors versus making the best returns for the shareholders in the investment company. Many of those seeking consulting contracts as additional revenue have incentives not to challenge the managers who award the contracts—a problem similar to that we find with accounting firms. The client-owned mutual funds (most notably Vanguard) or the nonprofits (CalPERS, TIAA-CREF) do not have these conflicts of interest, so we can expect them to be more attentive to monitoring issues.

The nonprofit institutional investors are discounted in some of the analytic literature as lacking the incentive to achieve high returns on investment because the pay levels do not attract the best people or motivate achievement. Others argue that nonprofit investment institutions do well enough; moreover, the idea that high pay is necessary to motivate high returns seems to them to have been assumed rather than empirically proven.

We find diverse orientations in other areas of the representational intermediary category. One wing of the corporate social responsibility movement, for example, has turned to shareholder activism to advance its goals. In so doing, it sometimes finds itself at odds with other activist investors who stress financial goals. To understand the role of representational intermediaries, therefore, requires us to recognize that politics and political processes may steer different segments of the representation intermediary category in different directions.

Labor

If investors have not played the role assigned to them in corporate governance literature, what about labor? Is it the resolute foe of minority shareholder protection, as the literature has supposed? Hall and Soskice, along with others, have shown that, as in the case of capital, labor's views are context dependent.[30] Recent research stresses the influence of pension investments on labor's position.[31] To varying degrees across countries and unions, labor union members have holdings in pension funds. This makes labor cross-pressured. Workers worry about jobs and pay, but also about the health of the firm providing their jobs. The politics varies with the size of pension holding in equities and with the political formulation of wage determination and job security. Countries with large privatized pension systems are more likely to have lobbies that worry about minority shareholder protection than are those with pay-as-you-go public pensions.[32] The shift from defined benefit to defined contribution plans may undermine the incentives to worry about corporate governance.[33]

In Germany, the institution of co-determination—where employees play a part in managing the company—gives a further incentive for unions to care about transparency. Cioffi and Hoepner argue that involvement on supervisory boards inclines employees to pay attention to shareholder demands for transparency; this makes them better able to understand what strategies managers are pursuing. Labor became part of the coalition for minority shareholder protection in Germany, where important reforms were enacted by a coalition of the Social Democratic Party (SPD) with the Free Democratic Party (FDP), opposed by the Christian Democratic Union (CDU), the party of Rhineland industry, and Germany's traditional conservative party.[34] Financial company executives may also be internally divided, being concerned with shareholder rights, on the one side, and managerial autonomy from shareholder pressure, on the other.[35]

In the United States, Democrats push for more minority shareholder protection rules, while Republicans oppose them, despite their claims to be the "investor party." This can be seen in Securities and Exchange Commission rulings, with GOP-appointed commissioners backing views of the Conference Board and other top management groups, while the Democratic appointees support rules on proxy voting and other provisions advocated by shareholder activists and pension fund groups. The SEC is driven less by the incentives of the officials to self-aggrandizement than by a desire to please political masters.

SEC actions reflect the results of elections, not what the aggrandizing bureau-
crats want. These splits are evident in opinions submitted to the SEC during
open comment periods.

This cleavage puts management on the side opposing minority shareholder protection, and labor on the side supporting it, contrary to what had
been the dominant view in the literature. Like the category of investors, labor
is internally driven, divided between its pension wing and its employment
wing. Union leaders may defend jobs, and so oppose the market for control,
which can lead to hostile takeovers, while the pension representatives may
push for policies that reward investments, thus supporting shareholder rights.
In the United States, employee pension funds pull them across the class divide. This may account for the activism in 2012 on resolutions regarding executive pay.[36]

Substantial legislative changes in many countries—for example, the 2006
Corporations Law in Japan and the 1998 Kontrag Law in Germany—have
enabled a variety of actions. Do these changes result in a new system, or a
hybrid?[37] Have countries moved toward the U.S. model? It is too soon to tell.[38]
For Culpepper, investors dominate the process of change, getting essentially
what they want, because the public does not focus its attention unless there is
crisis.[39] However, as we have seen, the category of investors is not unitary.
Political processes divide it in different ways.

Conclusions

The organization and activities of the firm cannot be understood through an
exclusive focus on incentives internal to the corporation. To secure their positions within the firm, players inside the firm must look outside of it to obtain
the policies and regulations they want and need. The private-market channel
influences practices around the world, as Western institutional investors visit
firms and governments armed with codes of good governance practices, demanding their adoption as a prerequisite for share purchasing. This has led to
changes in many places, in both private practice and state regulation. But the
outcomes for corporate governance practices are likely to be context dependent: corporate governance turns on the characteristics of the legal system,
the pattern of enforcement, policies toward competitive markets and antitrust, labor, educational training, and a host of other measures.[40] Changing
corporate governance by decreeing a change in legal family seems a fantasy of

causality. Locating regulation and law in the context of social and political institutions provides a more promising alternative.[41]

Corporate governance once lay within the domain of domestic arrangements, beyond the reach of international negotiations that would have violated norms of sovereignty. Today, however, the domestic/international boundary has eroded. As corporate governance becomes part of international disputes, it will face national interests and norms in contestation, as the European Union has already witnessed. Thus, international as well as domestic politics will shape the corporate form.

Private market forces produce good results by punishing badly run firms. However, they also allow the exploitation of market failures, collective action barriers to effective supervision, and other opportunities for capturing profit that hurt shareholders and generate systemic risk. Law and regulation can correct some of these problems, but the processes that produce them are vulnerable to capture by politics as well. That is true of all markets. There are no markets beyond the reach of politics. Building that reality into our analysis of the optimal seems crucial. We do not have a choice between markets free of politics and bad politics, but we do possibly have a choice between good and bad politics.[42] To have this latter choice, however, we have to acknowledge the role of politics in the first place.

The power of economic and management research, while huge, can never resolve all issues. What is the right balance today between austerity and economic stimulus in dealing with recession? The problem is not only technical but also a matter of values: what is more troublesome, the risk of inflation or the costs of unemployment? Value choices can only be resolved by political processes, where differing constituencies with different points of view come into an arena of contestation and alliance formation, their interactions giving rise to a collective result. In the 1930s, austerity was abandoned as governments were defeated or overthrown. Today, political change may be having similar effects as governments around Europe attempt to induce Chancellor Angela Merkel to shift German policy in the direction of growth and employment.

In the world of corporate governance, disputes over shareholder rights and managerial autonomy involve a battle over values. Resolving the disputes among different ways of interpreting Jensen, as I have shown, turns in some measure on political factors. Corporate governance is about the politics of the firm: who decides what about cash flow, employment, rewards, and so on. Shareholders, pensioners, employees, and contractors all have valid claims.

Asserting the primacy of shareholding does not resolve the problem of claims among them. Such a resolution would be possible only if all of the incentives harmoniously aligned. Recent experience suggests that incentives, in fact, do not align; the category of owners is itself internally diverse.

The ideas of Jensen were also used to justify no regulation. The claim was that intermediaries, such as banks and accountants, would have such a strong self-interest in preserving their reputations that they would exercise strict internal controls. Libor and other scandals have shown the absurdity of this idea. Given the powerful self-interest to abuse, why would they not? Why did the self-regulation idea prevail in the first place? Because of its power as an idea, to be sure, but also very substantially because the absence of regulation enabled many people to make a lot of money. In other words, embracing an antiregulatory stance, in this case, may itself be a political act, designed to serve certain specific interests as opposed to others.

In all these issues, politics plays an important part. Politics establishes the value parameters we need to choose among plausible alternatives in the face of uncertain information. We may understand the role of politics better if we see it not as a perversion of well-ordered theory—whether economic or legal—but rather as a necessary component of any theory that purports to explain empirical patterns of corporate governance and their variability around the world. Corporations exist not in a realm sealed off from the political, but rather in social worlds suffused with politics. To guide our reasoning about the possible and desirable futures of corporate governance in real-world situations, we need to grasp the role played by corporation-external political processes.

Chapter 12

The Nature and Futility of "Regulation by Assimilation"

Jonathan R. Macey

In finance, regulators and market participants ostensibly have overlapping, if not identical goals. At least in theory, both regulators and market participants want to be able to measure both risk and return accurately and in a timely fashion and to improve the enforceability and overall efficacy of contracts in order to enable firms to make credible commitments to investors and to cause scarce resources (capital) to flow to those market participants who can make the best use of it. Firms in search of investors and customers want to distinguish themselves from their rivals. Regulators want to enable investors and customers of companies to make better decisions about how to allocate their resources.

Regulators and market participants sometimes use different techniques in order to accomplish their parallel goals. Regulators threaten to punish fraud with jail time. Market participants use securities design, incentive-based compensation, and other contractual devices to signal that they are telling the truth. Increasingly, however, perhaps frustrated by their lack of success in detecting fraud and in identifying bubbles in the financial sector, regulators have abandoned traditional regulatory techniques in favor of promulgating rules that take the devices, mechanisms, and institutions being used in the private sector and assimilating them into regulations.

The most striking example of the phenomenon of regulation by assimilation in finance is the adaptation of the internal, often proprietary internal risk-assessment algorithms by regulators who use them to evaluate the financial condition of the banks that they regulate. Prior to the financial crisis, bank regulators noticed that financial institutions were using quantitative risk-measurement techniques in order to determine the riskiness of their own activities. These models attempted to evaluate not only loan performance but also loan quality and managerial processes such as internal risk controls. Recognizing "the extent to which bank risk management and supervisory capital requirements share common objectives,"[1] regulators assimilated banks' own internal risk models into regulation. As the FDIC observed:

> Of all the changes in capital regulation being considered by the Basel Committee on Banking Supervision, the most fundamental shift from current practice is that the risk-based capital requirements for the largest banks would no longer be based on a few pre-set ratios dictated by the regulators. Instead, these banks would play a major role in setting their own capital requirements by using their internal estimates of the underlying risk of each credit exposure as inputs into regulator-defined formulas called risk-weight functions. Collectively, this approach is known as the internal ratings-based (IRB) approach.[2]

This sort of "assimilation by regulation" is not limited to banks' internal risk assessments. The technique of regulation by assimilation has become very widespread, indeed ubiquitous, among regulators in the financial sector. The examples of regulation by assimilation examined in this chapter are the co-option of the ratings generated by credit rating agencies, the fairness opinions produced by investment banks and other financial firms, the outside audits performed by independent accounting firms, and finally and probably most importantly, the internal risk assessments generated by banks and investment banks to measure the riskiness of the assets held on and off of their balance sheets.

This chapter examines the removal of these devices from the purely private sphere and their assimilation into the broader regulatory framework. The analysis generates the conclusion that the co-option of voluntary market mechanisms inevitably corrupts these mechanisms and is likely to have contributed significantly to the recent financial crisis.

The analysis offered here is analytically related to a previous generation of scholarship about the distinction between and the relative merits of mandatory rules imposed by legal rule and enabling rules that can be opted into or out of. In the recent past, much progress has been made toward a fuller understanding of the vital distinction between such mandatory rules and enabling rules in corporate law and contracts.[3]

Largely ignored, however, is an analogous phenomenon of regulatory co-option. Just as lawmakers sometimes transform enabling rules that parties can contract around into mandatory rules that are immutable, so too do regulators sometimes decide to compel the use of certain market devices and mechanisms that have historically been used by market participants, if at all, on a voluntary basis. This is regulation by assimilation.

Mandatory market mechanisms begin their lives as enabling mechanisms just as all rules begin (in a state of nature if you will) as enabling rules.[4] For example, the credit ratings on government debt and on corporations and corporate debt issued by credit rating agencies began as purely private (enabling) institutions. Nobody was required to use credit ratings. Later, however, the Securities and Exchange Commission, followed over time by a dazzling array of other regulators, including state insurance regulators and state and federal banking regulators, decided to make credit ratings mandatory, for some companies under some circumstances. It was in this way that an enabling market institution gradually became mandatory for issuers.

All market mechanisms begin as enabling mechanisms that emerge to solve some problem or other that is plaguing market participants. But market mechanisms are often subtly co-opted by regulators who attempt to make certain regulations more efficient by incorporating the use of market mechanisms into the regulatory process. This chapter describes the process by which spontaneously generated market mechanisms are co-opted by government regulators. Each of these examples of co-option is more or less well known, if not to the public, at least to market participants. Indeed, by definition, such co-option is perfectly transparent. Moreover, co-option is often strongly encouraged by regulated firms for a variety of reasons discussed here.

The normative contribution of this chapter is to describe the corrupting influence of government co-option of naturally occurring market mechanisms. The analysis of the incidences of co-option examined in this chapter reveals that market mechanisms do not remain the same after they are incorporated into regulation. Most significantly, the original, demand-driven motivation for utilizing a particular market mechanism disappears when the market mechanism is incorporated into a rule. In place of the demand-driven motivation for utilizing a market mechanism, use of the market mechanism by private-sector actors becomes driven by regulation. When this happens, the process of implementing the market mechanism is corrupted.

The best-known example of government co-option of a private-sector institution is the co-option of private-sector credit rating agencies. Companies issuing securities originally procured credit ratings because the cost of the rating was less than the benefits that the rating provided to the issuer, which came in the form of a lower cost of capital on debt issues that had been vetted by independent, highly regarded rating agencies. In this unregulated environment, credit rating agencies had strong incentives to maintain their reputations for providing high-quality ratings, because if the ratings they issued were not credible to investors, the investors would not pay more for highly rated securities than for other securities, and issuers would have no incentive to incur the cost of procuring a credit rating for an issuance of debt. This market dynamic was corrupted once investors were *required* by regulators to purchase securities rated by the established credit rating agencies. Credit rating agencies were transformed into Nationally Recognized Statistical Rating Organizations (NRSROs). Upon achieving this official, quasi-governmental status, the rating agencies no longer had to compete on the basis of the quality of their ratings. They began to maximize profits by lowering the cost of producing ratings. This, in turn, lowered the quality of the ratings. But the lower quality no longer mattered, as issuers had to pay for ratings because most institutional investors could not buy securities that lacked a rating from a governmentally sanctioned NRSRO.

In other words, once credit ratings were incorporated into government regulation, the ratings themselves became corrupted and stopped serving the original purpose for which they were used in purely private, consensual transactions. Absent regulation, credit rating agencies had to generate very high quality information about issuers in order to survive. Thus, absent regulation, the credit rating agencies would not have become corrupted.

The notion that credit rating agencies do not generate information of value is fairly well known. What is not well understood is the fact that this was not always the case. Credit ratings used to be of high quality. The quality was corrupted when ratings were co-opted into regulation. Most important is the primary point of this chapter, which is that credit rating agencies are by no means unique. A number of important market mechanisms have been corrupted by regulation. In fact, it appears that whenever regulators attempt to co-opt a market mechanism, the market mechanism tends to become corrupted, even when the regulators are acting with the best of intentions.

The transformation of market institutions to enabling institutions has been curiously understudied, particularly since one observes it quite often. In addition to credit ratings, audits once were voluntary, but now they are mandatory for public companies. And corporations' internal risk assessments are being internalized into regulations.

Likewise, various sorts of advisory services, particularly the rendering of fairness opinions, which are professional opinions rendered by investment banks about whether the terms of major corporate transactions like mergers, corporate acquisitions, share repurchases, and leveraged buyouts going private are fair, began their existence as voluntary. They now are essentially mandatory in a wide variety of contexts. Fairness opinions are delivered, typically for hefty fees by investment banks in connection with their provision of financial advice, to corporations deciding whether to pursue important deals.[5]

The first section of this chapter contains an analysis of the economic rationales for the use of the market mechanisms described in this chapter. This section consists of a discussion of the specific market imperfections that private-sector institutions are attempting to solve through various innovations. Not surprisingly, these market imperfections manifest themselves in the form of the transaction costs that confront companies when they try to raise capital from outsiders and the agency cost problems that confront shareholders and creditors who are trying to monitor the firms in which they have invested.

The second section contains an analysis of four critical voluntary market institutions that have been incorporated (co-opted) by regulators in various ways. These institutions consist of: (a) the credit ratings generated by credit rating agencies; (b) the fairness opinions generated by investment banks; (c) the outside audits provided by independent auditing firms; and (d) the internal risk assessments (generally Value at Risk models) that financial institutions use to determine whether they have sufficient levels of capital to operate safely.

Market Mechanisms and Their Co-option and Corruption

In the realm of corporate governance and finance, the market mechanisms examined in this chapter were initially designed for the purpose of mitigating various contracting and agency problems facing entrepreneurs, managers, and investors. Fairness opinions from investment banks and credit ratings from credit rating agencies were meant to ameliorate the contracting problem that results from the fact that contracting parties possess radically asymmetric information about the assets over which they are contracting.

The audits performed by independent accounting firms similarly reduce contracting costs by allowing firms to make credible promises that the financial information they are providing to investors and others is accurate. In addition, outside, independent audits reduce agency costs by alerting directors and other corporate monitors about financial and accounting anomalies and irregularities that constitute red flags and require investigation.

Similarly, accurate internal risk assessments can serve the additional purpose of controlling agency costs within firms. More accurate assessments of risk not only help firms control their risks and establish minimum capital levels, they also enable companies to provide more accurate incentive-based compensation and other rewards. This, in turn, reduces the moral hazard that faces managers who are compensated on the basis of their performance because adjusting the realized outcomes of particular investments for their risk has the effect of decreasing the returns of projects deemed to be relatively risky, and concomitantly increasing the returns of relatively safe projects.

The consequences of subverting these market mechanisms described here can hardly be overstated. These market mechanisms served the function, in other words, of mitigating asymmetry of information problems, signaling problems, and credibility problems that if left uncorrected will, as George Akerlof famously explained, cause markets to implode.

Asymmetry of Information and the Inability to Make Credible Commitments

The analysis begins with the assumption that both private-sector actors and public officials are acutely interested in facilitating capital formation. Of course the private-sector actors are concerned about raising money for their particular firms, while public-sector officials are, presumably, less concerned about the fate of particular firms than they are about the general economic environment in which capital formation takes place.

One way that this commonality of interests among private and public actors manifests itself is that both groups have incentives to fashion remedies for the contracting problems that plague companies in search of capital and their potential investors. For example, when a company requires working capital or needs funding for a particular project, it will seek access to the public and private markets for debt or equity. The ability of companies to attract such capital will depend on their ability to convince investors that they will refrain from absconding with their investment dollars and will, instead, be able to offer a competitive rate of return on any funds entrusted to the company.

There are several ways that regulation and market forces attempt to overcome the credible commitment problem that makes it difficult for unknown market participants to attract capital. Among the most important potentially available strategies that may be deployed either separately or together are: (a) investing in reputation;[6] (b) submitting to an intensive regulatory regime in which fraud is pursued and punished assiduously; and (c) submitting to a trading environment characterized by high degrees of transparency and efficiency so that fraud and misrepresentations will quickly be ferreted out by rivalrous competition among market professionals such as arbitrageurs and stock market professionals.

In his seminal 1970 article titled "The Market for Lemons: Quality Uncertainty and the Market Mechanism," George Akerlof provided the theoretical foundation for the economic role of the strategies described above.[7] The fundamental cause of the problem in search of solutions is "information asymmetry," the situation that arises when one party to a transaction (usually the seller, though not always) has more and better information about the product or service than its counter-party. In cases where information asymmetries are large enough, markets will fail to the point of implosion unless something is done to restore the informational balance. Akerlof explained the conditions under which information asymmetries lead to market collapse with an illustration from the market for used cars. In American vernacular, the cars of the poorest quality in this market are dubbed "lemons," while cars of the highest quality are "cherries." In Akerlof's model, all other cars—those whose quality is somewhere between these two extremes—are lumped together as "average." In an ideal world of "perfect" (or costlessly available) information, all cherries will sell for the highest prices, all lemons for the lowest prices, and all average cars for prices in between. But consider what happens when we move from a world of "perfect markets" to one characterized by significant, even chronic, asymmetry of information—a world where sellers and buyers often do not know one another, do not engage in repeat dealings, and, to make things worse, have no reliable, well-informed reputational intermediaries to provide them with the information they lack. In this radically "imperfect," informationally challenged world, sellers of both lemons and average cars may be tempted to pass their cars off as cherries. But buyers are not stupid—and recognizing their own inability to distinguish among cars on the basis of quality, they reduce the price they are willing to pay by enough to compensate for the risk they are buying a lemon.

This set of arrangements and adjustments may work for a while. The problem, however, is that it is likely to lead to an unsustainable "non-equilibrium" in which some sellers of lemons receive a premium over the actual value of their cars, while many other sellers of cherries are offered significantly less for their cars than they are worth. Once the buyers of the lemons discover that they have paid too much, they—and those who hear their stories—will either withdraw from the market or dramatically reduce the prices they offer to the (now discredited) sellers in the market. And once the sellers of cherries observe that they can no longer obtain a fair price for their cars, many of those sellers—particularly those with the best cars—will decline to put their cars on the market and will resort to other means of sale that do not involve impersonal market transactions. Such alternatives are likely to include transactions within the sellers' "circle of trust," such as family members or those with a close religious or ethnic affiliation.

The withdrawal of the highest quality cars from the market results, of course, in a reduction in the average quality of the cars on the market. As cherries are withdrawn from the market, buyers will respond by adjusting downward the amount they are willing to pay to reflect the new, lower average quality of the cars in the market—and this then leads still more sellers to withdraw their cars from the market. Soon none of the best cars are available for sale, and even owners of average-quality cars begin to receive too little compensation for their vehicles. Once the average-quality cars start to disappear from the marketplace, buyers eventually recognize that the only cars available on the market are lemons and lower their prices accordingly. And this downward spiral in quality and price ultimately leads, as Akerlof's model posits, to the complete failure of the market—unless market participants figure out a way to solve the information problem confronting buyers and sellers.

Akerlof's model applies with particular force in the context of the capital markets in which securities trading occurs. First, these markets are characterized by acute information asymmetry. Sellers of securities, particularly issuers or banks that have designed a particular trading instrument, or developed the algorithm used to determine the value of the instrument, will have significant information advantages over their counter-parties.

Second, the intuition that buyers will manage this information problem by paying a price for assets that reflects the anticipated average quality of those assets to compensate for the risk of receiving low-quality assets seems particularly applicable to the world of corporate finance. Following the principles of modern portfolio theory, investors routinely attempt to construct diversified portfolios of securities to eliminate the "firm-specific" risk (which might be thought of as the possibility that a particular firm turns out to be a lemon) associated with a particular investment. Third, traditional strategies for overcoming the problem of asymmetric information at the heart of the lemons problem often do not work in the context of financial products.

Traditional strategies for confronting the lemons problem, such as offering product warranties, work well when the manufacturer is offering many units of the same product and consumers are concerned about the quality of the particular unit they are buying. But in the capital markets, the more typical concern is that an entire issue of securities will fail to perform as promised. Warranties, refunds, and exchanges, which are all forms of insurance for buyers, do not work in the context of securities offerings because when the issuer fails, all investors tend to suffer together. Finally, stark differences around the world in the quality of capital markets appear attributable to the fact that the lemons problem is particularly acute in countries with poorly developed legal and regulatory systems for the obvious reason that, in such countries, sellers of securities are unable to commit credibly to telling the truth simply by submitting themselves to the sanctions imposed by law.

Thus, developing mechanisms and institutions for coping with the contracting problems generated by asymmetric information is among the most important tasks for economists, lawyers, and policy makers. The credit ratings, fairness opinions, and audits by independent financial firms discussed in this chapter are among the most important mechanisms and institutions ever developed by markets. The degradation caused by their assimilation into regulation has proved very costly.

Agency Costs

As Jensen and Meckling famously explained, both investors and entrepreneurs seeking investments have strong incentives to find ways to reduce agency costs because the investors and entrepreneurs will share the gains associated with eliminating this source of inefficiency.[8] Among the farrago of mechanisms used to align the interests of agents and principals are profit sharing, commission, or piece-rate compensation; bonding through reputation building; and threats of firing or other disciplines.

But these sorts of rather crude mechanisms for addressing agency cost problems present problems of their own sometimes. Moreover, technological problems sometimes make it difficult to devise contractual solutions for agency problems. For example, firms often compensate employees on the basis of their performance. To do this, employees such as traders and professional money managers are compensated on the basis of the returns generated by the portfolios of assets they assemble and trade. But these returns must be adjusted for the risks associated with these investments, or else the incentive-based compensation can lead to the moral hazard of excessive risk-taking. Unfortunately, the measurement of risk is more difficult, more subjective, and less precise than the measurement of returns. The elaborate and expensive internal risk-assessment processes developed by financial firms were an important step on the path toward developing more accurate and precise measures of the risks associated with the assets held on and off of the balance sheets of these institutions. Unfortunately, as the following section shows, the internal risk-assessment process was corrupted when government regulators assimilated these internal risk assessments into their capital requirements for banks and other financial institutions.

From the Sublime to the Ridiculous: Four Tales of Co-option

Markets must innovate in order to survive. As transaction costs and agency costs become more acute, the need to innovate becomes correspondingly more acute. It is difficult to identify markets in which the transaction costs and agency cost problems are more acute than the securities markets. Firms in search of investors' capital must somehow credibly commit to being able to act in the best interests of the investors who part with their money and have very little capacity to monitor or control the firms in which they have invested. As Andrei Shleifer and Robert Vishny have provocatively observed:

> How do the suppliers of finance get managers to return some of the profits to them? How do they make sure that managers do not steal the capital they supply or invest it in bad projects? How do suppliers of finance control managers?
>
> At first glance, it is not entirely obvious why the suppliers of capital get anything back. After all, they part with their money, and have little to contribute to the enterprise afterward. The professional managers or entrepreneurs who run the firm might as well abscond with the money. Although they sometimes do, usually they do not.[9]

From a legal perspective, the problem facing shareholders is even more vexing than the problem facing suppliers of capital more generally (bondholders, banks, and other fixed claimants). Unlike fixed claimants, shareholders are not entitled to dividends, much less capital appreciation. Shareholders are residual claimants, and, as such, are paid only when, and if, the boards of directors of their firms deem it appropriate. And they won't as long as managers and directors think that a company can invest the free cash flow of a firm more efficiently than the shareholders could invest this money if the company paid taxes on it and then returned it to the shareholders in the form of dividends. Needless to say, shareholders are not entitled to any capital appreciation. Their economic rights are virtually nonexistent. And their voting rights are not much more effective in providing any assurance that their investments will not be appropriated at the first opportunity by self-interested and rapacious officers and directors.[10]

Despite all this, we actually observe, at least in some economies during some time periods, not only "the flows of enormous amounts of capital to firms," but also, perhaps even more astonishingly, the "actual repatriation of profits to the providers of finance."[11] It is worth observing that such capital flows and capital repatriation pre-dates the emergence of the modern regulatory state. Thus, it must be the case that the market mechanisms and institutions discussed in this section are able to overcome the vast contracting problems facing companies in search of capital and potential investors in such firms.

The Making and Unmaking of Mandatory Credit Ratings

In a series of seminal articles, Frank Partnoy explains the way that regulation has transformed a useful, but rather narrowly focused industry into a regulatory-enhanced juggernaut. As Partnoy points out, the regulatory environment created by the Securities and Exchange Commission, and perpetuated by a host of other state and federal regulatory agencies, conveys significant regulatory benefits on those credit rating agencies that have been fortunate enough to receive the SEC's designation as an NRSRO. As Partnoy points out, credit rating agencies are distinctly characterized by an "oligopoly market structure that is reinforced by regulations that depend exclusively on credit ratings issued by Nationally Recognized Statistical Rating Organizations (NRSROs)."[12]

Prior to the intervention by the SEC, the credit rating agencies enjoyed a significant boom during the 1920s and then fell into a period of decline in the wake of the stock market crash in 1929. That decline persisted until the early

1970s, when the SEC began to promulgate a series of highly technical and obscure regulations that transformed the credit rating agencies into powerful monoliths in the classic sense: the rating agencies that have the NRSRO designation are massive, unchanging, and difficult to deal with on a human scale.

In 1975 the SEC imposed a uniform "net capital rule" on broker-dealer firms. The purpose of this rule was to ensure that broker-dealer firms regulated by the SEC would have sufficient resources (capital) to meet their financial obligations to customers, counter-parties, and creditors. The SEC's strategy for ensuring that brokers had sufficient capital to meet their obligations was to require "every broker-dealer to maintain at all times specified minimum levels of liquid assets, or net capital, sufficient to enable a firm that falls below its minimum requirement to liquidate in an orderly fashion."[13]

Regulating capital is notoriously difficult to do. One of the bigger problems facing regulators is that not all assets are alike, particularly with respect to characteristics such as liquidity and risk. This problem is compounded by the fact that, unlike returns, which are easy to measure accurately in real time, risk and liquidity are extremely difficult to evaluate at all, and accurate measurements are virtually impossible, particularly in real time.

At one extreme on a continuum, measuring risk and liquidity would be short-term debt obligations of the U.S. government, which are highly liquid and virtually riskless. At the other extreme would be such things as unique, individually negotiated commercial loans from individual banks to small, obscure companies and complex, untraded derivative instruments. It would make no sense whatsoever to require companies to maintain the same amount of capital to support assets such as cash and U.S. government notes as they must maintain to support assets such as consumer loans, commercial loans, and investments in complex derivatives.

The SEC's solution to this problem was to create a new quasi-government institution out of an old private-sector institution. The old institution was the credit rating agency. The new institution into which the old credit rating agencies were magically transformed was the Nationally Recognized Statistical Rating Organization. In an apparently well-intended effort to inject some subtle gradations into its net capital rules, the SEC decided that bonds and other debt obligations held by broker-dealers that had high ratings from an NRSRO were safer (more liquid) than other, unrated obligations. As such, the SEC reasoned, broker-dealer firms should be required to hold less capital to offset the highly rated assets on their balance sheets than they are required to offset the unrated (or poorly rated) assets on their balance sheets.

And because capital is very expensive for financial firms, especially relative to debt, this meant that it was less costly for firms to hold rated securities than other assets, all else equal.[14] The use of the NRSRO designation to determine how much capital a broker-dealer was required to have in order to comply with the net capital rules was followed by an even more profound regulatory co-option of the private-sector role of credit rating agencies. Here the obscure regulation is SEC Rule 2a-7, which pertains to what are, arguably, the most important and fragile financial institutions in the SEC's domain: money market mutual funds.

Mutual funds, of course, are investment companies whose assets consist of investments in securities issued by other corporations. Money market mutual funds are a particular subset of mutual funds. Money market mutual funds are mutual funds that compete with commercial banks by holding themselves out to the public as offering stable asset prices that feature safe, stable repositories for liquidity. Money market mutual funds compete with bank checking accounts by maintaining a stable net asset value of one dollar per share. This, in turn, permits investors in money market mutual funds to enjoy check-writing privileges while still obtaining more competitive rates of return than are often available on bank checking accounts.

Money market funds are used by individuals. What is less widely known is that money market funds are extremely important providers of short-term liquidity to financial intermediaries.[15] Institutional investors use them as a cash management tool.[16] Money market mutual funds are by far the largest customers for commercial paper and repurchase agreements (repos) in the world.

In observing the emergence of money market mutual funds onto the mutual fund landscape, the SEC felt compelled to devise regulations that would limit the ability of mutual funds to deceive investors by calling themselves money market mutual funds but not investing in the very high quality and highly liquid assets that would enable the funds to be able to withstand large-scale efforts by investors to obtain liquidity by cashing in (redeeming) their investments simultaneously.

The SEC "solved" this problem by promulgating SEC Rule 2a-7. Rule 2a-7 restricts the kinds of securities that funds calling themselves money market mutual funds can invest in. The purpose of the rule is to make sure that the mutual fund invests in assets of sufficient quality and liquidity that the fund will be able to maintain a stable net asset value of one dollar even in times of significant stress and turmoil in the markets. Rule 2a-7, at the time of the financial crisis, provided that money market funds would be limited to investing in securities that are rated by an NRSRO in one of its two highest short-term rating categories (unless the board of directors determined that an unrated security was of comparable quality). Rule 2a-7 also required money market funds to monitor on a continuous basis the ratings of the securities in their portfolios and to respond appropriately in case of a downgrade.[17]

Over time the reliance by regulatory agencies on the SEC's NRSRO designation metastasized into the thousands, even defying scholars' efforts to quantify all of the regulations at the federal, state, and local levels that relied on the NRSRO designation.[18] The invention of the NRSRO designation was very good for credit rating agencies. It was because of the demand for ratings created by regulation that Thomas Friedman was able to say that there were only two superpowers in the world, the United States and Moody's, and that sometimes it wasn't clear which was more powerful.[19]

Astonishingly, as Frank Partnoy has observed, when Thomas Friedman made his famous quip, the credit rating agencies had not even begun their meteoric rise. Moody's, the only publicly traded NRSRO, has operating revenues, profitability, capitalization, and market share consistent with those of a participant in a government-protected cartel.[20] The value of Moody's stock increased more than 300 percent in the five-year period prior to the 2007 market crash, when the demand for rating agencies' services blossomed as more and more exotic credit derivatives were issued (and rated).

Also, significantly, around this period, the largest credit rating agencies, Moody's, Fitch, and Standard and Poor's, began to charge the issuers for ratings. Previously, these credit rating agencies generated revenue by selling subscriptions to publications that contained, among other material, the ratings they generated.[21]

The credit rating agencies designated as NRSROs "have benefited from an oligopoly market structure that is reinforced by regulations that depend exclusively on credit ratings issued by Nationally Recognized Statistical Rating Organizations (NRSROs). These regulatory benefits . . . generate economic rents for NRSROs that persist even when they perform poorly."[22]

And perform poorly they do. Empirical studies indicate that credit ratings contain little, if any, timely or accurate information about issuers.[23] While many have observed the poor performance of the credit rating agencies, and many have lamented the distortions caused by the NRSRO designation, none have suggested, as I do, that there is a causal link between the NRSRO designation and the rating agencies' poor performance. Partnoy, for example, takes the view that credit rating agencies never performed well. But if credit rating agencies always performed poorly, it is unclear why they were, at least at one time, of value to investors and issuers. Rather, it appears that credit rating agencies played a very modest role in corporate finance until the NRSRO designation uncoupled their profits from their performance.

Historically, the reason that rating agencies were able to charge fees at all was because "the public has enough confidence in the integrity of these ratings to find them of value in evaluating the riskiness of investments."[24] Before companies were required to obtain ratings for their newly issued debt (so that their customers would be permitted by regulators to buy such debt), the only rationale for paying for a credit rating was that the cost of obtaining the rating was lower than the benefit, which came in the form of lower borrowing costs for debt that was subjected to the scrutiny of the credit rating agencies.

It is not at all clear from the historical evidence that credit rating agencies were ever particularly good at generating accurate ratings. As Martin Fridson has observed, the historical evidence shows some massive mistakes (like Enron)[25] and a tendency toward ratings inflation, but there has also been a correlation between ratings, defaults and losses, and net returns, suggesting that ratings did historically generate some information of value to investors.[26] From this perspective, it appears that a major part of the problem that government regulation created in the credit rating context was that the NRSRO designation caused credit ratings to be taken too seriously. Credit ratings, which used to be a mere sideshow in American corporate finance, became the main attraction in the capital markets' biggest tents.

Moreover, to a large extent, credit ratings are a product of market inefficiency. Credit ratings are necessary in order to compensate for a lack of market-generated information. Over time, as information technology improves and competition among market participants increases, one would expect that the natural evolution of the capital markets would be toward less reliance on credit ratings over time. Instead, of course, because of the NRSRO designation, credit ratings have become more rather than less important.

The phenomenon of rising demand for credit ratings over time does not appear to be the result of either improving credit ratings or deteriorating capital markets. In fact, the data suggest the opposite. Empirical studies have documented that yield spreads of corporate bonds start to expand as credit quality deteriorates but before a rating downgrade.[27] These results cast doubt on the informational value of credit ratings because they indicate that prices in the capital markets generally anticipate future downgrades by the credit rating agencies. These data also suggest that differences in yields among securities (credit spreads), which show the increases (decreases) in rates of return that investors can expect when buying securities with higher or lower yields, reflect the increases (decreases) in risk associated with these various investments.

Once credit ratings were co-opted by the government's NRSRO designations, not only did their business explode, but their basic business model changed as well. Quality became less important because the NRSRO regulatory framework decoupled the quality of the ratings generated by the credit rating agencies from the demand for their services. Thus, the rational response from the credit rating agencies was to lower costs. As Partnoy suggests, the growth in size and profitability in credit ratings likely is attributable to cost savings:

> Both S&P and Moody's have high levels of staff turnover, modest salary levels and limited upward mobility; moreover, investment banks poach the best rating agency employees. These factors limit the ability of rating agencies to generate valuable information. In addition, the process agencies use today to generate ratings does not obtain any obvious advantages over competing information providers and analysts. Credit rating agencies do not independently verify information supplied to them by issuers, and all rating agencies get the same data. Both Moody's and S&P make rating determinations in secret. The agencies never describe their terms or analysis precisely or say, for example, that a particular rating has a particular probability of default, and they stress that the ratings are qualitative and judgmental. This secretive, qualitative process is not the type of process one would expect if the agencies had survived based on their ability to accumulate reputational capital. On the other hand, such processes make it more likely that an agency would be able to survive in a non-competitive market; if the rating process had been public or quantitative (rather than qualitative), other market entrants easily could have duplicated the rating agencies' technology and methodology.[28]

The consequences of the misguided decision to incorporate credit ratings into securities and capital markets regulations were severe. The evidence shows that, whatever the quality and reliability of credit ratings might have been prior to the end of the twentieth century, the rating agencies failed dismally between 2001 and 2008. As Thomas Gorman (echoing many others) has observed, "Credit rating agencies, and in particular, nationally recognized statistical rating organizations ('NRSRO'), have been thought by many to be at the center of much of what went on with the market crisis, particularly in the area of structured products. The agencies have come under significant criticism for their methodologies, lack of procedures and conflicts of interest."[29]

The evidence strongly suggests that credit rating agencies lowered their standards between 2001 and 2008, especially with respect to their ratings of structured financial instruments.[30] In particular, as Fridson points out, many credit default obligations received "undeserved Triple-A ratings"[31] during this period, making it simply "impossible to defend the agencies' . . . ratings of mortgage-related collateralized debt obligations"[32] because fully "89% of the investment grade mortgage-backed securities ratings that Moody's awarded in 2007 were subsequently reduced to speculative grade."[33]

Rating structured financial obligations such as collateralized debt obligations (CDOs) is particularly difficult for credit rating agencies, it seems because:

> when a rating agency rates a mortgage-related CDO, it may have greater difficulty controlling the conflict that arises from the issuer-pay model. To begin with, the issuer is not an existing company with a new need for capital. Rather, the prospective offering has come about because an underwriter has structured a financing around a pool of mortgages. The deal is contingent on selling the senior tranche to investors who will accept a comparatively low yield in exchange for a very high level of perceived safety. Therefore, if the bankers are not fairly confident of being able to obtain a Triple-A rating on the senior tranche, they will not even bother to commence work on the deal. In that case, the CDO will not be created and the rating agencies will receive no revenue.[34]

The NRSRO regulatory framework ultimately created a competitive environment, in which the cartel of well-known credit rating agencies issuing ratings would inevitably come to view the most rational business model to be that of supplying ratings not for the purpose of conveying information, but for the purpose of providing prophylactic protection against various risks, including litigation risk and the risk of underperforming one's rivals. In this environment, the rational, profit-maximizing strategy would be for firms offering fairness opinions to compete for market share by offering fairness opinions, with the results preferred by target company boards of directors.

In response to the simultaneous increased reliance on and deteriorating quality of ratings, regulators have recently begun to try to fix the problem they caused with the invention of the NRSRO designation. The Dodd-Frank Wall Street Reform and Consumer Protection Act created a new office of credit ratings that is responsible for administering the processes by which NRSROs calculate credit ratings. This office is tasked with conducting an annual audit of each NRSRO and issuing a public report on the NRSROs' performance.

In order to improve the flawed credit ratings, the SEC, which in my view actually caused the poor quality of the ratings by inventing the NRSRO concept in the first place, is now responsible for the corporate governance of the credit rating agencies. Each NRSRO is required by Dodd-Frank to have a board of directors that is responsible for overseeing a system of internal controls over the policies and procedures used to determine ratings, and other internal issues, such as promotion and compensation.

Dodd-Frank also requires the SEC to regulate credit rating agencies in a number of additional ways. New rules must be promulgated to: (a) preclude ratings from being influenced by sales and marketing; (b) define the meaning of rating symbols and require that they be used consistently; (c) require that NRSROs use distinct symbols to denote credit ratings for different types of instruments; (d) require that each NRSRO assess and disclose the probability that an issuer will default or otherwise not make payments in accord with the terms of the instrument; (e) establish the criteria for the qualifications, knowledge, experience, and training of persons who perform ratings; (f) require the disclosure of information that will permit the accuracy of ratings and foster comparability among the agencies to be evaluated; (g) require the disclosure, on a form that will accompany each rating issued, of information about the underlying assumptions, procedures, and methodologies employed as well as the data used in establishing the rating.[35] These provisions all are based on the idea that SEC regulation can improve the quality of the ratings generated by the NRSROs.

Dodd-Frank also makes it easier for investors to sue credit rating agencies. This provision, of course, is based on the notion that the threat of liability can improve quality of the ratings generated by the NRSROs.[36]

The sequence of events culminating the provisions of Dodd-Frank related to credit rating agencies is strongly supportive of the hypothesis of this chapter, which is that government co-option of private institutions tends to cause the deterioration of such institutions. First, government co-opted credit rating agencies by regulating them. This regulation ultimately distorted credit rating agencies' incentives and removed their prior, market-driven incentives to produce high-quality ratings. But the regulation also created more dependence on credit ratings than ever before. This in turn created an acute need for more regulation (which came in the form of Dodd-Frank), the new regulation being aimed at improving the poor performance of the credit rating agencies that the prior regulations caused in the first place.

Congress's recognition in Dodd-Frank of the failure of the regulators' co-option strategy for credit rating agencies went even further than simply increasing the regulation of credit rating agencies. Section 939A of the Dodd-Frank Wall Street Reform and Consumer Protection Act requires the SEC to review its myriad regulations referencing credit ratings and to modify those regulations so as to "remove any reference to or requirement of reliance on credit ratings."[37] In place of these credit ratings, the SEC must promulgate "standard of credit-worthiness as each respective agency shall determine as appropriate for such regulations."[38]

The implications of this rule change are manifold. In particular, the investment advisors who manage money market funds can no longer rely on the credit ratings generated by NRSROs when making investment decisions. Money market fund managers have to analyze their investments on their own. Removing reliance on the credit rating agencies reduces systematic risk by decreasing the tendency of mutual funds to have investments that are highly correlated with (i.e., the same as) the investments of other mutual funds. Prior to Dodd-Frank, mutual funds advisers and other money managers were tempted to pick the highest yielding assets within any particular ratings category, in order to maximize the risk-adjusted returns associated with their investments. Requiring money managers to make decisions on the basis of their own risk analysis rather than relying on credit rating agencies will, therefore, likely reduce the systemic risk caused by the "herd behavior" of money managers.

To the extent that regulators must now remove the regulatory co-option of the credit rating designation, then credit rating agencies will have to, once again, compete on the basis of the quality of their ratings as the artificial demand for their services created by regulation subsides. Ironically, this means that the quality of the ratings generated by the credit rating agencies should improve just as the professional money managers become less reliant on their use. In retrospect, the creation and expansion of the NRSRO designation can be viewed as an experiment with the regulatory co-option of privately generated credit ratings. Clearly, this experiment failed. The reason that the experiment failed was because the very act of incorporating credit ratings into the regulatory framework changed the incentives of the companies issuing such ratings and ultimately corrupted the quality of the ratings themselves.

Selling Indulgences: The Judicial Co-Option of Fairness Opinions

For officers and directors of the United States, public companies' fundamental corporate decisions are dangerous events. Even when officers and directors are negotiating and structuring transactions that promise huge profits for shareholders, the risk is great that the directors and officers considering these transactions will be sued by attorneys purporting to represent either shareholders, complaining that the price obtained by the company for its assets was too low, or creditors complaining that the price obtained by the company for its assets was too low or involved too much debt and thereby decreased the value of the creditors' claims.

The plaintiffs bringing these claims typically structure their lawsuits as class actions or derivative suits. The complaints generally allege that the corporate managers' approval of a significant transaction breached their common-law fiduciary duties of care or loyalty or good faith in making their decision. Litigation of this kind is considered to be, along with markets, contracts, norms, and other structural features, an important part of the corporate governance framework that constrains corporate managers.

In response to the omnipresent threat of litigation, corporate officers and directors seek guidance from lawyers about how to reduce the threat of litigation. These corporate officers and directors, of course, pay rapt attention to the suggestions that judges make about how corporate actors should conduct themselves when making major decisions.

One major defensive weapon in managements' arsenal is the fairness opinion. Fairness opinions generally take the form of letters addressed to the board of directors of a corporation that is in the process of making an important decision, which articulates the opinion of the issuer of the fairness opinion as to the adequacy or "fairness, from a financial point of view" of a particular course of action.[39] Fairness opinions generally contain detailed valuations of the company being bought and sold.

For years, courts have emphasized that board members can rely on fairness opinions as an integral part of their decision-making process. The use of such opinions is an important aid in the quest of directors to obtain the protections from liability provided by the business judgment rule.[40]

Over time, despite occasional protestations by courts to the contrary, as a practical matter, there developed "the widespread belief that a fairness opinion is required for protection under the business judgment rule."[41] For example, in the seminal case S*mith v. Van Gorkom*,[42] although the Delaware Supreme Court expressly observed that fairness opinions were not required under Delaware law, the court did impose liability on directors in that case, and the fact that the board had failed to obtain a fairness opinion clearly did not help their case. It seems plausible that obtaining a fairness opinion "would have insulated the directors from liability," and this, in turn, translated into the creation of what has accurately been described as "an informal requirement."[43] As a result of this opinion, since January 1985, when the Delaware Supreme Court ruled against the directors of Trans Union Corp. in *Smith v. Van Gorkom*, fairness opinions have become "customary."[44]

In this way, fairness opinions are no longer simply a source of information about a proposed transaction or financing. Obtaining a fairness opinion, rather, has become rather like the practice of buying indulgences prior to the Protestant Reformation, but for sins that one is about to commit instead of for past sins.[45] The practice is very widespread, but it isn't entirely legitimate.

In addition to the widespread use of fairness opinions, companies retained investment bankers to provide them with advisory services even more regularly than they retained such banks to furnish them with fairness opinions. Clearly, judges' opinions in fiduciary duty cases, particularly the opinion articulated in *Smith v. Van Gorkom*, increased the demand for financial advisory services. On average, 61 percent of target firms report obtaining fairness opinions. The percentage of firms using fairness opinions was in decline prior to *Smith v. Van Gorkom*, but the percentage increased dramatically following this decision. The frequency of firms reporting the use of investment banks' advisory opinions has, in contrast, held steady at over 90 percent.[46]

Significantly, in my view, the data show that the use of fairness opinions in corporate acquisitions was extremely widespread prior to the 1985 decision in *Smith v. Van Gorkom*. As shown in Figure 12.1,[47] for example, in 1980, fully 90 percent of target companies involved in acquisitions obtained fairness opinions. Figure 12.1 also shows that the use of fairness opinions was on a steady decline until 1982, when it experienced a one-year uptick before continuing its sharp downward trend that ended only in 1985 when *Smith v. Van Gorkom* was decided by the Delaware Supreme Court.[48]

This, in turn, strongly suggests that, at least prior to 1985, the demand for fairness opinions was driven by a genuine desire on the part of directors and officers to get the benefit of an investment banker's judgment about whether the price being considered in a particular control transaction was fair. During this period of time, investment banks and other firms generating fairness opinions were concerned about maintaining the value of their reputational capital. [49]

Following *Smith v. Van Gorkom*, however, the demand for fairness opinions became decoupled from the quality of those opinions for several reasons. First, the courts evaluating fairness opinions did not seem to care, particularly, about whether the bank generating the fairness opinion had a reputation

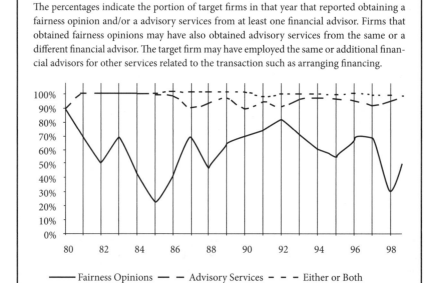

The percentages indicate the portion of target firms in that year that reported obtaining a fairness opinion and/or a advisory services from at least one financial advisor. Firms that obtained fairness opinions may have also obtained advisory services from the same or a different financial advisor. The target firm may have employed the same or additional financial advisors for other services related to the transaction such as arranging financing.

———— Fairness Opinions   — — Advisory Services   - - - Either or Both

All completed acquisitions announced between January 1, 1980 and December 31, 1999 between publicly traded, nonfinancial firms where the value of the transaction is at least $10 million. Data source: Thomson Financial, Inc.

Figure 12.1 Comparison of the Percentage of Target Firms Using Advisory Services and Fairness Opinions

Source: Helen Bowers, "Fairness Opinion and the Business Judgment Rule: An Empirical Investigation of Target Firms' Use of Fairness," 96 *Northwestern University Law Review* (2002), 573.

for producing accurate and reliable valuations. It appears that an opinion from any well-known investment bank would suffice. This, in turn, created a competitive environment, in which the cartel of well-known investment banks issuing fairness opinions would, rationally, see their business model as supplying opinions not for the purpose of conveying information, but for the purpose of providing prophylactic protection against litigation risk. In this environment, the rational, profit-maximizing strategy would be for firms offering fairness opinions to compete for market share by offering fairness opinions with the results preferred by target company boards of directors. Banks offering these sorts of opinions would, it would seem, be more likely to be retained by companies than competitors who suffered the reputation of offering fairness opinions with results that target management did not want to receive.

Providers of fairness opinions have little difficulty determining the precise opinions that their clients want to hear. Generally, the people generating fairness opinions know the terms of the deal they are evaluating, including the price of the offer. They also know whether the management or boards of directors who have retained them approve of the proposed deal or not. Advisors usually have experience with the management team that hires them to render a fairness opinion.[50]

There might be room for new entry into the business of offering fairness opinions by firms who can develop a reputation for offering reliable opinions. However, the co-option of fairness opinions into fiduciary duty analysis has distorted those incentives. Prospective new entrants are hobbled in the post-*Smith v. Van Gorkom* regulatory environment because such new entrants would, ironically, likely not be as useful in protecting boards' decisions from legal attack precisely because they are not well known to courts. Directors would find themselves in the awkward position of having to explain to skeptical plaintiffs' attorneys and judges why they decided to seek a fairness opinion from an unknown parvenu court instead of a well-known, long-established firm such as Goldman Sachs.

So, two facts emerge from this analysis. First, although fairness opinions are not, strictly speaking, required by law, bankers are almost always retained to offer fairness opinions in deals involving the sale of public companies or other transactions in which directors are likely to be sued.[51] At the same time, unfortunately, it is also the case that the banks that prepare fairness opinions never say that the transaction that they are evaluating is actually "unfair." Rather, the fairness opinion has been transformed into a mere rubber stamp that is used "to justify the deal under consideration to litigious investors."[52]

Even those who support the notion that fairness opinions might potentially be of use to investors in the current regulatory environment conclude that the banks issuing such opinions must be tightly regulated. Unfortunately, these scholars apparently ignore the fact that the reason why fairness opinions lack "meaning" and are devoid of a "useful role" is because they are no longer being commissioned by directors for the market-driven purpose of obtaining a thoughtful, sophisticated, unconflicted analysis of a proposed transaction.[53] Rather, such opinions are commissioned in order to guard against the imposition of liability from opportunistic plaintiffs.

In sum, absent the regulatory co-option described above, fairness opinions have to be accurate or else companies would have no incentive to procure such opinions, because they are costly. However, in the face of regulatory co-option, fairness opinions have become less reliable, since the basic motivation for seeking such opinions has now changed. Absent regulatory co-option, the motive for obtaining a fairness opinion is to obtain valuable information from a reliable source. After the fairness opinion was co-opted into the regulatory structure, the purpose of such opinions changed entirely. In the postregulatory environment, the purpose of fairness opinions is to insulate officers and directors from liability in anticipated derivative and class action litigation. This, in turn, has transformed and degraded the market for regulatory opinions.

Making Outside Audits Mandatory

Reliable information related to the financial condition and financial performance of companies is obviously of great importance to investors. Historically, companies in the capital markets have demanded the services of independent outside auditors in order to be able to signal that the financial results being reported by the company with which they are considering interacting are accurate.[54] This need to provide a credible signal of the integrity and reliability of financial statements is particularly acute in light of the strong incentives that managers have to misstate earnings and other indicia of financial performance:

> Auditors' reputations are central to the standard economic theory of auditing. Only auditors with reputations for honesty and integrity are valuable to audit-clients. The idea is that, absent a reputation for honesty and integrity, the auditor's verification function loses its value. In

theory, then, auditors invest heavily in creating and maintaining their reputations for performing honest, high quality audits. High quality audits by independent auditors who have good reputations are assured. The quality assurance is derived from the fact that performing poor-quality audits diminishes the value of the audit firm's investment in reputation.[55]

In previous work, Ted Eisenberg and I have described this as the "pre-Enron" view of the accounting industry. This model of the accounting industry, which was generally embraced by the law and economics movement,[56] predicted that accounting firms would compete in a healthy reputational "race to the top":

> There was a time that the audit function was carried out in a market environment that induced high quality financial reporting. In that era, accounting firms were willing to put their seal of approval on the financial records of a client company only if the company agreed to conform to the high standards imposed by the accounting profession. Investors trusted accountants because investors knew that any accounting firm that was sloppy or corrupt could not stay in business for long. Auditors had significant incentives to "do superior work" because "auditors with strong reputations could command a fee premium, and high fees signaled quality in the auditing market."[57]

Audit firms had incentives to provide high-quality audit services because they wanted to protect their reputation for independence and integrity.[58] As Ted Eisenberg and I observed previously, "in a world in which auditors have both invested in developing high quality reputations and in which no single client represents more than a tiny fraction of total billings, high audit quality seems assured. Under these conditions, any potential gain to an auditor from performing a shoddy audit, much less from participating in a client's fraud, would be vastly outweighed by the diminution in value to the auditor's reputation."[59]

Interestingly, even though companies can (and do) audit themselves, they can justify the expense of hiring outside auditors to enhance their financial reputation and credibility with a wide range of current and prospective claimants on their cash flows, including investors, suppliers, customers, and prospective employees. Under this reputational model, companies need independent audits to attract outside capital. The auditors performing these audits would be expected to quit an engagement before permitting a client to issue inaccurate or fraudulent financial statements. Thus, hiring a truly independent auditor under these conditions allowed companies, even companies that lacked reputations of their own to honesty and probity, to credibly signal the veracity of their reported financial results.[60]

The notion was that accounting firms that dismissed an audit client would lose only that client. But this loss would probably be more than offset, as the accounting firm would likely gain new clients by virtue of the enhancement in the reputation of the accounting firm that followed from firing the client. This theory, which I have dubbed the "law and economics 101" approach to auditing, reflects the view that, even though companies can and do impose their own financial controls and audit themselves, they hire outside auditors to capitalize on the audit firm's reputation for probity. Hiring an auditor, under this theory, allows client companies to "rent" the reputation of the accounting firm, which rents its reputation for care, honesty, and integrity to its clients. As one observer characterized the market for auditors' services: "Public accountants knew they had a lot to lose if their clients' information turned out to be false or misleading. Auditors who did a superior job would reduce the chance of their clients' issuing unreliable information and so reduce their own risk of being sued by aggrieved investors. Such suits are costly to auditors; even unsuccessful suits damage their valuable reputations."[61] Unfortunately, this reputational theory of auditors' services no longer has much, if any, explanatory power. In fact, the accounting industry is not characterized by robust competition, and investors do not trust the numbers generated by accounting firms.[62] Part of the explanation for this is that there are no detectable statistically significant distinctions among the big accounting firms with respect to quality.[63] Rather, the accounting firms all perform about the same, and there simply is no way for a company to distinguish itself for probity and honesty in its accounting standards through its selection of auditors, contrary to the assumptions of economic theory.[64]

Many explanations for the decline in audit quality have been offered.[65] Relevant to this analysis are the SEC rules that made outside audits compulsory for firms and required that such audits be carried out by auditors deemed by the SEC to be independent of management. The SEC's regulations have effectively cartelized the accounting industry by requiring that large, publicly held corporations be audited by accounting firms that obtain only a small proportion of their revenues from any one client. This, in turn, means large public companies can be audited only by very large accounting firms, which in turn has led to the massive consolidation that the accounting industry has experienced in recent decades.

The SEC's long-standing notion about what constitutes "auditor independence" has contributed significantly to the decline in the quality of the auditor-client relationship. Enron provides a useful example of the problem.

For regulatory purposes, Arthur Andersen was said to be independent of Enron because Enron accounted for less than 1 percent of Arthur Andersen's billings, but Enron appears to have accounted for all of the billings of the lead partner assigned to the Enron audit and for several members of his team. Worse, Arthur Andersen management in Chicago appears to have relied exclusively on its captured audit team not only for its information about the client, but also for how to report the financial information provided by the client. Unfortunately, although Andersen undoubtedly represented an extreme example of an auditing firm losing its internal controls, the general contours of the auditor-client relationship that characterized the Andersen and Enron scandals are quite common. The nature of this relationship suggests that investors have good reason to worry about the quality of the financial reporting provided by the national accounting firms, even when the SEC considers such firms "independent."

Thus, the role of accounting firms in capital markets and corporate governance is eerily similar to the role of credit rating agencies. What began as a subtle, reputation-based, highly efficient relationship has evolved into a relationship driven by regulatory requirements rather than genuine, market-driven demand. Specifically, while companies used to hire auditors to provide an independent, credible verification of their reported financial results, companies now hire auditors out of regulatory necessity. In both cases, rules emerged that transformed the once-voluntary relationship between companies and accountants into a compulsory relationship. Once the core purpose of the engagement with auditors became regulatory compliance rather than the provision of information for the company, the nature of the relationship changed. This shift, coupled with the auditor independence rule, which cartelized the accounting industry, and coupled with the removal of personal liability for accounting errors, had the cumulative effect, as Eisenberg and I previously observed,[66] of eliminating any quality distinctions that might once have existed among the accounting firms that audit large public companies. Absent the ability to make such quality distinctions among auditors, issuers must select auditors on the basis of other criteria, such as cost and malleability.

Making Internal Risk Modeling Mandatory

No private-sector innovation has captured the regulatory imagination more than the use by financial institutions of internal risk assessments. In the late 1980s, following the stock market crash of 1987, financial institutions— particularly the largest, most sophisticated, and complex banking and financial services firms—began to utilize state-of-the-art financial mathematics to measure and control their firms' financial risk. The methodology for doing this involves the utilization of a Value at Risk (VaR) model or similar algorithm, which measures the maximum loss that a financial company might experience under various sets of assumptions.

VaR models generate risk measures on the specific portfolios of financial assets that financial institutions have or may be considering. Starting with a particular firm's portfolio, and using various measures of probability and time horizons, a portfolio's VaR is the measure of the probability that the actual (marked-to-market rather than accounting) loss on the measured portfolio during the given time horizon will exceed a particular threshold value. Thus, for example, assigning to a particular portfolio of stocks a one-day 98.5 percent VaR of $100 million means that the financial institution assigning this VaR believes that there is a 1.5 percent chance that the portfolio will fall in value by more than $100 million over a one-day period.

Following the financial crisis of 1987, VaR models became widely used in measuring risk, in implementing financial controls, and in determining appropriate levels of capital. Stress testing is used as part of VaR calculations to measure the stability of a particular institution's balance sheet. Stress testing involves measuring the ability of a financial institution to withstand pressures in excess of normal operational levels in order to ascertain the point at which the entity will fail. Variations on the VaR modeling process such as "tail value at risk" (TVaR, also known as tail conditional expectation) permit firms to obtain measures of the severity of possible failures as well as the probability that failure will occur.

Regulators quickly incorporated VaR models into various regulatory frameworks for financial institutions. Beginning in 1997, the SEC began forcing investment banks to provide VaR information in the notes to their financial statements when they ruled that U.S. public corporations must disclose quantitative information about their derivatives activity. Major banks and dealers implemented the rule by presenting VaR models in their financial statements.[67]

Even more significantly, the Basel II capital guidelines, which would, if adopted, dictate the capital requirements for virtually every bank in the world, have adopted VaR throughout the regulations. VaR is the preferred measure of market risk. Significantly, the Basel capital guidelines permit VaR and other so-called internal ratings-based approaches to credit risk, thus permitting banks to rely on their own measures of a counter-party's risk and to determine their capital requirements using their own internal models.[68]

Under the version of the Basel II capital guidelines adopted in the United States by various federal regulators, including the Office of the Comptroller of the Currency (OCC), the Board of Governors of the Federal Reserve System (Board), the Federal Deposit Insurance Corporation (FDIC), and the (now abolished) Office of Thrift Supervision (OTS), a risk-based capital adequacy framework was adopted that requires certain banks, bank holding companies, and savings and loan associations to "use an internal ratings-based approach to calculate regulatory credit risk capital requirements and advanced measurement approaches to calculate regulatory operational risk capital requirements."[69]

Interestingly, regulators fully understand that the use of financial institutions' own internal risk assessment tools will occur in an environment in which banks' models are constantly evolving. Unfortunately, the regulators do not seem to have grasped the notion, central to the analysis in this chapter, that banks' incentives about how to utilize a market process such as an internal risk assessment tool change when it becomes incorporated into regulation.

Internal risk assessment tools are particularly subject to distortion by regulatory co-options.[70] Absent any regulatory overlay, internal risk assessment tools are useful for banks to see what sorts of potential problems they are facing. As soon as internal risk assessment tools become internalized into regulation, the consequences of using these tools change dramatically. Regulators and banks, after all, want to use internal risk assessments in order to calculate the amount of capital that banks must maintain to offset particular assets. Because capital is very expensive for firms relative to debt, once internal risk assessments become incorporated into regulation, then the use of such assessments can have significant costs for financial institutions. Banks understand that once internal risk assessments can be used to justify requiring banks to maintain more capital, they will have incentives to adjust their models, and to modify the way that their models are used, in order to mitigate the costs of using these models.

Besides the odd fact that regulators do not seem to realize that their regulations might actually have an influence on the development of banks' internal risk assessment tools, a second striking thing about the incorporation of
banks' internal risk assessment processes into the capital adequacy rules is the
amount of trust that the regulators apparently have in the banks.

The regulators understand that "a system is only as good as the inputs that
go into it."[71] As such, it also is the case that financial institutions permitted to
use their own internal risk assessments to measure risk are assumed able "to
measure the key statistical drivers of credit risk."[72] Strangely, there does not
appear to be any theoretical or statistical basis for assuming that banks can do
this, particularly in the absence of independent oversight. Moreover, there is
no generally accepted paradigm or protocol for determining which of the
myriad technical approaches to internal risk assessment represent best practices or even acceptable industry standards. Whatever banks come up with
themselves appears to be fine with the regulators. As one regulator observed,
"The Basel Committee clearly recognizes that there is more than one way to
[measure credit risk]." As such, the applicable capital rules should "provide
banks with the flexibility to rely on data derived from experience, or from
external sources, as long as the bank can demonstrate the relevance of the
external data to its own exposures."[73]

In other words, the banks get to design the very examinations that will be
used to evaluate their financial condition. The amazing thing is that regulators
are surprised by the pervasive grade inflation. Remarks on risk-based capital
by a top official of the Federal Reserve Bank of New York illustrate the extent
to which the capital guidelines relied on undeveloped and untested models
that depended on data that were not yet even available at the time.

As William Rutledge, executive vice president of the Federal Reserve Bank
of New York, observed when discussing the Basel Capital Accords:

> The Basel standards outline the data history banks will need in order
> to use the IRB approach. The [Basel] Committee recognizes that banks
> may not currently have all of the required information on hand. For
> this reason we have continued to engage market participants in a dia-
> logue on this issue.
>
> Given our desire for Basel II to be consistent with the best existing
> and *emerging* [emphasis in the original text] risk measurement and
> management practices, getting specific feedback from the industry is
> particularly critical. . . .

Time and effort has also been invested in developing richer and more meaningful data on past, and likely future, credit performance—data that are needed to fuel management information and control systems for senior management use. I expect that much of the cost to banks of adopting the advanced approaches of Basel II will come from pushing ahead on precisely these types of initiatives.[74]

In other words, as the credit crisis approached, regulators were increasingly allowing the financial world's largest financial institutions, primarily those with large market-risk positions, to use their own internal estimates of the risks associated with their activities in determining what their own capital requirements would be for regulatory purposes. This was allowed under the so-called market risk amendment to the original Basel Accord.[75]

Thus, financial institutions subject to minimum capital requirements were not merely allowed to determine for themselves whether they were in compliance with such requirements; they also were allowed to design for themselves the test that they would use for making this determination. As Partnoy observes, financial institutions used faulty VaR models due to legal rules. Regulators required firms to use and to disclose their VaR measures, but in doing so, the regulators were "inadvertently encouraging firms to misstate their own risks."[76]

Partnoy suggests that there was a problem with VaR models themselves, calling them "faulty" on the grounds that "all these models really did was compare historical measures of risk and return."[77] This observation, while true, is describing the first generation of VaR models developed in the mid- to late 1990s. The models, such as the ones used by failed firms, including Bankers Trust and Long Term Capital Management, were what were incorporated by the regulators.[78] Once these models were adopted by regulators, they became ossified. But if these models had not been incorporated into regulation, the companies using them would have had strong incentives to refine and improve them in order to make them more accurate and useful as internal evaluation mechanisms.

Regulatory assimilation distorted the incentives of the firms who developed the VaR model. The process of assimilation subverted the integrity of the very algorithms being co-opted. Unfortunately, like credit ratings, internal risk models, which were once a promising means for banks to improve their internal controls, have become largely discredited. For example, Sheila Bair, chairman of the Federal Deposit Insurance Corporation, observed that in the years preceding the financial crisis, under the advanced approaches of Basel II, regulators allowed the largest banks to use their own internal models to set individual risk-based capital requirements. Regulators permitted this on the premise that the largest banks did not need as much capital as smaller banks due to their sophisticated internal risk models and diversification. According to Bair, "the crisis demonstrated the fallacy of this thinking."[79]

Conclusion

In this chapter, the term regulation by assimilation is used to describe the process by which internal norms, rules, or practices of private firms are assimilated into regulation. The descriptive purpose of this chapter has been to point out the large role played by regulatory assimilation in the regulation of the financial markets. The normative purpose of the chapter has been to show that the very process of assimilation tends to undermine the efficacy of the very mechanisms and institutions being co-opted.

In recent decades, regulators have come to recognize the difference between mandatory and enabling rules, and in some cases, particularly in the corporate context, they have begun to consider with care the costs and benefits of making a particular legal rule mandatory or enabling.[80] At the same time, another, far less heralded, but similarly important, revolution in the regulatory approach to financial markets was taking place. This second, much quieter regulatory sea change consisted of the forced assimilation of market-based mechanisms and institutions into regulation. This chapter has examined four such assimilations. These insidious assimilations of credit ratings, fairness opinions, internal audits, and internal risk assessments into various regulations have had a corrupting influence on these mechanisms and institutions. Each of these market-generated devices has become less useful after being conscripted for use by regulators.

The diminution in the value of these market mechanisms was, in each case, an entirely unforeseen consequence of their co-option by regulators. In fact, and rather ironically, the regulators effectuating this assimilation thought that they were harnessing the efficiency of the market in the service of more effective and enlightened regulation.

The takeaway point of this chapter is not necessarily that regulators should avoid co-opting market mechanisms into regulations. Such a conclusion would be premature, because we have yet to consider whether a more enlightened regulatory approach might work. Such a regulatory approach will begin only when regulators recognize the fact that their efforts to co-opt market institutions into various regulatory frameworks risk distorting the very market processes that they wish to internalize into regulation. Though far from certain, it is at least conceivable that more carefully designed regulations that were sensitive to the risks of distorting the very market mechanisms being assimilated might avoid the problems identified in this chapter.

Chapter 13

Multinational Corporations as Regulators and Central Planners

Implications for Citizens' Voice

Katharina Pistor

Multinational corporations (MNCs) have been in the literature on business organizations and governance at least since the 1970s. Their size and economic power have raised questions about how best to govern these entities. While not fundamentally different from the governance issues that afflict domestic corporations, including but not limited to corporate governance, antitrust, and compliance with labor and consumer protection regulation, the fact that there is no unified political structure with the appropriate legal and regulatory instruments to control transnationally operative MNCs creates a governance vacuum.[1] Those who trust the forces of the marketplace view such concerns as vastly overstated. Given the scale of global markets, even large corporations rarely raise serious antitrust concerns, for example. Moreover, by pitching different national regulators against one another, MNCs might instill regulatory competition and thereby contribute to the selection of more efficient regulation.[2] In contrast, those less sanguine about the competitiveness of global markets or their impact on the governance of firms have sought new forms for holding MNCs accountable. The United Nations' Global Compact, a voluntary governance regime that commits MNCs to basic principles of human rights, labor, and environmental protection, is an example for using soft law to enhance the governance over MNCs.[3]

In this contribution I take a different perspective and treat MNCs not as the object, but as the subject of governance. Based on insights from the literature on transnational private regulation (TPR),[4] I suggest that MNCs themselves have become regulators. At some level every firm is a regulator of its internal affairs. Well beyond the organizational structures imposed on them by corporate law, firms develop monitoring and supervisory structures to ensure internal compliance with set standards. MNCs do that too, but their internal governance structure straddles multiple jurisdictions. As a result, MNCs become by default arbitrageurs of multiple legal and regulatory regimes in which their branches, subsidiaries, contractors, and suppliers operate. Moreover, they transmit and enforce regulatory standards from markets where they intend to sell their end products to the markets where their producers and suppliers are located along global production chains. MNCs may not have the power of coercion associated with nation-states,[5] but they have the power of exclusion: firms unwilling or incapable of complying with their standard will not be able to join their global supply and distribution networks.

MNCs are not only regulators; they are also central planners. Central planning has received a bad taste in light of the fate of former socialist economies. Yet, economists have long conceded that the very existence of firms suggests the need for organizational forms beyond the marketplace.[6] Standard economic theory suggests that when transaction costs are high or when parties make highly specific investment into joint production, vertical integration—that is, some level of central control of economic decision making—may be superior to the idealized arm's-length contracting.[7]

In the case of MNCs, central planning frequently goes well beyond the need to minimize transaction costs or avoid holdup problems that result from specific investments when control rights are shared.[8] Rather, MNCs use central planning to maximize returns for the parent. Foreign branches and subsidiaries are vehicles to achieve these ends, but are not utility maximizers in their own right. This works, because parent companies are shielded from the costs of subsidiary failure by limited liability.

Regulation and central planning are complementary means for advancing the interests of the MNC's core operations in a world of multiple legal orders that create costs while also offering opportunities for new actors able to exploit them. The costs arise from the need to comply with multiple sets of mandatory rules, where applicable. The opportunities stem from the ability of MNCs to arbitrage around rules, play regulators off against one another, and devise their own regulatory models beyond the reach of individual nation-states. To a large extent, realizing these opportunities is made possible by national legal systems. National legal systems lend enforcement authority to the contracts by which MNCs enforce regulatory standards. They endorse private regulation as "industry practices" or the specification of standards set by national law. In addition, they accommodate MNCs in devising specific rules and regulations in ways that are compatible with the MNCs' own standards—whether financial contracts or pollution standards for international transport and import companies. Moreover, by protecting the corporate shield, they support MNCs' central planning strategies, even if they come at the expense of other stakeholders in markets where foreign subsidiaries operate and their collapse may create substantial local costs. Viewed in this light, states are the handmaidens for the rise of MNCs as regulators and central planners.

The key question is where this leaves the citizens of countries around the globe where MNCs operate or where their impact is felt. They enter the picture mostly as consumers of products manufactured in global production chains or as the beneficiaries of regulations that ensure their safety or environmental soundness. Sometimes they also enter the picture as employees of companies that have become part of global production chains or plaintiffs in disputes that seek remedies for environmental or other damages they have caused. But they rarely enter the picture as citizens—that is, as political principals with preferences for different policies. Given that MNCs operate across multiple political systems, yet the rights of citizens are tied to territorially bounded nation-states, regulatory leverage of these polities over MNCs is increasingly limited.

As a possible response to this governance vacuum, I will invoke the concept of "regulatory capabilities."[9] It offers a normative framework for assessing the ability of all stakeholders in a given regulatory regime to contest or exit from it. At its core the regulatory capabilities approach suggests that the decentering of political power in today's globalized world may not be reversible and that, therefore, new approaches for creating a public space need to be created.

MNCs as Regulators

For more general theorists of firms and organizations, it comes as no surprise that MNCs govern their own internal affairs. As independent legal entities

they have the power to self-regulate, subject to mandatory constraints enshrined in the national legal systems that govern the corporate law under
which they incorporate; the contract law they use to govern their relations
with customers, suppliers, and creditors; the labor law that governs their employment relations; the environmental law that restricts their ability to exter-
nalize the costs of their production; or consumer protection regulations aimed
at minimizing the risks they impose on others. To be sure, all this could not
be taken for granted only two hundred years ago, when no legal system allowed for the free incorporation of just any business but required special approval on a case-by-case basis.[10]

The role of MNCs as regulators, however, goes well beyond internal governance. Regulation entails making rules with intentional third-party effect.
In areas where no national rules impose binding constraints, MNCs effectively have the prerogative to set rules, and they frequently use standardized
contracts to do so. Most legal systems endorse the autonomy of private parties
to design contracts as they wish, subject only to "public order," "duress," or
"good faith" constraints. Standard contracts are common not only for MNCs.
The critical point is that in the transnational space, standard contracts are the
mechanisms by which safety and quality standards are being established or
transmitted to producers and suppliers in different jurisdictions. These contractual devices are of great importance, especially in decentered multinational conglomerates. Over the past thirty years the vertically integrated
Fordist corporation has increasingly given way to global production chains
that rely less on equity (shareholder) ties and more on networks held together
by contracts.[11] Moreover, MNCs have outsourced production to many companies that are neither branches nor subsidiaries and govern these relations
by contracts.

In theory, contracts are negotiable for both parties. This distinguishes
them from regulation, which is set by one and binding on many. Bargain
power, however, varies substantially along global supply chains. Many small
producers that face a single buyer have little bargaining power. They also
rarely contribute highly specific input, which might increase their bargaining
power. Buyers have learned to diversify and source even specific inputs from
multiple suppliers and at times pitch them against one another.[12] Contracts
are also the predominant device for determining labor standards, subject to
two qualifications. First, employment contracts are frequently subject to state
regulation that establishes safety standards or imposes restrictions on the termination of labor relations, especially for long-term employees. And second,

firm-level labor standards are sometimes supplemented with monitoring schemes that involve third parties, such as nongovernmental organizations (NGOs) or labor unions.[13] This is more likely the case in MNCs with major brand names that have come under attack by NGOs or labor unions, or that seek partnerships with local stakeholders in an attempt to preempt such scrutiny.

State law or third-party monitoring does not reduce the need for contracting or internal monitoring mechanisms. Laws frequently serve as a focal point for firms for regulatory arbitrage to cut costs and thereby enhance their competitiveness. International diversification strategies are also a commonly used device for sidestepping national labor standards. MNCs have outsourced production to countries with low labor costs; they have used the lower standards and ineffective enforcement of foreign legal systems to maximize the flexibility of labor relations. The use of independently owned and operated firms as major production sites for goods they market globally is one such strategy. Another is to source directly from small producers, which feature as self-employed and therefore tend to escape labor law scrutiny.[14] In other cases, firms have reverted to temporary work arrangements.[15] Temporary workers typically do not get the same protection as long-term employees. The way to combine labor market flexibility and reliability of the workforce is to employ intermediaries who maintain long-term relations with well-qualified employees and refer them to firms.

While the above examples may suggest that companies can employ contracts with impunity to circumvent the constraints of mandatory labor laws, some have discovered that reputation effects place a limit on these practices. An example is Nike, which was successfully sued in California for anticompetitive conduct after it misrepresented labor practices in ads and public statements.[16] The firm had outsourced production to multiple sites in East Asia and had ignored the lack of minimum labor standards afforded to employees of its subcontractors. In an attempt to limit the damages to the brand name and improve its image, Nike developed its own labor standards and used a company-wide monitoring system to supervise compliance. The data the company had collected were analyzed by a group of researchers at MIT, who found that implementation of labor standards varied widely. Interestingly, there was a close affinity between compliance and the overall level of the rule of law in the country where the monitored firm was located.[17] This may suggest that the efficacy of MNCs as regulators is limited. Yet, the researchers also found that if and when efforts were made to tackle the root causes for poor working conditions, improvements could be made even in contexts where rule of law was weak.[18]

The means by which Nike imposes labor standards on subcontractors and ensures that monitors have access to their sites is through contracting. Contracts are also used to ensure compliance with product quality and safety standards, including state-imposed safety standards. Take the example of food safety standards set by regulators in importing countries, such as the United States. All goods, including foreign-grown or produced food, must meet these standards. The standards are often higher than local standards in producing countries. Importing firms must ensure compliance at production sites to ensure that they can sell the products to the destination market.

MNC parent companies monitor compliance and sanction noncompliance with remedies available for breach of contract, such as rescission and compensation. The contractual mechanisms are only part of a much more complex scheme for monitoring and implementing what are essentially foreign regulatory standards in the local settings of exporting countries. Government agencies and multilateral organizations frequently get involved to ensure that at least some producers can meet the requisite standards and thus participate in global production chains. They have developed tool kits for firms and entrepreneurs on how to meet "best practice" (read foreign) standards for different product categories. Ratcheting up product quality and labor standards has thus become an important aspect of transnational industrial policy.

Government agencies also get involved when things go wrong in order to protect local stakeholders, whether suppliers or consumers. In 2008, for example, the United States experienced a salmonella scare linked to imported jalapeños and tomatoes from Mexico.[19] Government regulators and diplomats from both countries intervened in what at first glance looks like a simple breach-of-contract case: Mexican farmers may have delivered "defective" products, or their importers may have failed to accept produce of the negotiated quality. The economic stakes on both sides were high. In Mexico, farmers were threatened with losses estimated between U.S.$100 million and $500 million, as they could not sell perishable produce to the United States, even though no proof had been offered that Mexican tomatoes or peppers were indeed responsible for the salmonella outbreak. U.S. importers were also confronting losses, although they were more diversified than the producers; in the United States regulators feared that food imports were contaminated. As a Mexican government official put it in a conference meeting, the negotiations had the flavor of pre-NAFTA (North American Free Trade Agreement) protectionism.[20] The United States began putting in place a system that would outsource Food and Drug Administration (FDA) monitoring to accredited private parties.[21] It remains to be seen what role MNCs will play in this new device.

Even in the absence of a delegated monitoring role, it is clear that MNCs have become critical standards setters and standard transmitters in global production chains. Local producers often have little choice but to comply or perish. Indeed, there is some evidence that larger firms that can afford the costs associated with compliance have crowded out small peasants who flock to the cities or across the borders in search of work. Thus, indirectly, MNCs also contribute to the restructuring of industries in exporting countries. Clearly, they themselves are subject to external pressures—regulatory standards in the importing countries, and market pressures for quality standards even in unregulated industries. The major point is that MNCs have increasingly assumed a role as regulators of their suppliers and producers. The latter have little choice but to tailor their production to the demands of MNCs. The MNCs' regulatory role is certainly to their own economic advantage. It enhances their bargaining powers and allows them greater scrutiny of the internal affairs of independent suppliers than they might otherwise have. They are also free to choose the means for regulatory standards that are most cost effective on their end.

In short, where MNCs exercise regulatory power, isomorphism[22] is most likely to occur around the regulatory standards they set. It makes little sense for local governments to deviate from these standards—at least with respect to products geared toward export markets. While one might argue that this will ultimately benefit local consumers as well, as their product quality will be ratcheted up to meet global standards, there are downsides to this strategy. Most important, it squeezes out smaller entities that cannot on their own meet the requisite standards. In fact, the same regulatory goals can often be met by different regulatory means, and not all might impose the same costs on producers. Moreover, they turn local governments into agents of global standard setters—both public and private. Local governments are less likely to invest in alternative regulatory approaches if confronted with the need to comply with what may be one of only a few major investors in their jurisdiction. More generally, the global division of the regulatory space gives entities that serve major consumer markets a comparative advantage in determining the shape and contents of that space. This raises profound questions of participation and democracy—issues addressed in greater detail below.

MNCs as Central Planners

MNCs not only set rules for themselves and others; they also engage in central planning. Management, or planning, distinguishes firms from the market-place according to standard economic theory. When Ronald Coase first formulated the question "why do firms exist?"[23] the most common answer was that hierarchy is needed to decide how best to allocate resources when leaving these decisions to markets is too costly.[24] While the theory has been disputed and alternative theories about why firms exist, including incomplete contract theory,[25] have been advanced, there is little dispute that inside firms, decisions are made in a fashion that is more akin to planning than to spot markets. MNCs have raised this principle to new heights as they have created transnational *internal* allocation systems for supplies and capital and the management of human capital. The literature often refers to these allocation systems as internal markets. But it should be remembered that access to these "markets" is limited to members of the MNC and that supply and demand are not determined exclusively or even primarily by the price mechanism. The size of these internal allocation systems is remarkable. It is estimated that intra-firm trade accounts for roughly 25 percent of all transnational trade; in the United States the share is estimated to be as high as 46 percent.[26] There is substantial variation across countries and products. Moreover, the estimates may be at the low end given that many independently operated firms are in fact part of international production chains.

These internal allocation systems are used for all kinds of inputs, including capital. There is, for example, a growing literature on debt shifting within MNCs. Tax arbitrage is an important motive for shifting debt among different entities that compose a multinational firm. Debt is shifted to subsidiaries that can get the best tax benefits, and the returns are shared at the group level.[27] Apparently, the scale of debt and profit shifting is much larger than can be explained by different tax treatment of debt alone. Another explanation for intra-firm movements of capital is that multinationals often support affiliates in their quest to raise debt finance by offering guarantees.[28] As a result, a parent firm and its affiliates become financially interdependent. If the parent guarantees the debt of its subsidiary, it has a vital interest that the subsidiary will be able to repay its debt. As a result, temporary cross-subsidization becomes more likely.

This trend is particularly pronounced in the banking sector. With the liberalization of financial markets, banking has become a global business.

Extensive privatization programs in Central, East, and South East Europe (CESEE) and Latin America in particular have resulted in extensive foreign ownership of domestic banks.[29] Prior to the global crisis the share of foreign bank ownership in CESEE ranged from a low of 36 percent in Slovenia to a high of 98 percent in Estonia.[30] In Latin America, foreign ownership was on average 43 percent.[31] During the global crisis, a number of banks sought to reduce their exposure to emerging markets in order to focus on their home economies.[32] Selling domestic banks to foreign investors helped raise capital to comply with capital adequacy standards that CESEE countries had to comply with when they joined the European Union (EU).[33] It also brought the promise of additional capital and the transfer of expertise. The belief at the time was that the acquisition of foreign subsidiaries was more akin to foreign direct investments than to portfolio capital flows. It was supposed to be more "sticky" and ensure that foreign banks would have a sufficiently long time horizon and not expose emerging markets to the types of risks typically associated with portfolio capital flows. This had come into disrepute in the Asian financial crisis of 1997/98, when the investors abandoned the region at the first signs of an economic downturn that had been triggered by unsustainable inflows of capital.[34]

The global financial crisis that started in 2007, however, demonstrated once more that "looks can be deceiving."[35] The stickiness and sustainability of foreign bank ownership and the capital flows associated with it depended largely on a peculiar form of funding them. Multinational groups sourced their funds for expanding in emerging markets primarily from international lending markets. Indeed, recent evidence suggests that, as a result, domestic subsidiaries of foreign parent banks cut back lending more significantly than did domestic entities that had sources of internal funding.[36] They thereby exposed emerging markets to the volatilities of international lending markets, which made them more akin to portfolio capital. Once international lending markets dried up, multinational banks faced liquidity problems and began to cut back and eventually withdraw capital from the periphery.

Countries in CEESE had to find out during the crisis that the rate of credit expansion in their countries, which peaked around 70 percent per annum in Bulgaria in the years leading up to the crisis,[37] had been fueled by the global credit boom. When international credit markets dried up, credit expansion came to a "sudden stop,"[38] and parent banks in neighboring countries sought to withdraw capital to protect the core of the banking group. CEESE countries threatened to ring-fence assets, and some imposed restrictions on capital out-

flows by preventing parents from repatriating dividends.[39] Only the intervention of several multilateral organizations spearheaded by the European Bank
for Reconstruction and Development (EBRD) prevented a disorderly withdrawal of capital.[40]

Viewed from the perspective of financial MNCs, the strategy they employed made perfect sense. Operating simultaneously in multiple markets
allows an MNC to exploit differences in interest rates and yields in funding
markets and investment markets, to source in one market and supply credit
in another, and to profit from the difference. When the strategy lost its appeal,
because interest rates in interbank lending markets skyrocketed—as happened after the collapse of Lehmann Brothers—the same logic forced MNCs
to contract: to cut their losses in the periphery and focus on the core. There is
little doubt that emerging markets benefited from this practice in the upturn,
as they experienced a substantial expansion in credit that helped fuel growth.[41]
Moreover, there is some evidence that in the first year of the crisis, countries
in CEESE with substantial foreign bank penetration benefited from capital
transfers by the parent banks. De Haas and colleagues attribute this to the
existence of internal financial markets within MNCs.[42] However, they do not
explore whether the same market can also be held responsible for an unsustainable credit expansion strategy. Neither do they discuss the conditions that
made cross-subsidization possible in the early stages of the crisis. Multinational banks benefited from measures taken by central banks around the
world to ensure financial markets remained liquid. The U.S. Federal Reserve
(the "Fed"), in particular, created numerous new funding facilities to allow
financial intermediaries to make up for the collapse of private markets.[43] This
included, among others, the Term Auction Facility that offered liquidity to
banks that had previously relied on asset-backed commercial paper markets
to manage short-term liquidity needs. However, these measures have not succeeded in stemming a reversal of capital flows to the region, as De Haas and
Van Lelyveld report in a 2012 paper.[44]

The above examples of debt and capital shifting suggest that the management of internal capital flows by MNCs is more akin to central planning than
to an ideal market. Indeed, it shares with socialist-style central planning one
key attribute—namely, the soft budget constraint. Janos Kornai has coined
this term and argued that it lies at the heart of the malfunctioning of the socialist system.[45] The basic argument is that the superior performance of the
capitalist system stems from the fact that firms face a hard budget constraint—
that is, they face the prospect of liquidation if they fail. They therefore have

the correct incentives for making efficient investment decisions. In contrast, in the socialist system, nonviable firms were constantly cross-subsidized, thereby undermining incentives throughout the system for firms to improve their performance. The logic of the central planning system required that efficiency considerations at individual firms were subordinated to the preservation of the overall system.

Financial MNCs follow a similar logic—to a point. Internally they operate according to the same logic as centrally planned economies by shifting capital to different entities to ensure welfare maximization at the group level. This may or may not imply profit maximization at the level of all subsidiaries. As it happened, in CEESE local subsidiaries benefited as long as the credit boom lasted, but suffered in the crisis. Local subsidiaries paid back profits to the foreign parent in the form of dividends. This meant that they lacked a cushion to protect themselves from the downturn when the crisis struck. Moreover, the rapid pace of credit expansion exceeded the ability of domestic fiscal authorities to bail out their banks, triggering a sovereign debt crisis when they tried nonetheless, or placing the countries ultimately at the mercy of the International Monetary Fund (IMF) and other multilateral lenders.[46] The major difference between centrally planned economies and financial MNCs is that the former lacked a final backstop when the system had run its course and could no longer sustain itself. It thus collapsed. In contrast, financial MNCs have found various backstops, at least for now. During the early stages of the crisis, Sovereign Wealth Funds stepped up to shore up the capital of major multinational banks.[47] When this proved insufficient, central banks in their home countries came to their rescue. In doing so they extended the soft budget constraint to the core operations of financial MNCs.[48]

Rethinking the Relation Between MNCs and Citizens

I have argued that MNCs are not simply the sites of production, or strategic or financial investors. They are also regulators and central planners. As such, they exert substantial power over people around the globe. This does not mean that states have disappeared or will any time soon. In fact, states have been instrumental in creating the preconditions for MNCs to evolve into transnational regulators and central planners. States have streamlined laws and regulations and thereby reduced the costs for multinationals to do business across state lines. They have facilitated legal arbitrage by allowing corporations to choose where to incorporate yet maintain operations on their territory. States also enforce contracts that MNCs use to govern their internal affairs. Last but not least, states have devolved regulatory and monitoring authorities to MNCs.

The rise of MNCs as private regulators and central planners poses new challenges to the relation between governors and the governed—between MNCs and citizens. In state-centered systems, it is assumed (even if not always the case) that governments operate as mediators between the interests of business and citizens, to set regulatory priorities and use their coercive powers to enforce the laws where voluntary compliance is lacking. In the more decentered systems that characterize the transnational space, many actors beyond the nation-state set policies, regulate, and plan specific regulatory domains in ways that affect many others.[49] Yet, those affected do not necessarily have a voice in the organizations or the regulatory domains they occupy, and not all have effective exit options.

A possible response to the rise of private regulation and the role MNCs play in its making and enforcement is to place states once more at the center of regulation, governance, and planning. Another is to ratchet up regulation from the state to the global level and create global regulators in key areas where MNCs produce negative externalities on many, such as pollution, finance, or nuclear energy.[50] The first option would mean a retreat from open trade and capital flows; the second would add a new layer of bureaucratic governance, the efficacy and equity of which is quite uncertain. The world is sufficiently heterogeneous to doubt that a central regulator would be able to find solutions deemed legitimate in the eyes of all affected by them or would be endowed with sufficient resources to implement such solutions in the absence of voluntary compliance.

It may well be that for some regulatory issues a consensus will evolve over time or for which a return to state governance or a move toward vertical integration at the global level is optimal. Yet, for many areas neither solution is attractive or feasible. This has prompted some to suggest that we are confronting a globalization trilemma.[51] It says that we need to choose between deep global integration, national sovereignty, and democracy, because we cannot have all three: deep integration undermines sovereignty and democratic governance, and sovereignty is at odds with deep integration though compatible with democracy. Critically, the trilemma is based on the assumption that nation-states are the primary source of transaction costs: their legal systems, customary rules, and policies create barriers to deep integration. It also assumes that nation-states are the only space where the common people can express their preferences.

The trilemma proposition stands or falls with the validity of the assumptions made. As we have seen, private actors are involved in making regulatory structures that are quite impenetrable to parties that are not members of the same organization or network. They are not only regulated, but also regulators. Moreover, state-made laws and regulations are not only the source of transaction costs, but are market *constituting*. States have promoted negative integration by breaking down borders and entry barriers to trades, guilds, and local markets.[52] They have helped construct transnational markets by making their courts available for enforcing foreign and international arbitral awards (though not necessarily court verdicts), harmonized regulatory standards or negotiated mutual recognition, and created international instruments to facilitate the enforcement of investor rights in the form of bilateral investment treaties. Last but not least, while democratic nation-states have so far provided the most comprehensive form of governance by the people, it is not inconceivable that the public space can be configured differently and give effective voice to people vis-à-vis transnational "power wielders."[53]

Indeed, the process of globalization has gone hand in hand not only with the rise of MNCs and their ascendency to important regulatory roles. We have also witnessed the proliferation of NGOs and—supported by new information technologies—transnational social networks on issues such as climate change or the governance of global finance.[54] National elections that give politicians a broad political mandate are not the only and not necessarily the most effective way in which citizens of the world can express their policy preferences. They can join organizations with global reach to advance specific causes, whether human rights, the environment, or other causes. And they can use these organizations to mobilize resources and launch campaigns against businesses or governments, including media campaigns or boycotts. Clearly, not all issues are amenable to such measures. Some causes are more likely to call attention and mobilize people than others. Some stakeholders may be too dispersed to generate much influence, or their cause may lack traction among a broader audience. These drawbacks notwithstanding, it should be clear that self-governance takes place not only within nation-states but also within organizations and in the transnational space, at least in areas where different entities compete for influence.

Thus, it is at least as plausible to characterize the process of global integration as a contest for regulation among different collective actors (states,

MNCs, and NGOs) as it is to presume that the global marketplace is an open, unstructured place for economic agents that engage in arm's-length transaction driven only by price signals. If we adopt the former perspective, the critical question is not so much which of the three policy parameters in the policy trilemma—deep integration, sovereignty, and democracy—we need to give up, but how to ensure that each is realized in an overall welfare-enhancing fashion. This requires a normative framework for incorporating democratic values in the governance of the transnational space that lacks a demos.[55]

In joint work with Fabrizio Cafaggi, we have developed the notion of regulatory capabilities to move the debate in this direction.[56] The concept is inspired by the work of Amartya Sen and Martha Nussbaum on individual capabilities,[57] and both Sen's as well as Susan Sturm's extension of these ideas to institutions and organizations.[58] Regulatory capability refers to the capacity and ability of institutions, organizations, and communities to regulate affairs of relevance to them and their citizens or stakeholders. A public, private, or nongovernmental entity possesses regulatory capabilities if it has both the option and capacity to make self-determinative regulatory choices. The basic premise is that it is normatively desirable for individuals and entities to regulate, not only to be regulated. The logic of this principle is that every regulator needs to respect the desire of others to regulate as well. Regulatory regimes that are imposed without contestation and grant neither voice nor exit do not live up to the standard of regulatory capabilities.[59]

Regulatory capability is an attribute of a collective rather than of a single individual; yet, it depends on and can help advance individual capabilities. Several of the individual capabilities Nussbaum has identified—the capabilities to associate with others, engage in practical reasoning, and control one's own life—are preconditions for the ability of individuals to become citizens of institutions and advance their regulatory capabilities through them. Conversely, as Sturm has emphasized, citizenship in institutions or organizations, including schools, universities, unions, or firms, is critical for advancing individual capabilities.[60] These institutions in turn are members or citizens of larger entities, such as cities, states, transnational networks, or associations. Entities that help advance individual capabilities internally may also project similar values in their interaction with other entities. In short, individual and regulatory capabilities mutually reinforce each other.

This sounds more utopian than it is in practice. Take the example of fair trade. Transnational corporations that use their bargaining power to unilaterally impose their preferred standards on small producers undermine their regulatory and individual capabilities. In response, NGOs have emerged that promote principles of fair trade and have developed certification programs. In doing so, they have effectively created a new regulatory domain aimed at enhancing the capabilities of small producers as well as consumers of these products. This is not to say that there are no conflicts of interests between producers and consumers, or that the self-interests of NGOs (that is, in protecting their own trademark) may not at times trump the interests of the constituencies they purport to advance. But it suggests that monopolizing narrowly defined regulatory domains without "other-regarding" preferences may not be a sustainable business strategy in all sectors. It is less effective in sectors in which consumer awareness is high and can be mobilized as a countervailing force. It appears to be least effective in areas such as finance, where the industry has successfully managed to protect itself by the sheer complexity and opaqueness of its undertakings, which has become difficult to penetrate for public regulators and nongovernmental organizations alike.

Bringing voice and principles of self-governance into the transnational space thus requires more than a single strategy. Any strategy must be able to adapt to the regulatory issue at hand, the strategy pursued by those seeking to monopolize a regulatory space, and their vulnerability to media, or consumer pressure. Where these avenues are not available, mobilizing governments or international organizations may be an alternative strategy.

Concluding Comments

In conclusion, MNCs should be analyzed not only as sites of production or promoters of investments, but also as regulators and central planners. The domains they regulate and plan at first sight appear to be more narrowly construed than that of nation-states. As sovereigns, nation-states have assumed general jurisdiction over all matters of social, economic, and political life bounded only by territorial limits on their jurisdiction. In contrast, MNCs are in principle confined to their line of business, but they may pursue more than one. They may also run their own foundation, support political parties, finance elections at home and overseas, set up or support NGOs, and thereby seek to influence competing regulatory agents or occupy other regulatory domains. As corporate entities, MNCs are rooted in national legal systems—which endow them with the privilege of legal personhood and limited liability—but they transcend the territorial boundaries of nation-states. In-

deed, they can swap identity to take advantage of differences in national leg-
islations and choose among different business forms to evade overtly
restrictive rules. Their capital often exceeds that of nation-states, and their
impact on the lives of not only their employees and suppliers, but also on
communities, polities, and environmental sustainability, can be considerable.
Importantly, existing states have enabled MNCs (along with domestic firms)
to exercise such powers with only few accountability strings attached. Tort
victims in particular have a hard time extracting remedies from MNCs. Limited liability rules allow MNCs to structure their business so that they can spin
off into bankruptcy subsidiaries saddled with excessive liabilities.[61] States have
also created liability ceilings for critical sectors, such as nuclear energy, and in
finance have frequently bailed out systemically important firms.[62] Further, tort
actions typically need to be pursued in the jurisdiction where the damages
were inflicted and are amenable to arbitration only if the other party agrees,
which an alleged tort perpetrator is unlikely to do. This makes it much harder
for tort victims to enforce claims internationally, as foreign court rulings don't
travel as easily as do foreign arbitral awards.[63]

MNCs are also important central planners. While we like to think of
global markets as an open space in which economic actors freely compete
based on the price mechanism, in reality we find that a substantial part of all
transnational commerce takes place within multinational firms. Inside firms'
resources are allocated by means that only remotely resemble open markets,
notwithstanding the widely used language of "internal markets"—a contradiction in terms. The fact that firms resort to internal markets is often depicted as a response to weak institutions or state interference. But it can just
as plausibly be explained as a deliberate choice by economic agents to enhance
certainty in an inherently uncertain world.[64] Planning may benefit the MNC;
it also imposes costs. Subsidiaries may be turned into vehicles that maximize
the interests of the parent, not their own, with likely negative repercussions in
their home market. Last but not least, planning can channel externalities to
places and constituencies that are least able to protect themselves against
them.

Importantly, MNCs are not the only regulators in the transnational realm.
Nation-states have sought to expand their jurisdiction extraterritorially as a
response to globalization, especially in areas such as antitrust or finance.
Transnational NGOs have taken up various public causes and have contested
MNCs' regulatory strategies in labor, environmental, and human rights do-
mains. Just like MNCs, NGOs have also learned how to manipulate the state's

legal system to pursue their goals. NGOs have taken MNCs to courts for anticompetitive conduct or tort actions. They have mobilized international organizations, such as the United Nations, to create "soft" governance regimes for MNCs in the form of the Global Compact.[65] In addition, they use the media, social networking, and other nonlegal means to give voice to other constituencies in the global realm.

Whether this will be sufficient to ensure that MNCs will increasingly incorporate other-regarding preferences[66] into their business strategies remains to be seen. The major point is that upon closer scrutiny the policy trilemma of globalization may be less binding than it appears at first sight. Resolving it requires a new perspective on MNCs not only as agents of economic integration, but also as agents of regulation and planning. The major challenge is to find new forms to contest their regulatory powers in ways that protect the quest for self-determination by those that MNCs purport to regulate.

Chapter 14

Ethnicity, Inc.

On the Affective Economy of Belonging

Jean Comaroff and John Comaroff

Prologue: Toward the Ethno-future

In October 2000, *Business Day*, a leading South African newspaper, published an extraordinary story. Its title read: "Traditional Leaders Form Private Firm for Investment."[1] Contralesa, the Congress of Traditional Leaders, is the voice of ethnicity in this post-colony. It speaks for culture, customary law, and the collective rights of indigenous peoples. Also for the authority of chiefs who, as a power bloc, seek to change the national constitution. Their objective is a nation-state that accords them sovereign autonomy over their realms, a nation-state that puts the dictates of indigeneity before the universal rights of citizens.

According to *Business Day*, Contralesa had decided to move ethnicity into the global marketplace: it was creating a corporation to invest in mining, forestry, industry, and tourism, that archetypical site for the commodification of culture. Said Patekile Holomisa, powerful Xhosa head of the organization, "We have concentrated for too long on the political fight for constitutional recognition." The time had come to empower their peoples by venturing out from their traditional capitals into the realm of venture capital. Since then, Contralesa has become a truly cosmopolitan concern, a multimillion dollar business with interests carefully diversified across the planetary economy.

Could it be, pace all social science orthodoxy, that the future of ethnicity—

or, at least, *a* future—lies, metaphorically and materially, in ethno-futures? In taking identity into the marketplace? In hitching it to the world of franchising and finance capital? Leruo Molotlegi, king of the Bafokeng,[2] a wealthy South African chiefdom, intimated as much in an address on "corporate ethnicity" at a leading American university. The Wealth of Ethno-Nations is a topic about which he knows a lot. His people are famed throughout Africa for their lucrative platinum holdings. In 2000, soon after he succeeded to his throne, Leruo was pictured on the cover of *Mining Weekly* under the caption "Meet the New CEO of Bafokeng Inc."[3]

Cut away to another time, another optic, another part of South Africa.

In 1994, in the North West Province, there appeared an op-ed piece in *The Mail*, the local weekly, by one Tswagare Namane. "Our futures," he predicted, are going to rely increasingly on tourism. To attract it, however, demands not just hotels or game parks. It requires "uncovering," and marketing, "what is authentically Tswana."[4] Recourse to the cargo of cultural tourism, as we all know, has become a global panacea, an autonomic reflex almost, for those with no work and little to sell; this despite the fact that it seldom yields what it promises. But Namane had in mind something more than simply the tourist dollar. The commercialization of identity, he argued—pace Frankfurt School orthodoxy—does *not* necessarily reduce it to a brute commodity. *Per contra*: marketing what is "authentically Tswana" is also a mode of self-construction, of *producing* Tswana-ness. And an assertion, thereby, of political subjectivity and universal being-in-the-world. "I have searched for something genuinely mine; something I can cherish as the achievement of my forebears, something to affirm my humanity and my equality," he wrote. This restless urge, he added, is most acutely felt by persons dispossessed of their past. Note the choice of term: "dispossession." It connotes property, propriety, prosperity, paradise lost. "What I am reclaiming," he insisted, "is my ethnicity, my heritage; not my 'ethnicism.'" The distinction, a striking piece of vernacular anthropology, is critical. *Ethnicity* refers here to membership in a population with distinctive ways and means; *ethnicism,* to the tribal allegiances "propagat[ed by] apartheid." Heritage, of course, is culture projected into the past, and, simultaneously, the past rendered into culture. It is identity in alienable form: identity whose objects and objectifications may be consumed by others and, therefore, delivered to the market. Its alienation, as Namane saw, has the curious capacity to confer upon ethnicity a currency at once moral, political, material, and affective. Even more—and here is the irony—in solidifying the stuff of difference, of locality and indigeneity, the circulation of that currency also holds out the promise of universal recognition: of entry into what, from the perspective of the parochial, is a global cosmopolis. To have culture is to be human—in an age in which "humanity" is *the* key trope of species being. If they have nothing *dis*tinctive to alienate, many rural black South Africans have come to believe, they face collective *ex*tinction. As a Tswana elder once said to us, "If we have nothing [of ourselves] to sell . . . does it mean that we *have* no culture? No presence in the world?"

To be sure, the sale of culture seems, in significant part, to have replaced the sale of labor in the Brave Neo South Africa, whose industrial economy, founded on racial capitalism, is currently under reconstruction. A new breed of consultancy firm, like African Equations, has arisen to advise communities on how best to market themselves and their cultural products.[5] There is a growing demand for their services. Ethno-businesses are opening up all over. Like Funjwa Holdings, established by the Mabaso Tribal Authority in KwaZulu-Natal and funded by a major bank, to "reap the sweets and cakes of free enterprise."[6] Seeking to draw "thousands of international visitors each year," the "Mabaso people" have invested in a wildlife park offering such "authentic" African activities as bow-hunting—which, being Zulu, they never did.[7] By these means they hope to find "empowerment." Mark this term. It has little to do with power or politics. What it connotes is access to markets and material benefits. Among ethnic groups, it is frankly associated with finding something essentially their own, something of their essence, to sell. In other words, a brand.

This, patently, is not just true of South Africa, or Africa, or that part of the World formerly known as Third. It is as true in the United States, where, as Marilyn Halter points out in *The Marketing of Ethnicity,* there is a large "industry [to remind] hyphenated Americans of how valuable heritage is *no matter how remote or forgotten it may be*" (our italics).[8] According to brandchannel.com, this has "spawned an array" of culture-conjurers, a.k.a. "ethnic marketing experts," whose commerce—referred to as the "ethnic industry," in an unwitting parody of Adorno—yields $2 billion a year. Even in Britain, long known for its indifference to difference, that industry is growing quickly. The English and Celtic "heritage" business is expanding in direct proportion to the decomposition of *Great* Britain as national imagining. Scotland the Brave has, literally, become Scotland the Brand.[9]

The juxtaposition of branding, marketing, culture, and identity—what Namane pointed to in seeking something "authentically Tswana" to sell—

finds echoes in recent scholarly discourse. Thus Martin Chanock suggests
that, in our age, in which "fantasies work where reality fails," advertising technologies, those neoliberal weapons of mass instruction, replicate the production and alienation of culture.[10] In particular, he says, the process of
branding—of creating an attachment to a commodity, to both its *object*-form
and to the *idea* of an association with it—is "full of clues to the ways in which
allegiance to culture [is] made." Note the term "allegiance to culture." It trans-
lates, with little slippage, into ethnic identity. But here is the heart of the matter. To survive, concludes Chanock, "cultures, like brands, must essentialise.
Successful, sustainable cultures are those that brand best." This calls to mind
a remarkable example of the willful "commodification of tradition" in South
Africa.[11] It concerns the *koma*, the initiation school of the Pedi of the Northern Province. Initiation rites, across Africa, are held to transmit "deep knowledge"; it is here that cultural secrets are passed on.[12] For Pedi, the *koma* is also
a lucrative business. This is not just because locals pay up to $250 to take
part.[13] It is also because many *non*-local youths—for whom the fee is much
higher—also enroll. Pedi-brand *koma* has become a niche product in a regional culture market. In this immiserated economy, the alienation of vernacular knowledge *is* both a means of self-construction and a source of income.
Cultural survival is giving way, in many places, to survival through culture.
But with a twist: the more successful an ethnic group is in commodifying its
difference, the quicker it may devalue itself. This is the irony, too, of the quest
of those who consume exotic cultures-as-commodity: the more they pursue
their alienated selves in the *geist* of others, the more that *geist* risks succumbing to the banality of the market.[14]

But not always. Ethno-commodities are queer things. Apart from all else,
their aura does *not,* as critical theory would have had it, inevitably diminish
with their mass production and circulation. As we have implied, ethnicity as
a fact-of-being-and-becoming seems often to take palpable, credible, creative
life in the very *process* of its commodification. Thus we read of Balinese
dances, designed for tourist consumption, which so captured the imagination
of "natives" that they ended up replacing the sacred, auratic originals previously performed only in the temple.[15] Observing similar things in China and
elsewhere, Phillip Felfan Xie arrives at an unwitting, counterintuitive syllo-
gism: that, far from destroying cultural value, the commodification of "tradition," insofar as it valorizes indigeneity, is as likely to be a "positive mechanism
in the pursuit of authenticity," a means of finding "true selves," individual and
collective, "through the appropriation of pastness." Almost like nationalism—

but not quite.[16] For the imagination, here, is propelled less by the conceit of homogeneous inclusion than by the impetus to produce identification and self-definition through meaningful difference. To echo Žižek, our current worldliness seems to conjure an endless quest for unalienated otherness as its "necessary supplement."[17]

What conclusions may be drawn from all this? Could it be that we are seeing unfold before us a metamorphosis in the production of identity and subjectivity, in the politics and economics of culture, and in the interpellation of indigeneity into worlds beyond itself? Does this imply, concomitantly, a shift in the ontology of ethnic consciousness and the nature of belonging? And why does ethnic genealogy provide an ever more compelling basis for human connectedness and collective life, often seeming more "authentic" than the putative horizontal fraternity that underlies liberal citizenship? Note that, in posing the problem thus, we treat ethnicity, culture, identity, and in-digeneity *not* as analytic constructs but as signs variously deployed by human beings across the planet in their quotidian efforts to inhabit sustainable worlds.

Ethnicity, in the Ongoing Present: One or Two Questions of Theory

Let us pause briefly here to offer two general observations about cultural iden-tity. One is ontological, the other, orientational.

First, Ontology

The oldest, most foundational question of all about ethnicity, *sui generis*— ethnicity as consciousness, ethnicity as a sociological formation, ethnicity as a sentiment deep enough to die for—is whether it is primordial or an instrumentally-motivated social construction.[18] Happily, this question— which once divided scholars, organic intellectuals, and militias—has receded in significance. Few social scientists would argue any longer for primordial-ism, pure and simple, although ethno-nationalists continue to kill for it. To many in academia, bromides about ethnicity really being *both*, part primor-dial and part social construction, offer a banal compromise, a way of distan-tiating an intractable problem. In fact, that compromise is itself incoherent, impossible: primordial attachment and the social construction of identity describe irreducibly different ontologies of being that cannot, logically or sociologically, dissolve into each other. Unless, of course, the primordial is treated not as an *explanation* for ethnic consciousness, but as a phenomenological description of how that consciousness is experienced from within by those who share it.[19] More important, for now, however, is the fact that the compromise itself—that ethnicity is part primordial, part social construction— actually *mimics* an ever more palpable social fact: the great existential irony that, in its lived manifestations, cultural identity *is* increasingly apprehended, simultaneously, as a function of voluntary self-production *and* the ineluctable effect of biology. In other words, *as both* construction and essence.[20] This doubling, we would argue, is not a contradiction at all: it is an endemic condition of identity in neoliberal times. Of which more in due course.

Second, Orientation

It is a matter of observation that, across the positivist social sciences, treatments of cultural identity, where they extend beyond its modes of expression and representation, tend overwhelmingly to orient towards its *political* dimensions; perhaps this is itself the corollary of the triumph of constructionist perspectives, for which the fabrication of *any* collective consciousness is, by definition, a political act.[21] Which is why *politics* and *identity* are so often locked in conceptual embrace, as if each completes the other. So much is this the case that the economics, ethics, and aesthetics of ethnicity are, by extension, almost invariably reduced to a rather unsubtle sense of politics: to the pursuit of shared social and material interests;[22] to struggles for recognition in the face of homogenizing hegemonies; to redress for histories, real or imagined, of injury, suffering, victimhood;[23] to the right to engage in "different" bodily and domestic practices, poetics, musics, moralities.

Patently, the politics of ethnicity *are* critical. All the more so because the neoliberal moment is commonly said to diffuse the political by submerging its ideological bases in the imperatives of economic efficiency and capital growth; in the fetishism of the free market, bioscience, and technology; in the dictates of security and social order; in the demands of "culture."[24] At the same time, the continued privileging of the *politics* of ethnicity—at least, of a politics crudely conceived—has a number of costs: it depends on an underspecified conception of the political, it reduces cultural identity to a utility function, and it confuses the deployment of ethnicity as a *tactical* claim to entitlement with the *substance* of ethnic consciousness. Indeed, it is arguable that ethnicity-as-*strategy* and ethnicity-as-*existential identity* are somewhat different phenomena, despite being conditions of each other's possibility. Ethnicity-as-tactical claims usually presents its cultural bases, often quite cynically, not in the "thick" terms of a living, inhabited order of signs and practices—that is, of ethnicity-as-culture—but in "thin," second-order terms that, purged of density, refer to very general, reified values.[25] Like Britishness, which stresses such things as fair play and civility. Or *ubuntu*, African "humanity," usually glossed in South Africa as a socially oriented sensibility by contrast to Western individualism.

But, most of all, the tendency to understand ethnicity in terms of a purely instrumental sense of politics misses precisely what we began this chapter with. Recall Contralesa, the trustees of culture in South Africa, who have taken identity into the realm of venture capital; recall, too, the king of the Bafokeng, with his emphasis on corporate ethnicity. Neither of their visions lacked a politics. But what they recognized is that the institutional topography of the world has shifted: that the current age is one in which the fiction can no longer be sustained that "the political" is apprehensible as an autonomous domain, with sovereignty over material life; that politics and economics, inseparable as never before, are anchored together at once in the market, the law, and the meaning of personal identity. Nor is this revelation confined to South Africa. In China, says Arif Dirlik, "ethnic groups, once defined politically, now perceive themselves as 'natural' economic groups."[26] Pay attention to the stress on *natural* economic groups. It will have echoes as we proceed.

These observations lead, in turn, to a Big Issue. To the extent that they are true, should it not follow that the *context* in which culture, identity, and politics are embedded is itself under radical reconstruction? That context is typically taken to be the nation-state and, ever more nowadays, the transnational order of which it is part. Or, more accurately, in which it is dialectically entailed.

It has become commonplace to bespeak the metamorphosis of the modernist polity under the impact of globalization, neoliberalism, empire, whatever. The more difficult question is *how* precisely to make sense of this unfolding history. And how to do so in such a way as to illuminate the variant species of political subjectivity taking shape within it.

The Nation-State and Its Subjectivities

Modernist European polities, according to Benedictine history—Benedictine, as in Benedict Anderson—were founded on a fiction of cultural homogeneity, on an imagined, often violently effected, sense of horizontal fraternity.[27] Much has been said about this imagining: that Euro-nationhood was always more diverse than its historiography allows, always a work-in-progress, always subject to a tenuous hyphenation with the states that ruled them. But that is another story, a narrative of the *longue duree* that begins with Westphalia and ends in the Failure of the West. (Now, tellingly, renamed the "global *North*.") Since the late twentieth century, those polities have had increasingly to come to terms with difference. Historical circumstance has pushed them toward a more heterodox nationhood.[28] Hence the growing literatures, scholarly and lay alike, on citizenship, sovereignty, multiculturalism, minority rights, and the limits of liberalism. Hence the xenophobia that haunts heterodoxy almost everywhere. Hence, too, our disciplinary concern with the curious counterpoint between cosmopolitanism and indigeneity, *both* variously understood. Hetero-nationhood seeks—usually for pragmatic, not ethical reasons—to accommodate cultural diversity within a civic order composed of universal citizens, all ostensibly equal before the law. And to embrace identity politics within a liberal, constitutionally founded conception of national community. Especially since 1989, global liberalization has not merely transformed the sovereignty of nation-states. It has actively compounded the degree to which they are both polymorphous and porous: we scarcely need mention, here, the ever more mobile demographics of wage labor; or the incapacity of many Western cosmo-polities to reproduce their social infrastructures without the discomforting presence of "aliens"; or the impact of the electronic commons on the planetary circulation of virtually everything—and everything virtual. All of which, plainly, are corollaries of the hegemony of the market, of its power both to breach *and* to buttress borders, to curtail *and* to extend the regulatory reach of states, to valorize the local *and* to cast it into economic force fields well beyond itself.

In this world, in which the political and the ethical are also swept up under the sign of the market, freedom presents itself ineluctably as choice: most of all, as choice of identities and modes of fashioning them. But these identities are also experienced in increasingly substantive, embodied terms. As other bases of aggregation—most notably, in a post-Marxian, post-Weberian world, class—are undermined, as they dissolve into empty metaphors, as the social itself appears ever less "real,"[29] as "the" nation is compromised by heterogeneity and relativism, individual and collective attachments come to inhere in what seem the unmediated, elemental bases of human life itself: race, gender, sexuality, generation, ethnicity, religion. Which is why there has been a radical intensification of claims made in the name of all of these things, and sometimes in constellations of them; claims that frequently transcend and transect national frontiers. Mark the move here from metaphor to metonym: from the body politic to the politicized body as *fons et origo* of concrete social connectedness.

Among these putatively "elemental" bases of human life, ethnicity has proven particularly compelling as a principle of similitude, recognition, attachment, of consociation and mobilization—the active components that together congeal into identity. Like the nation, ethnicity is rooted, presumptively, in shared blood, culture, and corporate interest, a conjuncture that seems all the more real as civic nationhood fails to pass itself off as fictive kinship, to hold difference in check, or to subsume it within a community imagined-as-one. In fact, ethnic consciousness has become the common language of exchange in the "trading pits of pluralist relativism," the stock in trade of hetero-nationhood.[30] While most people continue to live as citizens *in* nation-states, they tend more and more only to be conditionally citizens *of* nation-states. Thus, to return to South Africa, which seems fairly typical in this respect,[31] a recent study shows that less than 25 percent of the population regards itself primarily as South African. The "vast majority . . . principally think of themselves" as members of "an ethnic, cultural, language, religious, or some other group," to which they "attach their personal fate." At the same time, most of them do *not* reject their national identity.[32] Therein lies the complexity. The conditionality of citizenship, the fact that it is overlaid and undercut by a politics of difference, does not necessarily entail the negation of the national subject, merely its uneasy alignment with other priorities. Mostly, the priorities of otherness.

In addition, these developments all involve a stress on *legal* instruments: on copyright, intellectual property, and the like. The modernist polity has always rested on jural foundations, of course. But, of late, there has been a palpable intensification in the resort to legal ways and means. The signs are everywhere: in the development of a global jurisprudence far more elaborate than its internationalist predecessor; in the epidemic of new national constitutions since 1989; in the proliferation of legal nongovernmental organizations (NGOs) across the world; in the remarkable spread of human rights advocacy; in the subjection of ever more intimate domains of human life to litigation. People across the planet are being encouraged to behave as *homo juralis*. And collectivities of all kinds are given ever more reason to mimic bodies corporate.[33]

There is a critical corollary to all this. It concerns the relocation of politics in the legal domain. More and more are differences of *all* kinds being fought out in the courts—whether they involve private freedoms, property rights, or national resources; access to medical treatment or title to real estate; sovereignty or cultural knowledge. In ways unthinkable until recently, governments and their agencies, especially those that deal in death and taxes, are regularly sued by their citizens, and citizens are ever more litigious in respect of each other. What once happened in parliaments, street protests, and political councils now finds a new space of contestation. Even history is being re-politicized, redeemed, recouped in the courts. Britain, for one, is being sued by several formerly colonized peoples in East Africa, each demanding restitution for an old wrong: the Nandi, for the killing of their leader in 1905; the Nyoro, for a land seizure in 1900; the Samburu, for injuries inflicted by relict munitions. In all these class actions, the plaintiff is an ethnic group, reclaiming its past by jural means. And asserting a corporate identity in the process.[34]

Project the legal subject onto the terrain of cultural identity, add the reduction of culture to property, mix it with the displacement of politics into the domain of jurisprudence, and what is the result? It is, to return to where we began: Ethnicity, Inc.

Casino Capital, Cultural Property, and Incorporation

Neither the incorporation of ethnic groups nor the commodification of culture is new. In North America, it has had *legal* recognition since at least 1934, with the passage of the Indian Reorganization Act. In 1971, moreover, the Alaskan Native Claims Settlement Act *explicitly* reorganized indigenous peoples into corporations composed of shareholders whose rights were based on genealogy, whose traditional lands became private, alienable property, and whose cultural products, a growing proportion of them trademarked under brand names like the "Silver Hand," were directed toward the market.[35] But the *popular* prototype of Ethnicity, Inc., in the United States lies in the Native American casino-owning "tribe," its apotheosis in the Mohegan Sun Casino and the Pequot Foxwoods Resort, two enormous monuments to ethnomarketing and the architecture of vernacular kitsch; at Foxwoods are found such establishments as the Ethnic Concepts International Gift Shop. As it turns out, the Native American cases of ethno-incorporation are bewilderingly complex; their identity economies stretch far beyond the gaming house.

But most of them share five things that will turn out to be significant as we proceed.

The first is obvious: the more like profit-seeking corporations indigenous groups become, the more the terms of membership privilege birth, blood, and biology over social or cultural attachments—and the more they tend to be contested.[36] The second, by contrast, is counterintuitive: not infrequently, it is commercial enterprise that begets an ethnic group, not the other way around. *Vide* the Pomo Indians—Pomo in both name and spirit—that, in the 1950s, consisted of two families, without tribe or territory. These families lived on land set aside for homeless Native Americans until they secured reservation land and a casino license. Whereupon they became "the" Pomo. Or better yet, the case of the Augustine Cahuilla Indians, who consist of one woman, Mary-ann Martin, but who have been allowed to open a gaming house on an abandoned reservation in California. By these means does Ms. Martin constitute a certified ethnic group. Nor is she the only one-person ethno-corporation in North America.[37]

The third notable thing about the U.S. cases is that, in many of them, the creation of a corporate ethno-economy has been set in motion by venture capital from outside. Its source is usually non-Indian financiers, for whom real or virtual "tribes" are franchises licensed to make a killing. As this suggests, ethno-enterprise is mandated by culture, but may not originate in it. In fact, several officially recognized bands have little connection to vernacular life ways. Maryann Martin, the last living Augustine Cahuila, was raised African American. But, once on the road to incorporation, they typically begin to assert—if necessary, to discover or develop—their "traditions," which may then be merchandised (hence the Ethnic Concepts store on the Pequot reservation—and, close by, a state-of-the-art Museum and Research Center of Culture). The content of identity, as we all know, is often produced in response to the market. So, sometimes, is indigeneity.

The fourth matter of note is that, once recognized by the state, Native American groups tend to proclaim their sovereign autonomy against it.[38] Thus, for example, Indian tribes, now major contributors to political campaigns in California, refuse to report their donations; as "nations," they claim exemption from U.S. law (this pre-dated recent legislation that lifted limitations on corporate campaign spending). Predictably, such assertions provoke reactions; the State of California has litigated against several Indian tribes. Similarly, when the governor of New York insisted that cigarette sales on the Mohawk reservation be licensed by his state, indigenous leaders invoked sovereign exclusion; the Mohawk make their own tobacco products and, acting under the sign of ethno-preneurship, were determined to protect their market.[39]

Finally, the Indian cases indicate that ethno-incorporation strives for geospatial materiality.[40] To be sure, it often involves a land claim. Which is not surprising: real estate held in patrimonial tenure—*territory*, that is—is typically taken to be a founding principle of sovereignty. Note these five points. They will, we repeat, turn out to be critical.

The prototypical Native American instances of Ethnicity, Inc., those associated with casino ownership, *presumed* a cultural identity at their core. But the *substance* of that identity was incidental to their incorporation. There are exceptions to this. Or rather, inversions: "tribes" whose corporate history began *not* with casino capitalism[41] but with the copyrighting of their cultures. Take the Zia Pueblo,[42] who successfully sued New Mexico a few years back for the unauthorized use of their sun symbol on state flags. The design, with its spiritual powers, they said, was their wholly owned property. Or, also in New Mexico, the Indians of Sandoval County who, over centuries, developed a ritually valued variety of blue corn that, in the 1980s, became a fashionable health food. As a result, Five Sandoval Indian Pueblos, Inc., was established to superintend the sale of trademarked agri-goods, like "Hopi Blue."[43] Here, in sum, an ethno-corporation arose from distilling local knowledge into a brand that, in turn, sedimented sociologically into an ethnic federation—just the thing Chanock pointed to in saying that "sustainable cultures are those which brand best."[44]

The branding of culture has been facilitated by an implosion, in recent times, in the domain of intellectual property: in the laws governing its possession, the rights accruing to it, and the spheres of existence over which it extends. This has persuaded the United Nations and the World Intellectual Property Organization to recognize an "inherent" right of indigenous peoples to the fruits of their vernacular knowledge, one effect of which has been to accelerate yet further their incorporation in many places. Some of them in quite unexpected ways.

Which brings us to a Tale of Two Ethnicities. Two instances of Ethnicity, Inc., that draw together the various strands of our narrative by addressing an unresolved dialectic at its core: the dialectic between the incorporation of identity and the commodification of culture. It should be clear by now that they are *not* the same thing. Hence the contrast between (i) those Native American groups, exemplified by casino capitalists, that became bodies corporate by virtue of being shareholders in enterprises enabled by their sovereign legal status and (ii) those made into corporations by virtue of a shared copyright in vernacular signs, knowledge, or practices. The relationship between these two tendencies, it turns out, completes the dialectic. But we are running ahead of ourselves. Our Tale of Two Ethnicities returns us to where we began: southern Africa.

Ethno-futures, Again

The first takes us to the edge of the Kahalari Desert, to the Land of the San—known, pejoratively, as Bushmen. It involves the hoodia cactus, *xhoba,* which they have imbibed since time immemorial. In the past, when hunting in the desert, it stayed their appetites and thirst; it is used these days to stave off the effects of poverty. San suffered severely from the predations of colonialism: stigmatized, victims of various forms of violence, removed from their ancestral lands, prey to illness and alcohol, their numbers diminished greatly. Over the past century, in fact, most of their communities dispersed into the immiserated reaches of the South African "colored" population.

The hoodia saga was to unleash a global media frenzy: in the United States, *60 Minutes* attested to the efficacy of the plant and spoke in awe of its promise for the fat-fighting industry;[45] the BBC sent a reporter "deep into the Kalahari desert," to "one of the world's most primitive tribes," to sample the "extremely ugly cactus" that "kills appetite and attacks obesity with no side effects."[46] It all began in South Africa in 1963, when the Council for Scientific and Industrial Research (CSIR) became interested in the medicinal properties of the cactus;[47] this was stimulated by reports of its use by San trackers deployed by the army in its wars against the enemies of apartheid. The CSIR corroborated the cactus's appetite-suppressant properties, identified their bioactive component, and in 1997, patented it under the label P57.

The CSIR licensed P57 to Phytopharm, a British company—which, after extensive trials, licensed it on to Pfizer for $21 million; ironic perhaps, since *xhoba* was held by San to have some of the same properties as Viagra, Pfizer's most famed product. It is at this point that the story becomes especially interesting.

The San first heard about the patent when Phytofarm announced P57 to the media. Or, more precisely, it was Roger Chennells,[48] a human rights lawyer, who read a quote from the head of Phytofarm, Richard Dixey, to the effect that the people, from whom the knowledge of hoodia derived, were extinct. At the time, Chennells was representing the San in a land claim,[49] in the course of which there had emerged an NGO, the South African San Institute (SASI), one of many such organizations that surfaced with the end of apartheid, with liberalization, and with the postcolonial politics of identity.[50] Chennells told SASI that the San were victims of biopiracy, that the return on the patent could be considerable—its value in the United States is about $3 billion a year—and that this was an opportunity to assert a collective identity under the San Council, a new body created by SASI to give political shape to, and claim sovereignty for, their ethnic aspirations.[51]

Richard Dixey may have been disingenuous in asserting the extinction of the San; the advantages to Phytofarm were plain enough. When the San Council protested to the CSIR, it acknowledged the error of its ways, Dixey confessed his "embarrassment," and a profit-sharing agreement was signed. Since then, Pfizer has given way as licensee to Unilever. Since then, too, the San Trust, set up to manage the incoming funds, has received its first royalties; has begun to tackle the problems of distribution among the San peoples of South Africa, Nambia, and Botswana; and has filed suit against twenty-six illicit producers. Since then "the San," as an ethno-corporation, has taken ever more articulate shape.

In point of fact, Dixey had not been altogether wrong. The San may not have been extinct, but their *ethno*cide had gone a long way. Having been cast out of their social ecology, "they" did not evince much by way of a collective identity; their dispersal into the gray racial space of South Africa made it impossible to do so. But the assertion of intellectual property—coupled, significantly, with the land claim that preceded it—reanimated San "identity." And gave it ever "thicker," more dense substance; a symptom of this, interestingly, being a sudden increase in people accusing each other, on biological grounds, of "not being real San."[52] Thus it is that there has been a language revival, that genealogies are being collected to create a population register; that SASI has initiated a "cultural resources management project"; that programs have been designed for "San-controlled income generation" using indigenous knowledge in a sustainable manner; that a legal platform has been set up to protect the global interests and dignity of the San. All of which had the effect of re-indigenizing this "people" through the very act of interpellating them into a distinctly cosmopolitan sense of being-in-the-world. When we asked Roger Chennells whether a new ethnic identity had been produced in the process, he answered in the affirmative. He is correct. In fact, the presumption that "the" San actually *had* a shared identity—or a coherent ethno-sociology—prior to the colonial dispersal of a complex *population* of hunter-gatherers collectively called "Bushmen," is itself contentious: who or what "they" were has long been a subject of bitter debate.[53] But that does not matter anymore, at least not outside of the academy. Today they are a multi-national, ever more assertively cosmopolitan ethno-corporation: as we said, "the" San, and the San Council that makes manifest their sovereignty, now straddle three of the countries of southern Africa.

The other story involves the Bafokeng, the people made wealthy by plati-num, the people whose kings are spoken of as CEOs, the people actually re-ferred to in South Africa as Bafokeng, Inc.[54] The history of their incorporation begins, long ago, with land: one of their nineteenth-century chiefs realized that, to protect their territory from white settlers, his people ought to *purchase* it outright.[55] So he sent young men to the diamond fields and commissioned their wages to buy as much real estate as possible. The subsequent history of South Africa did not make it easy to hold on to this land. But, by establishing the Bafokeng as a private, corporate owner, the purchase enabled their chiefs to defend it from seizure,[56] especially after the discovery of platinum in 1924 and its leasing to Impala Platinum, a large company, in the 1960s.[57] The great-est challenge, in this respect, came when the puppet homeland government of Bophuthatswana, set up by the apartheid state, exiled the chief of the Bafo-keng, expropriated their mineral rights, and negotiated contracts directly with Impala; this sparked a lengthy series of legal actions that eventually yielded a victory for the "tribe" in 1999—and, with it, a lucrative profit-sharing arrange-ment.[58] All of which made the Bafokeng so adept at litigation that, as one journalist put it, "their traditional weapon became the law, not the club."[59]

The corporate growth of Bafokeng, Inc., in the wake of these legal pro-cesses has been breathtaking. This nation of 150,000 shareholders—membership is defined by patrilineality—has large stakes in a complex network of companies; their interest in Impala alone yielded $80 million in 2002. In addition, they have opened up two new mining operations each val-ued at $65 million;[60] established a profitable partnership with Exxon;[61] bought a huge construction company;[62] purchased 20 percent of South Africa's sec-ond largest packaging plant;[63] and own 33 percent of SA Chrome, now re-named Merafe Resources.[64] *Merafe* is Setswana for "nations." Nor does the story end there. Their sovereign government is vested in the Royal Bafokeng Administration; their global investments are overseen by Royal Bafokeng Fi-nances; a Royal Bafokeng Economic Board manages development within the

chiefdom; and their mineral interests are husbanded by Royal Bafokeng Resources—which recently became a *public* company.[65] By these means, "the
Bafokeng" chiefdom has become the ultimate ethno-enterprise: one in whose
present holdings and futures you or we might purchase stock.[66]

What is missing in all this? The *cultural* element of Bafokeng cultural identity. King Leruo and his money managers have long presented themselves as
highly cosmopolitan business people primarily concerned with a sustainable
future: Vision 2020 is their ambitious plan to develop Bafokeng into a "self-
sufficient," fully employed, globally oriented nation by, well, 2020.[67] Of late,
however, there has been much more culture talk, much more talk of indigeneity. Since being installed in a ritual saturated with the trappings of a tradition partly historical, partly made up, powerfully vernacular, the young king
has taken to essaying "African values," to celebrating "traditional governance,"
and to arguing that, in moving toward "Afro-*modernity*," his people must "affirm" their essence (the king has also hired a personal consultant with a Ph.D.
in anthropology).[68] In short, Bafokeng, Inc., the manifest commodification of
Bafokeng *identity*, appears to be reaching toward a cultural sensibility in order
to complete itself.

Running the San and Bafokeng together, then, the dialectic at the heart of
Ethnicity, Inc., reveals itself. Each of these cases evinces the five things fore-
shadowed in Native America, if in different proportions: membership in both
has come to be defined genealogically, with some contestation either evident
or imminent; in both, commercial enterprise has been instrumental either in
crystallizing or in reproducing the sociological entity in which cultural identity is presumed to inhere; in both, venture capital and legal expertise from
outside have been crucial; both have asserted their newfound sovereignty
against the state; and both have based their incorporation on land claims, past
or present. In both, moreover, the displacement of the political into the legal
has been demonstrable: both have fought their battles by means of lawfare. In
the process, they have both naturalized the trope of identity around which
their "rights" adhere—and interpellated into it a significant measure of affect.
This is particularly striking in the case of the San. It is arguable that knowledge
of the hoodia was produced not by "*the* San" at all—who may or may not have
existed at the time—but by hunters of the Kalahari, a class defined by their
relationship to a mode of production. The projection of a vernacular right to
intellectual property onto "the San," a putatively "primordial" collectivity, has
the effect of *ex*tinguishing a class of producers as it *dis*tinguishes and materi-
alizes a cultural identity—and, as it does so, giving ontological primacy to the

idea of identity itself. Thus, to reiterate, does ideology become ID-ology and hide itself in a sense of the natural, the inevitable, the given.

Most of all, though, the stories of the San and the Bafokeng, precisely because they *are* such extreme instances, demonstrate how and why it is that Ethnicity, Inc., rests on a dialectic between the incorporation of identity and the commodification of culture; and, at another level, between indigeneity and the human cosmopolis. Whether it starts with the incorporation of identity, as in the Bafokeng case, or with the commodification of cultural property, as in Kalahari, the process evinces a drive to complete itself in the other. Thus it is that a dispersed group of former hunters and gatherers have become, ever more explicitly, "*the* San," replete with a sovereign sense of their own ethnosociology, their own governance, their own affective economy, their own range of institutions to make it all real. Thus it is that Bafokeng, Inc., is turning to vernacular ways and means in the name of an Afro-modernity that it may inhabit as it reaches toward the future. Neither is fortuitous. After all, Ethnicity, Inc., to the degree that it naturalizes collective right, material entitlement, and sovereignty, *does* require both the incorporation of identity *and* cultural substance to realize, recognize, fulfill itself. Which is why it tends to begin in land, thence to make claims to sovereignty, to secure its cultural property, and to invest in the long run. The future of ethnicity *does* seem to lie, at least in one important respect, in ethno-futures.

Conclusion

We have come *not* to praise Ethnicity, Inc. Nor do we extol empowerment that depends on the commodification of culture or the Empire of the Market, let alone the creeping judicialization of politics or the naturalization of the ethnotrope of identity into a brute term of social being. Quite the opposite. Ethnicity, Inc., carries with it a host of costs and contradictions. What we seek to do here, in short, is to interrogate a worldwide phenomenon in the making; one that is much more complicated than it first appears.

In so doing, we have stressed that Ethnicity, Inc., has deep roots and many precedents. After all, nation-states have long sought to distinguish themselves by marking as unique their national cultures, their fraternal heritage, their essence as embodied in both utilitarian and aesthetic objects. French champagne, Italian *grappa*, German opera, British tea and . . . china, have long been branded *national* products. In ever more cases they carry trademarks. Implicitly, in other words, the modernist nation has always been a brand, with some strange consequences; note, in this regard, Jonathan Franzen's brilliant caricature of Lithuania, Inc., in *The Corrections*, the upshot of which is that its national economy is sold by a quite plausible mistake to a bank in Atlanta.[69] Note, too, the fact that Silvio Berlusconi, CEO extraordinaire, often referred to his country as *Azienda Italia*, "Italy, the Company."[70] Nor only nations. Religions too. The judiciary of Pakistan, in deliberating the dispute between Ulema, religious authorities, and the Ahmediya, whom they style as blasphemers, has recently chosen to treat Islam as intellectual property.[71] And the process is proliferating in time as well as space: *vide* the recent efforts of the Israeli national archive to establish in a court of law that, because he was a Jew, Kafka's works were rightfully the intellectual "assets" of the Israeli state as the guardian, in perpetuity, of Jewish heritage.[72] What is going on here, it seems, is the hyperextension of an old phenomenon. And its migration into places it has not gone before: into the domain of cultural being, where, as Clifford Geertz once reminded us, modernity was supposed to run up against its limits.[73] But the ethnically defined peoples of "traditional" Africa, Latin America, the United States, and Asia have become thoroughly modern, if each in their own ways. Even more, they have sometimes passed by the modern and, like that Indian group of which we spoke, leapt directly into the Pomo. Which, above all, refigures and sometimes renders absurd, the lineaments of modernity. We may or may not like what Ethnicity, Inc., promises. But we are going to have to live with it, and, even more, to fashion an engaged anthropology to deal with its unfolding logic, its ambiguous promises, its material and moral vision for times to come, the deep affective attachments that it engenders. Ethnicity, Inc., is the congealed product—a fusion both hot and cold, if you will—of three elemental features of the neoliberal tendency: the apotheosis of intellectual property and the reduction of culture to it; the migration of politics into the realm of the law; and the growing naturalization of the trope of identity as *the* taken-for-granted domain of collective action. These are all key stations on the Road to a Brave Neo World.

Chapter 15

Corporate Nostalgia?

Managerial Capitalism from a Contemporary Perspective

Karen Ho

From the standpoint of the contemporary moment, when socioeconomic inequality in the United States has surpassed even that of the Great Depression, is it possible that we might want to revisit and reconsider the strengths and potentials of bureaucratic managerial capitalism? While the modern corporation may have inflicted suffocating routinization and hierarchical segmentation on its employees, it was also remarkably stable and resilient in its organizational form, which allowed the formation and fostering of an employee social contract. What might it mean to reinterpret such bureaucracies as avenues for, even protectors of, class mobility, greater equality in compensation, and stable employment, although such opportunities were often limited, segregated, and only beginning to emerge in the aftermath of the civil rights struggle? In other words, have scholars, in their rightful critique of the hierarchies, exploitations, and repetitive cadences of the modern corporation, not fully analyzed the socioeconomic benefits of these organizations? Has fear of sanctioning the abuses of Fordism and Taylorism prevented us from looking backward in order to fully assess the costs of our current era of financialization?

The problem and politics of nostalgia is a useful starting point for my argument. My intention is not to advocate a "return to" or recuperation of bureaucracy and managerial capitalism. It is crucial to be mindful of the pitfalls of bourgeois nostalgia, which not only ignores the process of continual capitalist change that generates this quintessential experience of modernity in the first place, but also allows for the reconsolidation of powerful interests and culturally specific visions.[1] In contrast, this chapter attempts to make the case that nostalgia can be utilized critically and productively with careful attention to uneven power relations, as a way to ground our present, account for loss, and better imagine our socioeconomic futures.

While critical scholars have long acknowledged the social benefits of the welfare state (despite its manifold problems), and have challenged reactionary denunciations of "governmental bureaucracy" that have often served as code words to legitimate the dismantling of societal safety nets, I argue that the corresponding decline of large, centralized (corporate) organizations has not been sufficiently accounted for or theorized as a related phenomenon. A notable exception has been the debate about postindustrial work in the sociological literature, which has deeply engaged with the collapse of bureaucracy and the changing role of institutions.[2] In other words, while my point is not necessarily to advocate for the unproblematic return of the bureaucratic machine, it is unclear whether we have fully come to terms with the social loss that accompanied the organizational undermining of corporate America. It is perhaps only after the fact that critics have begun to recognize the social possibilities and pathways embedded within these disappearing bureaucracies.

A number of scholars and social critics have recently begun to conduct this kind of excavation. Mobilizing a considerable amount of evidence, which I will return to later, Gerald Davis, a scholar of business management, makes the important argument that over the past thirty years, the downsizing, restructuring, and selling/breaking up of the large public corporation in the United States has contributed to the demise of what he calls the "society of organizations."[3] For much of the twentieth century, corporate institutions and employers were a main focus of social reform and amelioration. In part due to long-standing struggles in U.S. welfare capitalism about the "legitimate" roles and responsibilities of government, not to mention larger contestations around what constitutes the social domains of "state" and "market," socially ameliorative policies, programs, and regulations, from environmental protection to equal employment initiatives, were scaffolded upon bureaucratic institutions (framed as located in the private sphere). The corporation was seen not only as one of the foundations of a stable society, but also as an appropriate venue in which to further struggles for inclusivity. Since corporations played a vital role in shaping and organizing daily middle-class life, a constellation of organizations and programs built up through and around them over decades of engagement. But now that public corporations are no longer robust, long-term institutions—converted from long-standing bulwarks of economic productivity into mere stocks in portfolios—our society of organizations has increasingly transformed itself into a short-term "portfolio society." This chapter thus encourages scholars of corporations, citizenship, democracy, and economy to confront the contradictory and unanticipated losses generated in the gutted corporate afterlives of extreme financialization.

In his provocative work *The Culture of the New Capitalism*, Richard Sennett records a striking change of heart on managerial capitalism. Given the seismic insecurities and even greater inequalities the values and practices of finance capitalism have wrought, he laments the demise of bureaucracy in the new economy and almost romanticizes "the iron cage" in retrospect. Surprised by his own admission, since he was a self-professed 1960s radical who raged against the machine, he explained that he was unable to predict the extent to which many ably resisted, negotiated, thrived in, and were in turn supported by such bureaucratic institutions.

The concept of the "iron cage" began with Max Weber, who used the German term *stahlhartes gehäuse* (hard steel casing) in *The Protestant Ethic and the Spirit of Capitalism*. The "iron cage" became a central symbol of the modern industrial age, evoking the rationalization, efficiency, and rigidity of the modern bureaucratic form such that individuals, and by extension the social order itself, were increasingly turned into "cogs" of a machine—stripped of autonomy and subjected to depersonalizing, calculable measures of conduct. As Weber writes, the order of modern life "is now bound to the technical and economic conditions of machine production which to-day determine the lives of all the individuals who are born into this mechanism, not only those directly concerned with economic acquisition, with irresistible force."[4] "Victorious capitalism" allowed the iron cage, derived from ethical and religious values and practices, to break loose from its origins and organize modern economic life as "mechanized petrification."[5]

To return to Sennett's argument, the very experience of the dislocations wrought by the new culture of capitalism allowed him to reinterpret the possibilities of the "old" modern corporation. In fact, he reframes normative critiques of Weber's iron cage to argue that not only was the lived experience of agency possible under the iron cage (people continually negotiated and transformed it), but also that the cage provided, to some extent, stability, steadiness of purpose, and "the gift of organized time."[6] I would argue further that, given the context of stability (as opposed to space and time experienced as continually and unpredictably in motion), employees and larger social movements were able to agitate for greater opportunities and to create alternative spaces beyond Taylorist limitations and designs.

In what follows, I first sketch the demise of the modern public corporation and examine some of the central reasons for its passing. I then analyze the changed employment trajectories for a particular set of workers—managers and mid-level employees who had hoped to one day "climb the corporate ladder"—and the macro-employment consequences of a workplace premised not on stable institutions but on ephemeral and shifting networks. I show how managerial corporations—just as they were about to be dismantled—had become important sites in the struggle for middle-class employment equality by women and people of color who had previously been excluded from such privileged workplaces. With the erosion of these bureaucratic institutions, those without historical resources faced significant downward mobility, while those who had access to elite networks reconsolidated their power. These networks, premised as they often are on "old" hierarchical exclusions yet often framed as merit-driven, further exacerbate and harden invidious distinctions of race, gender, and class. In conjunction with this discussion, I explore some of the complex reasons why many social scientists and cultural critics have either avoided the "rehabilitation" of the managerial corporation (and thus the correspondent recognition that such institutions supported some measure of employee potential and upward mobility) or have continued to approach corporations ahistorically, such that the "iron-cage" corporation of yesteryear is conflated with today's financialized network of contracts and "outfits."

Complementary research, such as Gerald Davis's work on the manifold consequences of the shift from society of organizations to portfolio society, has offered crucial macro-analysis of these sweeping changes through key corporate indicators, from the rise of Wal-Mart to the breakup of vertically integrated institutions to the emulation of the model of the weightless corporation. The contribution of this chapter to existing research is to theorize the ramifications of this new landscape on the everyday world of professional work and our conception of institutions. It parallels Richard Sennett's project in *The Corrosion of Character* and *The Culture of the New Capitalism*, where, using archetypes, he delves into the psyche and sentiments of workers to highlight fundamental changes the new economy has wrought in their understanding of time and space. This chapter tracks organizational changes in white-collar work structures and describes how many professional, mid-level employees have fallen through the cracks.

Financialization and Corporate America

Over the past thirty years and even more intensely during the past decade, the Wall Street-led financialization of the economy has catalyzed the demise and liquidation of corporate America, the U.S. public corporation. By financialization, I mean the dominant influence of financial interests, solutions, and values in our social economy, where accumulation is mainly through financial channels as opposed to industrial production or trade.[7] While Wall Street financial institutions and leaders have argued that financialization benefits corporate America (through increased efficiency, competitiveness, and so on) by aligning corporate practices and governance with the purported goal of increasing stock prices, I, in conjunction with many social critics and critical management scholars, have argued that to the contrary, Wall Street's particular enactment of a short-term shareholder value repertoire is actually destructive of corporations, generating multiple waves of restructuring, liquidation, and "crises."[8]

The economy of financialization, then, privileges the buying and selling of corporations, as well as the use of profits not necessarily to reinvest in productive enterprises such as research, development, or infrastructure building, but rather to engage in share-boosting activities such as stock buybacks. Corporations are thus shorn of multiple stakeholders, uprooted from local ties and constituents, and placed into a commoditized space of exchange where only stock price appreciations (or proclamations thereof) matter. According to Wall Street's worldview, corporations are equivalent to their stock price: they are not long-term social institutions, but disposable items in investment portfolios.

Simultaneously, as many scholars, from Judith Stein to Gerald Davis and Naomi Klein to Greta Krippner, have shown, from the late 1970s onward U.S. governmental policies began to encourage disinvestment from manufacturing while creating a "deregulatory" environment more favorably suited to the financial sector. In this context, billions of dollars of capital have flowed into the financial industry, and the financial institutions that managed and advised such investments have been able to consolidate their influence over corporations, emerging as central nodes, spokespeople, and executors for financial markets, which in turn are held to "speak" for corporate America.

The globalizing, yet local and institutional, culture of Wall Street financial institutions and investment funds has contributed to the demise and devaluation of corporate America. Rife throughout the financial world has been the understanding that bureaucratic corporations, with their multiple stakehold-ers and commitments, long-term workforce, and breadth and depth of infra-structure, were not only "underperforming" according to the financial values of short-term shareholder value (though by many other measures, many cor-porations were performing steadily), but also "unmeritocratic" in nature and deserving of massive downsizing. Utilizing the wedge of meritocracy to wrest corporate control away from the corporations themselves and to legitimate financial worldviews and practices was made possible by the long-standing construction of Wall Street as the pinnacle of meritocratic economic practice, buttressed by a culture of smartness.

Over the past thirty years, Wall Street bankers have framed themselves as "the smartest in the world," the "masters of the universe," through the strategy of recruiting their prestigious front-office employees only from the nation's most elite universities, such as Princeton and Harvard, in order to create a "halo effect" and capitalize on the status already cultivated by these bastions of elitism. Correspondingly, financial actors have actively positioned their own institutional culture as one characterized by speed, innovation, and bril-liance both by touting their specific culture of smartness *and* by explicitly framing the broader institutional culture of corporate America as slow, stag-nant, and excessively bureaucratic. Perhaps most damagingly, both the insti-tutions and the employees of corporate America are constructed as "slow," "run-of-the-mill," "mediocre," and "nine-to-five," or, more crudely, as "fat, dumb, and stupid."[9] This strategy of heralding financial actors and institutions at the expense of *and* in order to discredit corporate America helps to solidify the increasingly taken-for-granted assumption of large public corporations' ineptitude while instantiating a winner-versus-loser proposition where Wall Street is entrusted and justified to restructure corporate America according to its particular models and measures.

After thirty years of such restructuring, it is thus not surprising that Gerald Davis has observed that "the twilight" of the U.S. public corporation is at hand.[10] Lest such a proclamation sound too alarmist, Davis highlights the compelling evidence that today, investment firms and short-term investment vehicles, with trillions of dollars of corporate assets under management, actually "own" the largest share of corporate America. BlackRock, an investment management firm, is "the single largest shareholder of one in five" U.S. corporations; Fidelity, a financial services firm most widely known for its mutual funds, is a distant second, as the "largest shareholder of one in ten American corporations."[11] What is at stake in, and what are the massive implications of, having financial and investment management firms (from mutual to private equity funds) own corporate America? Of course, while the differences matter—whether a corporation is owned by passive investment management firms or actively "managed" private equity funds—the point is that being controlled by relatively short-term investors within an expedited timeframe is the new norm. Given the recent notoriety of Bain Capital, the private equity firm led by 2012 Republican presidential nominee Mitt Romney, which was heavily critiqued for profiteering on the buying, breaking up, and bankrupting of corporations, let us take the example of corporate ownership in the hands of private equity firms.

Private equity firms are composed of investment funds that acquire corporations, which these firms are supposed to actively manage by installing their own "management teams." (Of course, there is much contestation around whether private equity firms actually manage these complex institutions or simply extract fees from them.) These funds are characterized by explicit expiration dates—that is, a limited timeframe—usually five years or so, before the companies that make up the fund portfolio must be sold again because the investors that have provided the capital for the funds in the first place expect their return. In these contexts, corporations are bought, sold, and passed around every five years or so. Now, even *if* all private equity firms and funds are not homogenous and are not all in the business of extraction and liquidation, the point I underscore here is that private equity in general privileges a short-term temporality and continually packages corporate entities for sale. There is perhaps no better sign of the end of the public corporation as we knew it than its transformation into a short-term investment. When corporate America is owned by investment funds—coupled with the fact that over the past thirty years, Wall Street has valued companies that squeeze the most profits from the least assets—do not the previous premises and promises of a corporate-centered society evaporate?

One of the central ways in which finance has translated, marketed, and legitimated the transformation of corporations into fodder for financial portfolios (not to mention weightless brands and networks of contracts) has been to frame this shift as a boon for "shareholder democracy." This ideology, otherwise known as "investor populism" or the "ownership society," presumes that most Americans own shares of corporate America and thus their fortunes rise with the financial markets.[12] Thus it matters little that institutions have been dismantled, because individuals have (presumably) grafted themselves onto the new "safety net" of the capital markets. Of course, share ownership is both highly uneven, with the top 10 percent of American households accounting for 81 percent of the total value of stocks owned by households, and highly volatile—not to mention the fact that most individual investors do not have the timely, inside knowledge necessary to make the most of their investment capital.[13]

If the corporation today is little more than a "nexus of contracts," a collection of brands and other intellectual properties, or an asset in financial portfolios, to what extent is it still an organization? The shift from managerial to shareholder power in large companies created "a new source of lateral power . . . at the top," populated by Wall Street institutions, advisors, and institutional shareholders as well as corporate executives oriented toward financial growth. As Sennett and many others have argued, corporate America was transformed into structures "most attractive to empowered investors," designed to "look beautiful to a passing voyeur." Drawing from Weber, Sennett argues that historically corporations were "saved from revolution by applying military models of organization to capitalism," which in turn promoted stability, longevity, and greater employment. The desire and pursuit of all things sudden—sudden profits, sudden bubbles and bursts, sudden drives and ambition—have, he believes, de-layered and undermined the institution.[14]

The old model of the corporation, therefore, has been increasingly replaced with an investment model, where "the ownership society" is understood as an alternative that will solve or fill in the gaps left by the demise of corporate America. In the ownership society promoted by George W. Bush, home ownership and individual accounts tied to the financial markets would replace the safety net that was once provided by corporate employers (along with the state). Of course, in reality this financial "democratization" resulted in a re-concentration of control in the hands of financial intermediaries (mutual, pension, and other investment funds, and their advisors), not to mention the leveraging of these newly appropriated assets to further financial interests and projects. Finance capitalism bought up and reconfigured assets for a new era, attempting to solve particular problems and crises in production, inclusion, and the state[15] through finance and credit, thus creating new models that, in the end, imploded.

Dismantling Without Replacement

The dismantling of long-standing institutions that once shouldered much responsibility for important dimensions of human life has generated widespread angst. Examining this insecurity in his book *Twilight of the Elites: America After Meritocracy*, cultural observer and MSNBC talk show host Chris Hayes laments "the dark void left by the collapse of traditional institutional authority."[16] He continues: "Without some central institutions that have the inclination, resources, and reputational capital to patrol the boundaries of truth, we really do risk a kind of Hobbesian chaos, in which trust is overtaken by sheer will-to-power. . . . Without the social cohesion that trust institutions provide, we cannot produce the level of consensus necessary to confront our greatest challenges."[17] The dismantling of multiple kinds of organizational and corporate forms—from the media to corporate America—goes hand in hand with the repurposing of these institutions in the service of particular elites. And, for Hayes, the starkest evidence for institutional failure is our inability to face the threat of climate change. For example, "when our most central institutions are no longer trusted, we take refuge in smaller, balkanized epistemic encampments, aided by the unprecedented information technology at our disposal. As some of the encampments build higher and higher fences . . . we approach a terrifying prospect: a society that may no longer be capable of reaching the kind of basic agreement necessary for social progress," such as finding a solution to "catastrophic climate change."[18]

The void left by the twilight of the U.S. public corporation has yet to be sufficiently theorized and documented. In fact, I would argue that social critics' fear of recuperating powerful corporations, of going backwards to corporate paternalism (at best) or the numbing brutality of Taylorism (at worst), has prevented a necessary confrontation with the multiple consequences of large-scale institutional collapse. To make sense of this scholarly void, it might be helpful to briefly contextualize some critical, representative scholarly engagements with managerial capitalism and "big business." Not surprisingly, much of this scholarship has emphasized the absolute rigidity of the iron cage and the almost totalizing degradation of work and worker under Taylorism and Fordism.[19]

For example, Harry Braverman, in his seminal study *Labor and Monopoly Capital*, focused mainly on the profound consequences of labor de-skilling, of worker space, creativity, skill, and pride being completely appropriated by capitalist manufacturers and then "returned" to workers as "dead labor."[20] As Braverman pointed out, "It is only in its era of monopoly that the capitalist mode of production takes over the totality of individual, family and social needs and, in subordinating them to the market, also reshapes them to serve the needs of capital."[21]

According to this scholarly framework, management functioned in parallel as the direct hand of the capitalist to control and mechanize every inch of the process. For instance, in 1977, Barbara and John Ehrenreich described the professional, managerial class as "salaried mental workers who do not own the means of production and whose major function in the social division of labor" is "the reproduction of capitalist culture and . . . class relations."[22] Both management and labor were caught in an essentializing and hierarchical dichotomy where there was no outside to the domination of capital over labor. Corporations were mainly interpreted as large-scale institutions for social control.

And, yet, even under the most oppressive bureaucratic regimes, employees continually "interpreted" and "translated" their orders.[23] For example, while requiring workers to "submit to command and control," Taylorism and Fordism did not reject the simultaneous ideal that labor and the work ethic produced "independence."[24] Now, while one could argue that independence actually furthered the Taylorist project through individuating and internalizing the self-as-worker, one could also make the corollary argument that "Taylored lives" were never completely totalizing. Martha Banta argues that even Frederick Winslow Taylor himself, who sought to spread his "managerial ethos" into every facet of life through the proliferation of stories told by multiple interlocutors and disciples, could not remain "in full control of either the practices of narrativization or the theoretical analysis," as multiply positioned storytellers, from managers to workers, would differ, sometimes unexpectedly, in their "support" or "condemnation" of various versions of Taylorism.[25] Richard Sennett goes so far as to argue that "interpretive modulation" was built into any bureaucratic pyramid, and that "performing" these continual translations "afforded people in the corporation a sense of their own agency."[26] The crucial point here is that power is always already mediated and continually interpreted, and that stable, bureaucratic institutions gave employees and communities "the gift of organized time," not only to plan and navigate their lives, but also to plot the reform of these very institutions. One could argue that the denial of the possibilities of bureaucracy played its part in allowing "one of the great ironies of the new economy model": "taking apart the iron cage . . . only succeeded in reinstituting these social and emotional traumas in a new institutional form."[27]

Sociologist Vicki Smith sheds light on another aspect of this generation of critique and scholarship. She argues that it was precisely this presumption of the rigidity of bureaucracy that allowed progressive public policy analysts, social activists, and senior corporate executives to come together and "*converge* on the goal of dismantling the bureaucratic management structure" (emphasis mine).[28] Political scientist Kathy Ferguson's book *The Feminist Case Against Bureaucracy* is a case in point: she portrays feminism as antithetical to bureaucracy, asserting that the latter is one of the "primary source[s] of the oppression of women and men," as it "induces conformity," isolation, and depersonalization, as well as rigid relations of "dominance and subordinance for employees and clients at *all* levels of the organization" (emphasis mine).[29] Similarly, anthropologist Jane Collins points out that the central social scientific rationale for the dismantling of the Fordist order was the "rigidity in the system"—the "rigidity of fixed investments in large factories, the rigidity of labor contracts and lifelong bargains with workers, and the rigidity of the state's commitments to social programs."[30] The *form* of rigidity, in and of itself, indexed bureaucratic failure and became the primary locus of discontent that contained, manifested, and symbolized all that was "wrong" with bureaucracy. In a sense, then, the diverse, actual contexts and negotiations of social and economic practices mattered less; bureaucracy itself had literally become the enemy and its elimination was thus presumed to be liberating. Ironically, what many social analysts have realized in hindsight is that in this dismantling, "the social has been diminished," while "capitalism remains."[31] In other words, embedded within bureaucracy were social relationships and employment promises, along with a temporal anchor that allowed the development and actualization of these social and work relations.

Could it be, then, that the scholarly and activist critiques of "the iron cage" were so totalizing that they left little room for imagining possibilities within these frames? Did the rigidities of our scholarly frame reflect (or only allow us to see) the rigidities of the imagined bureaucracy? What many of us did not anticipate—given the equating of corporations with oppression—was that the "revulsion against bureaucratic routine and pursuit of flexibility has produced new structures of power and control, rather than created the conditions which set us free."[32] Capturing this ambivalence in the scholarly temper, Gerald Davis and Adam Cobb, who recently put forward an argument that there existed less inequality during the age of corporate bureaucracy, framed their findings in terms of a "paradox of hierarchy." They seemed relatively shocked that even though "*organizations are a primary mechanism for generating inequality in society,*" it is precisely the size of the "largest employers relative to the size of the labor force" that has generated lower levels of "economy-wide income inequality." In other words, the "pre-downsized" modern corporations built throughout the mid-twentieth century ("when employment concentration increased during the merger wave of the 1960s") contributed to "the lowest levels" of inequality on record. As corporations were whittled down due to "bust-up takeovers, spinoffs, layoffs, and outsourcing during the 1980s and 1990s, employment concentration declined, while inequality correspondingly increased." While Davis and Cobb "do not want to wax nostalgic for some lost golden era of the organization man," they come to the realization that "with the death of the bureaucratic career has come the death of clearly-defined pathways to mobility" and that bureaucratic rationalization, albeit hierarchical, brought compensation in line with organizational standards.[33]

Finally, progressive academic and populist social sentiment toward corporations today is perhaps best exemplified by the widespread expressions of incredulity and hostility toward 2012 Republican presidential nominee Mitt Romney's proclamation that "corporations are people, my friends." In one sense, of course, Romney's comment was interpreted as wildly out of touch, precisely because many people's experiences of corporations have been constituted through precarity, restructuring, and exploitation. As their share of the economic pie dwindles, they are faced with financier windfalls—continual Wall Street transactions and devotion to stock prices—with little concern for employees. But I would also argue that this easy, static characterization of corporations as always already predatory fails to make the important distinction between corporations today (which are financialized entities negotiating short-term shareholder value) and those of generations past (corporations as longer-term social institutions). Moreover, one could certainly make the case that Romney himself utilized a historical sleight of hand: by attempting to evoke a personable corporation, he not only equated the current financialized entity with the paternalistic corporation, but also perhaps attempted to obscure the heightened inequality generated by the former by conjuring the latter. Ahistorical templates of "the corporation," in the realms of critical scholarship and public discourse, thus prevent a thorough accounting of radical socioeconomic change.

Employment Consequences: The Demise of Ladders and the Rise of Consultants and Old Boys' Networks

Twenty years ago, in 1993, sociologists Alejandro Portes and Min Zhou began to observe a growing "downward assimilation" that ran counter to linear conceptualizations of the American Dream. They presciently argued that one of the key obstacles preventing, in particular, the second-generation children of immigrants from experiencing social mobility was the "evaporation of *occupational ladders* for intergenerational mobility."[34] The demise of the workplace ladder created an "hourglass economy" and an increasingly steep and narrow "bottleneck to occupations."[35] Linking into the argument of this article, the demise of the ladder, while usually attributed to macro-processes of global economic restructuring, is directly and intimately linked to the dismantling of corporations as long-term, bureaucratic social institutions.

This final section queries the employment consequences for multiple levels of employees when the demise of bureaucracy necessarily undermines the key "imaginative object" that coheres to it: the ladder. While the ladder organized the hierarchical relationship between management and worker, it also served as the device for developing employee self-understanding, planning, movement, and future goals. Moreover, one may "climb up or down or remain stationary but there is always a rung on which to step."[36] Climbing steps became a way of life, and in this light, a form of home, albeit hierarchical. Given that in practice, most workers did not conform to the psychology Weber presumed for the iron cage, the demise of the ladder undermined stability, potential mobility, and the creation of a work narrative.

The View from the Top: Power Without Authority, Control Without Commitment

Executives charged with running contemporary corporations are judged primarily by their "willingness to destabilize [their] own organization," which in turn sends "a positive signal" to the new power brokers of Wall Street. Given that continual, restructuring change is considered innovation and stability a sign of weakness, then the practice of management, in both temporality and content, becomes relinked to the cultural values of financialization. Just as financialized corporations are broadly conceptualized as mimicking "the market," workplace relations are framed as "internal markets," constructed to reassemble the imagined external marketplace. As such, the "visible hands" (bureaucratic planning structures) of prior corporations that were constructed to temper and protect the "internal" workings of the institution from the volatilities of "external" market forms and practices were reframed as unnecessary as well as illegitimate, for "the market" had become the proper measure for all corporate spaces. In hindsight, the construction and maintenance of the distinction between inside and outside allowed for a kind of protection and insulation of workplace conditions, where institutions negotiated with a variety of timeframes and measures that were industry and institutionally specific. Thus, the breaking down of these boundaries, while seemingly liberating, created in practice a reorientation and subjection to actors who spoke in the name of the market—that is, financial institutions, investment managers, and Wall Street analysts. Moreover, the consequence of market governance meant privileging particular kinds of networks and managers that exacerbated, not attenuated, socioeconomic inequality. It is important to underscore I am not so much arguing that bureaucratic, welfare-capitalist values were actually "internal," and market values were actually "external." Rather, I am pointing out that how they were framed and understood spatially indicated their historical relationship, and the growing hierarchy between the two.

Within this de-layered framework (characterized by a gutted middle management with centralized lateral power at the top and, not surprisingly, overrepresentation in the bottom ranks), *managing* and being a bold manager means sending out "edicts from above." Top executives presume that their status, position, "belief in their own mental prowess, and access to technology empower them to command immediate change from the top."[37] This new process of management is worth unpacking. The elimination of middle management layers helped give rise to the presumption that commands from the top did not need to be mediated. Importantly, whereas today's corporation is all too ready to dismiss the roles, practices, and functions of middle managers, in the past they often worked to interpret, translate, even mitigate such commands, and in so doing, rendered them local and understandable. Moreover, those at the top, driven by impatient finance capital, are trained to understand themselves as charismatic leaders and "corporate saviors" who can instantly enact their will. Harvard business school professor Rakesh Khurana critiques this notion of the "charismatic CEO" as detrimental to the organization, as it reframes the modern corporation as an "elaborate structure for enabling a handful of well-connected insiders to benefit at the expense of the average person."[38] Business school students are trained to embody and emulate this de-institutionalized persona. As Khurana describes it, the "leadership model currently taught in business schools" is one where MBA students learn to equate themselves with the "single CEO protagonist" and to lead as if there were no constraints or competing agendas. In fact, the entire business study is written from the point of view of the CEO, and the task of the student is to save the corporation and be the star, the "change agent," thus reinforcing the top-down, charismatic orientation that dominates contemporary discussions of leadership while simultaneously constructing unrealistic expectations and perpetuating a management style unequipped for long-term negotiations and resolutions.[39]

In general, however, and beyond the CEO, I would argue that management consultants, both as profession and metaphor, serve as the new ideal-typical models of the managerial profession, the manager par excellence. Interestingly, the fact that management consultants are imagined to be "outside" the organization while their object of fixation is the corporate organization itself captures precisely the encounter between different spheres consultants are prized for in the new financial economy. It is this externalized standpoint—combined with the commitment to bold and radical revisioning of the workplace and workflow processes—that legitimates consulting "objectivity" and claims to efficient restructuring. Consultants approach each project vis-à-vis an overarching template, which they "tweak" based on the organization, industry, department, or corporation. Consultants, based upon what they already know—their culture of professional practice—"do the painful work of reorganizing activities throughout the peripheries of the organization—forced retirements, abolition of departments, new duties for employees who survive."[40]

And yet, it is precisely what recommends consultants in this new landscape that renders their recommendations so damaging to organizations. Consultants, as unaccountable interlocutors with misplaced and decontextualized expertise, do not have intricate, deep, and historical knowledge about the organization, nor any sense of commitment to it. With their eye toward payment and departure, they come to know the business only "through restructuring," and as such, they are prone to excise central connectors, layers, and pockets of knowledge crucial to the longevity of the institutions.[41] But they believe that through their own brilliance and hard work, they can analyze and master an entire area, and then create recommendations for change. Again, old-line managers are presumed to be encumbered, too "inside," too subjective, and thus unwilling (or unable) to be bold. Management consultants understand big change as a sign of their own ingenuity. "Internal" managers are then called upon to enact, embody, and operationalize these plans, thus conflating these two visions of management.

In sum, the consequence of management consulting as management is that it "divorce[s] control from accountability" in the organization. Given that their work is both externally sanctioned and charged to deliver solutions in the form of concrete "transactions," the presence of consultants allows "internal" managers to deny responsibility for restructuring. Yet when the consultants leave, these same managers must carry through the consultants' recommendations; such a passing of the baton allows the consolidation of greater power by executives at the top of an organization without the responsibility of authority. Because the social purpose of consulting is to conduct a transaction that "improves" the organization through reductions designed according to the evaluative standards of highly financialized models and spreadsheets, it comes as no surprise that such a managerial process often leaves an "organization in disarray," and "increase[s] social distance" and inequality on the ground. As Sennett concludes, management consulting is a "celebration of self-management" that is "hardly innocent": a "firm need no longer think critically about its responsibilities to those whom it controls."[42]

Ladders Pulled: Institutional Chaos and the Resurgence of Privilege

Perhaps the starkest ramification of the active construction of "market values" as replacement for the bureaucratic form is the demise of the corporate ladder as the device for broader social mobility and promotion. In such a context, a broad range of white-collar employees within the corporation are understood as mini-entrepreneurs, out-competing each other and driven by personal initiative, with no need for institutional architecture and bureaucratic structure. However, when entrepreneurial teams and individuals are charged with beating each other out to produce the "best" ideas, sales, and products in an "internal market," the corporations are plagued with duplication, inefficiency, and high stress. A "winner-take-all" model sacrifices broad organizational development for quick, high-stakes prizes. Managers are routinely oriented less toward a long-term process of innovation, and more toward quick results with little structure.[43]

Corporations under managerial capitalism typically promoted from within. Doing so allowed employees to accrue social capital, and such practices fostered not only loyalty but also knowledge of the idiosyncrasies of the firm. Of course, one could certainly argue that at least through the 1960s, promoting from within directly excluded "outsiders," external candidates, and that the bureaucratic formalization of hiring often "included following patterns initially developed for heirs, such as rotating select men through various departments. . . . The successful *did* compete on their way to the top, but they competed only among others who . . . had access to the right ladders."[44] This is certainly true, but it ignores the struggles and strides of the civil rights and feminist movements to actively shape and reform the bureaucracy. These movements succeeded in grafting some commitments to inclusivity onto the stable infrastructure of these institutions, and in so doing, recast marginalized identities, which had previously been subject to an almost-totalizing exclusion, as potentially connectable, hireable, even promotable. These incipient developments, however unsatisfying and incomplete, were destabilized and undermined in the wake of massive restructuring spurred by financialization of the past thirty years. In the end, recruitment and hiring in the new capitalism did *not* level the playing field, nor bring in new groups, but rather limited the potential of minoritized groups to accrue social capital.

A brief look backwards into the historiography and sociology of corporate ladders might be instructive here. At the dawn of the civil rights movement, people of color and women were "absolutely shut out" of white-collar and elite positions in the corporation.[45] While the postwar period expanded access to white men *not* from the upper classes, people of color and women lost ground, as white firms were "encroaching" on "previously segregated markets" while refusing to open their own gates.[46] It was only through the struggles of the civil rights movement that previously exclusive job markets were opened up, albeit slowly and in hierarchical ways, such that institutions began to "redesign their initial screens to fit skills and characteristics certifiably linked to job performance" and began to hire outside of privileged employees' own networks.[47] Before the 1960s, companies did not match jobs to employees' skills, but rather hired from old boys' networks. The social movements of that decade created an important sea change: marginalized identities and experiences, though still discriminated against, no longer served as totalizing disqualification and grounds for exclusion and devaluation.

By the 1970s, many "business and industrial labor unions" seemed to have "made peace with affirmative action," and many Fortune 500 corporations, from Xerox to Western Electric to Ford, began to redesign recruitment practices to focus on "screening in" versus screening out, so as to not "waste" talent.[48] Many mid- and high-level managers within these institutions and beyond (and especially in the public sector) started to recognize that differential valuations and hierarchies of background, connections, and access created situations where not only were assessments of "hard work and talent" insufficient for hiring, but hiring itself did not mean automatic advancement. It was finally a combination of "semiformal caucuses" of peer networks, formalized programs with buy-in from top management, federal policy reinforcement, and pressure and consciousness-raising from social movements that challenged the naturalized mores and practices of the old boys' networks.

The privileged "workings of social capital," which were invisible and normative, and benefited those in power, were "uncovered *only through* civil rights and feminist activism," and "the tools disadvantaged people and their advocates uncovered, named, and made legitimate now serve everyone, including those in the mainstream, more effectively than ever."[49] The age-old exclusionary practices of privileged white men were thus called out and repurposed; marginalized people challenged and identified these "essential mechanisms, first as factors that limited their success, then as tools for advancement." Even into the 1970s, such terms as "role models," "mentors," and "networks" were not in "America's general workplace vocabulary," and it was the active creation of "synthetic social capital" within institutions that allowed the white-collar workplace to begin to temper the effects of inequality.[50] A crucial point needs to be emphasized here: contrary to the misleading and retrograde conservative argument that using affirmative action to recognize and include the formerly excluded was a zero-sum game that "preferenced" the marginalized, such actions and orientations, where implemented, actually benefited and enabled all employees. Quite a few taken-for-granted institutional procedures and practices—from advertising job openings to the idea of matching job skills to people (versus simply picking from within a rarified insider network regardless of skill), from the importance of mentoring and networking to the creation of formalized training programs—were only made possible through struggles for fairness of access and promotion.

Seen from a historical perspective, these mechanisms of advancement and inclusion were only activated and applied (relatively) broadly *through* their location within bureaucratic institutions, through the process of formalization, of creating "synthetic social capital" within the institution, rather than the mobilization of already existing, individually generated networks of family and familiarity that benefited the status quo. In fact, research has demonstrated that it was precisely structured, "formal programs" with strong upper-management support and an understanding of the wider benefit that made a difference for these newcomers and "strangers on the ladder." Drawing from the 1995 Glass Ceiling Commission report, *Good for Business,* Laird concludes, "Overall, 'comprehensive, systemic approaches' succeeded, whereas 'one-shot or ad-hoc approaches' failed." In fact, poorly executed programs without broad-based institutional or top management support succeeded only in further stigmatizing outsiders and undermining the belongingness of the marginalized. Barriers to access were overcome by implementing formal programs "with strong and visible CEO support for *all* employees; tracking improvements; and making managers and other gate-keepers accountable for progress."[51] Embedding development programs within institutions, whether it structured systems of peer networking or formal mentoring programs that encouraged information-sharing, was what differentiated companies such as Xerox and IBM. For example, "African American men at Xerox formed the most well known of the early corporate caucuses put together by newcomers. Thanks to the participants' diligence and an unusually supportive upper management, this system of peer networks yielded a dozen African American vice presidents at Xerox by 1987." Of course, it goes without saying that employees with substantive background networks and corporate connections succeeded in ways that "formal programs were unable to replicate." And yet, modest successes were achieved through mapping points of connection and mobility onto the corporate ladder itself.[52]

The erosion and de-layering, then, of the organization collapsed the corporate ladder, and the continual restructuring of management destabilized the incipient and fragile networks that were strategically being embedded within the organization. In contrast, bureaucracy—with its stable layers—had allowed for both accountability and formalized mobility. Such an organizational format was "stable enough to deliver the future rewards," and for employees, this stability meant that managers remained "in place long enough to witness employee performances," and employees could work toward and plan for the next promotion. For the marginalized, the "fixed-work bureaucracies" in particular "served as a promissory note for social inclusion": the next steps on which to climb, already fused onto the work process itself, were not arbitrary and presumably would not disappear once previously excluded employees arrived. Moreover, the bureaucratic personnel procedures and evaluative processes grafted onto job levels favored longevity and protected the socially disadvantaged from the sorts of privatized deliberation and discretion that usually privileged white male networks.[53]

In the past few decades, as institutions were liquidated, these synthetic networks were targeted and dismantled, while the dense family connections and networks of class, race, and gender privilege (reframed as meritocratic through pedigrees from elite institutions) remained. Whereas the privileged had "traditional" networks—a dense latticework of colleagues, relatives, and classmates that crisscrossed the corporation and existed both internal to and outside it—the marginalized mainly had these bureaucratic promises, which served as networks for people without useful or connectable social assets of their own. These incipient networks "operate[d] *through* institutions to provide people having little access to social capital with some combination of role models and mentors, practical and social skills, and liaisons with the gatekeepers of opportunity."[54]

Moreover, Sennett makes the striking observation that the new elite, already resourced with "thick networks" that serve as their safety net, are disincentivized to plan ahead; rather, they learn to embrace "strategic confusion" and a presentist orientation. In other words, stable promotion ladders are unnecessary, as "chance opportunities" and possibilities that seemingly arrive out of the blue are more likely to cohere to "the child of privilege because of family background and educational networks." In fact, elites are often rewarded and judged to be smart precisely for turning against—restructuring or gutting—the institution. In a context where they are actively encouraged to use their resources and expertise to finesse, circumvent, or outwit many of the core rules, procedures, and even laws governing an institution, the stability and coherence of the organization matters little. In stark contrast, the child of the less privileged has a different relationship to institutional chaos or vacuums. With sparse networks, few contacts, and a lack of belongingness and support, this employee "remains more institutional-dependent." Crucially, her survival, not to mention success, requires formal strategic thinking, and formal strategic thinking *requires a legible social map*" (my emphasis).[55] For most employees, then, the demise of the long-term social institution has not so much ushered in change-as-opportunity, and a corresponding self-renewal, as it has rendered the social map of the workplace unintelligible. The "cutting-edge" organization is defined by "deficits of loyalty, informal trust, and accumulated institutional knowledge," and yet the privileged few who thrive in this arena do so precisely because they are a corporation unto themselves.[56]

The corporation, redefined and restructured in financial capitalism, is no longer the long-term social institution of the twentieth century that attracted multiple constituents eager to belong. At the moment when the buying of a corporation's stock ceased to signify simply the ownership of that stock, but rather the ownership of the corporation itself, corporations became their stock and were no longer "self-governing" institutions. This radical transformation, whereby corporations came to be fully equated with their stock price and beholden to financial market demands, depended upon the mining of institutional infrastructure to redistribute to institutional shareholders and financial advisors. Short-term shareholder value essentially ate the bureaucratic organization. And in a gutted corporation, it comes as no surprise that elite employees, who carry their networks with them and have become (in effect) organizations in and of themselves, are the ones who can thrive.

My point in this chapter is not so much to advocate for reinstating the old corporate regime, but to productively harness the politics of nostalgia to reflect on the loss and disappearance of an unexpected locus for challenging workplace inequality and insecurity. I argue that in order to imagine and implement community and employee-centered workplaces that provide fulfillment and sustenance, it is worth reexamining the models, cultural practices, and commitments that had cohered in bureaucracy. In fact, it is perhaps through this kind of accounting for and recognition of the protections and the possibilities mapped onto bureaucracy that we can better move beyond it to support the multiplicity of organizational forms emergent in the contemporary moment: worker cooperatives, credit unions, professional and industry organizations and support groups, and Occupy Wall Street social movements, to name a few.

For example, organizational sociologists Stephen Barley and Gideon Kunda, in their ethnographic study of high-skilled contract workers in Silicon Valley, indict the collapse of bureaucracy for the crucial loss of "access to corporate professionalism's supports," and recognize the "ambiguities of self-reliance."[57] And yet they demonstrate that the current goal is not so much to try to resurrect institutions that no longer exist but to rebuild supportive structures, actions, and organizations that, while more mobile, are grounded in and informed by the everyday practices and contexts of employees' lives. They found that occupational associations, professional societies, and industry groups, not to mention access to health care through temporary staffing agencies or other institutions, are indispensable for supporting and stabilizing the lives of contemporary itinerant professionals. It was through these assemblages that their informants not only constituted their knowledge and identity as technical professionals, but were also able to create the decentralized networks to find employment in the first place. I would emphasize that Barley and Kunda's insights on the growing importance of occupational, "strategic alliances" in "postindustrial organizing" were sharpened and informed not only through their ethnographic engagement with the experiences of contract professionals themselves but also through their attention to the gaps left by the collapse of bureaucracy, the work that these institutions engaged in, and the necessity of employee support and stability.[58]

Finally, as we look backward to better imagine what we need to do next, a word of caution is necessary. It is worth recognizing the danger of overprivileging work. In other words, given the larger socioeconomic contexts of less work, fewer jobs, and the devaluation of labor, the solution for progressive politics is often to advocate for more growth and more jobs, not to fundamentally question the politics of work and the fact that one's employment status has become indicative of one's moral worth. Feminist scholar Kathi Weeks, in an unconventional critique of work, has made a compelling argument that because the work ethic has been so naturalized and the presumed inevitability of waged work has so permeated everyday life, critical scholars, despite their interventions against alienation and exploitation, reinscribe and recenter the employment relation and the equation of work with life itself. A post-work politics, then, that questions and unpacks this trajectory and set of assumptions should be front and center as we use the lessons of corporate nostalgia to reimagine our socioeconomic futures.

Chapter 16

Can For-Profit Corporations Be Good Citizens?

Perspectives from Four Business Leaders

Nien-hê Hsieh

Can for-profit corporations be good citizens? If being a "good citizen" means acting responsibly and contributing to the good of society, then a quick glance at public opinion would suggest that for many people, the answer is no. Various retellings of the financial crisis of 2007–2009, for example, assign a central role to the activities of business enterprises, including mortgage lenders, banks, and ratings agencies.[1] Public polls reveal growing distrust in business and dissatisfaction with the size and influence of major corporations.[2] And, for-profit corporations face continued criticism that they fail to act responsibly with respect to a variety of areas, including wages and working conditions, corporate governance, and the environmental impact of their activities.

At the same time, the views of many scholars would suggest that criticism along these lines is misplaced. According to a widely held view, most notably associated with Milton Friedman, the responsibility of corporate managers is to maximize shareholder returns. On this view, if "good citizenship" requires corporations to forgo profits in order to further non-shareholder interests beyond what is required by the market mechanism or the law, then "good citizenship" is something to be eschewed by corporate managers.[3] On this view—frequently referred to as "shareholder primacy"—if there is anything about the ideal of "good citizenship" that corporations can and should follow, it is compliance with the law.

According to another view, to apply the norms of citizenship to for-profit corporations is mistaken altogether.[4] The activities of for-profit corporations, for example, may be said to belong in the private sphere, whereas the norms of citizenship apply to activity in the public sphere.[5] Furthermore, it may be said that citizenship is a property of natural persons. To suggest that for-profit corporations can be good citizens is to blur an important boundary between the public and private spheres and invites attributing to for-profit corporations inappropriately the rights associated with citizenship.[6] This is not to deny the relevance of debating the responsibilities and purpose of the for-profit corporation. Rather, the point is simply that such debates are best conducted without reference to the concept of citizenship.

What then about those who in fact manage and lead for-profit corporations? Do they view it as their responsibility to focus solely on maximizing shareholder returns? Is there anything to the idea of characterizing the purpose and responsibilities of for-profit corporation in terms of good citizenship? With these questions in mind, what follows are reflections on the comments of four business leaders,[7] with an emphasis on common themes and points of divergence as they relate to contemporary scholarship. The leaders were John Abele (co-founder and director emeritus of Boston Scientific and former president of Medi-tech, Inc.), Gordon Bajnai (former prime minister and minister of development and the economy of Hungary and former managing director and deputy CEO of CA IB Securities Plc), Fedele Bauccio (co-founder and CEO of Bon Appétit Management Company), and William Cobb (chairman of the board and CEO of JM Smith and president of QS/1).

Interests and Profits

In contemporary scholarship about the purpose of the for-profit corporation, a common way in which to frame the debate is in terms of whose interests the for-profit corporation is meant to advance. Shareholder primacy, as noted above, holds that the for-profit corporation is meant to advance the interests of shareholders, which is generally held to mean the maximization of their financial return subject to the constraints of market mechanisms and the law. The most prominent alternative is stakeholder theory.[8] Stakeholder theory holds that the for-profit corporation is meant to advance the interests of all stakeholders. Stakeholders, on this view, are defined as parties who are affected by the activities of the corporation or parties who are instrumental to its success. In addition to shareholders, they may include creditors, employees, clients, customers, suppliers, and the general public. As *interest-based* accounts of corporate purpose, shareholder primacy and stakeholder theory can be characterized as embodying divergent views about the weights to assign the interests of different stakeholders.

In response to proponents of stakeholder theory, proponents of shareholder primacy claim it is often the case that advancing the interests of non-shareholders leads to improved corporate financial performance.[9] Many of the remarks from the panelists could be taken in support of this claim. In particular, the panelists highlighted three means by which advancing the interests of non-shareholders could further corporate financial performance. The first, as highlighted by John Abele, is that for-profit corporations need a license to operate and that requires meeting certain communal and societal standards, which may include advancing the interests of non-shareholders. Without meeting those expectations, there would be no opportunity to operate in the first place. Second, according to Abele, central to the corporation's success are loyalty and maintaining good relations with all of the corporation's stakeholders. For example, a company is able to hire talented workers because people want to work for a successful corporation with a good reputation.[10] Related to this is a third mechanism, which is direct investment in stakeholders. As pointed out by William Cobb, as the third largest employer in its community, JM Smith has a "vested interest" in improving local education given that they want to hire educated employees. According to Abele, it is a matter of "enlightened self-interest" to pay attention to all stakeholders. And in the words of Gordon Bajnai, "the company—for its own good—must also be mindful of its wider circle of stakeholders: employees, the environment, and the state."[11]

What then did the panelists think should be done when the interests of shareholders and other stakeholders do not align? In situations such as these, what is the task of the corporate leader? For Cobb, the task is to find a "balance" between the interests of shareholders, customers, employees, and other stakeholders, and in finding that balance, there is "no priority among stakeholders." In the case of shareholders, what this means is to provide a "good return" for them. Cobb points out, however, that the company he serves is small and private. He knows each of the five hundred shareholders by name. They are in it for the "long term," according to Cobb, and they "don't seek to earn every penny at the expense of others." In contrast, the situation for leaders of publicly traded corporations may be different, he suggested. They may lack the leeway he has in balancing the interests of all stakeholders.

This lack of leeway on the part of corporate managers was echoed by the remarks of other panelists. For example, Abele also saw the task as "all about balance," but for him, the balance that needs to be struck is between the interests of various stakeholders, on the one hand, and the continued financial success of the corporation, on the other. As he pointed out, a company that does not survive financially cannot be a good corporate citizen for long. Similarly, Bajnai stressed the relevance of financial constraints. According to Bajnai, in times of crisis, corporations "shall principally seek to please shareholders by producing goods and services for a profit, satisfying consumer demand, and raising shareholder value."[12] To be clear, neither panelist suggested that managers should ignore the interests of non-shareholders. The point seemed to be that considerations of profit and financial success hold a certain priority when thinking about balancing the interests of various stakeholders in the case that tradeoffs need to be made among them. This prioritization can be seen as more in line with taking shareholder primacy, rather than stakeholder theory, as the appropriate account of corporate purpose and responsibility.

In the context of interest-based accounts of corporate purpose, such as shareholder primacy or stakeholder theory, the generation of profit holds significance primarily as a means to advance the interests of shareholders. Corporate purpose is then framed in terms of the extent to which profits ought to be traded off against the interests of various other stakeholders. Another way in which to understand profit is in terms of its role as an indicator of the financial sustainability of a corporation's activities. This interpretation points to an altogether different way in which to frame the purpose of for-profit corporations, one that is distinct from the interest-based framework discussed thus far. The following section outlines this alternate approach to framing corporate purpose and responsibility.

Productive Activity

"Our goal, actually, is to provide value to society from the beginning. That's the business goal. To the extent that we execute that well, we do well." That is how Abele described the approach taken by the company he helped to found and run. The thought seems to be that in designing and manufacturing medical devices, the company provides value to society, and that people's willingness to pay for these devices results in revenue for the company. How does conceiving of the practice of business along these lines give rise to an account of corporate purpose that differs from an interest-based framework?

One place to start is to consider the way in which profits are understood to serve as a motive or rationale for engaging in business activity. According to an interest-based approach to corporate purpose, as discussed above, the generation of profits serves primarily as a means to further the interests of shareholders. On the approach put forward in this section, profits are understood as the result of producing goods and services for which there is a demand on the part of people who are able to pay for those goods and services. This is not to say that the generation of profits is unimportant on this approach. After all, if the corporation were not profitable, it would have to cease its operations. Nor is this to say that managers do not intend to make a profit. Rather, the thought is that the generation of profit is not so much an aim in itself, but rather the mark of having engaged successfully in business activity.

In response, it may be said that the production of goods and services for which there is a demand is, in fact, a means to generating profits and, in turn, a means to advancing the interests of shareholders. For some managers this may be the way in which they conceive of the production of goods and services that are in demand, and this would be consistent with an interest-based approach to corporate purpose and responsibility. However, this does not rule out the possibility of an alternative to an interest-based approach to framing the purpose of for-profit corporations. Indeed, Abele allowed that the approach he outlined is "not the case [for] every type of company." The point is simply that there is another way to frame the relevance of profits in the context of an account of corporate responsibility that stands in contrast to that of shareholder primacy. Profits may be understood as constitutive of what counts as successful business activity, but they are not the aim or motive for engaging in that activity.

This emphasis on the specific productive activity of the corporation in conceiving of the purpose of the corporation can be seen in Fedele Bauccio's discussion of how his company came to be:

> My dream was to do something different in the industry. I wanted to create a new economic model that would be able to serve really great fresh food with local suppliers in markets that I thought I could reach the community in, and I wanted to do it in what you call the contrac-

tor institutional marketplace. . . . I wanted to do something in a restaurant kind of a way. So my dream was to create a new model. There was a lot of competition in the marketplace at that time. I figured to myself, I needed to do something different in order to distinguish myself. . . . So twenty-five years ago, my whole thought was about flavor and food. . . . I started talking to our chefs about going out into the fields and working with local farmers and local artisans and cheese-makers and ranchers and so forth because I was concerned about flavor . . . and that is how I got to the issue of sustainability, which is critical to the DNA of this company and how it works.[13]

For Bauccio, it seems, what defines the purpose of his company is the provision of a certain kind of product and doing it in a certain kind of way, which in this case, is one that centers on environmentally sustainable business practices. Because this approach allows the company to differentiate itself, it helps to make it profitable. But profitability is not the reason for choosing a sustainable approach to doing business. Moreover, it is the productive activity itself that is at the heart of the purpose of his business. For purposes of this discussion then, let us call this alternative to an interest-based approach, a *production-based* approach to corporate purpose.

At this point it may be asked whether the production-based approach is simply a version of stakeholder theory. For example, in describing the mission of his company, Abele referred to the patients who use medical devices, and for Bauccio, part of what drives him is knowing that what consumers eat is safe. To categorize the production-based approach as a version of stakeholder theory, however, seems mistaken. To be certain, the production of goods and services does serve the interests of those who demand them and are able to pay for them. However, just because these stakeholders benefit from the activities of the for-profit corporation, it does not follow that the purpose of the corporation must be framed in terms of the advancement of the interests of these stakeholders. According to the production-based view, what makes the activity of the for-profit corporation socially valuable is that individuals are able to meet their wants and needs as a result of this productive activity. This conception of the value of the activities of for-profit corporations differs from a view in which the aim of their activities is to advance the interests of various stakeholders. The activity is socially valuable not because it aims to advance the interests of customers, but rather because the activity is the sort of activity that allows customers to meet their needs and wants. Indeed, there need not be any motivation to advance the interests of customers directly. What matters is engaging in productive activity.

Two points of clarification are in order. First, this approach need not be taken to suggest that what satisfies consumer demand is itself socially valuable. Rather, the thought is that there is social value in having a system in which consumers are able to have their needs and wants met through the purchase of goods and services. Second, this approach need not be taken to suggest that the value of what for-profit corporations do is determined in part by how well they perform their activities in relation to some independent ideal or perfectionist standard. Instead, if there is a standard of successful activity, it is activity that results in the production of goods and services whose purchase by consumers meets their needs and wants.

Citizenship

As noted at the outset of this chapter, to ask whether for-profit corporations can be good citizens is to inquire not only into the purpose and responsibilities of the for-profit corporation, but also into what, if anything, is distinctive about corporate purpose and responsibility when considered from the perspective of citizenship. This section takes up this issue, starting with the panelists' comments on assigning to for-profit corporations a right that is central to citizenship in a democracy—the right to participate in the political process.

With respect to participation in the political process, the panelists were in broad agreement about the need for limited involvement on the part of for-profit corporations. "Beyond contributing twenty-five dollars to the local sheriff's association, we'll take no role," stated Cobb. "We don't contribute to political parties or candidates. We stay neutral on that." Cobb pointed out that his company does encourage employees to vote. If you vote, said Cobb, "you are a hero that day." Similarly, for Abele and Bauccio, involvement of their respective companies in the political process extended as far as encouraging employees to vote. "We give them the time off," said Bauccio, "and stay out of it." Bauccio continued, "I think it is very dangerous for a company to play a role and to say, 'vote here, vote there.'" Bajnai echoed the need for strict limits on corporate involvement and strong requirements of transparency. "Corporations without proper transparency and a sort of rule-of-law control on their influence on politics," he said, "can be very dangerous to our democracy."

In contrast, panelists did not hesitate in extending to for-profit corporations the duties associated with citizenship. For example, in response to a question from the audience about whether it was appropriate to draw an analogy between citizens and for-profit corporations, Bauccio noted that one respect in which for-profit corporations are like citizens is that corporations are required to follow the same basic rules. For Bajnai, "the most fundamental form of corporate social duty" is a duty viewed by many as central to citizenship—a duty to pay taxes. The reason, according to Bajnai, is that "the state is ultimately responsible for social protection and provides those services through tax revenues."[14] Taken together, the comments of the panelists convey an ideal of the for-profit corporation as an entity with less than full citizenship. That is, while for-profit corporations are required to follow the law and to pay taxes, they are to have a limited role in the political process that sets those requirements.

This ideal of limited corporate citizenship is consistent with interest-based accounts of corporate purpose and responsibility, such as shareholder primacy. Recall that according to shareholder primacy, the purpose of the for-profit corporation is to maximize shareholder returns so long as this is done within the limits of the law. According to interest-based accounts, for-profit corporations do not have independent interests in the same way as citizens. Rather, their purpose is to advance the interests of their stakeholders, whether narrowly or broadly defined, through commercial activity in an economic context. When considered in relation to interest-based accounts, the ideal of limited corporate citizenship underscores the senses in which those accounts are both restrictive and permissive. On the one hand, the ideal of limited corporate citizenship restricts the means by which stakeholders of for-profit corporations may advance their interests. If stakeholders are to advance their interests through the political process, it is in their capacity as citizens, and not as stakeholders of a corporation. On the other hand, the ideal of limited corporate citizenship underscores a sense in which interest-based accounts are permissive. Under interest-based approaches to corporate purpose and responsibility, managers of for-profit corporations are to act in ways that further the interests of specific stakeholders without having to address broader societal considerations so long as they obey the law.

When considered in relation to interest-based accounts, one way to understand the ideal of limited corporate citizenship is in terms of the idea of rule following. On this interpretation, commercial activity can be conceived as a kind of a game played by various actors in which actors are free to pursue their individual ends so long as they play by "the rules of the game." A duty to pay taxes fits into this picture in two ways. At one level, the requirement to pay taxes is simply a matter of following the law. At another, taxes may be seen as required to cover some of the costs associated with free-market activity. These include costs associated with protecting economic actors, maintaining the background institutions and infrastructure required for economic activity to occur, and compensating parties for the negative externalities that arise as a matter of course in the context of economic activity, such as pollution.

As in the case of interest-based approaches to corporate purpose and responsibility, a production-based approach identifies the commercial sphere as the appropriate locus of activity for the for-profit corporation. In this manner, the ideal of limited corporate citizenship is also consistent with a production-based approach to corporate purpose and responsibility. At the same time, consideration of limited corporate citizenship in relation to a production-based approach allows for a way to frame corporate purpose and responsibility that is distinct from that of rule following. This is with reference to the idea of a societal division of labor. On this interpretation, the for-profit corporation is but one of many ways to organize the production of goods and services that are needed or desired from the perspective of members of society or society as a whole. The role of the state is to provide those goods and services along with protections that are not readily supplied by for-profit corporations and yet are deemed important from the perspective of society. To be clear, according to this view, for-profit corporations need not be considered surrogates for the state in the provision of goods and services. Rather, the thought is that the ideal of limited corporate citizenship frames the activity of the for-profit corporation as part of the broader productive activity that occurs within society. If the conception of economic activity under rule following is one in which actors compete with one another in a game, then the conception in this case is more along the lines of one in which economic actors each play distinct roles that when pursued together allow society to meet the needs and wants of its members.

Participation in the political process, as discussed thus far, largely concerns electoral politics. On this point, as noted above, panelists were clear about the need for restraint on the part of for-profit corporations. At the same time, the comments of the panelists did suggest other areas in which it would be appropriate for corporations to be involved in the functioning of government institutions. One area that came up, in particular, was the regulation of business.

The panelists did not deny the need for government oversight. Citing the case of financial regulation, for example, Cobb emphasized the need for regulation to protect ordinary investors. Instead, the panelists voiced concerns about having the right sort of government oversight. With respect to taxes, Bajnai stressed that while the state should be strict in enforcing tax rules and the payment of taxes, the rules it puts into place must be "competitive."[15] For Abele, one concern was the "one size fits all" approach taken by government regulators. Another was the lack of predictability in government policies, especially given the difficulties in legislating in the current political context. In this light, Abele suggested there now was "a great opportunity" for businesses "to set up systems themselves that act as models or laboratories" to try out new rules and regulations. For Bauccio, the call for involvement extended further. Describing ways in which the current U.S. agricultural system is "broken," Bauccio explained, "we have a responsibility, at least in our part of the industry, to work with Congress to change it . . . to make change for the benefit of society." He concluded, "I think that is part of our role."

How do these comments figure into the discussion about the ideal of limited corporate citizenship? Consider first the case of interest-based accounts of corporate purpose and responsibility. When considered in relation to an interest-based approach, the ideal of limited corporate citizenship holds that the activities of for-profit corporations ought to advance the interests of stakeholders so long as they follow the "rules of the game." If, however, it is appropriate for corporations to be involved in setting regulations, then an interest-based account needs to specify when it is appropriate for corporations to be involved in setting the rules and the considerations that ought to guide them. Specifying those conditions, however, presents something of a challenge. Under an interest-based approach, the rationale for corporate activity is to advance the interests of stakeholders, but to set the rules to advance their interests runs counter to the idea of having rules in the first place. The challenge then is to specify considerations to guide corporate activity in addition to that of advancing the interests of stakeholders.

Consider now the case of a production-based approach to corporate purpose and responsibility. According to a production-based approach, the rationale for corporate activity is not the advancement of any particular set of stakeholder interests. Instead, the purpose of the for-profit corporation is to engage in the sort of activity that allows customers to meet their needs and wants. As a result, the approach avoids the challenge for interest-based accounts in justifying corporate involvement in the setting of rules and regulations described above. The focus on productive activity also provides a rationale for such involvement on the part of for-profit corporations. The rationale lies in the thought that for-profit corporations have a certain economic knowledge that comes from engaging in productive activity. This knowledge may relate to their individual enterprises, the industry in which they operate, or the economy as a whole. Insofar as sharing this knowledge with regulators and policy makers allows for rules that enhance productive activity, then sharing that knowledge is consistent with the purpose of the for-profit corporation under a production-based approach. According to this approach, corporations and their managers are to be guided by sharing their expertise as producers, rather than the advancement of any set of interests. This in turn is meant to help preserve the ideal of limited corporate citizenship in the face of corporate involvement in the regulatory and legislative process.

Conclusion

Can for-profit corporations be good citizens? That was the question put to a panel of four business leaders. Framing the panelists' responses in relation to themes and debates in contemporary scholarship, this chapter inquired into the purpose and responsibilities of the for-profit corporation, and into what, if anything, is distinctive about corporate purpose and responsibility when considered from the perspective of citizenship.

The chapter outlined two approaches to conceptualizing the purpose and responsibilities of for-profit corporations. The first frames the purpose and responsibilities of the for-profit corporation in terms of whose interests the corporation is meant to advance. Shareholder primacy—the view that the for-profit corporation is meant to advance the interests of shareholders subject to the constraints of the law—is a prominent example of this approach. Much contemporary scholarship follows this interest-based approach, and many of the panelists' comments were found to be consistent with it.[16] At the same time, the panelists' comments suggested another approach to framing corporate purpose and responsibility. This second approach was termed a production-based approach. According to this approach, what lies at the heart of the purpose of the for-profit corporation is engaging in productive activity. This activity is socially valuable not because it aims to advance the interests of any particular set of actors, such as shareholders, employees, or customers. That is not the purpose or responsibility of the for-profit corporation or its managers. Rather, the activity is valuable because it is the sort of the activity that allows members of society to meet their wants and needs.

As for conceptualizing corporate purpose and responsibility in terms of the rights and duties associated with citizenship, both interest-based and production-based approaches, for the most part, are consistent with the ideal of limited corporate citizenship that emerged from the panel discussion. For example, panelists were clear about the need to limit the participation of corporations in electoral politics, a limitation supported by both the interest-based and production-based approaches. Where the two approaches differ is with respect to one area in which panelists held it would be appropriate for corporations to participate in the functioning of government institutions—namely, the regulation of business. Justifying corporate involvement in setting regulations and specifying limits to that involvement presents a challenge for interest-based accounts. The basic challenge is that under an interest-based approach, the rationale for corporate activity is to advance the interests of stakeholders, but to set the rules to advance their interests runs counter to the idea of having rules in the first place. In contrast, on a production-based approach, the involvement of corporations and their managers is to be guided by sharing their expertise as producers, rather than the advancement of any set of interests. The sharing of expertise provides both the rationale for corporate involvement in formulating regulation as well as the basis for specifying the limits of involvement.

In examining the purpose and responsibilities of the for-profit corporation and what is distinctive about this topic when considered from the perspective of citizenship, this chapter has covered a good deal of ground and has raised a number of issues without addressing them fully. This is particularly true in the case of the production-based approach to corporate purpose and responsibility. The chapter has put forward only a brief sketch of this alternative to an interest-based approach, leaving many details to be developed.

With that said, it is hoped the chapter has provided enough detail to stimulate further debate about this approach and others to thinking about the purpose and responsibilities of the for-profit corporation. This attempt to stimulate debate is in part a response to an additional issue that the reference to citizenship brings to mind. As discussed in this chapter, the purpose and responsibilities of the for-profit corporation reflect the legal and political system in which it operates. In the ideal, the legal and political system is open to the influence of citizens. To ask about the corporation as a citizen then is to ask citizens about their visions for the for-profit corporation. The continued public distrust in business suggests the need for greater dialogue on this topic. This chapter is offered as part of that conversation.

Chapter 1. Why For-Profit Corporations and Citizenship?

1. Brandon Bowers, "YouTube Video Goes Venti After Singing Starbucks Employee Fired in Chowchilla," *Merced Sun-Star*, Lifestyle section, September 21, 2011. Available at http://www.mercedsunstar.com/2011/09/21/2052357/youtube-video-goes-venti-after. html. Lyneka Little, "Starbucks Employee Fired for Satirical Song," *ABC News 20/20*, September 2012. Available at http://abcnews.go.com/Business/barista-fired-starbucks-rant-song-viral/story?id=14582329#.T6qdJL81eRY.

2. From "Message Communicated to the Two Houses of Congress at the Beginning of the First Session of the Fifty-seventh Congress," December 3, 1901. *Addresses and Presidential Messages of Theodore Roosevelt, 1902–1904*. New York: G. P. Putnam's Sons Knickerbocker Press, 1904.

3. Sarah Anderson and John Cavanagh, *Top 200: The Rise of Corporate Power* (Washington, D.C.: Institute for Policy Studies, 2000). However, a 2009 report indicates that the number of business corporations among the top 100 economies may have dropped to forty-four: Tracey Keys and Thomas Malnight, "Corporate Clout: The Influence of the World's Largest 100 Economic Entities," *Global Trends*, 2009. Available at http://www .globaltrends.com/knowledge-center/features/shapers-and-influencers/66-corporate-clout-the-influence-of-the-worlds-largest-100-economic-entities (accessed May 9, 2012).

4. Matthew Bristow, "Drugs Fade in Colombian Economy," *Wall Street Journal,* April 3, 2010. Available at http://online.wsj.com/article/SB10001424052702303960604575158 203628601096.html.

5. *Planetary Resources*, 2012, http://www.planetaryresources.com/mission (accessed June 25, 2012).

6. R. B. Gordon, M. Bertram, and T. E. Graedel, "Metal Stocks and Sustainability," PNAS 103 (2006): 1214. Available at http://www.pnas.org/content/103/5/1209.full.pdf +html (accessed June 15, 2012).

7. *Planetary Resources*, 2012, http://www.planetaryresources.com/mission (accessed June 15, 2012).

8. http://www.addictinggames.com/about/about-us.jsp (accessed June 11, 2012).

9. The characterization of corporations as "profitable philanthropies" I owe to John Abele, co-founder and former director of Boston Scientific Corporation, who participated in a roundtable discussion in connection with the development of this book. I am grateful to him and to the other participants in that roundtable, the results of which are discussed in the concluding section of this introductory chapter and in the book's final chapter, written by Nien-hê Hsieh.

10. Judith MacKay and Michael P. Eriksen, *The Tobacco Atlas* (Geneva: World Health Organization, 2002), 36. Available at http://www.who.int/tobacco/media/en/title.pdf.

11. John Keegan, *The Second World War* (New York: Penguin Books, 2005 [1990]), 12.

12. Centers for Disease Control and Prevention, National Center for Chronic Disease Prevention and Health Promotion, "Tobacco Use: Targeting the Nation's Leading Killer, at a Glance 2011." Available at http://www.cdc.gov/chronicdisease/resources/publications/AAG/osh.htm.

13. N. Hirschhorn, "Corporate Social Responsibility and the Tobacco Industry: Hope or Hype?" *Tobacco Control* 13 (2004): 449. Available at http://tobaccocontrol.bmj.com/content/13/4/447.abstract.

14. Adam Smith, *The Theory of Moral Sentiments*, par. IV.I.10.

15. M. Todd Henderson, "Everything Old Is New Again: Lessons from *Dodge v. Ford Motor Company*," John M. Olin Law and Economics Working Paper 373 (2007), 26.

16. Lynn A. Stout, "Why We Should Stop Teaching *Dodge v. Ford*," UCLA School of Law, Law and Economics Research Paper 07-11 (2007), 3.

17. Milton Friedman, "The Social Responsibility of Business Is to Increase Its Profits," *New York Times Magazine*, September 13, 1970, 32–33, 122, 124, 126. Available at http://scholar.google.com/scholar_url?hl=en&q=http://www.umich.edu/~thecore/doc/Friedman.pdf&sa=X&scisig=AAGBfm2ow5EKPpLLiXQRcI6D8HywHfWN0g&oi=scholarr.

18. Stout, "Why We Should Stop Teaching *Dodge v. Ford*," 7.

19. Stout, "Why We Should Stop Teaching *Dodge v. Ford*," 12.

20. Anthony P. Carnevale et al., *Help Wanted: Projections of Jobs and Education Requirements Through 2018*, Georgetown University Center on Education and the Workforce, June 15, 2010. Available at http://cew.georgetown.edu/jobs2018.

21. National Center for Education Statistics, Institute of Education Sciences, *Fall Enrollment and Number of Degree-Granting Institutions, by Control and Affiliation of Institution: Selected Years, 1980 Through 2009* (2010), Table 205. Available at http://nces.ed.gov/programs/digest/d10/tables/dt10_205.asp.

22. Amitai Etzioni, "Warning: Profit-making Colleges Are After You." *Huff Post, The Blog*, June 9, 2010. Available at http://www.huffingtonpost.com/amitai-etzioni/warning-profit-making-col_b_629213.html.

23. In the area of military defense, President Dwight D. Eisenhower in his farewell address on January 17, 1961, famously warned of the growing dangers of a "military-industrial complex."

24. Although the Penn State child sex abuse scandal makes obvious that public colleges and universities are not always themselves model citizens.

25. Bethany McLean and Peter Elkind, "The Guiltiest Guys in the Room," *CNN Money*, July 5, 2006. Available at http://money.cnn.com/2006/05/29/news/enron_guiltyest.

26. The joke can be found in differing forms on various websites. This version is from About.com's "Political Humor," http://politicalhumor.about.com/library/jokes/bljokecel lular.htm (accessed May 15, 2012).

27. See the Tea Party Patriots website, http://www.teapartypatriots.org/about (accessed May 5, 2012).

28. See the Occupy Wall Street website, http://occupywallst.org/about/ (accessed May 15, 2012).

29. The question of slavery's profitability has been long discussed, a classic formulation being that of Eric Williams (*Capitalism and Slavery* [Chapel Hill: University of North Carolina Press, 1994 [1944]), 6ff.), who argues that slavery was profitable under specific circumstances—namely, when free labor was in short supply.

30. Upton Sinclair, *The Jungle* (New York: Dover Thrift Editions, 2001 [1906]), 89.

31. Charles Duhigg and David Barboza, "In China, Human Costs Are Built into an iPad." *New York Times*, January 25, 2012. Available at http://www.nytimes.com/2012 /01/26/business/ieconomy-apples-ipad-and-the-human-costs-for-workers-in-china .html?pagewanted=all.

32. Peter Phillips, "The 1934–35 Red Threat and the Passage of the National Labor Relations Act," *Critical Sociology* 20 (1994): 27–50.

33. Franklin D. Roosevelt, "Statement on Signing the National Labor Relations Act," July 5, 1935. Available at http://www.intellectualtakeout.org/library/quotes/franklin-d -roosevelt-statement-signing-national-labor-relations-act-roosevelt (accessed June 21, 2012).

34. According to data presented in table A1 in Gerald Mayer, "Union Membership Trends in the United States," *Congressional Research Service, Library of Congress*, August 31, 2004. Available at http://digitalcommons.ilr.cornell.edu/cgi/viewcontent.cgi?article =1176&context=key_workplace (accessed June 21, 2012).

35. James Burnham, *The Managerial Revolution: What Is Happening in the World* (New York: John Day Company, 1941). See also Adolf A. Berle and Gardiner C. Means, *The Modern Corporation and Private Property* (New York: Harcourt, Brace & World, 1932 [1968]).

36. The exemption also covered outside sales staff, and has been expanded more recently to included computer experts. See U.S. Department of Labor, Wage and Hour Division, *Fact Sheet #17A: Exemption for Executive, Administrative, Professional, Computer and Outside Sales Employees Under the Fair Labor Relations Act* (Washington, D.C.: Department of Labor, 2008). Available at http://www.dol.gov/whd/regs/compliance/hrg .htm#8.

37. These figures are taken from table 3 in Jelle Visser, "Union Membership Statistics

in Twenty-four Countries," *Monthly Labor Review* 1 (2006): 45. Available at www.bls.gov /opub/mlr/2006/01/art3full.pdf.

38. Ben Klayman, Nick Zieminski, and Matthew Lewis, "U.S. Treasury Cuts Stake in GM to 7.3 Percent." Reuters, September 18, 2013. Available at http://www.reuters.com /article/2013/09/18/us-autos-gm-treasury-idUSBRE98H0KE20130918 (accessed September 27, 2013).

39. "China Buys Up the World," *Economist*, November 11, 2010. Available at http:// www.economist.com/node/17463473.

40. Paul R. Gregory, *The Political Economy of Stalinism* (Cambridge: Cambridge University Press, 2004), 27–28.

41. Gregory, *The Political Economy of Stalinism*.

42. Philip Hanson, "The Russian Economic Puzzle: Going Forwards, Backwards, or Sideways?" *International Affairs* 83 (2007): 869–89.

43. "Country Rankings," *Heritage*, 2012, http://www.heritage.org/index/ranking (accessed June 28, 2012).

44. Friedman, "The Social Responsibility of Business Is to Increase Its Profits," 33.

45. Karen Gullo, "S&P, Moody's Must Face Calpers Lawsuit over Ratings, Judge Rules," *Businessweek* January 13, 2012. Available at http://www.businessweek.com/news/2012 -01-13/s-p-moody-s-must-face-calpers-lawsuit-over-ratings-judge-rules.html.

46. Arindrajit Dube and Ken Jacobs, "Hidden Cost of Wal-Mart Jobs: Use of Safety Net Programs by Wal-Mart Workers in California," Center for Labor Research and Education, Institute of Industrial Relations, University of California, Berkeley, August 2, 2004.

47. Wal-Mart, "Wal-Mart Careers," 2012, http://careers.walmart.com/our-company (accessed June 29, 2012).

48. Wal-Mart "Supplier Sustainability Assessment," 2012, http://www.walmartstores .com/download/4055.pdf (accessed July 1, 2012).

49. Paul Baier, "Why Wal-Mart's Better Supplier Scorecard Is a Big Deal," Greenbiz. com, April 2012, http://www.greenbiz.com/blog/2012/04/19/why-walmarts-better-sup plier-scorecard-big-deal (accessed July 1, 2012).

50. John Morell, "Impact of the Wal-Mart Sustainability Scorecard [1]." Enivron mentalManger.org, 2009, http://www.environmentalmanager.org/index.php/category /topicsissues/toolsforsustainability/the-role-of-tacit-knowledge-in-information -transfer/ (accessed July 3, 2012).

51. Tamara Audi, "Los Angeles Unions Try a New Tack in Wal-Mart Battle," *Wall Street Journal,* July 2, 2012, A2.

52. Andreas Knorr and Andreas Arndt, "Why Did Wal-Mart Fail in Germany?" *Materialien des Wissenschaftsschwerpunktes "Globalisierung der Welt Wirtschaft," Universität Bremen* 24 (2003): 18. Available at http://www.iwim.uni-bremen.de/publikationen/ pdf/w024.pdf (accessed July 10, 2012).

53. Kate Norton, "Wal-Mart's German Retreat." *Bloomberg Businessweek,* July 28,

2006. Available at http://www.businessweek.com/stories/2006-07-28/wal-marts-german retreatbusinessweek-business-news-stock-market-and-financial-advice.

54. Knorr and Arndt, "Why Did Wal-Mart Fail in Germany?" 18.

55. Stout, "Why We Should Stop Teaching *Dodge v. Ford*," 3.

56. Michael Lewis, *The Big Short: Inside the Doomsday Machine* (New York: W. W. Norton, 2011), 258.

57. Karen Ho, "Situating Global Capitalism: A View from Wall Street Investment Banks," *Cultural Anthropology* 20 (2005): 89.

Chapter 2. Corporate Power and the Public Good

1. This chapter is based largely but not exclusively on my book with Joseph L. Bower and Herman B. Leonard, *Capitalism at Risk: Rethinking the Role of Business* (Boston: Harvard Business Review Press, 2011).

2. Examples of corporate mismanagement, influence buying, and wrongdoing in the news as of this writing include, respectively, the $2 billion to $9 billion hedging error by JPMorganChase; the discount VIP loans made to members of the U.S. Congress by Countrywide Financial and the flow of corporate dollars seeking to influence the U.S. 2012 elections; and the revelations of extensive bribery and corruption by Wal-Mart in Mexico. See, e.g., Julie Steinberg and Dan Fitzpatrick, "JP Morgan Models Get Regulatory Spotlight," *Wall Street Journal,* June 29, 2012, C1; John R. Emshwiller, "Complaints in Congress Helped Prompt VIP Loans," *Wall Street Journal*, July 5, 2012, A4; Mike McIntire and Nicholas Confessore, "Groups Shield Political Gifts of Businesses," *New York Times*, July 8, 2012, A1; Stephanie Clifford, "Bribery Case at Wal-Mart May Widen," *New York Times*, May 18, 2012, B1.

3. See, e.g., Lynn S. Paine, "Managing for Organizational Integrity," *Harvard Business Review* 72, no. 2 (March–April 1994); Lynn Sharp Paine, *Value Shift: Why Companies Must Merge Social and Financial Imperatives to Achieve Superior Performance* (New York: McGraw-Hill, 2003).

4. Bower, *Capitalism at Risk*, 19–20, note 3.

5. Richard Newfarmer et al., *Global Economic Prospects 2007: Managing the Next Wave of Globalization* (Washington, D.C.: World Bank, 2007), 29. "Measured as the difference in the number of poor in 2002 using the 1990 poverty incidence (headcount) and the actual number of poor (at the $1/day poverty line)."

6. The World Bank's report is found in Newfarmer et al., *Global Economic Prospects 2007*.

7. The ten first-order areas include the three areas discussed in this chapter—the global financial system, income distribution, and environment—as well as seven others: the trading system, mass migration, the rule of law, public health and education, the rise of state capitalism, evolution and pandemics, radical movements and terrorism. For detailed discussion, see Bower, *Capitalism at Risk*, 43–102.

8. "Trade to Expand by 9.5% in 2010 After a Dismal 2009, WTO Reports," World Trade

Organization, press release, March 26, 2010. On World Trade Organization website, at http://www.wto.org/english/news_e/pres10_e/pr598_e.htm, accessed September 3, 2012.

9. Newfarmer et al., *Global Economic Prospects 2007*, xvi, fig. 7.

10. Newfarmer et al., *Global Economic Prospects 2007*, xiii, fig. 2.

11. Newfarmer et al., *Global Economic Prospects 2007*, 60, table 2.3.

12. Newfarmer et al., *Global Economic Prospects 2007*, 83.

13. Newfarmer et al., 110, table 4.2.

14. Bower, *Capitalism at Risk*, 58 (quoting a forum participant).

15. Newfarmer et al., *Global Economic Prospects 2007*, 143, table 5.1.

16. Bower, *Capitalism at Risk*, 188 (quoting a forum participant).

17. This is not to ignore charitable giving by corporations, which is both accepted and routine. Two-thirds of U.S. states, including Delaware, have adopted some form of § 3.02 of the Model Business Corporation Act, which expressly authorizes corporations to "make donations for the public welfare or for charitable, scientific or educational purposes," and the American Law Institute Principles of Corporate Governance provide that "Even if corporate profit and shareholder gain are not thereby enhanced, the corporation, in the conduct of its business . . . (2) May take into account ethical considerations that are reasonably regarded as appropriate to the responsible conduct of business; and (3) May devote a reasonable amount of resources to public welfare, humanitarian, educational, and philanthropic purposes." See Model Business Corporation Act §3.02, at http://apps.americanbar.org/dch/committee.cfm?com=CL270000; American Law Institute, *Principles of Corporate Governance: Analysis and Recommendations*, §2.01 (1994, with supplements). While corporate charitable giving in the United States came to $15.29 billion in 2010, this amount is small as a percentage of corporate spending, at about 0.1 percent of revenues. See Giving USA Foundation (2011), *Giving USA 2011: The Annual Report on Philanthropy for the Year 2010, Executive Summary* (Chicago: Giving USA Foundation, 2011); Committee Encouraging Corporate Philanthropy, *Giving in Numbers, 2011 Edition*, at http://www.corporatephilanthropy.org/pdfs/giving_in_numbers/GivinginNumbers2011.pdf.

18. Bower, *Capitalism at Risk*, 107.

19. Bower, *Capitalism at Risk*, p. 189 (quoting a forum participant).

20. David Moss, "Fixing What's Wrong with U.S. Politics," *Harvard Business Review* (March 2012): 134–39, citing Nolan McCarty, Keith T. Poole, and Howard Rosenthal, *Polarized America: The Dance of Ideology and Unequal Riches* (Cambridge, Mass.: MIT Press, 2006), 136.

21. "Nike, Inc. Announces Strategic Partnership to Scale Waterless Dyeing Technology," Nike Press Release, February 7, 2012. Available at http://nikeinc.com/news/nike-inc-announces-strategic-partnership-to-scale-waterless-dyeing-technology.

22. "Impact Areas: Water," Nike, Inc., FY10/11 Sustainable Business Performance Summary, 2012, p. 60. Also available at http://www.nikeresponsibility.com/report/content/chapter/water.

23. Amount based on industry analyst estimates of expected polyester production

of 39 billion tons for 2015, estimated water use of 100 to 150 liters per kilogram of textile material, and U.S. Environmental Protection Agency estimates of municipal water consumption. Sources: http://nikeinc.com/press-release/news/nike-inc-announces -strategic-partnership-to-scale-waterless-dyeing-technology,   https://www.ceres.org/ roadmap-assessment/key-findings/performance/operations/water-management#18, http://www.prweb.com/releases/polyester_filament_yarn/polyester_staple_fiber /prweb8121171.htm, http://www.epa.gov/watersense/pubs/fixleak.html.

24. "Nike, Inc. Announces Strategic Partnership to Scale Waterless Dyeing Technology," Nike Press Release, February 7, 2012. Available at http://nikeinc.com/news/nike -inc-announces-strategic-partnership-to-scale-waterless-dyeing-technology.

25. For a full account, see William C. Kirby et al., "China Mobile's Rural Communications Strategy," HBS Case No. 309-034 (Boston: Harvard Business School Publishing, 2009). A description of China Mobile's rural communications strategy can also be found in Bower, *Capitalism at Risk*, 131–36.

26. This account is based on conversations with founding partner David Blood and on Sandra J. Sucher et al., "Generation Investment Management," HBS Case No. 609-057 (Boston: Harvard Business School Publishing, 2009).

27. The MSCI World index is a frequently used benchmark for assessing the performance of global stock funds. The index, which covers some 1,600 stocks, is maintained by MSCI, Inc., formerly Morgan Stanley Capital International.

28. Author communication with founding partner, May 2012.

29. For a full account, see the case study by Lynn S. Paine, Nien-hê Hsieh, and Lara Adamsons, "Governance and Sustainability at Nike (A)," HBS Case No. 313-146 (Boston: Harvard Business School Publishing, 2013).

30. Nike's "Project Rewire" undertaken in 2009 is a good example. See "Impact Areas: Labor," Nike, Inc. FY10/11 Sustainable Business Performance Summary (2012), 49. Available at http://www.nikeresponsibility.com/report/content/chapter/labor.

Chapter 3. How Big Business Targets Children

1. "Greater Public-Private Cooperation Needed to Strengthen Public Governance," International Business Leaders Forum. Press release, January 25, 2008. Available at http://www-dev.iblf.org/media_room/general.jsp?id=123983.

2. For the other two, see Joel Bakan, *Childhood Under Siege: How Big Business Targets Children* (New York: Free Press, 2011). The cases mentioned in this chapter, along with others, are discussed there in much greater detail.

3. Joel Bakan, *The Corporation: The Pathological Pursuit of Profit and Power* (New York: Free Press, 2004), 56–57.

4. I first discovered the game at AddictingGames.com. It has since been removed. A few examples of sites where Whack Your Soulmate can still be played include: Y8.com, ArcadeCabin.com, and Y3.com.

5. At the same sites as in the previous note, and also at AddictingGames.com.

6. As noted, Whack Your Soulmate was recently removed from the site as a result of complaints from the organization Campaign for a Commercial-Free Childhood. The ten million unique user figure comes from http://www.addictinggames.com/aboutus/about_ ag.php. Buried in AddictingGames.com's privacy policy is the requirement that individuals be at least thirteen years old and live in the United States in order to play. Based on an unscientific survey of my son's friends—all of whom visited the site, were under thirteen years old at the time and did not live in the United States (we live in Canada)—there is little knowledge of these requirements among users, and no hesitancy to ignore them once made aware of them. The site has no registration requirement, nor are players asked to indicate their age before playing. By one estimate, 13 percent of visitors to the site are between the ages of three and twelve, 44 percent are between the ages of thirteen and seventeen, and 53 percent are female. More than half (53 percent) of households where the game is played include children between the ages of three and twelve; 43 percent of such households include children between the ages of thirteen and seventeen. http:// www.quantcast.com/addictinggames.com/demographics?country=US.

7. Interview with Martin Lindstrom. Also see Martin Lindstrom, *Brandchild: Remarkable Insights into the Minds of Today's Global Kids and Their Relationships to Brands* (London: Kogan Page, 2005).

8. Lindstrom, *Brandchild.*

9. Victoria J. Rideout et al., *Generation M2: Media in the Lives of 8- to 18-Year-Olds* (Kaiser Family Foundation, 2010). Available at http://kaiserfamilyfoundation.files.word press.com/2013/01/8010.pdf.

10. The $15 billion figure quoted here is likely conservative, as it is an estimate from 2003. Still, that figure is more than double the number from 1992. See Susan Linn, *Consuming Kids: The Hostile Takeover of Childhood* (New York: The New Press, 2004), 1. A 2007 estimate of the amount spent marketing to kids is $17 billion, compared with just $100 million in 1983. See http://www.cbsnews.com/stories/2007/05/14/fyi/main2798401 .shtml.

As noted below, children's direct buying power combined with their influence over parents' purchasing tops $1 trillion per year, an exponential rise over the past several decades. See "Trillion-Dollar Kids," *The Economist*, November 30, 2008, available at http://www.economist.com/node/8355035?story_id=8355035.

11. Martin Lindstrom, *Brandwashed: Tricks Companies Use to Manipulate Our Minds and Persuade US to Buy.* (New York: Crown Business, 2011).

12. Federal Trade Commission, *Perspectives on Marketing, Self-Regulation and Childhood Obesity: A Report of the Federal Trade Commission and the Department of Health and Human Services* (Washington, D.C.: Federal Trade Commission, 2006), 1. Available at: http://www.ftc.gov/os/2006/05/PerspectivesOnMarketingSelf-Regulation&Childhood ObesityFTCandHHSReportonJointWorkshop.pdf.

13. Evidence of full-fledged addiction to gaming and other Internet activities is controversial, though there is widespread agreement that gaming can generate similarly

compulsive behavior to gambling. Interview with Dr. Douglas Gentile. See also C. H. Ko et al., "Brain Activities Associated with Gaming Urge of Online Gaming Addiction," *Journal of Psychiatric Research* 43 (2009): 739–47.

The American Psychiatric Association recently stated that it will continue to monitor the accumulating evidence on "Internet addiction," though it currently has no plans to include it as an official disorder in its *Diagnostic and Statistics Manual.* See http://www .dsm5.org/ProposedRevisions/Pages/Substance-RelatedDisorders.aspx.

14. According to the American Medical Association, "The preponderance of research from both sides of the debate does support, without controversy, the conclusion that exposure to violent media increases aggressive cognition, affect, and behavior, and decreases pro-social behavior in the short term." American Medical Association, *Report of the Council on Science and Public Health: Emotional and Behavioral Effects, Including Addictive Potential, of Videogames,* January 2007. Available at http://www.ama-assn.org /ama1/pub/upload/mm/467/csaph12a07.doc.

15. American Psychological Association, *Report of the APA Task Force on the Sexualization of Girls* (Washington, D.C.: American Psychological Association, 2007). Available at http://www.apa.org/pi/women/programs/girls/report-summary.pdf.

16. See Rick Mayes et al., *Medicating Children: ADHD and Pediatric Mental Health* (Cambridge, Mass.: Harvard University Press, 2009), 1. In the past decade alone, psychotropic drug use among two- to five-year-olds doubled. See M. Olfson et al., "Trends in Antipsychotic Drug Use by Very Young, Privately Insured Children," *Journal of the American Academy of Child and Adolescent Psychiatry* 49 (2010): 3–6. Available at http:// www.ncbi.nlm.nih.gov/pubmed/20215922. See also a 2009 report by the Food and Drug Administration's Center for Drug Evaluation and Research on children's use of antipsychotic drugs at http://www.fda.gov/downloads/AdvisoryCommittees/CommitteesMeet ingMaterials/PediatricAdvisoryCommittee/UCM191615.pdf. For more discussion of increased psychotropic drug use among youth, see Elizabeth Roberts, *Should You Medicate Your Child's Mind? A Child Psychiatrist Makes Sense of Whether to Give Kids Psychiatric Medication* (New York: Marlowe and Company, 2006).

17. Jim Rosack, "FDA Warns of Suicide Risk with Paroxetine," *Psychiatric News* 38 (2003): 1, available at http://pn.psychiatryonline.org/content/38/14/1.2.full. For a recent study confirming the link between SSRIs and suicidality in youth, see Corrado Barbui et al., "Selective Serotonin Reuptake Inhibitors and Risk of Suicide: A Systematic Review of Observational Studies," *Canadian Medical Association Journal* (2009): 180, 291.

18. This account of Caitlin McIntosh's story is drawn from the testimony of her father, Glen McIntosh, before the Food and Drug Administration (FDA) panel. Transcripts of that testimony can be found at http://www.ablechild.org/fda_hearing_testimonies%20 2-2-04.htm and also at http://www.ritalindeath.com/FDA-Hearing-Testimonies.htm.

19. Erick Turner et al., "Selective Publication of Antidepressant Trials and Its Influence on Apparent Efficacy," *New England Journal of Medicine* 358 (2008): 252–60.

20. Dr. Eric Campbell quoted in Bob LaMendola and Fernando Quintero, "Eli Lilly

Paid Area Doctors to Discuss Drugs," *Orlando Sentinel,* September 23, 2009, http://articles.orlandosentinel.com/2009-09-23/news/0909220159_1_lilly-payments-to-doctors-companies-pay-doctors.

21. As quoted in Shannon Brownlee, "Doctors Without Borders: Why You Can't Trust Medical Journals Anymore," *Washington Monthly* (April 2004).

22. See Philip Shabecoff and Alice Shabecoff, *Poisoned Profits: The Toxic Assault on Our Children* (New York: Random House, 2008), 44.

23. Shabecoff and Shabecoff, *Poisoned Profits.*

24. Recent biomonitoring data collected as part of wide-ranging government-sponsored study in Canada suggests that our—and our children's—bodies are polluted with numerous industrial chemicals. See Health Canada, *Report on Human Biomonitoring of Environmental Chemicals in Canada: Results of the Canadian Health Measures Survey Cycle 1 (2007–2009)* (Ottawa: Canada, 2010). Available at http://www.hc-sc.gc.ca/ewh-semt/pubs/contaminants/chms-ecms/index-eng.php.

25. See, for overview, Safer Chemicals, Healthy Families Coalition, *The Health Case for Reforming the Toxic Substances Control Act,* January 2010, 8. Available at http://healthreport.saferchemicals.org/PDFs/The_Health_Case_for_Reforming_the_Toxic_Substances_Control_Act.pdf.

26. U.S. Center for Disease Control and Prevention, *National Report on Human Exposure to Environmental Chemicals: Executive Summary* (Washington, D.C.: Government Printing Office, 2005). Available at http://www.cdc.gov/exposurereport/executive_summary.html.

27. Author interview with Dr. Leo Trasande.

28. Trasande is quoted in Jordana Miller, "Tests Reveal High Chemical Levels in Kids' Bodies," *CNNTech,* October 22, 2007, http://articles.cnn.com/2007-10-22/tech/body.burden_1_flame-retardants-chemicals-bodies?_s=PM:TECH.

29. Rachel Gordon, "Mayor Gavin Newsom Vetoes Fast-Food Toy Ban," *San Francisco Chronicle,* November 13, 2010, http://articles.sfgate.com/2010-11-13/bay-area/24830064_1_toy-ban-toys-in-kids-meals-vetoes; CTV Calgary, "McDonald's Slams San Francisco Happy Meal Ban," November 2010, http://calgary.ctv.ca.

30. U.S. Food and Drug Administration, *FDA Amendments Act of 2007, Public Law 110-85, Title VIII* (Washington, D.C.: Government Printing Office, 2007). Fines of up to $10,000 a day can be levied for breach of the registration requirements. Available at http://frwebgate.access.gpo.gov/cgibin/getdoc.cgi?dbname=110_cong_public_laws&docid=f:publ085.110.

31. Roger Collier, "Clinical Trial Registries Becoming a Reality, but Long-Term Effects Remain Uncertain," Ca*nadian Medical Association Journal* 180 (2009): 1007–1008. Available at http://www.cmaj.ca/cgi/reprint/180/10/1007.pdf.

32. Cal Woodward, "New U.S. Law Applies 'Sunshine' to Physician Payments and Gifts from Drug, Device Industries," *Canadian Medical Association Journal* 182 (2010): E467–E468. Available at www.cmaj.ca/cgi/reprint/182/10/E467.pdf.

33. David Michaels, *Doubt Is Their Product: How Industry's Assault on Science Threatens Your Health* (New York: Oxford University Press, 2008), 256.

34. "Lautenberg Introduces 'Safe Chemicals Act' to Protect Americans from Toxic Chemicals," Senator Frank Lautenberg, press release, April 15, 2010, on the Lautenberg website, http://lautenberg.senate.gov/newsroom/record.cfm?id=323863. The "EPA does not have the tools to deal with dangerous chemicals," Senator Lautenberg continued, and "parents are afraid because hundreds of untested chemicals are found in their children's bodies." On European regime, see Robert F. Service, "A New Wave of Chemical Regulations Just Ahead," *Science* 325 (2009): 692–93. Available at: http://www.chemicalspolicy.org/downloads/2009-0807Scienceonchemicalregs.pdf.

Chapter 4. Corporate Social Purpose and the Task of Management

1. Howard Bowen, *Social Responsibilities of the Businessman* (New York: Harper & Brothers, 1953), 6.

2. Archie B. Carroll, "A History of Corporate Social Responsibility: Concepts and Practices," in *The Oxford Handbook of Corporate Social Responsibility*, ed. Andrew Crane, Abagail McWilliams, Dirk Matten, Jeremy Moon, and Donald Siegel (New York: Oxford University Press, 2008), 19–46; A. Acquier, Jean-Pascal Gond, and Jean Pasquero, "Rediscovering Howard R. Bowen's Legacy: The Unachieved Agenda and Continuing Relevance of *Social Responsibilities of the Businessman*," *Business & Society* 50 (2011): 607–46. Abstract available at http://bas.sagepub.com/content/50/4/607.abstract.

3. Bowen, *Social Responsibilities of the Businessman*, 12.

4. Donna J. Wood, "Corporate Social Performance Revisited," *Academy of Management Review* 16 (1991): 691–718.

5. R. Edward Freeman, Jeffrey Harrison, and Andrew Wicks, *Managing for Stakeholders: Survival, Reputation and Success* (New Haven: Yale University Press, 2007).

6. William Evan and R. Edward Freeman, "A Stakeholder Theory of the Modern Corporation: Kantian Capitalism," in *Ethical Theory and Business,* 4th ed., ed. Norman Bowie and Tom Beauchamp (Upper Saddle River, N.J.: Pearson Prentice-Hall, 1993), 82.

7. R. Edward Freeman, "Managing for Stakeholders," in *Ethical Theory and Business,* 8th ed., ed. T. L. Beauchamp, N. E. Bowie, and D. G. Arnold (Upper Saddle River, N.J.: Pearson Prentice Hall, 2009), 56–69.

8. Clarkson Centre for Business Ethics, "Principles for Stakeholder Management," *Business Ethics Quarterly* 12(2002): 257–64.

9. R. Edward Freeman, Jeffrey Harrison, Andrew Wicks, Bidhan Parmar, and Simone de Colle, *Stakeholder Theory: The State of the Art* (Cambridge: Cambridge University Press, 2010), 213–16.

10. Despite aspirations to the contrary in his early work, and despite the ways in which his work has been used by his proponents, Freeman is less inclined in his later work to conceive of stakeholder theory as providing a normative foundation for managerial responsibility or a theory that otherwise aims to build an account of managerial

responsibility based on an overarching *social* purpose of the modern corporation. He emphasizes that stakeholder theory provides a pragmatic basis for how a corporation can achieve its entrepreneurial objective of creating value. He writes, for instance, that stakeholder theory "is about business and value creation" and is fundamentally "managerial" in its scope. Freeman et al., *Stakeholder Theory,* 12.

11. Michael Porter and Mark Kramer, "Strategy and Society: The Link Between Competitive Advantage and Corporate Social Responsibility," *Harvard Business Review* (2006): 1–13 (Reprint R0612D); Michael Porter and Mark Kramer, "Creating Shared Value," *Harvard Business Review* 89 (2011): 62–77.

12. Aneel Karnani, "Doing Well by Doing Good: The Grand Illusion," *California Management Review* 53 (2011): 69–86.

13. John Rawls, "Two Conceptions of Rules," *Philosophical Review* 64 (1955): 3–32.

14. For a slightly different use of Rawls on this point as it relates to business *as a practice* versus a particular *form of organization,* see Alexei Marcoux, "Business-Focused Business Ethics," in *Normative Theory and Business Ethics,* ed. Jeffery Smith (Lanham: Rowman & Littlefield), 17–34.

15. John R. Boatright, "Business Ethics and the Theory of the Firm," *American Business Law Journal* 34 (1996): 217–38; Karnani, "Doing Well by Doing Good."

16. John R. Boatright, "What's Right and What's Wrong with Stakeholder Theory," *Journal of Private Enterprise* 21 (2006): 107.

17. John R. Boatright, "Contractors as Stakeholders: Reconciling Stakeholder Theory with the Nexus-of-Contracts Firm," *Journal of Banking and Finance* 26 (2002): 1837–52; Ronald Coase, "The Nature of the Firm," *Economica* 4 (1937): 386–405; Steven N. S. Cheung, "The Contractual Theory of the Firm," *Journal of Law and Economics* 26 (1983): 1–22; Oliver E. Williamson, *The Economic Institutions of Capitalism* (New York: The Free Press, 1985); Michael C. Jensen, "Value Maximization, Stakeholder Theory and the Corporate Objective Function," *Business Ethics Quarterly* 12(2002): 235–56.

18. Henry Hansmann, "The Ownership of the Firm," *Journal of Law, Economics, and Organization* 4 (1988): 267–304.

19. Freeman et al., *Stakeholder Theory.*

20. Sarah Williams Holtman, "Three Strategies for Theorizing About Justice," *American Philosophical Quarterly* 40 (2003): 77–90.

21. John Rawls, *Political Liberalism* (New York: Columbia University Press, 2005).

22. John R. Boatright, "Does Business Ethics Rest on a Mistake?" *Business Ethics Quarterly* 9 (1999): 583–91.

23. Michael C. Jensen, "Value Maximization, Stakeholder Theory and the Corporate Objective Function," *Business Ethics Quarterly* 12 (2002): 235–56.

24. The exception to this is the managerial discretion needed—and accepted—by owners to secure their position as residual claimants. Boatright follows Macey and contends that the special fiduciary trust that managers owe owners would itself ideally be subject to the bargaining process between owners and those willing to assume the role

of managers. In less than ideal circumstances, however, features of corporate law stand in to assure the trust between owners and managers by conceiving of managers at the outset as fiduciaries of owners. John R. Boatright, "Is There an Internal Morality of Contracting?" *Academy of Management Review* 32 (2007): 293–97; Jonathan R. Macey, "Fiduciary Duties as Residual Claims: Obligations to Non-Shareholder Constituencies from a Theory of the Firm Perspective," *Cornell Law Review* 84 (1999): 1266–81.

25. Jeffrey D. Smith, "Moral Markets and Moral Managers Revisited," *Journal of Business Ethics* 61 (2005): 129–41.

26. John R. Boatright, "Ethics and Corporate Governance: Justifying the Role of the Shareholder," in *The Blackwell Guide to Business Ethics,* ed. N. E. Bowie (Oxford: Blackwell, 2002), 38–60.

27. Joseph Heath, "A Market Failures Approach to Business Ethics," in *The Invisible Hand and the Common Good,* ed. Bernard Hodgson (Berlin: Springer-Verlag, 2004), 69–89.

28. Joseph Heath, "Business Ethics Without Stakeholders," *Business Ethics Quarterly* 16 (2006): 533–57.

29. Heath, "A Market Failures Approach to Business Ethics," 84.

30. Heath, "Business Ethics Without Stakeholders," 551.

31. For a more involved discussion of the interplay between the responsibilities corporate managers have toward members of the corporation (such as employees), and the responsibilities they have toward other societal stakeholders who are not members of the corporation (such as local community members), see Dominic Martin, "The Contained Rivalry Requirement and a 'Triple Feature' Program for Business Ethics," *Journal of Business Ethics* (2012). doi 10.1007/s10551-012-1369-4. Abstract available at http://link.springer.com/article/10.1007%2Fs10551-012-1369-4.

32. Some may be unfamiliar with the notion of ends as practical constraints. Ends can serve as constraints on deliberation and planning—that is, agents can be obliged to *take into account* certain ends when deciding how to act, or, in this context, how to conduct business. Barbara Herman, *Moral Literacy* (Cambridge, Mass.: Harvard University Press, 2007). Heath's list of market-oriented constraints need not function as a list of exceptionless rules without any need for application in concrete circumstances. The constraint that negative externalities be minimized, for example, is a constraint that specifies an end that should be weighted into a manager's decision making. What that end requires in a specific case, whether it demands, say, a specific type of pollution be reduced and how much of an investment in abatement or technological improvement it includes, can remain an open question depending upon the circumstances.

33. Wayne Norman, "Business Ethics as Self-Regulation: Why Principles That Ground Regulations Should Be Used to Ground Beyond-Compliance Norms as Well," *Journal of Business Ethics* 102 (2012): 43–57.

34. Christopher McMahon, "The Public Authority of the Managers of Private Corporations," in *The Oxford Handbook of Business Ethics,* ed. G. Brenkert and T. Beauchamp (New York: Oxford University Press, 2010), 100–125; Christopher McMahon, "The Po-

litical Theory of Organizations and Business Ethics," *Philosophy and Public Affairs* 24 (1995): 292–313.

35. McMahon, "The Public Authority of the Managers," 107.

36. Amartya Sen, "The Moral Standing of the Market," *Social Philosophy and Policy* 2 (1985): 1–19.

37. For the purposes of this chapter, I assume, without defense, that there may be some morally important social values that are not realized—or possibly marginalized in importance—if their production is delegated to firms operating in markets, even markets without any noteworthy failures. Markets will gauge individuals' preferences for certain social values, but those preferences may not capture their worth from a moral point of view. The efficient satisfaction of *individuals' preferences* for national defense, education, public health, and the like does not entail that those values themselves are being sufficiently produced, in relation to, and in comparison with, each other.

38. McMahon, "The Public Authority of the Managers," 120.

39. McMahon, "The Public Authority of the Managers," 121.

40. Christopher McMahon, "Managerial Authority," *Ethics* 100 (1989): 33–53.

Chapter 5. Corporate Purpose and Social Responsibility

In revising this chapter, we have benefited from the perceptive commentary Walter Licht provided on our first draft and from the bibliographic suggestions given us by Christy Chapin. We are grateful as well for the astute leadership and assistance of Greg Urban.

1. Adolf A. Berle and Gardiner C. Means, *The Modern Corporation and Private Property* (New York: Macmillan, 1932).

2. For an excellent discussion of the customary concept of corporate governance, see Mary A. O'Sullivan, *Contests for Corporate Control: Corporate Governance and Economic Performance in the United States and Germany* (New York: Oxford University Press, 2000).

3. Alfred D. Chandler, Jr., *The Visible Hand: The Managerial Revolution in American Business* (Cambridge, Mass.: Belknap Press, 1977); and Alfred D. Chandler, Jr., *Scale and Scope* (Cambridge, Mass.: Belknap Press, 1990). On the Great Merger Movement, see Naomi Lamoreaux, *The Great Merger Movement* (New York: Cambridge University Press, 1988). See also Louis Galambos, "The U.S. Corporate Economy in the Twentieth Century," in *The Cambridge Economic History of the United States*, vol. 3, ed. Stanley L. Engerman and Robert E. Gallman (New York: Cambridge University Press, 2000), 927–69; and William Lazonick and David J. Teece, eds., *Management Innovation: Essays in the Spirit of Alfred D. Chandler, Jr.* (New York: Oxford University Press, 2012).

4. See, for instance, Philip Scranton, *Endless Novelty* (Princeton, N.J.: Princeton University Press, 1997).

5. Robert H. Wiebe, "The House of Morgan and the Executive, 1905–1913," *American Historical Review* 65 (1959): 49–60; Vincent R. Corosso, *The Morgans: Private International Bankers, 1854–1913* (Cambridge, Mass.: Harvard University Press, 1987).

6. See Susan B. Carter et al., eds., *The Historical Statistics of the United States,* vol. 4 (New York: Cambridge University Press, 2006), 935; and vol. 5, 81. The total railroad funded debt was more than four times the size of the federal debt.

7. As the late Thomas C. Cochran pointed out in his study of railroad leaders, the concept of conflict of interest—between the railroad executives, for instance, and the construction companies they owned—was neither well understood nor invoked in the U.S. business system in the Gilded Age. Thomas C. Cochran, *Railroad Leaders, 1845–1890: The Business Mind in Action* (New York: Russell & Russell, 1965).

8. Thus the leaders of the great corporate enterprises of this period—John D. Rockefeller, Henry Ford, and others—became the founders of the new general-purpose foundations that carved out a new role for the nonprofit sector in twentieth-century America. For a recent analysis, see Olivier Zunz, *Philanthropy in America: A History* (Princeton, N.J.: Princeton University Press, 2012).

9. As Brian Balogh and William J. Novak have cogently pointed out, the states had exercised substantial powers throughout the nineteenth century. Our analysis focuses on the transition at the federal level, where interstate commerce was the major concern. But see Balogh's *A Government out of Sight: The Mystery of National Authority in Nineteenth-Century America* (New York: Cambridge University Press, 2009); and Novak's "Long Live the Myth of the Weak State?" in *American Historical Review* 115 (2010): 792–800.

10. Louis Galambos, *The Creative Society—and the Price Americans Paid for It* (New York: Cambridge University Press, 2012), especially chapter 3 on "State Crafting—American Style."

11. Susan B. Carter et al., eds., *The Historical Statistics of the United States,* vol. 1 (New York: Cambridge University Press, 2006), 104. The disparity is reduced if you add to the rural population those living in small towns with populations under 2,500.

12. Archie B. Carroll, "A History of Corporate Social Responsibility: Concepts and Practices," in *The Oxford Handbook of Corporate Social Responsibility*, ed. Andrew Crane, Abagail McWilliams, Dirk Matten, Jeremy Moon, and Donald S. Siegel (New York: Oxford University Press, 2008), 19–46, is extremely useful—as are many of the other essays included—but we believe developments before 1940 demand more attention than they received in this chapter. Geoffrey Jones and Jonathan Zeitlin, eds., *The Oxford Handbook of Business History* (New York: Oxford University Press, 2007), does not include material specifically on corporate social responsibility, but readers will find informative the comparative analysis in the chapters by Robert Millward, "Business and the State," 529–57, and Kenneth Lipartito, "Business Culture," 603–28.

13. William Henry Vanderbilt apparently said this to a reporter in the 1880s.

14. Richard Tedlow, *Keeping the Corporate Image: Public Relations and Business, 1900–1950* (Greenwich, Conn.: JAI Press, 1979).

15. Richard Gillespie, *Manufacturing Knowledge: A History of the Hawthorne Experiments* (New York: Cambridge University Press, 1991); and Richard Edwards, *Contested Terrain: The Transformation of the Workplace in the Twentieth Century* (New York: Basic Books, 1980).

16. There is a great body of literature on the Bell System. The interested reader can start with the citations in Peter Temin and Louis Galambos, *The Fall of the Bell System: A Study in Prices and Politics* (New York: Cambridge University Press, 1987), and then turn to Paul J. Miranti, Jr., "Probability Theory and the Challenge of Sustaining Innovation: Traffic Management at the Bell System, 1900–1929," and Kenneth Lipartito, "Rethinking the Invention Factory: Bell Laboratories in Perspective," in *The Challenge of Remaining Innovative: Insights from Twentieth-Century American Business*, ed. Sally H. Clarke, Naomi R. Lamoreaux, and Steven W. Usselman (Stanford, Calif.: Stanford University Press, 2009), 132–59.

17. Brian Balogh, "Reorganizing the Organizational Synthesis: Federal-Professional Relations in Modern America," *Studies in American Political Development* 5 (1991): 119–72. Balogh describes the emerging system as the "pro-ministrative state."

18. See two remarkable essays in *The Cambridge Economic History of the United States*, vol. 3: *The Twentieth Century*, ed. Stanley L. Engerman and Robert E. Gallman (New York: Cambridge University Press, 2000): Claudia Goldin, "Labor Markets in the Twentieth Century," 549–623, 1096–1100; and Christopher L. Tomlins, "Labor Law," 625–91, 1100–1113.

19. Chandler's emphasis throughout was on the internal, not the external, forces driving structural change in these organizations. Since three of the four giant firms that led the way in this phase of reorganization lost antitrust suits or had other problems with public policy during the early decades of the twentieth century, we feel safe in suggesting this altered perspective on causation (as well as results).

20. On the changes that accompanied the Third Industrial Revolution (also called the Digital or Information Age), see Naomi R. Lamoreaux, Daniel M. G. Raff, and Peter Temin, "Beyond Markets and Hierarchies: Toward a New Synthesis of American Business History," *American Historical Review* 108 (2003): 404–33. Also see Giovanni Dosi and Louis Galambos, eds., *The Third Industrial Revolution in Global Business* (New York: Cambridge University Press, 2013).

21. Most important in this regard is Carroll, "A History of Corporate Social Responsibility," 19–46. The entire *Oxford Handbook* in which this essay appears provides an excellent guide to the development of this field of study and instruction.

22. See, for instance, José Salazar and Bryan W. Husted, "Principals and Agents: Further Thoughts on the Friedmanite Critique of Corporate Social Responsibility," in Crane et al., eds., *The Oxford Handbook of Corporate Social Responsibility*, 137–55.

23. Patrick Despres-Gallagher conducted a study for us of the Fortune 50 companies (n.p., 2013). As the report indicates, all of the firms had at least one executive—either a vice president or senior vice president—of either corporate responsibility or corporate citizenship. In some cases there were multiple vice presidents with responsibility for different initiatives. Two fairly recent changes include an increase in public corporate social responsibility reports and the employment of corporate responsibility consulting firms.

24. See Jennifer Delton, *Racial Integration and Corporate America, 1940–1990* (New

York: Cambridge University Press, 2009); and Nathan D. B. Connolly, "Games of Chance: Jim Crow's Entrepreneurs Bet on 'Negro' Law and Order," in *What's Good for Business: Business and American Politics Since World War II*, ed. Kim Phillips-Fein and Julian E. Zelizer (New York: Oxford University Press, 2012).

25. Samuel P. Hays, *Beauty, Health, and Permanence: Environmental Politics in the United States, 1955–1985* (New York: Cambridge University Press, 1989); and Samuel P. Hays, *A History of Environmental Politics Since 1945* (Pittsburg, Pa.: Pittsburg University Press, 2000); Philip Shabecoff, *A Fierce Green Fire: The American Environmental Movement*, rev. ed. (Washington, D.C.: Island Press, 2003).

26. An exception was provided by the domestic tire manufacturers, which attempted to stay at home and meet the European competition of radial tires. After an extended competitive struggle, however, only one company remained in U.S. control. The others failed and were bought by foreign corporations.

27. See Louis Galambos, "The American Solution, 1981 to 2001," in *The Creative Society—and the Price Americans Paid for It* (New York: Cambridge University Press, 2012).

28. A recovery is under way, but domestic employment is seriously and uncharacteristically lagging. According to recent articles in the *Wall Street Journal*, U.S. multinationals are adding jobs overseas faster than in the United States; the U.S. jobs are being added at about the same pace as the growth of the U.S. GDP. A number of developing economies (the BRICS in particular) are, however, growing faster than the United States, and that is where more of the jobs are being added. Scott Thurm, "U.S. Firms Add Jobs, but Mostly Overseas," *Wall Street Journal*, April 27, 2012, http://online.wsj.com/article/SB10001424052702303990604577367881972648906.html. See also Ben Casselman, "Slowing Growth Stirs Recovery Fears," *Wall Street Journal*, April 28–29, 2012, http://online.wsj.com/article/SB10001424052702304811304577369640809969900.html, for comparative figures on recovery (including employment) as the economy began to pull out of recessions in 1975, 1980, 1991, 2001, and 2009.

29. We refer to the years between 1945 and roughly 1970 as the "American Century." The breakdown in American economic power on a global scale actually began in the late 1960s in several leading industries; the oil crisis of 1973 accelerated the downturn—1970 is just a convenient date.

30. The literature on this subject is vast. We have found the following sources particularly helpful: Christy Chapin, "Ensuring America's Health: Publicly Constructing the Private Health Insurance Industry, 1945–1970" (Ph.D. dissertation, University of Virginia, 2012); and Christy Chapin, "The Health Insurance Association of America, American Medical Association, and Creation of the Corporate Healthcare System," *Studies in American Political Development* 24 (2010): 143–67; Jennifer Klein, *For All These Rights: Business, Labor, and the Shaping of America's Public-Private Welfare State* (Princeton, N.J.: Princeton University Press, 2003); Paul Starr, *The Social Transformation of American Medicine* (New York: Basic Books, 1983); and Paul Starr, *Remedy and Reaction: The Peculiar American Struggle over Healthcare Reform* (New Haven, Conn.: Yale University Press, 2011).

31. See, for instance, Helene L. Lipton et al., "Pharmacy Benefit Management Companies: Dimensions of Performance," *Annual Review of Public Health* 20 (1999): 361–401.

32. See Dominique A. Tobbell, *Pills, Power, and Policy: The Struggle for Drug Reform in Cold War America and Its Consequences* (Berkeley: University of California Press, 2011), on pharmaceutical policy and political realities in these years.

33. The classic account is Randy Shilts, *And the Band Played On: Politics, People, and the AIDS Epidemic* (New York: St. Martin's Press, 1987). See also Steven Epstein, *Impure Science: AIDS, Activism, and the Politics of Knowledge* (Berkeley: University of California, 1996).

34. For a captivating account by a central actor in these developments, see Peter Piot, *No Time to Lose: A Life in Pursuit of Deadly Viruses* (New York: W. W. Norton & Company, 2012); Among many other sources on the global HIV/AIDS response since the 1980s, see Victoria A. Harden, *AIDS at 30: A History* (Dulles, Va.: Potomac Books, 2012); Jeffrey L. Sturchio, "Partnership for Action: The Experience of the Accelerating Access Initiative, 2000–04, and Lessons Learned," in *Delivering Essential Medicines: The Way Forward*, ed. A. Attaran and B. Granville (London: Royal Institute of International Affairs, 2004), 116–51; Bernhard Schwartländer, Ian Grubb, and Jos Perriëns, "The Ten-Year Struggle to Provide Antiretroviral Treatment to People with HIV in the Developing World," *The Lancet* 368 (2006): 541–46; Stefano Vella et al., "The History of Antiretroviral Therapy and of Its Implementation in Resource-Limited Areas of the World," *AIDS* 26 (2012): 1231–41; the essays in the July 2012 issue of *Health Affairs* on "Assessing the President's Emergency Plan for AIDS Relief," http://content.healthaffairs.org/content/31/7.toc; *Global HIV/AIDS Response: Epidemic Update and Health Sector Progress Towards Universal Access, 2011 Progress Report* (Geneva: World Health Organization, UNAIDS, and UNICEF, 2011), http://www.who.int/hiv/pub/progress_report2011/summary_en.pdf and *Together We Will End AIDS* (UNAIDS, 2012), 9, http://www.unaids.org/en/media/unaids/contentassets/documents/epidemiology/2012/jc2296_unaids_togetherreport_2012_en.pdf.

35. On Mectizan, see Brenda Colatrella and Jeffrey L. Sturchio, "Successful Public-Private Partnerships in Global Health: Lessons from the MECTIZAN Donation Program," in *The Economics of Essential Medicines*, ed. Brigitte Granville (London: Royal Institute of International Affairs, 2002); Roy Vagelos and Louis Galambos, *The Moral Corporation: Merck Experiences* (New York: Cambridge University Press, 2006); William C. Campbell, "Ivermectin as an Antiparasitic Agent for Use in Humans," *Annual Reviews of Microbiology* 45 (1991): 445–74; B. Thylefors, M. M. Alleman, and N. A. Y. Twum-Danso, "Operational Lessons from Twenty Years of the Mectizan Donation Program for the Control of Onchocerciasis," *Tropical Medicine and International Health* 13 (2008): 689–96; and Mectizan Donation Program, www.mectizan.org (accessed October 15, 2012). For subsequent developments, see Shereen El Feki, "Face Value: the Acceptable Face of Capitalism," *The Economist*, December 12, 2002, http://www.economist.com/node/1491753; "Prescription for Change," *The Economist*, June 16, 2005, http://www.economist.com/node/4053970; "Merck's Migraine," *The Economist*, December 1, 2005,

http://www.economist.com/node/5253901er; and "Winds of Change," *The Economist,* December 11, 2008, http://www.economist.com/node/12673331. Sturchio followed these developments while employed by Merck, and Galambos was a consultant on history projects for the company.

36. Christopher Culp and Steve H. Hanke, "Empire of the Sun: An Economic Interpretation of Enron's Energy Business," *Policy Analysis,* no. 470 (2003), http://www.cato.org/sites/cato.org/files/pubs/pdf/pa470.pdf; Paul M. Healy and Krishna G. Palepu, "The Fall of Enron," *Journal of Economic Perspectives* 17 (2003): 3–26. Alan D. Anderson, "Uneven Playing Fields: Enron and the Transformation of the U.S. Natural Gas Industry, 1968–1993," *Organization of American Historians Annual Meeting,* March 19, 2011, http://www.oah.org/meetings/annual_meeting/program/sessions/Enron_and_the_Gas_Industry.pdf.

37. *Global Status Report on Non-Communicable Diseases, 2010* (Geneva: World Health Organization, 2011), http://www.who.int/nmh/publications/ncd_report_full_en.pdf.

38. See Soeren Mattke et al., "Improving Access to Medicines for Non-Communicable Diseases in the Developing World," *Rand Report* OP 349 (2011), http://www.rand.org/pubs/occasional_papers/OP349.html; and Montserrat Meiro-Lorenzo et al., "Effective Responses to Non-Communicable Disease: Embracing Action Beyond the Health Sector," *World Bank HNP Discussion Paper* (2011), http://siteresources.worldbank.org/healthnutritionandpopulation/Resources/281627-1095698140167/Effective ResponsestoNCDs.pdf, especially the section "Action by Both Public and Private Actors."

39. The fact that these positions even exist can be related to the same forces making for functional specialization that earlier produced departments of public relations. Dr. Sturchio was vice president for corporate responsibility at Merck, before his retirement in 2008.

40. The creation of such "shared value" is at the heart of recent work by Michael Porter and Mark Kramer: see, for example, their essays on "Strategy and Society: The Link Between Competitive Advantage and Corporate Social Responsibility," *Harvard Business Review,* December 2006, http://hbr.org/2006/12/strategy-and-society-the-link-between-competitive-advantage-and-corporate-social-responsibility/ar/1; and "Creating Shared Value," *Harvard Business Review,* January 2011, http://hbr.org/2011/01/the-big-idea-creating-shared-value.

Chapter 6. Education by Corporation

For very helpful comments and suggestions, the author would like to thank Sigal Ben-Porath, Joan Goodman, Doug Lynch, and Greg Urban.

1. Osamudia R. James, "Predatory Ed: The Conflict Between Public Good and For-Profit Higher Education," *Journal of College and University Law* 38 (2011): 49. See also Joseph Shipley, Note, "For-Profit Education and Federal Funding: Bad Outcomes for Students and Taxpayers," *Rutgers Law Journal* 64 (2011): 267, 273–74 (providing different metrics of FPs' rapid growth).

2. Robin Wilson, "For-Profit Colleges Change Higher Education's Landscape; Nimble Companies Gain a Fast-Growing Share of Enrollments," *Chronicle of Higher Education*, February 7, 2010.

3. James, "Predatory Ed," 50.

4. Wilson, "For-Profit Colleges Change Higher Education's Landscape."

5. See, e.g., Nick DeSantis, "A Boom Time for Education Start-Ups Despite Recession; Investors See Technology Companies' 'Internet Moment,' " *Chronicle of Higher Education*, March 18, 2012.

6. See, e.g., Derek Bok, *Universities in the Marketplace: The Commercialization of Higher Education* (Princeton, N.J.: Princeton University Press, 2003); Brian Pusser, Bruce M. Gansneder, Ned Gallaway, and Nakia S. Pope, "Entrepreneurial Activity in Nonprofit Institutions: A Portrait of Continuing Education," *New Directions for Higher Education*, 129 (Spring 2005). Cf. Martha Minow, "Public and Private Partnerships: Accounting for the New Religion," *Harvard Law Review* 116 (2003): 1229, 1229.

7. This is referred to as the "nondistribution constraint." See, e.g., Usha Rodrigues, "Entity and Identity," *Emory Law Journal* 60 (2011): 1257, 1263. See generally James, "Predatory Ed."

8. Andrea Fuller, "Share of Students Receiving Federal Aid Climbs, Especially at For-Profit Colleges," *Chronicle of Higher Education*, May 24, 2012.

9. The discussion was held at the University of Pennsylvania on January 19, 2012. The principal panelists were: Jonathan Harber, CEO of a division of Pearson, Inc., the leading pre-K–12 curriculum, testing, and software company in the United States; Peter Smith, senior vice president of academic strategies and development for Kaplan Higher Education, which includes more than seventy campuses in twenty states, as well as online offerings including Concord Law School; and Michael Moe, an advisor to GSV Advisors and founder of GSV Asset management, a strategic advisory firm focused on the education sector, providing merger, advisory, and private placement services to investors and companies involved in for-profit education.

10. Wilson, "For-Profit Colleges Change Higher Education's Landscape."

11. See, e.g., Gary A. Berg, *Lessons from the Edge: For-Profit and Nontraditional Higher Education in America* (Westport, Conn.: Praeger, 2005), 94.

12. "University of Phoenix Lawsuit Settles for a Record 78.5 Million," geteducated.com, 2010, http://www.geteducated.com/online-education-facts-and-statistics/latest-online-learning-news-and-research/312-university-of-phoenix-lawsuit-settles-for-a-record-785-million (accessed June 4, 2012).

13. United States Government Accountability Office, "Highlights of GAO-10-948T: Undercover Testing Finds Colleges Encouraged Fraud and Engaged in Deceptive and Questionable Marketing Practices," August 4, 2010, http://www.gao.gov/assets/130/125202.pdf.

14. Ibid.

15. Ibid.

16. "For Profit Online Colleges Named in Government Investigation of Education

Fraud, Deceptive Marketing," geteducated.com, August 10, 2010, http://www.getedu
cated.com/online-education-facts-and-statistics/latest-online-learning-news-and
-research/369-for-profit-online-colleges-named-in-government-investigation-of-educa
tion-fraud-deceptive-marketing (accessed June 4, 2012).

17. James, "Predatory Ed," 46.

18. Ibid., 68.

19. Michael Stratford, "Obama to Crack Down on Deceptive Practices by Colleges
that Recruit Veterans," *Chronicle of Higher Education*, April 27, 2012. In response to the
suspected abuses, President Obama issued an executive order on April 27, 2012, calling
for enhanced transparency in the recruitment and loan information provided to military
personnel and veterans. Ibid.

20. James, "Predatory Ed," 46.

21. Fuller, "Share of Students Receiving Federal Aid Climbs."

22. Ibid.

23. Amitai Etzioni, "Warning: Profit-Making Colleges Are After You," *Huffington Post*,
June 29, 2010, http://www.huffingtonpost.com/amitai-etzioni/warning-profit-making
-col_b_629213.html. See also Goldie Blumenstyk, "Q & A: What For-Profit Colleges Are
All About," *Chronicle of Higher Education*, February 7, 2010; Paul Basken, "New Grilling of
For-Profits Could Turn up the Heat for All of Higher Education," *Chronicle of Higher Education*, June 22, 2010 (noting that the FP higher education industry is sometimes "carica-
tured as an opportunistic outlier that peddles low-value education to unprepared high
school dropouts"); Joseph Sipley, "For-Profit Education and Federal Funding: Bad Outcomes for Students and Taxpayers," *Rutgers Law Review* 64 (2011): 267, 278 ("for-profit
schools receive significantly more in tuition money than their traditional counterparts. . . .
The increased tuition largely goes to pay shareholders and management . . . yet the taxpayer takes all the downside risk by providing loan guarantees").

For their part, FP advocates contend that the charge that FP courses lack value is
nothing more than self-serving hypocrisy. Traditional institutions decline to award
transfer credit to the FP's courses, the objection goes, not because the FP's courses genuinely fall short of the traditional institutions' standards but instead because traditional
institutions want to maintain their turf. In this way, traditional colleges function like a
"prestige cartel, used to marginalize the [for-profit] sector and the students it serves."
Tressie McMillan Cottom, "Essay on Significance of Last Week's Proposal for Higher Ed
Outsourcing in California," *Inside Higher Ed*, March 18, 2013.

24. Tamar Lewin, "Senate Committee Report on For-Profit Colleges Condemns
Costs and Practices," *New York Times*, July 29, 2012.

25. Etzioni, "Warning." See also Basken, "New Grilling of For-Profits" (quoting
Glenn Harlan Reynolds, a law professor at the University of Tennessee at Knoxville, who
also characterizes the FP higher education sector as an economic bubble).

26. Goldie Blumenstyk, "The Morality of a For-Profit College, in One Act," *Chronicle
of Higher Education*, April 3, 2012.

27. Ibid.

28. Basken, "New Grilling of For-Profits." Jackson Toby, an emeritus sociology professor at Rutgers, has proposed that eligibility for federal subsidized education loans be conditioned on a demonstrated ability to handle and succeed at college. See ibid.

29. See, e.g., Wilson, "For-Profit Colleges Change Higher Education's Landscape" (reporting that Keiser University, a Florida for-profit school, "has been the No. 1 producer of associate-degree graduates in health professions and related sciences in the state for three of the last five years [i.e., 2005–2010]").

30. Basken, "New Grilling of For-Profits."

31. See, e.g., Tamar Lewin, "Obama Signs Order to Limit Aggressive College Recruiting of Veterans," *New York Times*, April 27, 2012.

32. For a version of this concern as it arises in the K–12 education context, see, for example, Kathleen Conn, "For-Profit School Management Corporations: Serving the Wrong Master," *Journal of Law and Education* 31 (2002): 129.

33. Sam Dillon, "Troubles Grow for a University Built on Profits," *New York Times*, February 11, 2007.

34. Ibid. In a similar vein, others, including Andrew Rosen, CEO of Kaplan, have acknowledged the potential tensions between students' and managers' interests. See, e.g., Andrew S. Rosen, *Change.edu: Rebooting for the New Talent Economy* (New York: Kaplan, 2011), 174 ("There will always be some leaders who choose to manage for the short term . . . particularly when they hold the highly liquid equity stakes that the leadership of private-sector institutions sometimes receive as part of their compensation. This isn't a theoretical issue; it has happened").

35. These concerns have arisen as well in the face of for-profit forays into K–12 education. See, e.g., Lisa M. Fairfax, "Doing Well While Doing Good: Reassessing the Scope of Directors' Fiduciary Obligations in For-Profit Corporations with Non-Shareholder Beneficiaries," *Washington & Lee Law Review* 50 (2002): 409, 470–72.

36. Wilson, "For-Profit Colleges Change Higher Education's Landscape."

37. Lewin, "Senate Committee Report on For-Profit Colleges."

38. Blumenstyk, "Q & A."

39. Ibid.

40. Wilson, "For-Profit Colleges Change Higher Education's Landscape" (quoting from an interview with Gregory M. St. L. O'Brien, who had moved from administrative positions at the University of New Orleans and then the University of South Florida to the presidency of for-profit Argosy University). See also Blumenstyk, "Q & A."

41. American Law Institute, *ALI Principles of Corporate Governance*, 2.01. See generally Jill E. Fisch, "Measuring Efficiency in Corporate Law: The Role of Shareholder Primacy," *Journal of Corporate Law* 31 (2006): 637. Lisa Fairfax has argued that concern about tensions between profit-making and educational quality are overblown, since the law permits directors to attend to students' interests even when doing so requires forsaking profitable opportunities. Fairfax, "Doing Well While Doing Good." It is worth noting,

though, that the law's permission does not entail that the FP educational institution will necessarily serve students' interests at shareholders' expense, and the empirical evidence Fairfax adduces is inconclusive at best.

42. Basken, "New Grilling of For-Profits."

43. Paul Fain, "Kaplan's CEO Faces Tough Questions from Public University Leaders," *Chronicle of Higher Education*, November 16, 2010. See also Basken, "New Grilling of For-Profits" (quoting Peter Smith, who states that the country can meet Obama's goal only if institutions enroll "students who are now considered unwilling to [do] or incapable of the work").

44. Nick DeSantis, "Three Start-Up Announcements from the Education Innovation Summit," *Chronicle of Higher Education*, April 18, 2012 (quoting Paul Friedman, CEO of Altius, a FP "transfer college" whose goal is to provide students with a bridge program from high school to a traditional four-year college).

45. Wilson, "For-Profit Colleges Change Higher Education's Landscape."

46. Ibid.

47. Elite institutions may be moving toward greater flexibility as they produce and disseminate massive open online courses (MOOCs), the class sessions for which can be watched whenever the enrolled student finds it convenient to do so. See, for example, Tamar Lewin, "Universities Abroad Join Partnerships on the Web," *New York Times*, February 20, 2013.

48. Ibid.

49. Minow, "Public and Private Partnerships," 1243. It may be worth noting that the incursion of FP entities into the K–12 education arena does not appear to have produced gains in educational quality. See, e.g., Brian P. Gill et al., *Inspiration, Perspiration, and Time: Operations and Achievement in Edison Schools* (Santa Monica, Calif.: RAND Education, 2005); Robert Bifulco and Helen F. Ladd, "The Impacts of Charter Schools on Student Achievement: Evidence from North Carolina," *Education Finance and Policy* 1 (2006): 50; Helen F. Ladd, "School Vouchers: A Critical View," *Journal of Economic Perspectives* 16 (2002): 3. Cf. Martin Carnoy, "National Voucher Plans in Chile and Sweden: Did Privatization Reforms Make for Better Education?" *Comparative Education Review* 42 (1998): 309.

50. Nathan Heller, "Laptop U: Has College Moved Online?" *The New Yorker*, May 20, 2013, http://www.newyorker.com/reporting/2013/05/20/130520fa_fact_heller?current Page=all.

51. "Access to information about services and results also decreases if the information becomes private." Minow, "Public and Private Partnerships," 1235.

52. Rohit Chopra, "Our Student Loan Complaint System Is Open for Business," Consumer Financial Protection Bureau, March 5, 2012, http://www.consumerfinance.gov /blog/our-student-loan-complaint-system-is-open-for-business.

53. Minow, "Public and Private Partnerships," 1243. See generally Galit Sarfaty, "Regulating Through Numbers: A Case Study of Corporate Sustainability Reporting," *Virginia Journal of International Law* 53 (2013): 575.

54. See Carol Ascher et al., *Hard Lessons: Public Schools and Privatization* 54 (1996)

(describing a focus on test scores in the context of assessing privatization of a Baltimore school as "eclipsing" all other measures of teaching).

55. Cf. Minow, "Public and Private Partnerships," 1249–52 (describing analogous concerns in the context of K–12 school "choice").

56. Wilson, "For-Profit Colleges Change Higher Education's Landscape."

57. See Blumenstyk, "Q & A," interviewing Peter Smith, who argues that society can be served both by training students in free inquiry and conferring upon them specific skills. Traditional and for-profit institutions do not "serve the society the same way, and I think that's OK," he maintains.

58. There is yet a third concern about the interplay between for-profit educational ventures and democracy—namely, that allowing for-profit entities to provide a good traditionally furnished by government involves a potentially unconstitutional delegation of governmental powers. See, e.g., Gillian E. Metzger, "Privatization as Delegation," *Columbia Law Review* 103 (2003): 1367. I do not address this concern here since it pertains mostly to K–12 education, and since it is occasioned by NFP and FP institutions alike.

59. The connection between democracy and education is perhaps even better established at the K–12 level. See, e.g., *Plyler v. Doe*, 457 U.S. 202, 221 (1982) ("Public schools are the most vital civic institution for the preservation of a democratic system of government") (internal citations omitted); *Abington Sch. Dist. v. Schempp*, 374 U.S. 203, 241–42 (1963) (Brennan, J. concurring) ("It is implicit in the history and character of American public education that the public schools serve a uniquely *public* function: the training of American citizens"); *Brown v. Bd. of Educ.*, 347 U.S. 483, 493 (1954) ("Education is perhaps the most important function of state and local governments"); *W. Va. State Bd. of Educ. v. Barnette*, 319 U.S. 624, 637 (1943) (noting that public schools are "educating the young for citizenship"). See generally Fairfax, "Doing Well While Doing Good," 427 and n. 89.

60. James, "Predatory Ed," 58.

61. Ibid., 59.

62. For a general account of the historic role of higher education in preparing citizens for self-governance, from the seventeenth century onward, see R. Claire Snyder, "Should Higher Education Have a Civic Mission? Historical Reflections," in *Agent of Democracy: Higher Education and the HEX Journey,* ed. David W. Brown and Deborah Witte (Dayton, Ohio: Kettering Foundation, 2008).

63. James F. Shekleton, "Strangers at the Gate: Academic Autonomy, Civil Rights, Civil Liberties, and Unfinished Tasks," *Journal of College and University Law* 36 (2010): 875, 936.

64. "AAUP 1915 Declaration of Principles," in *Academic Freedom and Tenure: A Handbook of the American Association of University Professors,* ed. Louis Joughin (Madison: University of Wisconsin Press, 1969), 155, 160–61. See generally Risa L. Lieberwitz, "The Corporatization of the University: Distance Learning at the Cost of Academic Freedom?" *Boston University International Law Journal* 12 (2002): 73, 80–85 (detailing the AAUP's conception of the university through the various articulations of its statement of principles).

65. Campus Compact, "Presidents' Declaration on the Civic Responsibility of Higher Education," available at http://www.compact.org/resources-for-presidents/presidents-declaration-on-the-civic-responsibility-of-higher-education. See also Harry C. Boyte, "Public Work: Civic Populism Versus Technocracy in Higher Education," in *Agent of Democracy*, ed. Brown and Witte, 79 (describing institutions of higher learning as the "'agents and architects'" of democracy).

66. Kathryn Hoffman, Charmaine Llagas, and Thomas D. Snyder, *Status and Trends in the Education of Blacks* (Washington, D.C.: U.S. Department of Education, National Center for Education Statistics, 2003), 124 (finding enhanced voting rates among both White and Black graduates of institutes of higher learning).

67. See David Karen and Kevin J. Dougherty, "Necessary but Not Sufficient: Higher Education as a Strategy of Social Mobility," in *Higher Education and the Color Line: College Access, Racial Equity, and Social Change,* ed. Gary Orfield et al. (Cambridge, Mass.: Harvard Education Press, 2005), 33.

68. James, "Predatory Ed," 63.

69. See, e.g., Amy Gutmann and Dennis Thompson, *Why Deliberative Democracy?* (Princeton, N.J.: Princeton University Press, 2004), 137 ("The[re are] three principles that provide the content of deliberative democracy—basic liberty, basic opportunity, and fair opportunity. . . . Those basic opportunities typically include adequate health care, education, security, work, and income").

70. Milton Friedman, "The Role of Government in Education," in *Capitalism and Freedom* (Chicago: University of Chicago Press, 1962).

71. Martha C. Nussbaum, *Not for Profit: Why Democracy Needs the Humanities* (Princeton, N.J.: Princeton University Press, 2010), 10.

72. Richard Ruch, *Higher Ed, Inc.: The Rise of the For-Profit University* (Baltimore: Johns Hopkins University Press, 2001), 72–73.

73. Nussbaum, *Not for Profit*; Amy Gutmann, *Democratic Education* (Princeton, N.J.: Princeton University Press, 1999 [1987]).

74. Minow, "Public and Private Partnerships," 1253. Henry Levin has demonstrated that, at the K–12 level, greater school choice leads to greater socioeconomic and racial segregation of students. Henry M. Levin, "Educational Vouchers, Effectiveness, Choice and Costs," *Journal of Policy Analysis and Management* 17 (1998): 373.

75. Elizabeth Anderson, "Fair Opportunity in Education: A Democratic Equality Perspective," *Ethics* 117 (2007): 595, 597. See also Nussbaum, *Not for Profit,* 10.

76. James, "Predatory Ed," 67.

77. Alex Molnar, "Charter Schools: The Smiling Face of Disinvestment," *Educational Leadership* 54 (1996): 9, 15.

78. See, e.g., Michael Oakeshott, "The Character of a University Education," in *What Is History? And Other Essays,* ed. Luke O'Sullivan (Charlottesville, Va.: Imprint Academic, 2004), 373, 386 ("Not being comparable to a light-industry [having no product, in the strict sense], nor to a store [having no sales-list of items for disposal], a university

is apt to confound the accounts. Profit and loss, cost and return on capital are not easily calculable; indeed, there is something inappropriate in making the calculations").

79. Minow, "Public and Private Partnerships," 1235.

80. Ibid.

81. Mark Rosenman, "Commercializing the Public Good," *Huffington Post*, June 8, 2011: http://www.huffingtonpost.com/mark-rosenman/commercializing-the-publi_b_869265.html.

82. Ibid. See generally Michael J. Sandel, *What Money Can't Buy: The Moral Limits of Markets* (New York: Farrar, Straus and Giroux, 2012). Cf. Rodrigues, "Entity and Identity," 1264 ("A for-profit entity that proposes to save the dolphins or feed the hungry is incoherent because the knowledge that the firm's owner is ultimately in business to make money will dim the self-same warm glow that a donor seeks in giving to the organization in the first place").

83. Cf. Alan Wertheimer, "Exploitation in Clinical Research," in *Exploitation and Developing Countries: The Ethics of Clinical Research*, ed. Jennifer S. Hawkins and Ezekiel J. Emanuel (Princeton, N.J.: Princeton University Press, 2008), 63, 84 ("Just because a transaction would not occur under nonideal conditions, it does not follow that it is wrong for it to occur under nonideal conditions").

84. Kevin Carey, "Freemium Higher Education?" *Chronicle of Higher Education*, April 3, 2012. See also Blumenstyk, "Q & A" (quoting Peter Smith saying that state education budgets are getting smaller and public funding for higher education is focusing more and more on student choice—both trends that speak in favor of allowing FP institutions to complement their more traditional counterparts).

85. The general strategy is, of course, that of John Rawls, *A Theory of Justice* (Cambridge, Mass.: Belknap Press of Harvard University Press, 1999 [1971]), 215–28. But see Amartya Sen, *The Idea of Justice* (Cambridge, Mass.: Belknap Press of Harvard University Press, 2009) (rejecting the notion that one should derive principles of justice for a nonideal world from those that would reign in the ideal world).

86. Margaret Jane Radin, *Contested Commodities* (Cambridge, Mass.: Harvard University Press, 1996), 102–4.

87. Jeffery Smith, "Corporate Social Purpose and the Task of Management," in this volume.

88. See, e.g., Minow, "Public and Private Partnerships," 1236 ("Public values, which themselves require public deliberation, should guide assessments of the specific benefits and limitations of competition and the quality of services delivered by for-profit or religious providers in partnership with government to meet basic human needs").

89. Cf. Wertheimer, "Exploitation in Clinical Research," 84 ("Given the nonideal background circumstances under which people find themselves, there should be a very strong presumption in favor of principles that would allow people to improve their situation if they give appropriately robust consent, if doing so has no negative effects on others, and this even if the transaction is unfair, unjust, or exploitative").

90. In any event, as Amy Gutmann argues, we ought not to count on higher educa-tion as the exclusive provider of the final stages of training for citizenship, since many individuals might just as soon end their formal education after high school, and they should have the liberty to do so without forsaking the opportunity to be productive and participating citizens. Gutmann, *Democratic Education,* 172–73.

Chapter 7. Enron and the Legacy of Corporate Discourse

1. A "big business" is usually defined as one employing 10,000 people or more.

2. See Ari Adut, *On Scandal: Moral Disturbances in Society, Politics, and Art* (New York: Cambridge University Press, 2008).

3. Jack Beatty, *Colossus: How the Corporation Changed America* (New York: Broad-way Books, 2001), xix.

4. Businessweek/Harris Poll, cited in Beatty, *Colossus,* xix.

5. Louis Galambos, *The Public Image of Big Business in America, 1880–1940: A Quan-titative Study in Social Change* (Baltimore: Johns Hopkins University Press, 1975), 220.

6. Adolf A. Berle and Gardiner C. Means, *The Modern Corporation and Private Prop-erty* (New York: Macmillan, 1932).

7. Guido Palazzo and Andreas Georg Scherer, "Corporate Legitimacy as Delibera-tion: A Communicative Framework," *Journal of Business Ethics* 66 (2006): 72.

8. Ibid., 72.

9. Jack Blicksilver, *Defenders and Defense of Big Business in the United States, 1880––1900,* ed. Stuart Bruchey (New York: Garland, 1985), 398.

10. Galambos, *Public Image of Big Business in America,* 63.

11. E.g., ibid., 69–71.

12. Blicksilver, *Defenders and Defense of Big Business,* 74, 79–80.

13. Charles F. Adams and Henry Adams, *Chapters of Erie and Other Essays* (New York: Henry Holt, 1886), 134, quoted in Beatty, *Colossus,* 117–18.

14. Irving S. Michelman, *Business at Bay: Critics and Heretics of American Business* (New York: A. M. Kelley, 1969), 24.

15. Ibid., 14.

16. Ibid., 166.

17. As the New Deal's National Recovery Administration illustrated, this was not an entirely unfounded suspicion. Here an effort to bolster the American corporate-capitalist order took the form of government-sanctioned industrial cartels, encouraged—where they were not even supposed to be allowed—to cooperate in strategies of production, distribution, and price-setting (among others). The Supreme Court recognized the NRA as anathema and ruled it unconstitutional in 1935. Such a form of social organization was actually more in line with fascism than socialism. The fact that it was nonetheless more often associated with the latter may speak to Americans' relative confidence in private organizations as partners to the state—or at least to paranoia about industrial nationalization.

18. Blicksilver, *Defenders and Defense of Big Business*, 67, 71.

19. Galambos, *Public Image of Big Business in America*, 220.

20. See ibid.,78, for one early example.

21. Michelman, *Business at Bay,* 77–78; Galambos, *Public Image of Big Business in America*, 185.

22. Richard P. Adelstein, "'The Nation as an Economic Unit:' Keynes, Roosevelt, and the Managerial Ideal," *Journal of American History* 78 (1991): 160–87.

23. Beatty, *Colossus* (2001): xxii; David Skeel, *Icarus in the Boardroom: The Fundamental Flaws in Corporate America and Where They Came From* (New York: Oxford University Press, 2005), 210–11, 215.

24. Mark S. Mizruchi, "Berle and Means Revisited: The Governance and Power of Large U.S. Corporations," *Theory and Society* 33, no. 5 (2004): 580.

25. Harvard Law Review Association, "Developments in the Law: Corporations and Society," *Harvard Law Review* 117, no. 7 (2004): 2176.

26. Julia C. Ott, *When Wall Street Met Main Street: The Quest for an Investors' Democracy* (Cambridge, Mass.: Harvard University Press, 2011), 3–5.

27. Michael Zakim, "Producing Capitalism: The Clerk at Work," paper presented to the Penn Economic History Forum, December 2011. Available at http://www.history.upenn.edu/economichistoryforum/docs/zakim_11.pdf.

28. Rosalie Genova, "Building Dodd-Frank's New Regulatory Institutions: Lessons from the Case of the SEC," ms. presented at Kenan Institute for Ethics Symposium, "Rethinking Regulation," June 2011; Jessica Wang, "Imagining the Administrative State: Legal Pragmatism, Securities Regulation, and New Deal Liberalism," *Journal of Policy History* 17 (205): 272, 274, 276, 282–83.

29. Jennifer Karns Alexander, *The Mantra of Efficiency: From Waterwheel to Social Control* (Baltimore: Johns Hopkins University Press, 2008), 6.

30. Paul S. Adler, "Market, Hierarchy and Trust: The Knowledge Economy and the Future of Capitalism," *Organization Science* 12 (2001): 216, 222.

31. Yaron Ezrahi, *The Descent of Icarus: Science and the Transformation of Contemporary Democracy* (Cambridge, Mass.: Harvard University Press, 1990), 33, 35, 198, 203, 210.

32. William H. Whyte, *The Organization Man* (New York: Simon & Schuster, 1956; rpt. Philadelphia: University of Pennsylvania Press, 2002).

33. See Skeel, *Icarus in the Boardroom*.

34. Ibid., 6.

35. Beatty, *Colossus,* 271; Michelman, *Business at Bay,* 33.

36. E.g., Galambos, *Public Image of Big Business in America*, 52–53, 59, 66.

37. Blicksilver, *Defenders and Defense of Big Business*, 229, 241; see also Galambos, *Public Image of Big Business in America*.

38. Galambos, *Public Image of Big Business in America,* 68–69.

39. Ibid., 72.

40. Though see the chapter by Jeffery Smith, as well as others in this volume, for

arguments that corporate managers do, indeed, play a public role, even if they are not democratically elected officials.

41. For one approach to classifying explanations in technical terms as opposed to using "codes," "conventions," or "stories," see Charles Tilly, *Why?* (Princeton, N.J.: Princeton University Press, 2006).

42. Pauline Maier, "The Revolutionary Origins of the American Corporation," *William and Mary Quarterly* 50 (1993): 51–84.

43. Blicksilver, *Defenders and Defense of Big Business*, 248. Here I am quoting the author.

44. Beatty, *Colossus,* 256.

45. Paul Johnson, "The Prospering Fathers," *Commentary* 108 (1999): 66.

46. Ibid., 16; Perry Miller, "The Shaping of the American Character," *New England Quarterly* 28 (1955): 435–54.

47. Galambos, *Public Image of Big Business in America*, 6.

48. Beatty, *Colossus,* 275.

49. Edward J. Bander, ed., *The Corporation in a Democratic Society* (New York: H. W. Wilson Co., 1975), 38.

50. *The Insider,* directed by Michael Mann, released November 5, 1999 (Beverly Hills, CA: Spyglass Entertainment, 2000), DVD; *Erin Brockovich,* directed by Steven Spielberg, released March 17, 2000 (Los Angeles: Jersey Films, 2005), DVD; *Michael Clayton,* directed by Tony Gilroy, released October 12, 2007 (Las Vegas, NV: Castle Rock, 2008), DVD.

51. George Chapman, Ben Jonson, and John Marston, *Eastward Hoe!* quoted in Beatty, *Colossus*, 7.

52. *Modern Times,* directed by Charlie Chaplin, released February 25, 1936 (New York: Criterion Collection, 2010), DVD.

53. Michelman, *Business at Bay*, 188.

54. Ibid., 154.

55. *Office Space,* directed by Mike Judge, released February 19, 1999 (Los Angeles: Twentieth Century Fox, 1999), DVD; *Arrested Development,* created by Mitchell Hurwitz, (Culver City, CA: Twentieth Century Fox Television, aired 2003–13); *The Office,* created by Ricky Gervais (Los Angeles: NBC Universal Television, aired 2005–13); Scott Adams, *Dilbert* (Andrews McMeel Publishing, 1989–present), comic strip.

56. Joseph Heller, "The Office in Which I Work," quoted in Beatty, *Colossus,* 324.

Chapter 8. Saving TEPCO

This chapter is based on the most recent phase of my longitudinal ethnographic research on Japanese derivatives traders I have conducted since 1998. Early drafts of the chapter were presented at the Australian National University, Cornell University, McGill University, the University of Hong Kong, the University of Melbourne, the University of Pennsylvania, the University of Pittsburgh, and the University of Sydney. I benefited a great deal from comments by the following colleagues and friends: Laura C. Brown, Jessica Cattelino, Cheris Chan, Lieba Faier, James J. Fox, Chris Gregory, Akhil Gupta, Ghassan

Hage, Holly High, Waheed Hussain, Casper Jensen, Margaret Jolly, Naoki Kasuga, Peter Katzenstein, Eduardo Kohn, Purnima Mankekar, Jeffrey Martin, Atsuro Morita, Morten Pedersen, Tobias Rees, Annelise Riles, Kathryn Robinson, Mark Selden, Colin Smith, Rogers Smith, Greg Urban, Helen Verran, Jeff Weintraub, and Clark West.

1. Peter J. Katzenstein and Stephen Nelson, "Worlds in Collision: Uncertainty and Risk in Hard Times," in *Politics in the New Hard Times: The Great Recession in Comparative Perspective*, ed. Miles Kahler and David A. Lake (Ithaca, N.Y.: Cornell University Press, 2013), 233–52.

2. Hirokazu Miyazaki, "Economy of Dreams: Hope in Global Capitalism and Its Critiques," *Cultural Anthropology* 21 (2006): 147–72; Hirokazu Miyazaki, *Arbitraging Japan: Dreams of Capitalism at the End of Finance* (Berkeley: University of California Press, 2013).

3. Chester W. Hartman and Gregory D. Squires, eds., *There Is No Such Thing as a Natural Disaster: Race, Class, and Hurricane Katrina* (New York: Routledge, 2006).

4. "Josen kanrenhi 6,095 okuen, jisshihi 1,257 okuen zo no 4,978 okuen" [The budget for expenses related to radioactive substance clean up, 609.5 billion yen, expenses related to clean up itself, 497.8 billion yen, an increase of 125.7 billion yen]. *Fukushima-minpo*, January 30, 2013, available at http://www.minpo.jp/pub/topics/jishin2011/2013/01/post_6094.html.

5. As of March 2011, Japan's sovereign debt was over 924 trillion yen (approximately $11 trillion at the exchange rate of the time). Japan's debt/GDP ratio was over 200 percent at that time (http://www.mof.go.jp/jgbs/reference/gbb/2303.html).

6. Despite some efforts to deregulate Japan's energy markets, Japan's ten electric power companies have enjoyed a virtual regional monopoly in their respective service areas. Takeo Kikkawa, *Tokyo denryoku/shippai no honshitsu: "kaitai to saisei" no shinario* [Tokyo Electric Power Corporation/the essence of its failure: A scenario for "dissolution and rebirth"] (Tokyo: Toyokeizai-shinposha, 2011), 88–92. The regional monopoly system was established in the 1950s when the utility companies were privatized. The privatization of the power companies coincided with the incorporation of power-generating business into power-distributing business (ibid., 133–36).

7. The Tokyo Metropolitan Government is also a large shareholder of TEPCO for a historical reason.

8. Makoto Saito, *Genpatsukiki no keizaigaku: shakaikagakusha toshite kangaetakoto* [The economics of the nuclear crisis: A social scientist's thoughts] (Tokyo: Nihonhyoronsha, 2011), 192–93.

9. K. William Kapp, *The Social Costs of Private Enterprise* (Cambridge, Mass.: Harvard University Press, 1950).

10. Oshima Ken'ichi, *Genpatsu no kosuto: enerugitenkan eno shiten* [The cost of nuclear power: A perspective on energy change] (Tokyo: Iwanami-shoten, 2011), i–ii.

11. Ibid., iv (my translation).

12. Ibid., 193–202.

13. David Graeber, *Debt: The First 5,000 Years* (New York: Melville House, 2011); Chris A. Gregory, "On Money Debt and Morality: Some Reflections on the Contribution of Economic Anthropology," *Social Anthropology* 20 (2012): 380–96; Jane I. Guyer, "Obligation, Binding, Debt and Responsibility: Provocations About Temporality from Two New Sources," *Social Anthropology* 20 (2012): 491–501; Holly High, "Re-reading the Potlatch in a Time of Crisis: Debt and the Distinctions that Matter," *Social Anthropology* 20 (2012): 363–79; Gustav Peebles, "The Anthropology of Debt and Credit," *Annual Review of Anthropology* 39 (2010): 225–40.

14. Graeber, "Debt"; Karen Ho, *Liquidated: An Ethnography of Wall Street* (Durham, N.C.: Duke University Press, 2009); Alexandra Ouroussoff, *Wall Street at War: The Secret Struggle of the Global Economy* (Cambridge, U.K.: Polity Press, 2010); Gillian Tett, *Fool's Gold: How the Bold Dream of a Small Tribe at J. P. Morgan Was Corrupted by Wall Street Greed and Unleashed a Catastrophe* (New York: Free Press, 2009).

15. Annelise Riles, "Too Big to Fail," in *Recasting Anthropological Knowledge: Inspiration and Social Science*, ed. Jeanette Edwards and Maja Petrovic-Šteger (Cambridge: Cambridge University Press, 2011), 31–48; Annelise Riles, "Market Collaboration: Finance, Culture and Ethnography after Neoliberalism," *American Anthropologist* (forthcoming).

16. High, "Re-reading the Potlatch," 364.

17. Hirokazu Miyazaki and Naoki Kamiyama, "Corporate Shares as Gifts" (n.d., n.p., on file at the East Asia Program, Cornell University).

18. Ibid.

19. Japan Securities Dealers Association Study Group to Vitalize the Corporate Bond Market, "Toward Vitalization of the Corporate Bond Market" (June 22, 2010), Attachment 8 "Comparison of Japanese and American Corporate Bond Markets," Plate 4 "Holding of Corporate Bonds and Other Bonds by Types of Investors," available at http://www.jsda.or.jp/katsudou/kaigi/chousa/shasai_kon/files/100930_finalreport_e.pdf

20. The trading volume of corporate bonds in Japan is relatively low compared with its U.S. counterpart. See Koshasaihikiuke-kyokai (Bond Underwriters' Association of Japan), "Wagakuni shasaishijo no genjo to tenbo" (The current state and the prospect of our country's corporate bond markets), in *Koshasaishijo no shintenkai* (New developments in government and corporate bonds), ed. Koshasaihikiuke-kyokai (Bond Underwriters' Association of Japan) (Tokyo: Toyokeizai-shinposha, 1996), 27. The underdeveloped status of Japan's corporate bond market has been widely noted; see Peter G. Szilagyi, "Recent Developments in Japan's Corporate Bond Market," in *Japan's Fixed Income Markets: Money, Bond and Interest Rate Deriva*tives, ed. Jonathan A. Batten, Thomas A. Fetherston, and Peter G. Szilagyi (Amsterdam: Elsevier, 2006). It has been attributed to both structural and cultural factors, such as the "extreme risk aversion of Japanese households" (Szilagyi, "Recent Developments," 34). As Szilagyi notes, "The low demand for junk bonds by institutional investors is largely driven by internal investment eligibility rules rather than a quantitative risk-return assessment. Notably, many pension funds follow the guidelines set by the Government Pension Investment Fund, which prohibit investment in junk

bonds and command the sell-off of investment-grade bonds downgraded to junk" (43). Holders of corporate bonds are mostly banks, insurance and pension funds (Szilagyi, "Recent Developments," 45). See also Katsuyuki Tokushima, *Gendai shasaitoshi no jitsumu* [An up-to-date practical guide to investment in corporate bonds], 3rd edition (Tokyo: Zaikeishoho-sha, 2008), 58.

21. One of the reasons often cited for the inactive nature of Japan's corporate bond market is that Japanese corporations have long relied on low-interest bank loans for their financing. As a result, banks were the dominating issuers of bonds. In addition, corporate bonds were only issued as secured bonds from the 1950s until the 1980s. For the historical developments of corporate bonds in Japan, see Koshasaihikiuke-kyokai [Bond Underwriters' Association of Japan], *Koshasaishijo no shintenkai* [New developments in government and corporate bonds], ed. Koshasaihikiuke-kyokai [Bond Underwriters' Association of Japan] (Tokyo: Toyokeizai-shinposha, 1996). Many of these accounts note the ambiguous distinction between corporate shares and corporate bonds in the early years of securities trading in Japan; see Koshasaihikiuke-kyokai, "Wagakuni shasaishijo no genjo to tenbo," 7. All these accounts point to the significance of *shasaijoka-undo* ("corporate bond cleaning-up campaign") in the 1930s. The campaign orchestrated by banks ostensibly sought to make all corporate bonds secured bonds. Kazumasa Ni'imi draws attention to the fact that this campaign coincided with the shift from utility companies to chemical and heavy industry companies as the primary issuers of corporate bonds in Japan. See Kazumasa Ni'imi, "Detto fainansu niokeru shasai: wagakuni shasaishijo no henkakukanosei" [Corporate bonds in debt finance: The possibility of transforming our country's corporate bond markets] in *Koshasaishijo no shintenkai* [New developments in the government and corporate bond markets], ed. Koshasaihikiuke-kyokai [Bond Underwriters' Association of Japan] (Tokyo: Toyokeizai-shinposha, 1996), 326–27.

22. Koshasaihikiuke-kyokai [Bond Underwriters' Association of Japan], "Wagakuni shasaishijo no genjo to tenbo," 25.

23. Tokushima, *Gendai shasaitoshi no jitsumu*, 30–31.

24. In the 1970s, utilities companies' corporate bonds began to be widely held among individual investors; Koshasaihikiuke-kyokai [Bond Underwriters' Association of Japan], "Wagakuni shasaishijo no genjo to tenbo," 12. In the 1980s, the market was deregulated further, and nonsecured bonds were allowed to be issued (ibid., 12–13). However, Japanese corporations continued to rely heavily on bank loans. See, e.g., Yoshio Shima, *Nihon no kurejittoshijo: sono tanjo, hatten to kadai* [Japan's credit market: Its birth, development and problems] (Tokyo: Sigma Base Capital, 2006), 21.

25. Miyazaki, "Economy of Dreams"; Hirokazu Miyazaki, "The Temporality of No Hope," in *Ethnographies of Neoliberalism*, ed. Carol Greenhouse (Philadelphia: University of Pennsylvania Press, 2010), 238–50.

26. Riles, "Market Collaboration."

27. "Moody's Slashes Ratings on Tepco," *Japan Times,* April 1, 2011, available at

http://www.japantimes.co.jp/news/2011/04/01/business/moodys-slashes-ratings-on
-tepco/#.UZsaNL8zLww; Bill Koenig, "Tepco's Rating Cut to BBB+ From A+ by S&P,
May Be Cut Further," www.bloomberg.com, April 1, 2011, available at http://www
.bloomberg.com/apps/news?pid=newsarchive&sid=a0buWzAti2Jg.

28. Chisa Fujioka and Kevin Krolicki, "S&P Cuts Tepco's Credit Rating to Junk,"
http://www.reuters.com, May 30, 2011, available at http://www.reuters.com/article
/2011/05/30/us-tepco-credit-idUSTRE74T1U020110530; Rakteem Katakey and Katrina
Nicholas, "Tepco Rating Slashed to Junk by Moody's," www.bloomberg.com, June 20,
2011, available at http://www.bloomberg.com/news/2011-06-20/tepco-rating-slashed-
to-junk-by-moody-s.html.

29. "First of all, following the disaster, I think it was on March 31, new extra financing was provided to TEPCO in view of its responsibility to contain the situation at the
nuclear power station. This current issue [whether to inject public funds to TEPCO while
banks have not written off their loans made to the utility company before the disasters]
should be viewed separately. I believe that efforts must be made to make the public fully
aware of the situation. With regard to financing provided prior to the March 11 disaster,
at the current point that is a matter between private sector bodies and I should therefore
take care in what I say, but if you are asking me whether the public would be understanding of this matter, my own view is that it would be impossible to gain public understanding." Press Conference by the Chief Cabinet Secretary, May 13, 2011, Prime Minister's
Office, available at http://www.kantei.go.jp/foreign/incident/110513_0956.html.

30. By the summer of 2012, the Japanese government had set up a special fund and
mechanism for financing TEPCO's massive compensation payment into which over
three trillion yen of public funds has been injected so far. The crisis of TEPCO continues
as the state of the Fukushima Dai'ichi nuclear plant and the future of nuclear energy
remain uncertain.

31. Yoshio Shima and Yuko Kawai, *Kurejitto deribatibu nyumon* [An introduction to
credit derivatives] (Tokyo: Nihonkeizaishinbunsha, 2007), 27–30.

32. Miyazaki, *Arbitraging Japan.*

33. Ibid.

34. Ibid.

35. Ibid.

36. Annelise Riles, Hirokazu Miyazaki, and Yuji Genda, *Re-tooling: Techniques for an
Uncertain World* (n.d., n.p., manuscript on file at the Clarke Program in East Asian Law
and Culture, Cornell University).

37. Hirokazu Miyazaki, *The Method of Hope: Anthropology, Philosophy, and Fijian
Knowledge* (Stanford, Calif.: Stanford University Press, 2004); Miyazaki, "Economy of
Dreams"; Hirokazu Miyazaki, "The Economy of Hope: An Introduction," in *The Econ-
omy of Hope*, ed. Hirokazu Miyazaki and Richard Swedberg (Philadelphia: University of
Pennsylvania Press, forthcoming); Hirokazu Miyazaki, "Obama's Hope: An Economy of
Belief and Substance," in *The Economy of Hope*, ed. Miyazaki and Swedberg.

Chapter 9. The Rise and Embedding of the Corporation

1. Walter Licht, *Industrializing America: The Nineteenth Century* (Baltimore: Johns Hopkins University Press, 1995), 166–97.

2. On the limits to shareholder influence, see Mark J. Roe, *Strong Managers, Weak Owners: The Political Roots of American Corporate Finance* (Princeton, N.J.: Princeton University Press, 1994); and Dalia Tsuk Mitchell, "Shareholders as Proxies: The Contours of Shareholder Democracy," *Washington & Lee Law Review* 63 (2006): 1503–78. Roe argues that neither individuals nor bloc holders of shares ever have sufficient votes to challenge management; Dalia traces the absence of effective shareholder democracy to government regulations.

3. Alfred F. Conard, *Corporations in Perspective* (Mineola, N.Y.: Foundation PR, 1976), 128–32; Vikramaditya S. Khanna, "The Economic History of the Corporate Form in Ancient India," paper presented at Yale Law School, November 17, 2005, http://www .law.yale.edu/documents/pdf/cbl/khanna_ancient_india_informal.pdf (accessed September 27, 2013).

4. Om Prakash, *European Commercial Enterprise in Pre-Colonial India* (New York: Cambridge University Press, 1998).

5. Classic studies on early American corporations include Louis Hartz, *Economic Policy and Democratic Thought: Pennsylvania, 1776–1860* (Cambridge, Mass.: Harvard University Press, 1948); Mary Handlin and Oscar Handlin, *Commonwealth: A Study of the Role of Government in the American Economy, 1774–1861* (Cambridge, Mass.: Harvard University Press, 1947); Harry Schreiber, *Ohio Canal Era: A Case of Government and the Economy, 1820–1861* (Columbus: Ohio University Press, 1969); Ronald Seavoy, *The Origins of the American Business Corporation, 1784–1855: Broadening the Concept of Public Service During Industrialization* (Westport, Conn.: Greenwood Press, 1982).

6. The great Chandler works include *Strategy and Structure: Chapters in the History of Industrial Enterprise* (Cambridge, Mass.: Harvard University Press, 1962); *The Visible Hand: The Managerial Revolution in American Business* (Cambridge, Mass.: Harvard University Press, 1977); *Scale and Scope: The Dynamics of Industrial Capitalism* (Cambridge, Mass.: Harvard University Press, 1990).

7. Adolf Berle and Gardiner Means, *The Modern Corporation and Private Property* (New York: Transaction, 1932); James Burnham, *The Managerial Revolution: What Is Happening in the World* (New York: Transaction, 1941).

8. For an encyclopedic academic work on John D. Rockefeller and his Standard Oil Company, see Ralph W. Hidy and Muriel E. Hidy, *Pioneering in Big Business, 1882-1911. Vol. 1. History of Standard Oil Company (New Jersey)* (New York: Harper, 1955); for a recent popular rendition, see Ron Chernow, *Titan: The Life of John D. Rockefeller, Sr.* (New York: Random House, 1998).

9. For statistics on mergers, 1895–1904, see Naomi Lamoreaux, *The Great Merger Movement in American Business, 1895–1904* (New York: Cambridge University Press, 1985), 1–4.

10. Key critiques of "Fordism" include Charles F. Sabel, *Work and Politics: The Divi-*

sion of Labor in Industry (New York: Cambridge University Press, 1982); Michael J. Piore and Charles F. Sabel, *The Second Industrial Divide: Possibilities for Prosperity* (New York: Basic Books, 1984). See also essays anthologized in Steven Tolliday, *The Rise and Fall of Mass Production*, vol. 2 (Cheltenham, U.K.: Edward Elgar, 1998).

11. William G. Roy, *Socializing Capital: The Rise of the Large Industrial Corporation* (Princeton, N.J.: Princeton University Press, 1997), 21–40; Jeremy Atack, "Industrial Structure and the Emergence of the Modern Industrial Corporation," *Explorations in Economic History* 2 (1985): 29–52.

12. Philip Scranton, *Proprietary Capitalism: The Textile Manufacture at Philadelphia, 1800–1885* (New York: Cambridge University Press, 1983); Philip Scranton, *Figured Tapestry: Production, Markets, and Power in Philadelphia Textiles, 1885–1941* (New York: Cambridge University Press, 1989).

13. Philip Scranton, *Endless Novelty: Specialty Production and American Industrialization, 1865–1925* (Princeton, N.J.: Princeton University Press, 1997).

14. Robert Lewis, *Chicago Made: Factory Networks in the Industrial Metropolis* (Chicago: University of Chicago, 2008).

15. Naomi Lamoreaux et al., "Beyond Markets and Hierarchies: Toward a New Synthesis of American Business History," *American Historical Review* 108 (April 2003): 404–33.

16. Peter Cappelli et al., *Change at Work: How American Industry and Workers Are Coping with Corporate Restructuring and What Workers Must Do to Take Charge of Their Own Careers* (New York: Oxford University Press, 1997).

17. Roy, *Socializing Capital*, 41–78.

18. Colleen Dunlavy, *Politics and Industrialization: Early Railroads in the United States and Prussia* (Princeton, N.J.: Princeton University Press, 1994); Frank Dobbin, *Forging Industrial Policy: The United States, Britain, and France in the Railway Age* (New York: Cambridge University Press, 1994).

19. Jürgen Kocka, "The Rise of the Modern Industrial Enterprise in Germany," in *Managerial Hierarchies: Comparative Perspectives on the Rise of the Modern Industrial Enterprise,* ed. Alfred D. Chandler, Jr., and Herman Daems (Cambridge, Mass.: Harvard University Press, 1980), 77–116.

20. On the role of law and finance capital in the 1890s, see Roy, *Socializing Capital*, 115–258; Lamoreaux, *The Great Merger Movement*, 1–4.

21. Ron Chernow, *The House of Morgan: An American Dynasty and the Rise of Modern Finance* (New York: Grove Press, 1990).

22. Roy, *Socializing Capital*, 176–258.

23. For nuanced treatments of legal decisions imparting personhood to corporations and drawing distinctions between reasonable and illegal market dominance, see Morton Horowitz, *The Transformation of American Law, 1870–1960: The Crisis of Legal Orthodoxy* (New York: Oxford University Press, 1992), 65–108; and Martin J. Sklar, *The Corporate Reconstruction of American Capitalism, 1890–1916: The Market, the Law, and Politics* (New York: Cambridge University Press, 1988).

24. Charles Perrow, *Organizing America: Wealth, Power, and the Origins of Corporate Capitalism* (Princeton, N.J.: Princeton University Press, 2002), 141–57. Corporate leaders may have gained political favors, but that did not guarantee that they would effectively manage their businesses; for corruption and mismanagement, see Richard White, *Railroaded: The Transcontinentals and the Making of Modern America* (New York: W. W. Norton & Company, 1911). Even with political access, corporate leaders did not always control the regulatory process; see Gerald Berk, *Alternative Tracks: The Constitution of American Industrial Order, 1865–1917* (Baltimore: Johns Hopkins University Press, 1994).

25. Gabriel Kolko, *The Triumph of Conservatism: A Reinterpretation of American History, 1900–1916* (New York: Free Press of Glencoe, 1963), 26–29.

26. Olivier Zunz, *Making America Corporate, 1870–1920* (Chicago: Chicago University Press, 1990).

27. James Livingston, "The Social Analysis of Economic History and Theory: Conjectures on Late Nineteenth-Century American Development," *American Historical Review* 92 (February 1987): 69–95.

28. Robert Jackall, *Moral Mazes: The World of Corporate Managers* (New York: Oxford University Press, 1988).

29. The legendary strikes of American history are vividly portrayed in Jeremy Brecher, *Strike!* (Boston: South End Press, 1972).

30. Congress, *United States Congressional Serial Set,* 53rd Cong., 3rd sess., 1894–95 (Washington, D.C.: U.S. Government Printing Office), 110.

31. Walter Licht, "The Dialectics of Bureaucratization: The Case of MidNineteenth Century American Railwaymen," in *Life and Labor: Dimensions of American Working-Class History,* ed. Charles Stephenson and Robert Asher (Albany: SUNY Press, 1986), 92–114.

32. Licht, *Industrializing America,* 166–86.

33. Sanford Jacoby, *Employing Bureaucracy: Managers, Unions and the Transformation of Work in American Industry, 1900–1945* (New York: Columbia University Press, 1985).

34. Walter Licht, "Fringe Benefits: A Review Essay on the American Workplace," *International Labor and Working-Class History* 53 (1998): 164–78.

35. Basic works on the organizing of mass production workers in the 1930s under the aegis of the CIO include Robert Zieger, *CIO: 1935–1955* (Chapel Hill: University of North Carolina Press, 1995); Lisabeth Cohen, *Making a New Deal: Industrial Workers in Chicago, 1919–1939* (New York: Cambridge University Press, 1991).

36. This chapter was composed before the flowering of the Occupy Movement in the fall of 2012. However one judges the tactics and impact of this upsurge, it bears an interesting resemblance to the antimonopoly protests of the nineteenth century noted in this essay.

Chapter 10. Citizens of the Corporation?

1. Barry Hirsch, "Unions, Dynamism, and Economic Performance," in *Research Handbook on the Economics of Labor and Employment Law,* ed. Cynthia L. Estlund and Michael L. Wachter (Northampton, MA: Edward Elgar Publishing, 2012).

2. Richard Freeman and Joel Rogers, *What Workers Want* (Ithaca: Cornell University Press, 2006).

3. Ibid., 81–92.

4. Ibid., 84–88.

5. Ibid.

6. Ibid., 88–91.

7. Simon Deakin and Aristea Koukiadaki, "Capability Theory, Employee Voice and Corporate Restructuring: Evidence from UK Case Studies," in *Comparative Labor Law and Policy Journal* 33 (2012): 379–416.

8. Freeman and Rogers, *What Workers Want*.

9. Ibid.; Daphne Taras, "Why Non-Union Representation Is Legal in Canada," *Relations Industrielles/Industrial Relations* 52 (1997): 763–86. In particular, most Canadian provinces require joint worker-management safety committees that would likely be illegal under U.S. law.

10. John Godard and Carola Frege, "Labor Unions, Alternative Forms of Representation, and the Exercise of Authority Relations in U.S. Workplaces," *Industrial and Labor Relations Review* 66 (2013): 142–68; see also Daphne G. Taras and Bruce E. Kaufman, "Non-union Employee Representation in North America: Diversity, Controversy, and Uncertain Future," *Industrial Relations Journal* 37 (2006): 513–42; Freeman and Rogers, *What Workers Want*, 92–93.

11. Godard and Frege, "Labor Unions, Alternative Forms."

12. By way of comparison, unions got high marks from 41 percent of members (for consulting with members) and 54 percent (sticking up for members). Ibid., 16.

13. Ibid., 23–24.

14. The argument made in this and the next major section of this chapter is elaborated at greater length in prior work. Cynthia Estlund, "*Why Workers Still Need a Collective Voice in the Era of Norms and Mandates*," in *Research Handbook on the Economics of Labor and Employment*, ed. Cynthia L. Estlund and Michael L. Wachter (Northampton, Mass.: Edward Elgar Publishing, Inc., 2012); Cynthia Estlund, *Regoverning the Workplace: From Self-Regulation to Co-Regulation* (New Haven: Yale University Press, 2010).

15. Michael L. Wachter, "The Striking Success of the National Labor Relations Act," in *Research Handbook on the Economics of Labor and Employment*, ed. Estlund and Wachter.

16. Cynthia Estlund, "Wrongful Discharge Protections in an At-Will World," *Texas Law Review* 74 (1997): 1655–92.

17. Estlund, *Regoverning the Workplace*.

18. Bruce Kaufman, "Economic Analysis of Labor Markets and Labor Law: An Institutional/Industrial Relations Perspective," in *Research Handbook on the Economics of Labor and Employment Law*, ed. Estlund and Wachter; Cass Sunstein, "Constitutionalism After the New Deal," *Harvard Law Review* 101 (1987): 421–51.

19. Michael Wachter, "Labor Unions: A Corporatist Institution in a Competitive World," *University of Pennsylvania Law Review* 155 (2007): 581–634.

20. Freeman and Rogers, *What Workers Want*; Paul Weiler, *Governing the Workplace: The Future of Labor and Employment Law* (Cambridge, Mass.: Harvard University Press, 1990).

21. Kim Bobo, *Wage Theft in America: Why Millions of Working Americans Are Not Getting Paid—and What We Can Do About It* (New York: The New Press, 2009); Steven Greenhouse, *The Big Squeeze: Tough Times for the American Worker* (New York: Alfred A. Knopf, 2008); Eileen Appelbaum and Annette Bernhardt, *Low-Wage America: How Employers Are Reshaping Opportunity in the Workplace*, ed. Richard J. Murnane (New York: Russell Sage Foundation, 2003); Annette Bernhardt et al., "Unregulated Work in the Global City: Employment and Labor Law Violations in New York," Brennan Center for Justice, technical report, June 2007, at New York University School of Law, available at http://brennan.3cdn.net/d6a52a30063ab2d639_9tm6bgaq4.pdf; David Weil, "Compliance with the Minimum Wage: Can Government Make a Difference?" working paper, 2003, available at http://papers.ssrn.com/sol3/papers.cfm?abstract_id=368340.

22. Bernhardt et al., "Unregulated Work in the Global City"; Michael J. Wishnie, "Emerging Issues for Undocumented Workers," *University of Pennsylvania Journal of Labor and Employment Law* 6 (2004): 497–524.

23. Brooke E. Lierman, "'To Assure Safe and Healthful Working Conditions': Taking Lessons from Labor Unions to Fulfill OSHA's Promises," *Loyola Journal of Public Interest Law* 12 (2010): 1–37; Thomas O. McGarity and Sidney A. Shapiro, *Workers at Risk: The Failed Promise of the Occupational Safety and Health Administration* (Westport, Conn.: Praeger, 1993).

24. John F. Burton and James R. Chelius, "Workplace Safety and Health Regulations: Rationale and Results," in *Government Regulation of the Employment Relationship*, ed. Bruce E. Kaufman (Madison, WI: Industrial Relations Research Association, 1997), 253–94.

25. Richard B. Freeman and James L. Medoff, *What Do Unions Do?* (New York: Basic Books, 1984); Alison D. Morantz, "Coal Mine Safety: Do Unions Make a Difference?" *Industrial and Labor Relations Review* 66 (2013): 88; Weiler, *Governing the Workplace*.

26. James T. Bennett and Bruce E. Kaufman, *The Future of Private Sector Unionism in the U.S.: Assessment and Forecast* (Armonk, N.Y.: M. E. Sharpe, 2002); James J. Brudney, "Reflections on Group Action and the Law of the Workplace," *Texas Law Review* 74 (1996): 1563–1600.

27. The obvious utility of joint health and safety committees has led many employers to ignore the proscriptions of Sec. 8(a)(2) in this area, and it has led even the NLRB's general counsel to offer a fig leaf of an argument against federal preemption, to states that require such committees. See Estlund, *Regoverning the Workplace*, at 172–75. Still, most functioning nonunion health and safety committees are probably in technical violation of 8(a)(2).

28. See Civil Rights Act of 1964, Pub. L. No. 88-352, §703, 78 Stat. 241, 255 (codified as amended at 42 U.S.C. §2000e-2 [2000]).

29. See Age Discrimination in Employment Act of 1967, Pub. L. No. 90-202, 81 Stat.

602 (codified as amended at 29 U.S.C. §§621-634 [2000]); Pregnancy Discrimination Act, Pub. L. No. 95-555, 92 Stat. 2076 (1978) (codified at 42 U.S.C. §2000e (2006); Americans with Disabilities Act of 1990, Pub. L. No. 101-336, 104 Stat. 327 (codified as amended at 42 U.S.C. §§12101–12213 [2000]); Genetic Information Nondiscrimination Act of 2007, S. 358, H.R. 493, 110th Cong. (2007); Civil Rights Act of 1991, Pub. L. No. 102-166, 105 Stat. 1071 (1991).

30. Before 1991, race discrimination plaintiffs could seek damages and a jury trial under 42 U.S.C. §1981(a). After the 1991 amendments, a jury trial and damages (subject to caps) were available under Title VII itself.

31. Clyde W. Summers, "Employment at Will in the United States: The Divine Right of Employers," *University of Pennsylvania Journal of Labor and Employment Law* 3 (2000): 65–86.

32. See, e.g., *Luedtke v. Nabors Alaska Drilling, Inc.,* 768 P.2d 1123, 1136–37 (Ala. 1989) (discharge for refusing random drug tests); *Petermann v. Int'l Bhd. of Teamsters, Local 396,* 344 P.2d 25, 27 (Cal. Ct. App. 1959) (discharge for refusing to give perjured testimony); *Nees v. Hocks,* 536 P.2d 512, 516 (Or. 1975) (discharge for serving jury duty).

33. See *Wal-Mart Stores, Inc. v. Dukes,* 131 S.Ct. 2541 (2011); *AT&T Mobility LLC v. Concepcion,* 131 S.Ct. 1740 (2011).

34. Michael L. Wachter, "The Striking Success of the National Labor Relations Act," in *Research Handbook on the Economics of Labor and Employment Law*, ed. Estlund and Wachter; Oliver E. Williamson, Michael L. Wachter, and Jeffrey E. Harris, "Understanding the Employment Relation: The Analysis of Idiosyncratic Exchange," *Bell Journal of Economics* 6 (1975): 250–78.

35. Collective bargaining offers a potential solution to the problem of employer opportunism; see Michael L. Wachter and Randall D. Wright, "The Economics of Internal Labor Markets," *Industrial Relations* 29 (1990): 240–62; Kenneth G. Dau-Schmidt, "A Bargaining Analysis of American Labor Law and the Search for Industrial Peace," *Michigan Law Review* 91 (1992): 419–514; Weiler, *Governing the Workplace*. But collective bargaining, even with nonjudicial enforcement of the collective contract, still entails substantial contracting costs that may undermine the economic logic of the firm's decision to "make" through employees rather than 'buying' through outside contractors; Wachter, "Labor Unions: A Corporatist Institution in a Competitive World."

36. Michael L. Wachter, "Neoclassical Labor Economics: Its Implications for Labor and Employment Law," in *Research Handbook on the Economics of Labor and Employment Law*, ed. Estlund and Wachter; Edward B. Rock and Michael L. Wachter, "The Enforceability of Norms and the Employment Relationship," *University of Pennsylvania Law Review* 144 (1996): 1913–52; Wachter and Wright, "The Economics of Internal Labor Markets."

37. Rock and Wachter, "The Enforceability of Norms."
38. Wachter, "Neoclassical Labor Economics."
39. Rock and Wachter, "The Enforceability of Norms."

40. David H. Autor et al., "The Costs of Wrongful-Discharge Laws," *Review of Economics & Statistics* 88 (2006): 211–31.

41. See, e.g., *Woolley v. Hoffman-La Roche, Inc.*, 491 A.2d 1257 (N.J. 1985).

42. Estlund, *Regoverning the Workplace*.

43. Except for promises regarding compensation for work that has already been done; such claims will likely be deemed "vested" and thus enforceable. Rock and Wachter appear to concede the legal enforceability of "vested benefits"; see Rock and Wachter, "The Enforceability of Norms," 1936, n. 47.

44. Samuel Issacharoff, "Contracting for Employment," *Texas Law Review* 74 (1996): 1783–1812.

45. Pauline T. Kim, "Bargaining with Imperfect Information: A Study of Worker Perceptions of Legal Protection in an At-Will World," *Cornell Law Review* 83 (1997): 105–60.

46. Cynthia Estlund, "Between Rights and Contract: Arbitration Agreements and Non-Compete Covenants as a Hybrid Form of Employment Law," *University of Pennsylvania Law Review* 155 (2007): 379–445.

47. The TEAM Act—Teamwork for Employees and Managers—of 1997, which would have amended Section 8(a)(2) to allow for certain forms of nonunion employee representation, was passed by Congress over union opposition but vetoed by President Clinton.

48. Frank Dobbin, *Inventing Equal Opportunity* (Princeton, N.J.: Princeton University Press, 2009).

49. Ibid.; Lauren B. Edelman et al., "Diversity Rhetoric and the Managerialization of Law," *American Journal of Sociology* 106 (2001): 1589–1641.

50. It is clear, after the Supreme Court's ruling in *Wal-Mart v. Dukes*, 564 U.S. 131 (2011), that claims of sex discrimination cannot proceed in the form of a single nationwide class action. But individual or store- or region-specific lawsuits involving many thousands of plaintiffs have followed.

51. According to EEOC data, the percentage of professionals in the private sector who belong to a "minority" group (Black, Hispanic, Asian/Pacific Islander, American Indian/Alaskan Native, Native Hawaiian, or mixed race) rose from 3.9 percent in 1966 to 23.8 percent in 2007; among private-sector "officials and managers," minority representation rose from 1.8 percent in 1966 to 19.5 percent (and Black and Hispanic representation rose from 1.5 percent in 1966 to 14.6 percent) in 2007. Available at http://archive.eeoc.gov/stats/jobpat/2007/indicators.html. Of course, minority group (and black and Hispanic) representation in the labor force as a whole also rose during this period, but to a far lesser extent.

52. Those pressures are muffled in the more centralized bargaining systems of Europe, for example. Indeed, most of the developed world embraces the idea, and has put in place institutional structures, for taking wages largely out of competition.

53. David J. Doorey, "A Model of Responsive Workplace Law," *Osgoode Hall Law Journal* 50 (2012): 47–91.

Chapter 11. Politics and Corporate Governance

1. Daniel Yankelovich, *Profit with Honor* (New Haven: Yale University Press, 2006).

2. Gretchen Morgenson, "Employees, Too, Want a Say on Boss's Pay," *New York Times,* April 21, 2012.

3. John Cioffi, *Public Law and Private Power: The Comparative Political Economy of Corporate Governance Reform in the Age of Finance Capitalism* (Ithaca, N.Y.: Cornell University Press, 2010), 304; Ulrike Schaede, *Choose and Focus: Japanese Business Strategies for the Twenty-first Century* (Ithaca, N.Y.: Cornell University Press, 2008).

4. David Easton, *A Framework for Political Analysis* (New York: Prentice-Hall, 1965).

5. Daniel Kahneman, *Thinking Fast and Slow* (New York: Farrar, Straus and Giroux, 2011).

6. Rafael La Porta et al., "Investor Protection and Corporate Governance," *Journal of Financial Economics* 58 (2000): 3–27.

7. Ibid.

8. Ibid.

9. Ibid.

10. Raghuram Rajan and Luigi Zingales, "The Great Reversals: The Politics of Financial Development in the Twentieth Century," *Journal of Financial Economics* 69 (2003): 5–50.

11. Peter Gourevitch, "Politics, Institutions and Society: Seeking Better Results," in *World Bank Legal Review: Law Equity and Development* 2, ed. Ana Palacio (The Hague: Martius Nijhoff, 2006), 263-92.

12. A. A. Berle and G. Means, *Theory of the Firm: Managerial Behavior, Agency, and Ownership Structures* (New York: Transaction Publishers, 1932). Michael Jensen and William Meckling, "Theory of the Firm: Managerial Behavior, Agency Costs and Ownership Structure," *Journal of Financial Economics* 3 (1976): 305–60.

13. Mark Roe, *Political Determinants of Corporate Governance* (Oxford: Oxford University Press, 2003), 5.

14. Ibid.

15. Marco Pagano and Paolo Volpin, "The Political Economy of Corporate Governance," *Centre for Economic Policy Research Discussion Paper* 2682 (2001); Marco Pagano and Paolo Volpin, "The Political Economy of Finance," *Oxford Review of Economic Policy* 17 (2001): 502–19.

16. Peter Hall and David Soskice, *The Varieties of Capitalism* (Oxford: Oxford University Press, 2000); see also Andrew Schonfeld, *Modern Capitalism* (New York: Oxford University Press, 1965); and Ronald Dore, *Stock Market Capitalism, Welfare Capitalism* (New York: Oxford University Press, 2000).

17. Michael Hiscox, *International Trade and Political Conflict* (Princeton, N.J.: Princeton University Press, 2002).

18. Edward Glaeser et al., "Coase vs. the Coasians," *Quarterly Journal of Economics* 116 (2001): 853–900.

19. Frank Dobbin and Jiwook Jung, "The Misapplication of Mr. Michael Jensen: How Agency Theory Brought Down the Economy and Why It Might Again," in *Markets on Trial: The Economic Sociology of the U.S. Financial Crisis: Part B*, ed. Michael Lounsbury and Paul Hirsch *(Research in the Sociology of Organizations)* 30 (2010): 29–64.

20. Jensen and Meckling, "Theory of the Firm."

21. Dobbin and Jung, "The Misapplication of Mr. Michael Jensen."

22. Gretta Krippner, *Capitalizing on Crisis: The Political Origins of the Rise of Finance* (Cambridge, Mass.: Harvard University Press, 2011).

23. Dobbin and Jung, "The Misapplication of Mr. Michael Jensen."

24. Arthur Lupia and Mathew McCubbins, *The Democratic Dilemma* (New York: Cambridge University Press, 1998); Peter Gourevitch et al., *The Credibility of Transnational NGOs: When Virtue Is Not Enough* (Cambridge: Cambridge University Press, 2012).

25. Roe, *Political Determinants of Corporate Governance,* 5.

26. Bernard Black and John Coffee, "Hail Britannia: Institutional Investor Relations Under Limited Regulation," *Michigan Law Review* 92 (1994): 1997–2087.

27. Gerald Davis and E. Han Kim, "Business Ties and Proxy Voting by Mutual Funds," *Journal of Financial Economics* 85 (2007): 552–70.

28. U.S. Court of Appeals, D.C. Circuit, *Business Roundtable v. SEC* (Washington, D.C.: U.S Court of Appeals, 2011).

29. Peter Gourevitch, "What Do Corporations Owe Citizens? Pensions, Corporate Governance and the Role of Institutional Investors," in *What Do We Owe Each Other: Rights and Obligations in Contemporary American Society,* ed. Howard Rosenthal and David Rothman (New Brunswick, N.J.: Transaction, 2008), 45–60.

30. Hall and Soskice, *The Varieties of Capitalism.*

31. Peter Gourevitch and James P. Shinn, *Political Power and Corporate Control: The New Global Politics of Corporate Governance* (Princeton, N.J.: Princeton University Press, 2005).

32. Ibid.; James Shinn, "Portfolio Politics in the New Hard Times: Crises, Coalitions, and Shareholders in the United States and Germany," in *Politics in the New Hard Times: The Great Recession in Comparative Perspective,* ed. Miles Kahler and David A. Lake (Ithaca, N.Y.: Cornell University Press, 2013), 169–89.

33. Michel Goyer, *Contingent Capital: Short-Term Investors and the Evolution of Corporate Governance in France and Germany* (Oxford: Oxford University Press, 2011).

34. John Cioffi and Martin Hoepner, "The Political Paradox of Financial Capitalism: Interests, Preferences, and Center-Left Party Politics in Corporate Governance Reform," *Politics and Society* 34 (2006): 463–502.

35. Cioffi, *Public Law and Private Power,* 304.

36. Morgenson, "Employees, Too, Want a Say on Boss's Pay."

37. Schaede, *Choose and Focus.*

38. Cioffi, *Public Law and Private Power,* 304.

39. Pepper D. Culpepper, *Quiet Politics and Business Power: Corporate Control in Europe*

and Japan (Cambridge: Cambridge University Press, 2011), 248; Bruce Kogut, "Corporate Governance Reform: A *cri de coeur* for Two Decades," *French Politics* 9 (2011): 404-12.

40. Daniel Berkowitz et al., "Economic Development, Legality, and the Transplant Effect," *European Economic Review* 47 (2003): 165–95; also Curtis J. Milhaupt and Katharina Pistor, *Law and Capitalism: What Corporate Crises Reveal About Legal Systems and Economic Development Around the World* (Chicago: University of Chicago Press, 2008).

41. Daron Acemoglu and James Robinson, *Why Nations Fail* (New York: Random House, 2012).

42. Ibid.

Chapter 12. The Nature and Futility of "Regulation by Assimilation"

I am grateful for comments and suggestions from Bruce Ackerman, Ian Ayres, Jacqueline Carter, Jonah Gelbach, Daniel Hemel, Luis Nario, and Yair Listoken. This chapter is a slightly different treatment of the regulatory pathologies discussed previously in Jonathan R. Macey, "The Regulator Effect in Financial Regulation," *Cornell Law Review* 98 (2013): 591–636.

1. William L. Rutledge, "Implementing the New Basel Accord," *Bank for International Settlements*, March 13, 2003. Available at http://www.bis.org/review/r030217a.pdf (accessed Nov. 17, 2011).

2. Federal Deposit Insurance Corporation, Update on Emerging Issues in Banking, "Risk-Based Capital Requirements for Commercial Lending: The Impact of Basel II," *Federal Deposit Insurance Corporation,* April 21, 2003. Available at http://www.fdic.gov/bank/analytical/fyi/2003/042103fyi.html (accessed Nov. 18, 2011).

3. Ian Ayres and Robert Gertner, "Filling Gaps in Incomplete Contracts: An Economic Theory of Default Rules," *Yale Law Journal* 87 (1989): 99 (observing that "the legal rules of contracts and corporations can be divided into two distinct classes. The larger class consists of 'default' rules that parties can contract around by prior agreement, while the smaller, but important, class consists of 'immutable' rules that parties cannot change by contractual agreement. Default rules fill the gaps in incomplete contracts; they govern unless the parties contract around them. Immutable rules cannot be contracted around; they govern even if the parties attempt to contract around them").

4. All rules begin as enabling rules in the sense that, in the absence of mandatory rules or other regulatory constraints, firms can adopt more or less any system of private ordering that they choose. Later, regulators codify these arrangements, choosing for various reasons to make some rules mandatory for firms and individuals and leaving others as enabling.

5. See Marie Leone, "Fairness Opinions Neutrality Questioned," *CFO Magazine*, Feb. 2, 2006. Available at http://www.cfo.com/article.cfm/5465857 (accessed Feb. 24, 2011).

6. Hiring one or more reputational intermediaries can serve as a substitute for a direct investment in reputation. Companies without reputations must either use reputa-

tional intermediaries or confine themselves to the loan market, where commercial banks and other lenders perform intensive (and costly) ongoing monitoring and use various protective covenants and other restrictions on borrowers to protect themselves against opportunistic behavior. Jonathan Macey, "The Value of Reputation in Corporate Finance and Investment Banking (and the Related Roles of Regulation and Market Efficiency)," *Journal of Applied Corporate Finance* 22 (2010): 18–29.

7. George Akerlof, "The Market for 'Lemons': Quality Uncertainty and the Market Mechanism," *Quarterly Journal of Economics* 84 (1970): 488–500.

8. Michael C. Jensen and William C. Meckling, "Theory of the Firm: Managerial Behavior, Agency Costs and Ownership Structure," *Journal of Financial Economics* 3 (1976): 305.

9. Andrei Shleifer and Robert W. Vishny, "A Survey of Corporate Governance," *Journal of Corporate Finance* 52 (1997): 737–83.

10. See Jonathan R. Macey, *Corporate Governance: Promises Kept, Promises Broken* (Princeton, N.J.: Princeton University Press, 2008), 29: "One of the most remarkable aspects of modern economic life is the fact that hundreds of millions of investors have been persuaded to part with hundreds of billions of dollars in exchange for residual claims on the cash flows of companies. The securities that represent these residual claims offer their owners virtually nothing in the form of formal, legal protections. Shareholders do not have the right to repayment of their principal, ever. Companies issuing the equity claims have no obligation to repurchase the shares from investors, regardless of how well or poorly the issuing companies perform. These companies are not under any obligation to pay dividends or make any other sort of payments to equity claimants."

11. See Shleifer and Vishny, "A Survey of Corporate Governance," 737.

12. Frank Partnoy, "How and Why Credit Ratings Agencies Are Not Like Other Gatekeepers," in *Financial Gatekeepers: Can They Protect Investors?* ed. Yasuyuki Fuchita and Robert E. Litan (Baltimore: Brookings Institution Press and the Nomura Institute of Capital Markets Research, 2006)

13. "Net Capital Requirements on Introducing Brokers' Proprietary Accounts Assets Held by Clearing Brokers," NYSE Interp. Memo 98–10 (Dec. 10, 1998), 1998 WL 34299912.

14. "Debt Is Cheap and Equity Is Expensive." From "Should Banks Hold More Capital? It Worked Out Great for REITs," *Seeking Alpha*, Feb. 6, 2011. Available at http://seekingalpha.com/article/251069–should-banks-hold-more-capital-it-worked-out-great-for-reits (accessed Feb. 28, 2011).

15. Markus K. Brunnermeir, "Deciphering the 2007–08 Liquidity and Credit Crunch," *Journal of Economic Perspectives* 23 (2009): 77–100.

16. "Statement of Paul Schott Stevens, President, Investment Company Institute, Before the Committee on Banking, Housing, and Urban Affairs," *U.S. Senate on Assessing the Current Oversight and Operation of Credit Rating Agencies*, March 7, 2006. Available at http://banking.senate.gov/public/index.cfm?FuseAction=Files.View&FileStore_id=31 6a0acc-f3bc-4d8b-b09f-d013fb60e81b (accessed Feb. 28, 2011).

17. "Statement of Paul Schott Stevens, President, Investment Company Institute, Before the Committee on Banking, Housing, and Urban Affairs," *U.S. Senate on Assessing the Current Oversight and Operation of Credit Rating Agencies*, Mar. 7, 2006. Available at http://banking.senate.gov/public/index.cfm?FuseAction=Files.View&FileStor _id=316a0acc-f3bc-4d8b-b09f-d013fb60e81b (accessed Feb. 28, 2011).

18. Frank Partnoy, "The Paradox of Credit Ratings," in *Ratings, Rating Agencies, and the Global Financial System*, ed. Richard M. Levich, Giovanni Majnoni, and Carmen M. Reinhart (Norwell, Mass.: Kluwer Academic Publishers, 2002), 65–84.

19. Thomas L. Friedman, interview, *NewsHour with Jim Lehrer,* PBS, February 13, 1996.

20. Partnoy, "How and Why Credit Rating Agencies are Not Like Other Gatekeepers."

21. Lawrence White, "The Credit Rating Industry: An Industrial Organization Analysis," Paper prepared for World Bank Conference on the Role of Credit Reporting Systems in the International Economy, February 12, 2001, draft. Available at http://papers .ssrn.com/sol3/papers.cfm?abstract_id=1292667 (accessed March 7, 2011). White attributes this shift to the spread of low-cost photocopying, which prevented the credit rating agencies from preventing free-riding on the ratings they generated by nonpayers.

22. Partnoy, "How and Why Credit Rating Agencies Are Not Like Other Gatekeepers."

23. Frank Partnoy, "The Siskel and Ebert of Financial Markets: Two Thumbs Down for Credit Rating Agencies," *Washington University Law Quarterly* 77 (1999): 619–712.

24. Jonathan R. Macey, "Wall Street Versus Main Street: How Ignorance, Hyperbole, and Fear Lead to Regulation," *University of Chicago Law Review* 65 (1998): 1487.

25. Claire A. Hill, "Why Did Anyone Listen to the Rating Agencies After Enron?" *Journal of Business and Technology Law* 4 (2009): 283–94.

26. Martin Fridson, "Bond Rating Agencies: Conflicts and Competence," *Journal of Applied Corporate Finance* 22 (2010): 56.

27. Doron Kliger and Oded Sarig, "The Information Value of Bond Ratings," *Journal of Finance* 55 (2000): 2879–2902. Available at http://finance.wharton.upenn.edu/~sarig/ sarigo/ratings.pdf. Koresh Galil, "The Quality of Corporate Credit Rating: An Empirical Investigation," EFMA 2003 Helsinki Meetings. European Financial Management Association (Helsinki, Finland), June 25, 2003. Available at http://papers.ssrn.com/sol3 /papers.cfm?abstract_id=406681 (accessed March 7, 2011).

28. Partnoy, "The Paradox of Credit Ratings."

29. Thomas Gorman, "Dodd-Frank Credit Rating Agencies, Part I," *SEC Actions,* Aug. 23, 2010. Available at http://www.secactions.com/?p=2507.

30. Structured finance is the catchall term for financial transactions that created new, often complex, legal entities (special-purpose vehicles) whose sole purpose was to issue debt securities on a standalone basis (meaning the entities had no business of their own apart from issuing securities) in which the repayment of principal and interest on the securities created was based on the cash flows generated by assets such as mortgages, credit card receivables, and car loans. Structured financial instruments include a wide

variety of securities issued by specialized entities, primarily: asset-backed securities, mortgage-backed securities, collateralized mortgage obligations, collateralized debt obligations, collateralized bond obligations, and collateralized obligations of hedge funds and private equity funds. In technical terms, structured investments typically "(i) combine traditional asset classes with contingent claims, such as risk transfer derivatives and/ or derivative claims on commodities, currencies or receivables from other reference assets, or (ii) replicate traditional asset classes through synthetication or new financial instruments. Structured finance is invoked by financial and nonfinancial institutions in both banking systems and capital markets if either (i) established forms of external finance are unavailable (or depleted) for a particular financing need, or (ii) traditional sources of funds are too expensive for issuers to mobilise sufficient funds for what would otherwise be an unattractive investment based on the issuer's desired cost of capital. Structured finance offers issuers enormous flexibility to create securities with distinct risk-return profiles in terms of maturity structure, security design, and asset type, providing enhanced return at a customised degree of diversification commensurate to an individual investor's appetite for risk. Hence, structured finance contributes to a more complete capital market by offering any mean–variance trade-off along the efficient frontier of optimal diversification at lower transaction cost. The increasing complexity of the structured finance market, and the ever-growing range of products being made available to investors, however, invariably create challenges in terms of efficient management and dissemination of information." Andreas Jobst, "A Primer on Structured Finance," *Journal of Derivatives and Hedge Funds* 13 (2007): 199–213.

31. Fridson, "Bond Rating Agencies," 56.

32. Ibid.

33. Ibid.

34. Ibid., 58.

35. Dodd-Frank Act §932(a)(2)(B)(3), 124 Stat. at 1879–80. The act mandates that the SEC require NRSROs to "prescribe a form to accompany the publication of each credit rating that discloses" assumptions used, data, and use of servicer or remittance reports, as well as "information that can be used by investors and other users of credit ratings to better understand credit ratings in each class of credit rating issued by the nationally recognized statistical rating organization." §932(a)(8)(s)(1).

36. Dodd-Frank Act §931(3), 124 Stat. at 1872.

37. Dodd-Frank Act §939A(b), 124 Stat. at 1887.

38. Ibid.

39. For some examples of fairness opinions in significant transactions, see Credit Suisse Fairness Opinion in connection with a spinoff transaction, available at http://edgar.sec.gov/Archives/edgar/data/789388/000119312505074184/dex99c2.htm; "Opinion of Merck's Financial Advisor," *United States Securities and Exchanges Commission*, 2009, available at http://sec.gov/Archives/edgar/data/310158/000095012309009217/y77207 sv4.htm#169; "Opinion of Perella Weinberg, Financial Advisor to the Special Commit-

tee," *United States Securities and Exchanges Commission,* 2011, available at http://edgar
.sec.gov/Archives/edgar/data/1051251/000119312510274106/dprem14a.htm#toc121900
_28a.

40. Where the business judgment rule applies to a corporate decision, the directors
making the decision are presumed to make their decision on the basis of a "bona fide
regard for the interests of the corporation whose affairs the stockholders have committed
to their charge" *Gimbel v. Signal Cos.,* 316 A.2d 599, 608 (Del. Ch. 1974). Where directors
have the protection of the business judgment rule, they are insulated from liability except
in the exceedingly rare situation where the plaintiff is able to prove that the "directors, in
reaching their challenged decision, breached any one of the triads of their fiduciary
duty—good faith, loyalty, or due care." *Cede & Co. v. Technicolor, Inc.,* 634 A.2d 345, 361
(Del. 1993). Unless the plaintiff cannot sustain the burden of proving bad faith, disloy-
alty, or gross negligence, the plaintiff "is not entitled to any remedy unless the transaction
constitutes waste. 906 A.2d 27 (Del. June 8, 2006).

41. Helen M. Bowers, "Fairness Opinions and the Business Judgment Rule: An Empirical Investigation of Target Firms' Use of Fairness Opinions," Northwestern University
Law Review 96 (2002): 567, 571.

42. *Smith v. Van Gorkom* 488 A.2d 858 (1985).

43. Charles M. Elson, "The Duty of Care, Compensation, and Stock Ownership,"
University of Cincinnati Law Review 63 (1995): 649, 677; Bill Shaw and Edward Gac,
"Fairness Opinions in Leveraged Buy Outs: Should Investment Banks Be Directly Liable
to Shareholders?" *Securities Regulation Law Journal* 23 (1995): 293 (observing that "over
the last decade, the fairness opinion has become a necessary and integral aspect of every
major corporate control transaction. Directors feel they must seek the advice and blessing of investment banks before engaging in any action that requires them to enter the
thicket of conflicting interests"; Stephen Glover and Doketra Vansimme, "Fairness Opinion Issues: Anything but Routine," *National Law Journal,* April 15, 2006, C13; Michael J.
Kennedy, "Functional Fairness—The Mechanics, Functions and Liabilities of Fairness
Opinions," in *Handling High-Tech M&As in a Cooling Market: Ensuring That You Get
Value,* Corporate Law and Practice Handbook Series No. B-1255 (New York: Practice
Law Institute, 2001), 605, 607 (noting that fairness opinions are delivered "in almost any
transaction of note involving public companies"); Daniel R. Fischel, "The Business Judg-
ment Rule and the Trans Union Case," *Business Lawyer* 40 (1985): 1437, 1453 (asserting
that after Van Gorkom, "no firm considering a fundamental corporate change will do so
without obtaining a fairness letter"); Shaw and Gac, "Fairness Opinions in Leveraged Buy
Outs," 293 ("Over the last decade, the fairness opinion has become a necessary and integral aspect of every major corporate control transaction"); Andrew Ross Sorkin, "A Dual
Role for Lehman in Deal Talks," *New York Times,* June 3, 2005.

44. Paul Sweeney, "Who Says It's a Fair Deal?" *Journal of Accountancy* 188 (1999): 44, 45.

45. In the Catholic faith, an indulgence is a reduction or diminution in the punishment that otherwise would be owed for a sin committed. Abuses in selling and granting

indulgences provided a significant motivation for the Protestant Reformation initiated by Martin Luther in 1517.

46. Helen Bowers, "Fairness Opinions and the Business Judgment Rule: An Empirical Investigation of Target Firms' Use of Fairness Opinions," *Northwestern University Law Review* 96 (2002): 565–77.

47. Ibid., 573.

48. Henry Horsey, *Smith v. Van Gorkom,* 488 A.2d 858 (Del. 1985).

49. Stephen Choi, "Market Lessons for Gatekeepers, *Northwestern University Law Review* 92 (1998): 916.

50. Bowers, "Fairness Opinions and the Business Judgment Rule," 577.

51. As one popular investor website observes, "while they're not technically required by law, Fairness Opinions almost always get issued for deals that involve the sale of public companies due to lawsuits: no matter how much a company sells for, someone is bound to sue them"). Brian DeChesare, "Investment Banking Fairness Opinions: Profitable and Prestigious, or Glamorless Gruntwork?" MergersandInquisitions.com, http://www.mergersandinquisitions.com/investment-banking-fairness-opinions (accessed February 2, 2011).

52. Ibid. See also Lucian Arye Bebchuk and Marcel Kahan, "Fairness Opinions: How Fair Are They and What Can Be Done About It?" *Duke Law Journal* 27 (1989): 29–38 (discussing the substantial preparer discretion with respect to a fairness opinion); William J. Carney, "Fairness Opinions: How Fair Are They and Why We Should Do Nothing About It," *Washington University Law Quarterly* 70 (1992): 523 (criticizing fairness opinions for lack of precision and inability to predict price); Charles M. Elson, "Fairness Opinions: Are They Fair or Should We Care?" *Ohio State Law Journal* 53 (1992): 951 (criticizing fairness opinions for having "dubious" value); Michael W. Martin, Note, "Fairness Opinions and Negligent Misrepresentation: Defining Investment Bankers' Duty to Third-Party Shareholders," *Fordham Law Review* 60 (1991): 133, 140–41 ("During the mergers-and-acquisitions boom of the 1980s, the rendering of a fairness opinion became a mere formality performed after a deal was structured"); Dale Arthur Oesterle and Jon R. Norberg, "Management Buyouts: Creating or Appropriating Shareholder Wealth?" *Vanderbilt Law Review* 41 (1988): 207, 214 ("The chicanery of using made-to-order fairness opinions is probably widespread"); Bernard Black and Reinier Kraakman, "Delaware's Takeover Law: The Uncertain Search for Hidden Value," *Northwest University Law Review* 96 (2002): 521, 555–57 (criticizing fairness opinions for their "doubtful" value); Charles M. Elson, Arthur H. Rosenbloom, and Drew G. L. Chapman, "Can They Be Made Useful?" *Securities Regulation and Law Reporter* 35 (2003): 1–8 (discussing various criticisms of investment bank fairness opinions); David Henry, "A Fair Deal—But for Whom?" *Business Week,* Nov. 24, 2003, 108 (criticizing investment banks rendering fairness opinions for lack of objectivity and conflicts of interest).

53. Steven Davidoff, "Fairness Opinions," *American University Law Review* 55 (2006): 1608–9.

54. Theodore Eisenberg and Jonathan R. Macey, "Was Arthur Andersen Different? An Empirical Examination of Major Accounting Firm Audits of Large Clients," *Journal of Empirical Legal Studies* 1 (2004): 263, 266.

55. Ibid., 266.

56. Ibid.

5.7 Jonathan R. Macey and Hillary Sale, "Observations on the Role of Commodification, Independence, and Governance in the Accounting Industry," *Villanova Law Review* 48 (2003): 1167, 1168.

58. Independence is measured by the percentage of an audit firm's billings that are derived from a particular client. For example, Andersen was said to be independent of Enron because Andersen had 2,300 other audit clients, and Enron accounted for only about 1 percent of Andersen's total revenue from auditing (Andersen's Enron revenues were reported in 2001 as $100 million, as compared with $9.34 billion in 2001 audit revenue). Ibid., 1176, n. 33. Of course, Andersen's independence as a firm did not extend to the partners responsible for doing the actual audit work for Enron. Ibid., 1168.

59. Eisenberg and Macey, "Was Arthur Andersen Different?" 267.

60. Being fired by an accounting firm has serious implications for the client. The resignation of an auditor sends a very powerful negative signal to the capital markets and can have dire consequences not only for the firm whose auditor resigns, but also for the managers of the firm. See, e.g., Martin Fackler, "Drawing a Line: Unlikely Team Sets Japanese Banking on Road to Reform," *Wall Street Journal,* Aug. 6, 2003, A1 (describing how auditors' failure to sign off on financial projections of a large Japanese bank caused a crisis that forced the bank to seek a $17 billion government bailout that put the financial institution under government control).

61. Daniel B. Thornton, "Financial Reporting Quality: Implications of Accounting Research," Submission to the Senate (Canada) Standing Committee on Banking, Trade and Commerce, Study on the State of Domestic and International Financial System, May 29, 2002.

62. According to a 2002 Gallup poll, 70 percent of U.S. investors stated that business accounting issues were hurting the investment climate "a lot." SEC Commissioner Paul Atkins, Remarks at the Federalist Society 20th Annual Convention, November 14, 2002, available at http://www.sec.gov/news/speech/spch111402psa.htm.

63. Eisenberg and Macey, "Was Arthur Andersen Different?"

64. Ibid.

65. Explanations include: (a) The demise in civil liability and changes in organizational form, which resulted in a diminution in incentives for accounting firms to monitor themselves. The shift of organizational form from the general partnership form to the limited liability partnership form reduced the threat of liability faced by audit firm partners not directly involved in auditing a particular client. This, in turn, may have resulted in a diminution in the incentives of accounting firm partners to monitor the performance of their colleagues. The removal of aider and abettor liability risk reduced auditors' incentives to monitor one another. *Central Bank of Denver v. First Interstate Bank of*

Denver, 511 U.S. 164 (1994), holding that Section 10(b) and SEC Rule 10b-5 prohibit only "the making of a material misstatement (or omission) or the commission of a manipulative act" and do not prohibit the aiding and abetting of such acts. This decision was thought to have alleviated substantially the legal risks to outside advisors such as auditors and lawyers. This reduction in incentives was exacerbated in 1995 by passage of the Public Securities Litigation Reform Act (PSLRA). Pub. L. No. 104–67 (codified at 15 U.S.C. §78 [1998]). The PSLRA established new rules of pleading that require plaintiffs' complaints to "state with particularity all facts giving rise to a strong inference that the defendant acted with the required state of mind" when making a misstatement or omission in financial reporting. The PSLRA also delayed the beginning of discovery until after a court has decided whether to allow the case to go forward on the basis of the heightened pleading standards. Prior to passage of the PSLRA, plaintiffs' attorneys could begin to gather documents and interview witnesses as soon as their complaint was filed. PSLRA also sharply limited the doctrine of "joint and several liability," which ensures that victims can recover full damages even if one or more of the parties to the fraud cannot pay. Under PSLRA, those whose reckless misconduct contributes to the fraud can be held responsible for only their proportionate share of victims' losses. As a result, when the primary perpetrator of the fraud is bankrupt, investors cannot fully recover their losses from other entities, such as accounting firms. (b) Changes in the complexity of financial transactions, which made financial reporting more difficult. Auditing became more complex as new and more sophisticated methods of financing proliferated, and as the audit rules themselves became more technical and complex. As a consequence, audit firms that were engaged by large public companies found that the "audit engagement teams" they assigned to perform audits had to spend increasingly large percentages of their time performing audit services for that client. (c) The provision of consulting services by accounting firms upset the traditional balance of power between issuers and auditors, and contributed to the capture of accounting firms by their clients. Where accounting firms also provide consulting services, accounting firms might be tempted to use auditing work either as a loss leader or "as a mechanism for 'opening the door' with a client for the purpose of pitching their (higher margin) consulting services." Macey and Sale, "Observations on the Role of Commodification," 1178. Providing consulting services further erodes auditor independence by shifting the balance of power away from the auditor and in the direction of the audit client when auditors are discussing audit work and retention issues. Worse, consulting services provide a means by which audit clients can reward auditors for succumbing to the client's wishes about what accounting treatment should be used to report novel or complex transactions and business practices (ibid.). Where auditors only offer clients audit services, the client's only option is to fire the auditor if the client does not think that the auditor is being sufficiently aggressive or compliant. But when the accountants also are peddling consulting services, the client can employ a "carrot-and-stick" strategy that rewards the accounting firm for being compliant and punishes the firm for being inflexible. This pressure is particularly acute in an environment in which the firm is the only client of the engagement partner from the accounting firm that is performing the audit, since a partner's inability to procure lucrative consulting work would be reflected in the salary, promotion, and bonuses of the partner. It is well known that it is difficult for an audit client to fire its auditor because such dismissals invite "potential public embarrassment, public disclosure of the reason for the auditor's dismissal or resignation, and potential SEC intervention." Where a company is both an audit client as well as a consulting client of a particular accounting firm, "the client can easily terminate the auditor as a consultant or reduce its use of the firm's consulting services, in retaliation for the auditor's intransigence." Jonathan Macey and Hillary Sale, "Observations on the Role of Commodification, Independence, Governance, and the Demise of the Accounting Profession," *Villanova Law Review* 48 (2003): 1167. When the client terminates the high-margin consulting services provided by the accounting firm and retains only the low-margin auditing services, there is no need to make any public disclosure. This means that there is no risk that firing the auditor from a consulting engagement will provoke heightened scrutiny from investors, the SEC, or plaintiffs' class action law firms.

66. Eisenberg and Macey, "Was Arthur Andersen Different?"

67. Philippe Jorion, *Value at Risk: The New Benchmark for Managing Financial Risk* (New York: McGraw-Hill, 2006).

68. See "Risk-Based Capital Standards: Advanced Capital Adequacy Framework—Basel II," *Federal Register*, December 7, 2007. Available at http://www.federalregister.gov /articles/2007/12/07/07-5729/risk-based-capital-standards-advanced-capital-adequacy -framework---basel-ii (accessed February 24, 2011).

69. Ibid.

70. See Tanya Styblo Beder, "VaR: Seductive but Dangerous," *Financial Analysts Journal* September–October 1995, 12–24 (showing how VaR calculations are "extremely dependent on parameters, data, assumptions and methodology, and demonstrating that different methods of calculating VaRs can yield significantly different risk assessment," and observing that VaR calculations "are not sufficient to control risk").

71. Federal Reserve Bank of New York, March 13, 2003, speech of William L. Rutledge before the British Bankers Associations at the Basel 2 / CAD (capital adequacy directive) Conference, March 13, 2003. Available at http://www.newyorkfed.org/news events/speeches_archive/2003/rut031303.html (accessed March 3, 2011).

72. Ibid.

73. Ibid.

74. Ibid.

75. "Overview of the Amendment to the Capital Accord to Incorporate Market Risks," Basle Committee on Banking Supervision. Available at http://www.bis.org/publ /bcbs23.pdf.

76. Frank Partnoy, *Infectious Greed: How Deceit and Risk Corrupted the Financial Markets* (New York: PublicAffairs, 2009), 262.

77. Ibid., 262.

78. Ibid., 261–62.

79. Sarah Borchersen-Keto, "FDIC Moves on Dodd-Frank Capital Requirements," *CCH Financial Reform News Center*, Dec. 14, 2010. Available at http://financialreform .wolterskluwerlb.com/2010/12/fdic-moves-on-dodd-frank-capital-requirements.html (accessed March 3, 2011).

80. Jonathan Macey, "Corporate Law and Corporate Governance: A Contractual Perspective," *Journal of Corporate Law* 18 (1993): 187; John C. Coffee, Jr., "The Mandatory/Enabling Balance in Corporate Law: An Essay on the Judicial Role," *Columbia Law Review* 89 (1981): 1618–91.

Chapter 13. Multinational Corporations as Regulators and Central Planners

1. Ruth Grant and Robert O. Keohane, "Accountability and Abuses of Power in World Politics," *American Political Science Review* 99 (2005): 29–43.

2. Stephen J. Choi and Andrew T. Guzman, "Portable Reciprocity: Rethinking the Internatioanl Reach of Securities Regulations," *South California Law Review* 71 (1998): 903.

3. John G. Ruggie, "Reconstituting the Global Public Domain: Issues, Actors, and Practices," *European Journal of International Relations* 10 (2004): 499–531.

4. Fabrizio Cafaggi, "New Foundations of Transnational Private Regulation," *Journal of Law and Society* 38 (2011): 20–49.

5. Geoffrey M. Hodgson, "On the Institutional Foundations of Law: The Insufficiency of Custom and Private Ordering," *Journal of Economic Issues* 43 (2009): 143–66.

6. Ronald H. Coase, "The Nature of the Firm," *Economica* (Nov. 1937): 386–405.

7. Oliver Hart and John Moore, "Property Rights and the Nature of the Firm," *Journal of Political Economy* 98 (1990): 1119–58; Oliver Williamson, "Transaction-Cost Economics: The Governance of Contractual Relations," *Journal of Law and Economics* 22 (Oct. 1979): 233–61; Hart and Moore, "Property Rights and the Nature of the Firm."

8. Oliver Williamson, "Transaction-Cost Economics: The Governance of Contractual Relations," *Journal of Law and Economics* 22 (Oct. 1979): 233–61.

9. Fabrizio Cafaggi and Katharina Pistor, "Regulatory Capabilities," forthcoming in *Regulation and Governance* (2014).

10. Katharina Pistor, Yoram Keinan, Jan Kleinheisterkamp, and Mark West, "The Evolution of Corporate Law," *University of Pennsylvania Journal of International Economic Law* 23 (2002): 791–871.

11. W. W. Powell, "Neither Market Nor Hierarchy: Network Form of Organization," *Research in Organizational Behavior* 12 (1990): 295–336; Josh Whitford, *The New Old Economy: Networks, Institutions, and the Organizational Transformation of American Manufacturing* (Oxford: Oxford University Press, 2006).

12. Whitford, *The New Old Economy.*

13. Richard Locke, Fei Qin, and Alberto Brause, "Does Monitoring Improve Labor Standards? Lessons from Nike," *Industrial and Labor Relations Review* 61 (2007): 3.

14. In India, for example, the Tata group has given back the land to tea farmers to operate it as self-employed, yet Tata remains the only buyer. In fact the relation between farmers and the company has changed, but Tata has been able to devolve the responsibility for the health, safety, and productivity of labor entirely onto them. Note, however, that in India the self-employed are in principle subject to labor regulations, but these regulations are difficult to enforce. See P. K. Krishnakumar, "Tata Tea Handed Control of Its Tea Plantations to Workers to Make Profit," *Economic Times,* October 13, 2010.

15. Gilton Klerck, "Rise of Temporary Employment Industry in Namibia: A Regulatory 'Fix,'" *Journal of Contemporary African Studies* 27 (2009): 85–103.

16. Locke, Qin, and Brause, "Does Monitoring Improve Labor Standards?" 3.

17. Ibid.

18. Ibid.

19. See Julie Schmit, "Salmonella Fears Take Zing out of Pepper Biz," *USA Today,* July 14, 2008. Available at http://www.usatoday.com/money/industries/food/2008-07-13-peppers_N.htm (accessed April 23, 2012).

20. Conference on "Transnational Integration Regimes," Interamerican Development Bank, Washington, D.C., February 23–24, 2012. Notes on file with the author.

21. Michael R. Taylor, Deputy Commissioner for Foods, U.S. Food and Drug Administration, Remarks before America Trades Produce Tubac, Arizona, March 22, 2012. Available at www.fda.gov/food (accessed April 23, 2012).

22. Foundational on isomorphism, see Paul diMaggio and W. W. Powell, "'The Iron Cage Revisited': Institutional Isomorphism and Collective Rationality in Organizational Fields," *American Sociological Review* 48 (1983): 147–60. For an application to MNCs, see Peter S. Davis, Ashay B. Desay, and John D. Francis, "Mode of International Entry: An Isomorphism Perspective," *Journal of International Business Studies* 31 (2000): 239–58.

23. Coase, "The Nature of the Firm."

24. Ibid. Critically, however, Alchian and Demsetz, "Production, Information Costs, and Economic Organization" 62 *American Economic Review* (1972): 777–95, argue that firing an employee is no different from firing a supplier or contractor in the marketplace.

25. Oliver Hart, "An Economist's Perspective on the Theory of the Firm," *Columbia Law Review* 89 (1989): 1757–74.

26. Andrew Bernard, "Intrafirm Trade and Product Contractibility," *100 American Economic Review* 100 (2010): 444–48.

27. Thiess Buettner and Georg Wamser, *Internal Debt and Multinationals' Profit Shifting: Empirical Evidence from Firm-Level Panel Data* (Munich: If Institute and MLU, 2009).

28. Ibid.

29. Bank for International Settlements, "Foreign Direct Investment in the Financial Sector of Emerging Market Economies," CGFS Publications no. 22 (Mar. 2004). Available at http://www.bis.org/publ/cgfs22.htm.

30. Charles Enoch, "Credit Growth in Central and Eastern Europe," in *The Causes*

and Nature of the Rapid Growth of Bank Credit in the Central, Eastern and South-Eastern European Countries, ed. C. Enoch and I. Ötker-Robe (New York: Palgrave Macmillan, 2007).

31. Ibid.

32. According to BIS data there has been a substantial reduction in cross-border claims since the onset of the global crisis. See BIS, "Statistical Release: preliminary locational and consolidated internatinoal banking statistics at end-December 2011," *BIS Statistical Releases* 12 (2012) available at http://www.bis.org/statistics/rppb1210.pdf. A full update on ownership changes is not yet available.

33. Katharina Pistor, "Into the Void: The Governance of Finance in Central and Eastern Europe," in *Economies of Transition: The Long-run View*, ed. G. Roland (New York: Palgrave Macmillan, 2012), 132–52.

34. Steven Radelet and Jeff D. Sachs, "The Onset of the East Asian Financial Crisis," *HIID Working Paper* (1998). Available at http://www2.cid.harvard.edu/hiidpapers/eaonset2.pdf.

35. This is borrowed from the title of a paper that deals with the fallacy of relying on the law on the books alone to determine the similarity between U.S. and Japanese securities laws. See Beller, Alan, Tsunemasa Terai and Richard M. Levine, "Looks Can Be Deceiving: A Comparison of Initial Public Offering Procedures under Japanese and U.S. Securities Laws," *Law and Contemporary Problems* 55 (1992): 77–118.

36. Ralph de Hass and Iman van Lelyveld, "Internal Capital Markets and Lending by Multinational Bank Subsidiaries," *Journal of Financial Intermediation* 19 (2010): 1–25.

37. Sandor Gardor and Reiner Martin, "The Impact of the Global Economic and Financial Crisis on Central, Eastern and South-Eastern Europe: A Stock-Taking Exercise," *Occasional Paper Series, European Central Bank*, June (2010).

38. Stijn Claessens et al., "Lessons and Policy Implications from the Global Financial Crisis," *IMF Working Paper* 10/44 (2010). Available at http://www.imf.org/external/pubs/ft/wp/2010/wp1044.pdf.

39. Katharina Pistor, "Real vs. Imagined Markets: The Regulatory Challenge," in *INET: A Paradigm Lost*, ed. IfNET (Berlin: IfNET, 2012).

40. EBRD, *Vienna Initiative: Moving to a New Phase* (London: European Bank for Reconstruction and Development, 2011); Katharina Pistor, "Governing Interdependent Financial Systems: Lessons from the Vienna Initiative," *Globalization and Development* 2 (forthcoming).

41. Sandor Gardor and Reiner Martin, "The Impact of the Global Economic and Financial Crisis on Central, Eastern and South-Eastern Europe: A Stock-Taking Exercise," *Occasional Paper Series, European Central Bank* 114 (June 2010).

42. Ralph De Haas and Iman Van Lelyveld, "Internal Capital Markets and Lending by Multinational Bank Subsidiaries," *Journal of Financial Intermediation* 19 (2010): 1–25.

43. Perry Mehrling, *The New Lombard Street: How the Fed Became the Dealer of Last Resort* (Princeton, N.J.: Princeton University Press, 2011).

44. Ralph De Haas and Iman Van Lelyveld, "Multinational Banks and Global Financial Crisis: Weathering the Perfect Storm?" *EBRD Working Paper Series* 0135 (2012).

45. Jonos Kornai, Eric Maskin, and Roland Gerard, "Understanding the Soft Budget Constraint," *Journal of Economic Literature* 41 (2003): 1095–1136.

46. Pistor, "Into the Void."

47. Katharina Pistor, "Global Network Finance," *Journal of Comparative Economics* 37 (2009): 552–67.

48. Others have pointed out finance in capitalist economies has strong traits of the SBC. See Mathias Dewatripont and Gerard Roland, "Soft Budget Constraint, Transition, and Financial Systems," Mimeo (1999); Mathias Dewatripont and Gerard Roland, "Soft Budget Constraint, Transition, and Financial Systems," Mimeo (1999). Others have argued that the SBC is by no means limited to socialist economies. See Eric Maskin, "The Soft Budget Constraint," *American Economic Review* 89 (1999): 421–25.

49. Clearly, nation-states have never been the monopoly regulators as which they are portrayed, even domestically. Religious groups, social and economic associations, political parties, and self-regulatory organizations have always coexisted with state legislation and regulation; Fabrizio Cafaggi, "New Foundations of Transnational Private Regulation," *Journal of Law and Society* 38 (2011): 20–49.

50. Joseph Stiglitz, *Making Globalization Work* (London: W. W. Norton, 2006).

51. Dani Rodrik, "How Far Will International Economic Integration Go?" *Journal of Economic Perspectives* 14 (2000): 177–86.

52. Geoffrey M. Hodgson, "On the Institutional Foundations of Law: The Insufficiency of Custom and Private Ordering," *Journal of Economic Issues* 43 (2009): 143–66.

53. Ruth Grant and Robert O. Keohane, "Accountability and Abuses of Power in World Politics," *American Political Science Review* 99 (2005): 29–43.

54. Jessica Matthews, "Power Shifts," *Foreign Affairs* (1997): 50–66.

55. In this context it may be worth pointing out that a nation, the quintessential demos in the age of nation-states, is not a natural constituency, but had to be actively created. See Benedict Anderson, *Imagined Communities: Reflections on the Origin and Spread of Nationalism* (New York: Verso, 1983).

56. Cafaggi and Pistor, "Regulatory Capabilities."

57. Amartya Sen, *Commodities and Capabilities* (Amsterdam: North-Holland, 1985); Amartya K. Sen, *Development as Freedom* (New York: Random House, 1999); Martha Nussbaum, *Creating Capabilities: The Human Development Approach* (Cambridge, Mass.: Belknap, 2011).

58. Susan Sturm, "The Architecture of Inclusion: Advancing Workplace Equity in Higher Education," *Harvard Journal of Law and Gender* 29 (2006): 247–334.

59. Albert O. Hirschman, *Exit, Voice, and Loyalty; Responses to Decline in Firms, Organizations, and States* (Cambridge, Mass.: Harvard University Press, 1970).

60. Sturm, "The Architecture of Inclusion."

61. David W. Leebron, "Limited Liability, Tort Victims, and Creditors," *Columbia Law Review* 91 (1991): 1565–1650.

62. Hyman Minsky, *Stabilizing an Unstable Economy* (New Haven: Yale University Press, 1986).

63. Karen Mills, "Judicial Attitudes to Enforcement of Arbitral Awards and Other Judicial Involvement in Arbitration in Indonesia," *Arbitration* 68 (2002): 106–14.

64. Neil Fligstein, *The Transformation of Corporate Control* (Cambridge, Mass.: Harvard University Press, 1990).

65. Georg Kell and David Levin, "The Global Compact Network: A Historic Experiment in Learning and Action," *Business and Society Review* 108 (2003): 151–81.

66. This term is borrowed from Margaret M. Blair and Lynn A. Stout, "Trust, Trustworthiness, and the Behavioral Foundations of Corporate Law," *University of Pennsylvania Law Review* 149 (2001): 1735–1810.

Chapter 14. Ethnicity, Inc.

1. See "Traditional Leaders to Form Private Firm for Investment," *Business Day* (web edition), Oct. 10, 2000; available at http://www.bd.co.za/bday/content/direct/1,3523,717426-6078-0,00.html. See also Barbara Oomen, *Chiefs in South Africa: Law, Power and Culture in the Post-Apartheid Era* (New York: Palgrave, 2005), 97, who goes on to note that, in establishing its business trust in 1999 to join a mining consortium, "Contralesa sought to further the business interests of the chiefs and to capitalise on the 'Africanist' value of its constituency" (ibid., 143).

2. *Kgosi*, in Setswana, is usually translated as "chief." Among Bafokeng, however, it tends to be rendered as "king," itself an assertion of ethnic power. We are grateful to Dr. Susan Cook, who told us of Leruo's visit to Brown University in October 2002 and who alerted us to the edition of *Enterprise* which carried the supplement. Dr. Cook is presently doing highly original work on corporate ethnicity among Bafokeng; our work and hers, to which we shall return, have long informed each other.

3. Martin Creamer's *Mining Weekly* 6 (41), Nov. 17–23, 2000. Available at www.miningweekly.co.za.

4. Tswagare Namane, "Searching for Tswana Heritage," *The Mail*, March 4, 1994, 8.

5. We are grateful to Silvana Dantu, of *African Equations*, for an account of the company, which is run by an estimable group of women of color in Cape Town. We met Ms. Dantu and Shareen Parker, the director, in August 2002.

6. See Craig Bishop, "Community Reserve Launched," *Natal Witness*, Oct. 15, 2001; the version we cite—kindly made available to us by Ilana van Wyk, of the University of Pretoria, to whom we wish to express our gratitude—is copied from the SA Media holdings of the University of the Free State (Ref No. 5653, Topic 19).

7. There are other enterprises that sell "experiences" of the African wild. The Original Coffee Bay Backpacker, for example, offers "African Huts" and "Tribal Family Care" at its Bomvu site in the "true tribal Transkei" on the "Marijuana Trail." This information is

contained on its advertising leaflet, which offers contact information via bomvu@int
kom.co.za. But it is unclear whether or not this is an "ethnic" enterprise. Private companies also deploy the signs of African "authenticity" to market their tourist services.

8. Marilyn Halter, *Shopping for Identity: The Marketing of Ethnicity* (New York:
Schocken Books, 2000).

9. "Democratic Devolution in the UK: Scotland's Quiet Revolution," *Le Monde Di-
plomatique*, English edition, April 1998. Available at www.mondediplo.com/1998
/04/09scotland (accessed Aug. 8, 2006).

10. Martin Chanock, "'Culture' and Human Rights: Orientalising, Occidentalising
and Authenticity," in *Beyond Rights Talk and Culture Talk: Comparative Essays on the
Politics of Rights and Culture*, ed. Mahmood Mamdani (New York: St. Martin's Press,
2000). Chanock's comment is made in the context of a critique of the part played by
"culture talk"—indeed, of the ontological reduction of difference to culture—in the politics of the ex-colonial world. The interpellation into his argument of the "weapons of
mass instruction," is our own; so, too, is the definition of branding in the next sentence,
which goes somewhat further than his. Mahmood Mamdani, "Introduction," in *Beyond
Rights Talk and Culture Talk*, 2.

11. Oomen, *Chiefs in South Africa*, 161.

12. Jean Comaroff, *Body of Power, Spirit of Resistance: The Culture and History of a
South African People* (Chicago: University of Chicago Press, 1985).

13. Oomen, *Chiefs in South Africa*, 161–62.

14. Elizabeth A. Povinelli, "Consuming Geist: Popontology and the Spirit of Capital in
Indigenous Australia," in *Millennial Capitalism and the Culture of Neoliberalism*, ed. Jean
Comaroff and John L. Comaroff (Durham, N.C.: Duke University Press, 2001), 241–70.

15. Annette Sanger, "Blessing or Blight? The Effects of Touristic Dance-Drama on
Village Life in Singapadu, Bali," in *Come Mek Me Hol' Yu Han': The Impact of Tourism on
Traditional Music* ed. Olive Lewin and Adrienne Kaeppler (Kingston: Jamaican Memory
Bank, 1988), 99–100.

16. Philip Felfan Xie, "The Bamboo-Beating Dance in Hainan, China: Authenticity
and Commodification," *Journal of Sustainable Development* 11 (2003): 5–16.

17. Slavoj Žižek, "Move the Underground: What's Wrong with Fundamentalism, Part
II," (forthcoming). Available at http://www.lacan.com/zizunder.htm.

18. The theoretical literature surrounding this question is huge; there is no need to
annotate it here. In respect of Africa, however, Crawford Young's typology, which enu-
merates three approaches to the analysis of cultural identity—the primordialist, the con-
structivist, and the instrumentalist—is fairly representative of efforts to lay out the
discursive field. Crawford Young, "The Dialectics of Cultural Pluralism: Concept and
Reality," in *The Rising Tide of Cultural Pluralism: The Nation-State at Bay?* ed. C. Young
(Madison: University of Wisconsin Press, 1993).

19. Jean Comaroff and John L. Comaroff, "Ethnicity, Nationalism, and the Politics of
Difference in an Age of Revolution," in *The Politics of Difference: Ethnic Premises in a*

World of Power, ed. Edwin N. Wilmsen and Patrick A. McAllister (Chicago: University of Chicago Press, 1996).

20. Marilyn Strathern, "Enabling Identity? Biology, Choice and the New Reproductive Technologies," in *Questions of Cultural Identity*, ed. Stuart Hall and Paul Du Gay (London: Sage, 1996), 38–45. Marilyn Strathern makes a similar point, albeit not in respect of cultural identity but of kinship statuses. These, she says—speaking of what she calls "Euro-America"—"bring out contradictory appeals to choice and to genes" (38). She also cites Janet Dolgin, who, in speaking of motherhood in the United States, points to a fundamental tension between "biological certainties" and "negotiation and choice." Janet Dolgin, "Status and Contract in Feminist Legal Theory of the Family: A Reply to Bartlett," *Women's Rights Law Reporter* 12 (1990): 103–13.

21. Stuart Hall, "New Ethnicities," in *Stuart Hall: Critical Dialogues in Cultural Studies*, ed. David Morley and Kuan-Hsing Chen (New York: Routledge, 1996), 442f.

22. Courtney Jung, *Then I Was Black: South African Political Identities in Transition* (New Haven: Yale University Press, 2001).

23. Wendy Brown, *States of Injury: Power and Freedom in Late Modernity* (Princeton, N.J.: Princeton University Press, 1995).

24. Jean Comaroff and John L. Comaroff, "Millennial Capitalism: First Thoughts on a Second Coming," in *Millennial Capitalism and the Culture of Neoliberalism*, 1-56.

25. Jung, *Then I Was Black,* 22–24.

26. Arif Dirlik, "Reversals, Ironies, Hegemonies: Notes on the Contemporary Historiography of Modern China," in A. Dirlik, V. Bahl, and P. Gran, eds., *History After the Three Worlds: Post-Eurocentric Historiographies* (Lanham, Md.: Rowman & Littlefield, 2000), 129.

27. Benedict Anderson, *Imagined Communities: Reflections on the Origin and Spread of Nationalism* (London: Verso, 1983).

28. Comaroff and Comaroff, "Ethnicity, Nationalism, and the Politics of Difference in an Age of Revolution."

29. Bruce Kapferer, ed., *The Retreat of the Social: The Rise and Rise of Reductionism* (New York: Berghahn Books, 2005).

30. Tom Vanderbilt, "The Advertised Life," in *Commodify Your Dissent: Salvos from the Baffler*, ed. Thomas Frank and Matt Weiland (New York: W. W. Norton, 1997), 140.

31. See the *International Social Survey Program: National Identity II* (ISSP 2003), available at http://zacat.gesis.org/webview/index.jsp?object=http://zacat.gesis.org/obj/fStudy/ZA3910 (accessed Dec. 13, 2006). On Israel, in particular, see Uri Ram, "National, Ethnic or Civic? Contesting Paradigms of Memory, Identity and Culture in Israel," *Studies in Philosophy and Education* 19 (2000): 405-422.

32. James L. Gibson, *Overcoming Apartheid: Can Truth Reconcile a Divided Nation?* (New York: Russell Sage Foundation, 2004). Gibson's study was widely reported in the South African media. The citations here are from an insightful analysis of that study, Jan Hofmeyr, "Our Racially Divided City Can Ill Afford Another Fear-Based Election Campaign," *Cape Times* (Aug. 2005), 11.

33. Jean Comaroff and John L. Comaroff, "Law and Disorder in the Postcolony: An Introduction," in *Law and Disorder in the Postcolony*, ed. Jean Comaroff and John L. Comaroff (Chicago: University of Chicago Press, 2006); John L. Comaroff and Jean Comaroff, *Ethnicity Inc.* (Chicago: University of Chicago Press, 2009).

34. All of these stories are readily accessible in media archives. For the Nandi story, for example, see "Nandi to Sue Britain over Leader's Killing," *Daily Nation On The Web*, available at http://nationaudio.com/News/DailyNation/Today/News/News150920037.html; on the Bunyoro one, see Solomon Muyita, "Ugandan Monarchy Applies to Sue Britain," *Daily Nation* (Kenya) (Oct. 2004), 13; and for the Samburu case, which has received wide coverage, see http://www.nationaudio.com/News/DailyNation/Supplements/weekend/current/story24014.htm.

35. We are grateful to Caroline Brown, a doctoral student at the University of Chicago, for pointing us in the direction of the relevant literature on ACSA; we have also drawn, in this paragraph, from an early draft of her Ph.D. dissertation: Caroline Brown, *Native, Inc.: A Geography of Alaskan Native Politics* (PhD dissertation draft, Department of Anthropology, University of Chicago); Julie Hollowell-Zimmer, "Intellectual Property Protection for Alaska Native Arts," *Cultural Survival* 24 (2001). Available at http://www.culturalsurvival.org/publications/csq/ index.cfm?id=24.4.

36. A spectacular case that made the international press is that of the Penchanga Band of the Luiseno Mission Indian Reservation in San Jacinto, California, whose casino resort yields $184 million p.a. In 2003, its enrollment committee expelled 130 of the 990 members, apparently on genealogical grounds. Tribal elders responded to the ensuing lawsuit by arguing that, having "sovereign immunity," the tribe could not be challenged in court; see Louis Sahagun, "Battle over Rights to Casino-Fuelled Gravy Train Pits Grandparents Against Kids," *Sunday Independent* (Feb. 2004), 16.

37. See Donald L. Bartlett and James B. Steele, "Wheel of Fortune," *Time*, Dec. 16, 2002, 46, 58. For another case of a one-person tribe, also involving a casino complex, see John M. Broder and Charlie LeDuff, "California Looks to Casinos for Revenue: New Deal with Indian Tribes Could Mean $1.5 Billion More a Year," *New York Times*, Feb. 2, 2003, 14.

38. We owe the development of this point to an exchange with our colleague, Jessica Cattelino, whose highly original work on the topic has informed our own. Says Cattelino (pers. communication): "Public debate overlooks the sovereign dimensions of Native American enterprise, which is seen to grow out of 'special rights' rather than sovereignty. The conflation of indigeneity with ethnicity has . . . trapp[ed] Indians between the discourses and policies of multiculturalism and those of sovereignty-based rights." Jessica R. Cattelino, "Casino Roots: The Cultural Production of Twentieth-Century Seminole Economic Development," in *Native Pathways: Economic Development and American Indian Culture in the Twentieth Century*, ed. Brian Hosmer and Colleen O'Neill (Boulder: University of Colorado Press, 2004); Jessica R. Cattelino, *High Stakes: Florida Seminole Gaming and Sovereignty* (Durham, N.C.: Duke University Press, 2008).

39. James C. McKinley Jr., "End to State and Tribe Dispute Removes Obstacle to Casino," *New York Times*, May 10, 2003, A16. The disagreement had become an obstacle to the settlement of the Mohawk land claim, pursuant to the establishment of a new casino in the Catskills.

40. Virtually all of the examples cited above, from the Mohegan case through those of the Californian bands to the Mohawk dispute with the State of New York, at one or another stage involved a land claim, if only for the formal recognition of real estate as a tribal reservation—and, with it, of sovereignty.

41. The term "casino capitalism," of course, has been used to describe neoliberal economies, *tout court*, a matter we discuss elsewhere (Comaroff and Comaroff, "Millennial Capitalism: First Thoughts on a Second Coming"). See Susan Strange, *Casino Capitalism* (Oxford: Blackwell, 1986).

42. Michael F. Brown, "Can Culture Be Copyrighted," *Current Anthropology* 19 (1998): 193–222.

43. Sandra Lee Pinel and Michael J. Evans, "Tribal Sovereignty and the Control of Knowledge," in *Intellectual Property Rights for Indigenous Peoples: A Sourcebook*, ed. Tom Greaves (Oklahoma City: Society for Applied Anthropology, 1994), 45.

44. Ibid., 5.

45. An account of the *60 Minutes* story, broadcast on November 21, 2004, may be found, under the title "African Plant May Help Fight Fat," at http://www.purehoodia.com/cbs_news.htm.

46. Tom Mangold, "Sampling the Kalahari Cactus Diet," *BBC News*, May 30, 2003. Available at http://www.purehoodia.com/bbc.htm.

47. Gavin Evans, "'Extinct' San Reap Rewards," in *Mail and Guardian Bedside Book 2003*, ed. Shaun de Waal and Mondli Makhanya (Bellevue, South Africa: Jacana, Jan. 2003), 12.

48. John Comaroff interviewed Roger Chennells in Stellenbosch (South Africa), Feb. 24, 2005; we are grateful to him for sharing with us the information recorded here.

49. Rupert Isaacson, *Healing Land: A Kalahari Journey* (London: Fourth Estate, 2002); see also Steven Robins, "Whose Modernity? Indigenous Modernities and Land Claims After Apartheid," *Development and Change* 34 (2003): 12–14.

50. As will be clear from the *SASI Annual Review*, Apr. 2001–Mar. 2002. We have drawn extensively on this review for our summary account here. Available at http://www.san.org.za/sasi/ann_rep_2002.htm.

51. Evans, "'Extinct' San Reap Rewards."

52. *SASI Annual Review*, Apr. 2001–Mar. 2002, 8. The other citations in this paragraph, unless otherwise specified, are taken from the same *Annual Review*, 4–9.

53. The so-called Kalahari Bushman debate concerns the way in which economy, society, and culture among the San-speaking peoples are to be characterized: whether these peoples ought to be seen as "prehistoric" hunters and gatherers, having been "authentically" such since time immemorial (e.g., Richard B. Lee and Irven Devore, *Man the*

Hunter [Chicago: Aldine, 1968]); or whether, as revisionist scholars argue—Edwin N. Wilmsen, *Land Filled with Flies: A Political Economy of the Kalahari* (Chicago: University of Chicago Press, 1989); James R. Denbow and Edwin N. Wilmsen, "Paradigmatic History of San-Speaking Peoples and Current Attempts at Revision," *Current Anthropology* 3 (1990): 489–524—their predicament is a relatively recent historical effect of their relations with other populations in the region. For overviews of the debate, especially for contemporary archaeology, see A. B. Smith, "The Kalahari Bushman Debate: Implications for Archaeology of Southern Africa," *South African Historical Journal* 35 (1996): 1–15; and Karim Sadr, "Kalahari Archaeology and the Bushman Debate," *Current Archaeology* 38 (1997): 104–12.

54. Lani Holtzhausen, "Bafokeng Will Diversify Income, Says New CEO," *Mining Weekly*, Nov. 17–23, 2000, 2–3. This report suggests that the reigning king, Leruo Molotlegi, "views himself not as royalty, but as the CEO of Bafokeng Inc., an apt description of a nation that has built up considerable wealth on the back of its platinum interests." Professor Susan Cook, an anthropologist who has worked among Bafokeng for many years and enjoys the confidence of Leruo (see above, note 2), suggests otherwise (personal communication): the young king, she says, sees himself *both* as the royal leader of his people *and* as a thoroughly modern business figure. This is also the impression that John Comaroff came away with on first meeting him in 2003.

55. Susan E. Cook, "Caught in the Act: Implications of Communal Land Reform in South Africa," paper presented at the Annual Meetings of the African Studies Association, New Orleans, Nov. 2004.

56. Ibid., 6 and throughout.

57. We rely here, again, on Susan Cook's work ("Caught in the Act"; Cook, *Language, Ethnicity, and Nation in the New South Africa* [forthcoming]), itself based on her own research, on a manuscript by Bernard Mbenga and Andrew Manson, *A History of the Bafokeng of Rustenburg District, South Africa: And the Contest over Platinum Royalties*, and on other unpublished materials not available to us. Cook's essay also explores a topic that is crucial to the future of Ethnicity, Inc., in South Africa, but which is beyond our present scope: the effects of the Communal Land Rights Act of 2004.

58. Impala Platinum announced the agreement on February 8, 1999. The settlement gave the Royal Bafokeng Nation 22 percent of taxable income from Impala's operations (up from 14.9425 percent), a minimum royalty of 1 percent of the gross selling price of metals mined on Bafokeng land, and one million shares in Impala Platinum Holdings Ltd. See http://www.implats.co.za/press/press21.html.

59. Holtzhausen, "Bafokeng Will Diversify Income," 2.

60. Both agreements were signed in August 2002. On the first, see Rob Rose, "Bafokeng and Angloplat in R4bn Deal," *Business Day*, August 12, 2002, electronic edition. The details of the second were announced electronically on October 15, 2002, by Bell Dewar and Hall, who acted as legal advisers to the Bafokeng. Available at http://www.belldewar .co.za/news/articles_financiallaw/finlaw_article_20020815.htm.

61. Both were announced on www.Mbendi.co.za, a major African business site. The first, "Mobil and Royal Bafokeng in Joint Venture," appeared on Sept. 9, 1998; the second, "Mobil Oil South Africa and The Royal Bafokeng Administration Clinch Shareholding Deal," on June 1, 2001. See http://www.mbendi.co.za.

62. The company bought by the Bafokeng was Murray Construction, renamed Bafokeng Construction; it won, among other contracts, one to upgrade Durban harbor and another to build the Bakwena platinum corridor, both worth billions of rand. The corporation was closed in 2002 "to make way for the emerging construction industry within the [Bafokeng] community." See Carli Lourens, "Bafokeng Construction to Close Shop This Year," *Business Day*, Aug. 19, 2002, electronic edition.

63. Wiseman Khuzwayo, "Astrapak Investors Agree to Sell 20% of Equity to Royal Bafokeng Finance," *Cape Times*, Business Report, Jan. 13, 2005, 1.

64. See "Bafokeng's Cunning Plan," David McKay, *Miningmx*, Oct. 13, 2004. Available at http://www.miningmx.com/mining_fin/388082.htm. Miningmax is an online mining investment service, a joint initiative of South Africa's *Finance Week*. It is not clear what the current 33 percent Bafokeng stake in Merafe is worth at present; their initial equity of 22 percent was valued at R100m in February 2001; see Ilja Graulich, "Bafokeng Nation Extends Portfolio," *Business Day*, Feb. 28, 2001, electronic edition. Its dollar worth has probably multiplied several times, especially given the rise in the value of the South Africa rand over the past two years.

65. Paula Gray, "People of the Dew," *Leadership* (Aug. 2003), 16.

66. Julie Bain, "Royal Bafokeng Nation May Eventually Seek to List Extensive Mining Interests," *Business Day*, Aug. 30, 2002, electronic edition.

67. Paula Gray, "People of the Dew," *Leadership* (Aug. 2003), 13–14.

68. Ibid., 14.

69. Jonathan Franzen, *The Corrections* (New York: Farrar, Straus and Giroux, 2001).

70. Andrea Muehlebach, *The Moral Neoliberal: Welfare and Citizenship in Italy* (Chicago: University of Chicago Press, 2012), 16.

71. Asad Ahmed, "Adjudicating Muslims: Law, Religion, and the State in Colonial India and Post-Colonial Pakistan" (Ph.D. dissertation, University of Chicago, 2006).

72. Judith Butler, "Who Owns Kafka?" *London Review of Books* 33 (Mar. 2011): 3–8.

73. Clifford Geertz, "The Integrative Revolution: Primordial Sentiments and Civil Politics in the New States," in *Old Societies and New States*, ed. C. Geertz (New York: Free Press, 1963).

Chapter 15. Corporate Nostalgia?

1. Marshall Berman, *All That Is Solid Melts into Air: The Experience of Modernity* (New York: Penguin Books, 1988).

2. Stephen R. Barley and Gideon Kunda, *Gurus, Hired Guns, and Warm Bodies: Itinerant Experts in a Knowledge Economy* (Princeton, N.J.: Princeton University Press, 2004).

3. Gerald Davis and Adam Cobb, "Corporations and Economic Inequality Around the World: The Paradox of Hierarchy," in *Research in Organizational Behavior*, ed. A. Brief and B. M. Staw (Oxford: Elsevier, 2003).

4. Max Weber, *The Protestant Ethic and the Spirit of Capitalism* (Mineola, N.Y.: Dover, 2001), 123.

5. Weber, *The Protestant Ethic,* 124.

6. Richard Sennett, *The Culture of the New Capitalism* (New Haven: Yale University Press, 2007), xxx.

7. Greta Krippner, *Capitalizing on Crisis: The Political Origins of the Rise of Finance* (Cambridge, Mass.: Harvard University Press, 2011).

8. Karen Ho, Liquidated: An Ethnography of Wall Street (Durham, N.C.: Duke University Press. 2009); William Lazonick and Mary O'Sullivan, "Maximizing Shareholder Value: A New Ideology for Corporate Governance," Economy and Society 29 (2000); Lynn Stout, The Shareholder Value Myth: How Putting Shareholders First Harms Investors, Corporations, and the Public (San Francisco: Berret-Koehler, 2012).

9. Ho, *Liquidated,* 102–4, 130.

10. Gerald Davis, "The Twilight of the Berle and Means Corporation," *Seattle University Law Review* 34 (2011), 1121-1138.

11. Gerald Davis, "After the Corporation," *Politics & Society* (forthcoming).

12. Thomas Frank, *One Market Under God: Extreme Capitalism, Market Populism, and the End of Economic Democracy* (New York: Random House, 2000).

13. Edward Wolff, "The Asset Price Meltdown and the Wealth of the Middle Class," NBER Working Paper No. 18559 (2012).

14. Sennett, *The Culture of the New Capitalism,* 39.

15. Krippner, *Capitalizing on Crisis.*

16. Chris Hayes, *Twilight of the Elites: America After Meritocracy* (New York: Crown, 2012), 134.

17. Ibid., 136.

18. Ibid., 107.

19. Harry Braverman, *Labor and Monopoly Capital: Degradation of Work in the Twentieth Century* (New York: Monthly Review Press, 1974); Barbara Ehrenreich and John Ehrenreich, "The Professional-Managerial Class," *Radical America* 11 (1977): 7–31.

20. Braverman, *Labor and Monopoly Capital,* 227.

21. Ibid., 271.

22. Ehrenreich and Ehrenreich, "The Professional-Managerial Class," 13.

23. Sennett, *The Culture of the New Capitalism,* 34–35.

24. Kathi Weeks, *The Problem with Work: Feminism, Marxism, Antiwork Politics, and Postwork Imaginaries* (Durham, N.C.: Duke University Press, 2011), 54–55.

25. Martha Banta, *Taylored Lives: Narrative Productions in the Age of Taylor, Veblen, and Ford* (Chicago: University of Chicago Press, 1995), 4.

26. Sennett, *The Culture of the New Capitalism,* 35.

27. Ibid., 47.

28. Vicki Smith, *Managing in the Corporate Interest: Control and Resistance in an American Bank* (Berkeley: University of California Press, 1990), 165.

29. Kathy Ferguson, *The Feminist Case Against Bureaucracy* (Philadelphia: Temple University Press), ix–11.

30. Jane Collins, *The Opposite of Fordism: Wal-Mart Rolls Back a Regime of Accumulation* (Madison: University of Wisconsin Press, 2006), 101.

31. Sennett, *The Culture of the New Capitalism*, 81–82.

32. Richard Sennett, *The Corrosion of Character* (New York: W. W. Norton, 1998).

33. Davis and Cobb, "Corporations and Economic Inequality Around the World."

34. Alejandro Portes and Min Zhou, "The New Second Generation: Segmented Assimilation and Its Variants," *Annals of the American Academy of Political and Social Science* 530 (1993): 83.

35. Ibid., 85.

36. Sennett, *The Culture of the New Capitalism*, 24.

37. Ibid., 43.

38. Rakesh Khurana, *Searching for a Corporate Savior: The Irrational Quest for Charismatic CEOs* (Princeton, N.J.: Princeton University Press, 2004), xii.

39. Ibid., 214.

40. Sennett, *The Culture of the New Capitalism*, 56.

41. Ibid., 56–57.

42. Ibid., 58–61.

43. Ibid., 52–53.

44. Pamela Laird, *Pull: Networking and Success Since Benjamin Franklin* (Cambridge, Mass.: Harvard University Press, 2007), 114.

45. Ibid., 262.

46. Moreover, according to Laird, "white middle- and upper-class women" possessed "a great advantage over ethnic minorities, for "whether as members of executive men's families or as private secretaries and assistants, they were in a position to see those social patterns at work" and not completely excised from patterns of power, as were most racialized groups (Laird, *Pull*, 262).

47. Ibid., 198.

48. Ibid., 215; Nancy Maclean, *Freedom Is Not Enough: The Opening of the American Workplace* (Cambridge, Mass.: Harvard University Press, 2006), 251.

49. Laird, *Pull*, 335–36.

50. Ibid., 265–67.

51. Ibid., 324–27, 331.

52. Ibid., 2, 282, 325–26.

53. Sennett, *The Culture of the New Capitalism*, 74–78.

54. Laird, *Pull*, 188.

55. Sennett, *The Culture of the New Capitalism*, 80–81.

56. Ibid., 77–82.

57. Barley and Kunda, *Gurus, Hired Guns, and Warm Bodies,* 289, 301.

58. Ibid., 294, 304.

Chapter 16. Can For-Profit Corporations Be Good Citizens?

1. For one review of various books on the topics, see Andrew Lo, "Reading About the Financial Crisis: A Twenty-One-Book Review," *Journal of Economic Literature* 50, no. 1 (2012): 151–78.

2. Frank Newport, "American's Anti-Big Business, Big Gov't," *GALLUP Politics,* January 19, 2012, http://www.gallup.com/poll/152096/Americans-Anti-Big-Business-Big -Gov.aspx; "Annual Global Study," *Edelman Trust Barometer Executive Summary,* January 22, 2012, http://www.scribd.com/doc/79026497/2012-Edelman-Trust-Barometer-Exe cutive-Summary.

3. In the frequently quoted *New York Times Magazine* article from 1970, Friedman provides a slightly different formulation of managerial responsibility. He writes: "In a free enterprise, a private property system, a corporate executive is an employee of the owners of the business. He has a direct responsibility to his employers. That responsibility is to conduct the business in accordance with their desires, which generally will be to make as much money as possible while conforming to the basic rules of the society, both those embodied in law and those embodied in ethical custom." Strictly speaking, this formulation opens two avenues for managers to follow standards above and beyond what is required by the law: the desires of shareholders and ethical custom. However, most commentators interpret Friedman's view as consistent with the weak constraints view. Milton Friedman, "The Social Responsibility of Business Is to Increase Its Profits," *New York Times,* September 13, 1970, available at http://www.colorado.edu/studentgroups/libe tarians/issues/friedman-soc-resp-business.html.

4. For a collection of articles that engage in this debate, see the special issue of *Business Ethics Quarterly* 18, no. 1 (2008).

5. On the need to separate business activity and the norms associated with it from other spheres of life, see Elizabeth Anderson, *Value in Ethics and Economics* (Cambridge, Mass.: Harvard University Press, 1993); Michael Sandel, *What Money Can't Buy* (New York: Farrar, Straus and Giroux, 2012); Debra Satz, *Why Some Things Should Not Be for Sale* (Oxford: Oxford University Press, 2010); Michael Walzer, *Spheres of Justice* (New York: Basic Books, 1983).

6. Consider the debate around *Citizens United v. Federal Election Commission,* 558 U.S. 50 (2010) on whether First Amendment protections extended to corporations and unions with respect to political expenditures.

7. On September 15, 2011, for the opening event of the 2011–2012 Penn Program on Democracy, Citizenship, and Constitutionalism, four business leaders met onstage at the National Constitution Center to address the question, "Can for-profit corporations be good citizens?" I served as moderator of the panel. A complete recording of the event

can be viewed at iTunes U, available at https://itunes.apple.com/gb/itunes-u/penn
-program-on-democracy/id485011846.

8. For an overview, see R. Edward Freeman, Jeffrey S. Harrison, Andrew C. Wicks, Bidhan L. Parmar, and Simone de Colle, *Stakeholder Theory: The State of the Art* (Cambridge: Cambridge University Press, 2010).

9. For an overview of the literature surrounding this claim, see Joshua Margolis and James Walsh, *People and Profits? The Search for a Link Between a Company's Social and Financial Performance* (Mahwah, N.J.: Lawrence Erlbaum Associates, 2001).

10. In an op-ed piece to accompany the panel, Abele writes, "A good reputation requires respect. And respect has to be earned, not bought. Relationships with each of these constituencies are built on a combination of trust, openness, respect, judgment, and accountability." John Abele, "The Good Corporate Citizen," *Philadelphia Inquirer*, September 13, 2011, available at http://articles.philly.com/2011-09-13/news/30149662_1 _malden-mills-corporate-citizen-respect.

11. From his op-ed piece to accompany the panel. Gordon Bajnai, "Companies Must Be Mindful of the Wide Circle of Stakeholders in the Community," *Philadelphia Inquirer*, September 13, 2011, available at http://articles.philly.com/2011-09-13/news/30149676_1 _corporate-citizen-social-responsibility-companies.

12. Ibid.

13. Fedele Bauccio, speaking at the Penn Program described in note 7.

14. Bajnai, "Companies Must Be Mindful."

15. Ibid.

16. For an overview of theories of corporate responsibility, see Domènec Melé, "Corporate Social Responsibility Theories," in *The Oxford Handbook of Corporate Social Responsibility*, ed. Andrew Crane, Abagail McWilliams, Dirk Matten, Jeremy Moon, and Donald S. Siegel (Oxford: Oxford University Press, 2008), 47–82.

JOEL BAKAN is Professor of Law at the University of British Columbia. His work examines the social, economic, and political dimensions of law, and he has published in leading legal and social science journals as well as in the popular press. His books include *The Corporation: The Pathological Pursuit of Profit and Power* and *Childhood Under Siege: How Big Business Targets Your Children*.

JEAN COMAROFF is Alfred North Whitehead Professor of African and African American Studies and of Anthropology at Harvard University, and Honorary Professor of Anthropology at the University of Cape Town. Her research focuses on processes of social and cultural transformation in South Africa—the making and unmaking of colonial society, the nature of the postcolony, and the late modern world viewed from the Global South. Among her books co-authored with John Comaroff are *Ethnicity, Inc.* and *Theory from the South, or How Euro-America Is Evolving Toward Africa*.

JOHN COMAROFF is Hugh K. Foster Professor of African and African-American Studies and of Anthropology, and Oppenheimer Research Scholar in African Studies, at Harvard University. His current research focuses on the workings of the state, democracy and difference, and postcolonial politics. Among his books co-authored with Jean Comaroff are *Ethnicity, Inc.* and *Theory from the South, or How Euro-America Is Evolving Toward Africa*.

CYNTHIA ESTLUND is the Catherine A. Rein Professor of Law at the New York University School of Law. Her research focuses on labor and employment law, and she has written extensively on the relationship between the workplace and democracy. Among her publications are: *Working Together: How Workplace Bonds Strengthen a Diverse Democracy* and *Regoverning the Workplace: From Self-Regulation to Co-Regulation.*

LOUIS GALAMBOS is Professor of History and Editor, The Papers of Dwight David Eisenhower, at The Johns Hopkins University. He is the author of numerous books on modern institutional development in America, the rise of the bureaucratic state, and the evolution of the professions. His most recent book is *The Creative Society—and the Price Americans Paid for It.*

ROSALIE GENOVA holds a Ph.D. in history from the University of North Carolina at Chapel Hill. Her dissertation is entitled "Big Business, Democracy and the American Way: Narratives of the Enron Scandal in 2000s Political Culture." She was most recently a postdoctoral fellow in the University of Pennsylvania's Program on Democracy, Citizenship, and Constitutionalism.

PETER GOUREVITCH is Professor Emeritus in the Department of Political Science at the University of California, San Diego, where he was also founding dean of the School of International Relations and Pacific Studies. His books include *Politics in Hard Times: Comparative Responses to International Economic Crises* and *Political Power and Corporate Control: The New Global Politics of Corporate Governance.* Well-known papers include the "Second Image Reversed," published in *International Organization,* a journal of which he was later co-editor with David Lake. A graduate of Oberlin College in 1963, he earned a Ph.D. at Harvard in 1969, and taught at Harvard and McGill before moving to University of California, San Diego, in 1979.

KAREN HO is Associate Professor of Anthropology at the University of Minnesota. Her research centers on the problematic of understanding and representing financial markets, sites that are resistant to cultural analysis. Among her publications is *Liquidated: An Ethnography of Wall Street,* based on three years of fieldwork among investment bankers and major financial institutions. Her latest book project excavates an alternative cultural history of financial risk through the ethno-historic investigation of three central sites—corporations, investment practices, and investment funds—from the mid-twentieth century until the present moment.

NIEN-HÊ HSIEH is Associate Professor of Business Administration at Harvard Business School. He teaches and writes about ethical issues that arise in global economic activity. His current work focuses on developing a framework for business managers operating under institutions that are weak, incomplete, or contested, and on ways to conceptualize the purpose of business. Previously he was an Associate Professor at the Wharton School, University of Pennsylvania. He has held visiting fellowships at Harvard University, Oxford University, and the Research School for Social Sciences at the Australian National University.

WALTER LICHT is Walter H. Annenberg Professor of History at the University of Pennsylvania. He teaches courses in American economic and labor history, and his research interests lie in the history of work and labor markets. His most recent book publication is the award-winning, co-authored *The Face of Decline: The Pennsylvania Anthracite Region in the Twentieth Century,* and he is completing a book tentatively titled *American Capitalisms: A Global History.*

JONATHAN R. MACEY is Sam Harris Professor of Corporate Law, Corporate Finance, and Securities Law at Yale University, and Professor in the Yale School of Management. In addition to scholarly articles, he has written numerous editorials for such publications as *the Wall Street Journal*, *Forbes*, *the Los Angeles Times*, and *the National Law Journal*. His books include the two-volume treatise *Macey on Corporation Laws.*

HIROKAZU MIYAZAKI is Director of the East Asia Program and Professor of Anthropology at Cornell University. His current work introduces anthropological perspectives into the ongoing debate about financial markets and their regulation. Among his publications are *Arbitraging Japan: Dreams of Capitalism at the End of Finance* and *The Method of Hope: Anthropology, Philosophy, and Fijian Knowledge.*

LYNN SHARP PAINE is John G. McLean Professor and Senior Associate Dean for Faculty Development at Harvard Business School, where she co-founded the required MBA course on Leadership and Corporate Accountability and currently co-chairs the Senior Executive Program for China. Her research focuses on the leadership and governance of companies that meld high ethical standards with outstanding financial results. Her publications, including more than 200 case studies, have appeared in a variety of books, periodicals, and scholarly journals. She is most recently co-author of *Capitalism at Risk: Rethinking the Role of Business.*

KATHARINA PISTOR is the Michael I. Sovern Professor of Law at Columbia Law School and the Director of the School's Center on Global Legal Transformation. She has conducted extensive research on corporate governance in Central and Eastern Europe, Russia, and East Asia, and more recently focused on the impact of globalization on the transformation of law and legal institutions in the areas of finance, property rights, and transnational regulation. Her publications include *Law and Capitalism: What Corporate Crises Reveal About Legal Systems and Economic Development Around the World.*

AMY J. SEPINWALL is assistant professor of Legal Studies and Business Ethics at Penn's Wharton School. She holds a Ph.D. in philosophy from Georgetown University and a J.D. from Yale Law School. She has published widely on responsibility for financial and corporate wrongdoing. She has two current research streams, one addressing corporate constitutional rights, and the other interrogating the commodification of civic values.

JEFFERY SMITH is the Nancy Schaenen Visiting Scholar at the Prindle Institute of Ethics and visiting associate professor at DePauw University. He was the founding Director of the Banta Center for Business, Ethics and Society and continues as associate professor of business ethics at the University of Redlands School of Business. His current research focuses on the moral foundations of corporate social responsibility, the human rights obligations of corporations, and ethical decision making within organizations. His writings have appeared in *Business Ethics Quarterly*, the *Journal of Business Ethics, Business Ethics: A European Review,* and other journals.

JEFFREY L. STURCHIO is senior partner at Rabin Martin, a global health strategy consulting firm based in New York. Before joining the firm in 2011, he served as president and CEO of the Global Health Council, vice president of corporate responsibility at Merck & Co., Inc., president of The Merck Company Foundation, and chairman of the U.S. Corporate Council on Africa. Dr. Sturchio is also a visiting scholar at the Johns Hopkins Institute of Applied

Economics, Global Health, and the Study of Business Enterprise and a senior associate at the Center for Strategic and International Studies.

GREG URBAN is Arthur Hobson Quinn Professor of Anthropology at the University of Pennsylvania. His long-term research explores the forces affecting cultural motion. He is currently engaged in the ethnographic study of modern business corporations. His publications include *Metaculture: How Culture Moves Through the World*.

Index

Acknowledgments

Do corporations serve or subvert the public interest? Are democratic institutions up to the task of overseeing the enormous power unleashed by the corporately organized pursuit of profit? These are surely among the pressing questions of our time. The premise of this book is that an adequate assessment of such questions demands scrutiny from multiple perspectives.

Correspondingly, the project that gave rise to it has been from the outset a collective one. I am lastingly grateful to Rogers Smith (Professor of Political Science at the University of Pennsylvania), as well as Walter Licht (Professor of History at the University of Pennsylvania), Nien-hê Hsieh (Harvard Business School), Amy Sepinwall (Wharton), Doug Lynch (former Vice Dean of the Graduate School of Education at Penn), Erin Graham (formerly with Penn Press), and Jill Fisch (Penn Law School). Stephan Stohler and Andrew Russell provided invaluable research assistance. I counted on help as well from Chloe Bakalar and Chelsea Schafer.

This volume would not have been possible without support from the Mellon Foundation; Wharton's Zicklin Center for Business Ethics Research; and at the University of Pennsylvania, the Anthropology Department, the Philosophy Department, the Center for East Asian Studies, and the Graduate School of Education.

Philadelphia's National Constitution Center sponsored a panel discussion in September 2011, "Can For-Profit Corporations Be Good Citizens?" The panel featured four distinguished CEOs: John Abele (Boston Scientific), Fedele Bauccio (Bon Appétit Management Company), William Cobb (JM Smith Corporation), and Gordon Bajnai (former deputy CEO of CA IB Securities Plc, as well as former Prime Minister of Hungary). In the final chapter of this book, Nien-hê Hsieh discusses their observations and ideas.

Doug Lynch and Amy J. Sepinwall co-organized a roundtable discussion that took place in January 2012 on "For-Profit Educational Corporations." The discussion featured Jonathan D. Harber (founder and former CEO of School Net, Inc.), Peter Smith (Senior Vice President at Kaplan Higher Education), and Michael Moe (founder of GSV Asset Management). Amy J. Sepinwall's chapter in this volume draws on that discussion as well as other work.

In addition to being world-class scholars, the volume contributors have exhibited an impressive commitment to this collective endeavor, as well as a willingness to share with others, thereby making my life easier. The stamp of the trenchant, albeit anonymous Penn Press review is evident in the chapter organization of this volume. Finally, for his never-flagging support, I owe a debt to Peter Agree, editor-in-chief at Penn Press.